MW01061785

JEWISH LITERARY CULTURES

JEWISH LITERARY CULTURES

VOLUME 2, THE MEDIEVAL AND EARLY MODERN PERIODS

DAVID STERN

The Pennsylvania State University Press
University Park, Pennsylvania

Library of Congress Cataloging-in-Publication Data

Names: Stern, David, 1949– author.
Title: Jewish literary cultures / David Stern.
Description: University Park, Pennsylvania : The Pennsylvania State University
Press, [2019] | Includes bibliographical references and indexes.
Summary: "A collection of essays and studies of diverse texts and topics in
medieval and early modern Jewish literature, using contemporary critical
approaches and textual analysis to explore larger ideas and themes in rabbinic
Judaism."—Provided by publisher for volume 2.
Contents: Volume 1. The ancient period.
Identifiers: LCCN 2015012690 | ISBN 9780271084831
(volume 2 : cloth : alk. paper)
Subjects: 1. Jewish literature—History and criticism. I. Title.
Classification: PJ5005.S74 2015 | 809'.88924—dc23
LC record available at https://lccn.loc.gov/2015012690

The Pennsylvania State University Press is a member of the
Association of University Presses.

It is the policy of The Pennsylvania State University Press
to use acid-free paper. Publications on uncoated stock
satisfy the minimum requirements of American National
Standard for Information Sciences—Permanence of Paper
for Printed Library Material, ANSI Z39.48–1992.

In Memory of

Alan Mintz

ז״ל

CONTENTS

ILLUSTRATIONS

ACKNOWLEDGMENTS

The chapters in this volume of Jewish Literary Cultures all appeared in somewhat different forms in the following places, each of which I wish to acknowledge for their permission to allow me to reprint them in revised form here:

"Just Stories: From the Mishnah to Ma'aseh Yerushalmi," in *The Faces of Torah: Studies in the Texts and Contexts of Ancient Judaism in Honor of Steven Fraade*, ed. Michal Bar-Asher Siegal, Chris Hayes and Tzvi Novick, The Journal of Ancient Judaism, Suppplements, 22 (Göttingen: Vandenhoeck & Ruprecht, 2017), 545–66.

"The Alphabet of Ben Sira and the Early History of Parody in Jewish Literature," in *The Idea of Biblical Interpretation*, eds. Hindy Najman and Judith Newman (Leiden: Brill, 2004): 423–48.

"The Hebrew Bible in Europe in the Middle Ages," *Jewish Studies Internet Journal* 11 (2012): 1–88.

"The Making of the Rabbinic Bible," in *The Hebrew Book in Early Modern Italy*, ed. Adam Shear and Joseph Hacker (Philadelphia: University of Pennsylvania Press), 78–108, 252–68.

"The Topography of the Talmudic Page," in *The Visualization of Knowledge*, ed. Marcia Kupfer et al. (Turnhour: Brepols, forthcoming).

"'Jewish' Art and the Making of the Medieval Prayerbook," in *Ars Judaica: A Journal of Jewish Art* 6 (2010): 23–44.

"Mapping the Redemption: Messianic Cartography in the 1695 Amsterdam Haggadah," in *Studia Rosenthaliana* 42/43 (2010–2011), 43–63.

In the case of all these chapters, I was greatly assisted by many colleagues and friends whom I acknowledged in the original publications of the articles. Without repeating their names, I wish to acknowledge their help and generosity once again.

Patrick Alexander, the Director of Penn State University Press, has shown patience longer than God's in waiting for this manuscript. Patrick's encouragement has been a constant support throughout this project (which is still not yet complete).

And finally, this volume would not be as technically perfect and visually attractive without the assistance of three graduate students of mine, past and present. Allison Hurst was invaluably diligent in gathering all the images and permissions for this volume. Alex Ramos, now Production Editor for Penn State University Press, lent his conscientious intelligence to the thankless task of trying to impose consistency upon me in copyediting the manuscript and the countless shelf marks in chapter 3. And last of all, Eric Jarrard lent his diligent eye to proofreading and indexing this book. It was a rare privilege to be assisted and overseen by all three.

As always, this volume and the chapters in it would never have been written without the love of my closest reader and companion in life, Kathryn Hellerstein.

The dedication of this volume to the memory of Alan Mintz is explained at the conclusion of the introduction to this volume.

INTRODUCTION

This volume of *Jewish Literary Cultures*, the second in a series of three, collects seven revised essays I have written on Jewish literature in the medieval and early modern periods. (The first volume of *Jewish Literary Cultures* was devoted to essays on ancient Jewish literature; the third volume will focus upon the modern and contemporary periods.) Among other topics, the essays in this volume deal with an early medieval narrative about a Jew who marries a demoness, one of our earliest examples of parody in Hebrew literature, illustrations in medieval prayerbooks, the history of the talmudic page, the types of Bibles Jews used and read in the Middle Ages, the story of the Rabbinic Bible, and the eschatological significance of an unusual map in the most famous Passover Haggadah printed in the late seventeenth century.

For all their disparate subjects, the articles in this volume share a common concern with the continuity of Jewish literature as it spanned multiple historical periods across the numerous geographic centers of the Jewish Diaspora. The essays also span the length of my scholarly career. The first two chapters go back to the first book I published, *Rabbinic Fantasies: Imaginative Narratives from Classical Hebrew Literature*, an anthology of scholarly translations of fictional texts from rabbinic and medieval Hebrew literature. The idea for the book was not mine. It came from my coeditor, the novelist Mark Mirsky. Mark and I met through Ben Zion Gold—the legendary rabbi at Harvard Hillel while I was a graduate student—when, on Passover in 1978, the three of us found ourselves standing in the cafeteria line at Hillel. We began talking, and when Mark learned that I was writing a dissertation on midrash, he broached the idea of our coediting a volume of erotic stories from classical Jewish literature to appear in a journal he ran called *Fiction Magazine*. I liked the idea but I warned Mark that the volume might be very, very slim. As we continued to talk over the next months, we decided to broaden the collection's topic to include imaginative narratives more generally, or rabbinic "fantasies," as Mark called them, because many of the texts stretched fiction into the realm of magical realism. In 1985, the *Fiction* volume appeared, and it was so successful we decided to expand it into a full book with some sixteen translations, ranging from rabbinic parables to Hasidic dream-narratives by Nahman of Bratslav.

Editing *Rabbinic Fantasies* was a formative experience, because it exposed me to all the possibilities and challenges of dealing with questions of continuity in Jewish literature. As I pointed out in its introduction, there is no word for "fiction" in classical Hebrew, nor is it possible to speak of a genuine tradition of fictional narrative in that literature. On the other hand, the various works we collected did testify to a persistent if not continuous presence of imaginative writing in Jewish literature before the modern period, and there was much to say about that abiding presence, even if it did not constitute a conventional genre of writing. For one thing, the very identification of these texts as works of imaginative writing was an achievement that had eluded most previous scholarship on Hebrew literature (with the single exception of a scholarly monograph that appeared shortly before our collection). Moreover, some of the texts we identified seemed in our judgment to be among the greatest works of imaginative writing in the entire history of Hebrew literature. These texts deserved to be known and read.

The first two chapters in this volume deal with the two works translated in *Rabbinic Fantasies* that etched themselves most indelibly in my imagination. The first essay, "Just Stories: From the Mishnah to *Ma'aseh Yerushalmi*," deals with a remarkable novella-length narrative that developed from a genre of very brief anecdotes used as legal precedents in the Mishnah that claim to have actually taken place even though the plots of these narratives are so literally fantastic that they challenge credibility. In *Ma'aseh Yerushalmi*, or *The Tale of a Jerusalemite*, this rhetoric of incredibility is pushed to its limits through the tale of a hapless Jew who marries a demoness and ultimately comes to ruin—not because of his marriage to the demoness, but on account of his *faithlessness* to her. As I suggest in my reading, the tale is an extraordinary allegory of the Jewish encounter with Otherness—namely, the world of Gentiles—and how and why it is that Jews are doomed to live under the rule of the Other—that is to say, Gentile domination. As I also suggest, the story may also have been a veiled criticism of a certain type of legalistic scrupulousness that was endemic to the highly scholastic world of Geonic Babylonia in the tenth century, the probable place and time of the work's composition.

The second essay treats arguably the most loudly denounced work in all classical Jewish literature, the *Alphabet of Ben Sira*, a text that one of the earliest modern scholars to write about it deemed "worthy to be burned on Yom Kippur even if the fast day coincided with the Sabbath." (Other medieval sages used the text as a precedent for legal rulings dealing with the permissibility of artificial insemination.) The precise purpose of this work and its character have been extensively debated by scholars, but I suggest that at least part of the composition—it is clearly a composite work—is a genuine literary parody of two identifiable rabbinic passages, one midrashic, the other talmudic. Who would have been entertained by such a parody? Only a reader who would have recognized the texts being parodied—namely, a rabbinic scholar, probably one living in the same general environment as the audience of *The Tale of a Jerusalemite*. Both works, in other words, reveal dimensions of early medieval Jewish culture that otherwise would be virtually undocumented.

The five remaining chapters in this volume of *Jewish Literary Cultures* all date from a later period in my scholarly career, after my research shifted to the history of the Jewish book. A few words about the background to the shift may help the reader appreciate the context for these later essays. The first phase of my career as a scholar focused upon classical Jewish literature in its more conventional sense, sometimes on works like *The Tale of a Jerusalemite* or the *Alphabet of Ben Sira*, but for the most part on midrash and the literature of rabbinic biblical interpretation. I have written elsewhere about what drew me initially to the literature of midrash—its unusual literary discourse, which seemed to flourish in the in-between space between commentary and imaginative fiction; its singular hermeneutics, with its extraordinary attentiveness to the biblical text and its simultaneous, seemingly unbounded freedom of invention; and the overall (and superficial) resemblance of its literary forms to the fragmented, self-reflexive literary structures of postmodernism. When I first encountered them, these various incongruous features of midrash appeared to me like a virtual puzzle calling out, to paraphrase a famous rabbinic formulation, "Solve me!" and it was to the solution of this midrashic puzzle that most of my earlier work was directed.

By the time I completed my first two books on midrash, however, I felt I had more or less solved the puzzle, those problems that had initially intrigued me. While my love for studying midrash and teaching students what I had learned about midrash had not abated, the intense curiousity that had inspired and driven my scholarship had more or less been satisfied. I found myself in the midst of a scholarly midlife crisis. I did not know exactly what I wanted to do next, or whether or not I would even find another subject that would draw my attention as passionately as midrash had. And then the unexpected happened (and as things often happen, in a completely happenstance way).

A colleague of mine at the University of Pennsylvania, Peter Stallybrass, had founded a weekly faculty workshop seminar on the History of the Material Text. Papers given at the seminar ranged over every conceivable topic connected to books as physical artifacts—from the history of the comma, to the wax tablet and tablets of memory, to contemporary South African pornographic comics. In short, the seminar was very intellectually stimulating, and I had begun to attend its meetings solely because they were so fascinating. Neither then, nor earlier, had I worked seriously on anything even remotely connected to the history of the book.

After I had been attending the seminar for about a year—or rather, "lurking" there, listening but not actively participating—an invited guest speaker cancelled on Peter at the last moment, and left him desperately looking for a replacement. He asked me if I was willing to give a seminar presentation. I was flattered by the invitation, and felt obligated to accept, but I was not working on anything connected to the material text and had no idea what I could present. When I confessed my quandary to Peter, he asked, "Well, what about that book of yours with that strange page format, the one with the text in the center and all the commentaries around it?" "The Talmud?" I responded. "Yes, the Talmud. Where does that page format come from?" I had never even thought about that question! "Well," he answered. "Why don't you give a paper on that?" Reluctantly, I agreed, and after I started researching the question, I almost instantly became obsessed with the topic. I gave that seminar and thus entered the field of the history of the book. Some twenty years later, I finally completed the paper. It appears in this volume.

In point of fact, I had long had a very marginal interest in books as objects. When I was a graduate student, I audited a course in early English printing where we handled First Folio editions of Shakespeare, among other extremely rare printed books. Through my close friendship with the novelist and theologian Arthur Cohen, who was also a dealer in rare art books, I briefly toyed with the idea of a becoming a rare book dealer, until the little business sense I had kicked in and quickly convinced me I would never be successful enough to make a living from the business. But all of my previous scholarly and intellectual work had dealt with essentially abstract and intangible problems—hermeneutics, textuality, issues of interpretation. The pleasure of dealing with the book as a material artifact, something one could physically touch and actually look at, was palpable; it came almost as an enormous intellectual relief. Around the time I first became interested in the history of the Jewish book, I also met the eminent Israeli palaeographer and codicologist Malachi Beit-Arié, who was a fellow at Penn's Center for Judaic Studies at the time and who subsequently became my mentor in the field. When I asked Malachi for advice as to how I should learn about the history of the Jewish book, he told me, "Begin by looking at books, go through them, folio by folio—and smell the parchment!" Not long after our conversation, I was invited to give the Stroum Lectures at the University of Washington, and somewhat recklessly, I volunteered to give the three talks on Jewish books. At that point, I suddenly realized how little I knew!

There are many different approaches to the history of the book. To give only two examples: some use the book as a key to historical change, while others look at different material aspects of the book, like its illustrations or marginal notes, and investigate their relationship to the text in the book. My own interest focused on specific types or genres of Jewish books—such as the Talmud, the siddur and maḥzor (the Jewish prayerbooks), and the Passover Haggadah, the three of which were the subjects of my Stroum lectures—and their histories as material artifacts from beginning to end, as it were, from antiquity to the present day, and, as the physical shapes of these books changed, how they can help us understand the evolving place of these books in Jewish culture. As I began to understand the field more deeply, it became clear to me that the materiality of the book was the interface between the text and the world in which the book's producers and readers lived. The material text, in other words, was a window through which one could understand what these books meant to their readers, not only as conveyors of words but as objects with meanings in their own right.

Initially, it did not seem to me that there was much of a connection between this new research agenda and my earlier work on midrash and other forms of ancient Jewish literature. The lack of a connection did not bother me, but it was only when I first began working on the history of the Jewish Bible—the term I use to refer to the Hebrew Bible in all its shapes and forms that Jews have actually held in their hands—that I realized that there was in fact an intimate relationship between the two scholarly projects. That realization came when I first understood the obvious but profound fact that we do not read "texts." What we read are texts that have been inscribed upon a specific type of writing "platform"—a scroll, a codex, a digital screen—in a particular way (with commentaries on the page, or with illustrations, or with the words alone in their naked splendor), and the particular way in which the text is inscribed has a deep impact on how we understand—*interpret*, in the largest sense of the term—the meaning of a text. The history of the book thus leads directly to the history of reading, away from hermeneutics and toward practice. The textual and material sides of the book were not only connected but deeply implicated in one another. With this realization, I suddenly understood that I had not truly left behind my earlier work; by looking at the material dimension of an inscribed text, I had merely added a rich layer of meaning to be studied and analyzed.

The five remaining essays in the book all deal with material aspects of the four pillars of classical Jewish literature. The first two essays—on the Hebrew Bible in Europe in the Middle Ages and on the making of the Rabbinic Bible— were written along with a third essay, about the first Jewish codices and the early history of Jewish reading (which appeared as the final chapter in the first volume of *Jewish Literary Cultures*), as preliminary studies for my book *The Jewish Bible*. In all three essays, I presented original research and provided arguments for conclusions that I later summarized in *The Jewish Bible*; these articles provide the scholarly background and foundation. The next chapter in this volume, on the talmudic page, traces the history of this distinctive page layout and its impact on Talmud study; as I show, the format originated in Christian scribal culture but was transformed, first by Jewish scribes and later by printers of Jewish books (many of them Christians), into what eventually becomes the iconic image of the Jewish book. The following chapter deals with the medieval Ashkenazic maḥzor, or holiday prayerbook, and its remarkable illustrations, whose meaning and function I seek to define within their context as visual *piyyutim*, or liturgical poems, a venerable tradition of the Jewish liturgy. Rather than being merely decorative or illustrative, the representational images in these prayerbooks picture the world of the congregants using the prayerbook and serve them as an instrument for expressing their communal identity, a function that the Jewish liturgy also serves in addition to being a medium of worship. In this way, I try to show how a book like the maḥzor can be understood as a "whole book," its poetry and illustrations and text all at once. In the final essay, I turn to another liturgical text, the Passover Haggadah, which becomes *the* Jewish book of redemption par excellence, and show how the map of the biblical land of Israel in the 1695 Amsterdam

Haggadah—the most famous of all printed haggadot, and the first map to appear in a haggadah—was intended not only to illustrate the historical journey of the Israelites from Egypt to the land of Canaan but also meant to serve as an eschatological diagram, a map to lead the Jews back to their homeland in the soon-to-arrive time of their imminent redemption. Alas, the redemption did not arrive, but the map survives in the haggadah, even until today, a vivid proof of how the Jewish book remains the repository of Jewish dreams.

* * *

While I was completing the revisions on this book, my close friend Alan Mintz died very suddenly. To me, as to many others, Alan's death came as a terrible blow, a horrible, sobering shock. We first met in 1971, in New York City, at Columbia—I was an undergraduate, he was a graduate student—but we truly bonded a few years later, in Cambridge, Massachusetts, when we were both studying at Harvard. At the time, each of us was in search of a vocation, a calling, and we found ourselves jointly in the midst of turning from goyish to Jewish literature—Alan toward modern Hebrew literature, I in the opposite direction. It was Alan, in fact, who introduced me to midrash—he asked me one day if I wanted to join him in studying Shirta, the section of the Mekhilta dealing with the Song at the Sea, along with Judah Goldin's book-length commentary on the midrash. Despite my yeshivah education, that was the first time in my life I had ever opened a midrash collection. As our friendship continued over the years, it deepened. We read each other's work, we critiqued each other, and we supported each other. Alan's commitment to the totality of Hebrew literature, from the Bible to modernity, nearly every period of which he wrote about at some point, inspired my own commitment to the whole of Hebrew literature. The essays in the three volumes of this series only begin to suggest the enormity of Alan's influence upon me and his impact upon my work. It is a privilege, and a great sadness, for me to dedicate this volume to his memory. *Yehi zikhro barukh.*

1

JUST STORIES

From the Mishnah to *Ma'aseh Yerushalmi*

Over the past two or three decades, scholarly interest in narrative in classical Jewish literature from the rabbinic and medieval periods has grown exponentially. The sheer importance of these narratives, the critical position they occupy in classical Hebrew literature, and the contribution these narratives make to legal discourse in particular have been increasingly recognized. Even so, crucial aspects of the phenomenon of narrative in this literature remain to be explored, and none more so than the nature of fictionality in the classical Jewish imagination. What did the authors of these narratives believe about these narratives? Did they believe the stories they told actually took place, or were they able to recognize a tale as invented, or partly invented? Did fiction, imagined narrative, have a place in classical Jewish discourse?

In this chapter, I wish to explore these questions by looking at one specific genre of narrative, the *ma'aseh*, or anecdote, particularly as it figures in legal discourse, and trace its development as a narrative form from the Mishnah through the Geonic period in the early medieval period, with special attention in the later period to a novella-length narrative entitled *Ma'aseh Yerushalmi*. Before beginning this journey, however, a few words are necessary about the general background to the subject of fictionality in early rabbinic literature and about the various stances toward fictionality taken in regard to the different types of rabbinic narrative.

We can begin with the observation that classical Hebrew has no word for fiction. The closest one comes to an explicit discussion of the fictionality of a narrative—in this case, a biblical narrative—is the brief discussion about Ezekiel's vision of the resurrection of the dead bones (Ezek 37) in *b. Sanhedrin* 92b where the Babylonian sages R. Judah and R. Nehemia explore the question as to whether the prophetic vision was *emet*, "reality," an actual occurrence, or a *mashal*, usually translated as "allegory" or "parable" or "proverb" but, when juxtaposed with *emet*, a term that has more of the meaning of an invented tale, a fiction.[1] The same word is used in a similar fashion in *b. Bava Batra* 15a in a discussion over whether Job was an actual historical figure or a *mashal*. In both cases, however, the primary subject of discussion is the ontology of the biblical story—whether the event or person discussed in the text actually occurred or lived—and not the generic status of the text itself.

The fact that rabbinic Hebrew does not possess a word for "fiction" does not mean, of course, that the rabbis did not imagine such narratives. At least as seen from our perspective today, it is clear that imagined or invented (or partly imagined or partly invented) narrative existed as part of rabbinic literature virtually from the moment of its inception. Furthermore, there were several different genres of such narratives—the *mashal*, the narrative parable (as distinct from the word as used for a fiction, as just discussed); the *sippur darshani*, or exegetical narrative; and the *ma'aseh*, or anecdote.[2] Each of these genres takes a somewhat different stance toward the question of its fictionality.

The *mashal* is the easiest to discuss because it is the only one of these genres to self-consciously acknowledge its fictionality, even if that fictionality was a source of ambivalence.[3] Thus a famous passage in *Shir Ha-Shirim Rabbah* (1:1:8) describes the purpose of the *mashal*—by (typically) using the literary form of the *mashal*—as follows:

> Do not consider the *mashal* a trivial thing, for it is by means of the *mashal* that a man is able to arrive at the words of Torah. It is like (*mashal le-*) a king who lost a gold piece or a precious gem. Does he not find it with a penny candle?[4]

The *mashal* has the value of a penny candle. Its worth is trivial, and the source of that triviality is its fictionality: what validates the literary form and rescues it from triviality is the *mashal*'s utility as a tool for understanding Torah—namely, its exegetical function. But in fact, as any reader knows, the *mashal*'s literary power derives as much from its imaginative force as from its exegetical acumen. The rabbis, however, do not acknowledge that force as a source of any intrinsic value.

The fictionality of the *sippur darshani*—the many tiny narratives (and strands and fragments of narrative) that can be found throughout rabbinic literature, particularly in midrash, where they are used to solve exegetical problems in the biblical text—is a more complicated matter because it is tied to the question of the historicity of these exegetical narratives. The *sippur darshani* exists in a kind of nether-space between the biblical narrative and the sphere of the imagination of the exegete.[5] Did the rabbis consider these extrabiblical legends as historically authentic as the biblical narrative? We do not have a clear answer to this question, but the status occupied by these narratives may be most akin to the one occupied by myth in Greco-Roman Late Antiquity, an area that Paul Veyne has explored and defined as possessing a reality inherently different from that of the world in which we live but as nonetheless "real" in its own terms, with a kind of plasticity that makes it infinitely adaptable to different purposes.[6] While Veyne's exploration of the "constitutive" status of myth (or rabbinic aggadah) is far from satisfying, his approach does suggest that our contemporary terms—"fiction," "history," "reality"—may not be the most helpful categories for considering the status of these narratives.

The ontological status of the *sippur darshani* may have resided precisely in its "traditionality," the fact that it was acknowledged to be *aggadah*, transmitted tradition, and that its tradent-authors believed that the plain narratives or exegetical narratives they recounted were not invented by themselves but were received from past tradition or derived from the biblical text as acceptable midrashim. Insofar as they believed that they were not themselves the original authors of the traditions, they could not have believed them to be truly invented fictions. Either they were "in" the biblical text (the way all midrashim are "in" the Bible), or the fact that they were traditional meant that they were not simply made up by the sages who transmitted them.

In contrast to both the *mashal* and the *sippur darshani*, the *ma'aseh* largely avoids the question of its invented status by, explicitly or implicitly, claiming to have taken place exactly as it is narrated. This claim must not be confused with the entirely separate question as to whether or not these narratives actually did take place as they claimed. In contrast to the other narrative genres, the author of a *ma'aseh* makes a radical assertion of his narrative's authenticity and historicity and utterly denies its fictionality or inventedness. In some cases, as we shall see, that claim can be problematized, but it always characterizes the *ma'aseh* generically as a virtual condition of its existence.

As an identifiable genre of rabbinic discourse, the *ma'aseh* first appears in the Mishnah. Frequently, though not always, the subgenre can be identified by the fact that its narrative begins with the formula *ma'aseh be-*, which can be translated freely as "The following incident actually happened to . . ."[7] In a recent work, Moshe Shoshan-Simon has expertly categorized the two main types of *ma'asim* found in the Mishnah. The first of these, the case story, describes a particular situation in which (typically) a halakhic problem arose to which a sage (or sages) offered a ruling in the form of a pronouncement; the second, the exemplum, is a narrative that relates how a sage acted in a particular situation, usually one that posed a halakhic problem to which the sage responded by acting as he did.[8] As a device of legal discourse, the *ma'aseh* has partial analogues in Roman legal discourse.[9] The genre also has parallels in the *chreia*, anecdotal stories told about Greco-Roman sages and philosophers that were used as subjects of rhetorical exercises.[10]

Most *ma'asim* in the Mishnah are very brief, and nearly all presumably appear as illustrations or exemplifications or extensions of the halakhot discussed in the Mishnah.[11] As Shoshan-Simon shows, however, *ma'asim* are rarely transparent illustrations or unambiguous demonstrations of the halakhot that they accompany. There nearly always exist disparities between the narratives and their textual legal contexts. Either the *ma'asim* display too much information or detail—an excess that undermines their transparency—or they present significant lacunae, slippages, and other gaps and discontinuities within the *ma'asim* themselves or between the narratives and their halakhic contexts, such that they raise more questions than they answer. As a result, the *ma'asim* can rarely be read as simple applications or unmediated illustrations or transparent extensions of the more propositional parts of mishnaic discourse.[12]

There is no easy and obvious way to resolve or explain away these discontinuities, nor do we know how the author(s) or editor(s) of the Mishnah viewed them, or whether they were even fully aware of the problems these disparities introduce into the text. Paradoxically, the discontinuities and incongruities within *ma'asim* and between the narratives and their contexts actually serve to confirm their verisimilitude and claim to historicity, inasmuch as they provide for the reader visible proof that the Mishnah's redactor did not tamper with the *ma'asim* in order to make them fit the narratives' legal context perfectly. Typically, the disparities are noticeable—that is, if one is prepared to recognize them. The fact that they are recognizable may also help us appreciate the memorability of the *ma'aseh* as a literary form in the Mishnah. Perhaps their very incongruity—the fact that their disparities called for attention and interpretation—was part of their memorability.

For all their manifold incongruities, however, the narratives of the *ma'asim* in the Mishnah rarely raise issues of credibility or stray into the realm of the fantastic or the unbelievable. The *ma'asim* that come closest to being incredible (in the literal sense) are probably those about Ḥoni Ha-Me'ageil (the Circle-Maker) in *m. Ta'anit* 3:8, but even there what is at issue is Ḥoni's own status in the rabbis' eyes (specifically, within the Mishnah itself, Shimeon ben Shetaḥ's), not the historicity of the miracles that Ḥoni is able to work, which seems to be taken for granted.[13]

In Amoraic literature, particularly in the Babylonian Talmud, the *ma'aseh* expands as a genre to include not only "halakhic narratives" but also far lengthier and ambitious stories including "historical" accounts (like those concerning the destruction of the Temple and the founding of Yavneh) as well as many tales about sages that have no halakhic connection or implication. In many of these narratives, the claim to historicity becomes problematized. Supernatural figures—Elijah, angels, and demons (*sheidim*)—appear in them (although the mere fact of these figures' presence in these narratives does not necessarily weaken their claim to historicity since there is no question that the rabbis believed in their existence).[14] More important for our concerns, the narratives themselves, with or without supernatural characters, begin to stretch the limits of credibility, if not utterly transgress them. The result of these challenges to verisimilitude is not, however, the abdication of the claim to historicity or an acknowledgment of the invented nature of the *ma'asim* but, rather, an intensification of the claim to veracity. This is especially true of halakhic *ma'asim*, which will remain our focus here. The more unlikely the narrative, the stronger its claim to have taken place exactly as narrated. And the stronger that claim, the more powerfully the narrative enforces the halakhah it either illustrates or exemplifies. In other words, in these halakhic narratives the claim to historicity is used for both substantive and rhetorical purposes.

Consider the following passage from the Babylonian Talmud (*Berakhot* 53b), which comments on the Mishnah in *Berakhot* 8:7. The Mishnah builds upon the basic halakhah (never stated explicitly in the Mishnah) that a person must recite the "grace after meals" in the place where s/he ate. The Mishnah itself explicitly deals with the case of a person who ate a meal and *forgot* (*shakhah*) to say grace and then left the place where s/he ate and later remembered that s/he had not recited the prayer. According to the House of Shammai, the person must return to the place where s/he ate; according to the House of Hillel, the person can say grace wherever s/he remembers that s/he had forgotten. The Mishnah does not explain the rationale behind either House's opinion. The following is the Gemara:[15]

> R. Zevid, and some say R. Dimi bar Abba,[16] said: The dispute [between the Houses of Hillel and Shammai] is only in a case where the person genuinely forgot [to say grace]. But where the person acted deliberately (*be-meizid*) [and did not say grace and then regretted his omission and wished to say it], everyone agrees that s/he must go back to the place where s/he ate and bless.
>
> This is obvious! The Mishnah taught: "and forgot."
>
> [No!] For you might have said that it is the same [namely, that the two Houses disagree) even where he acted deliberately (*be-meizid*), and that the reason why the Mishnah said "and forgot" was to demonstrate to you the stringency (*kohan*) of the House of Shammai [in making the person go back *even* in a case where the omission was unintentional]. Therefore, [Rav Zevid's qualification of] "and forgot" was necessary [so as to make it clear that the House of Hillel says that the person does *not* need to go back *only* in a case where he actually forgot.]
>
> B. It was taught: The House of Hillel said to the House of Shammai: "According to your opinion, a person who ate at the top of a castle (*rosh ha-birah*) and then forgot and descended without saying grace—will he return to the top of the castle[17] and say grace?!"
>
> The House of Shammai responded to the House of Hillel: "And according to your opinion, would not a person who forgot his [or her] purse on the top of a castle[18] go back and retrieve it? If a person will go back for his own sake, then all the more so should he go back for the sake of heaven!"[19]
>
> C. There were two disciples. One acted accidentally (*be-shogeig*)[20] [and forgot to say grace], followed the House of Shammai, [and went back to where he had eaten, and said grace], and found a purse of gold![21]
>
> The other disciple acted deliberately (*be-meizid*)[22] [and omitted the grace], followed the House of Hillel, [and did not return,] and a lion ate him!

D. Rabba bar bar Hanna was traveling in a caravan (*shayyarta*).[23] He ate and was sated (*ishtalei*)[24] and did not say grace. He said: "What shall I do? If I tell them that I forgot to say grace, they will tell me, 'Bless here. Wherever you say the blessing, you are blessing the Merciful One.' It is better that I tell them that I forgot a golden dove."

He said to them, "Wait for me, for I have forgotten a golden dove."

He went back and said grace, and found a golden dove.[25]

And why a dove?

Because the community of Israel is likened to a dove, as it is written, "The wings of the dove are covered with silver, and her pinions with the shimmer of gold" (Ps 68:14). Just as the dove is saved only by her wings, so Israel is saved only by the commandments.[26]

This Gemara is remarkable for several reasons. In the first place, it clearly privileges the view of the House of Shammai, thereby violating the general rabbinic rule of following the House of Hillel.[27] Furthermore, this privileging is essentially accomplished through the narratives in the *sugya*, two of which, sections C and D, are recognizable *maʿasim*. B is not formally a *maʿaseh*, but it nonetheless contains a great deal of what Shoshan-Simon calls "narrativity," the specificity and dynamism that are elemental to narrative.[28]

This section, an exchange between the two Houses, follows upon the opening statement of R. Zevid that redefines the disagreement between the two Houses and effectively makes the House of Hillel concede to the House of Shammai in all but one case (where the person actually forgot). The exchange between the two Houses stages a mock dialogue in which each school posits a hypothetical case. First, the Hillelites, with apparent incredulity, question the Shammaites as to whether they would actually require a person who had honestly forgotten to say grace to climb all the way back up to the top of the castle solely in order to fulfill the requirement. To this the House of Shammai responds, with thoroughly unrhetorical curtness: if a person would "willingly" return all the way up to retrieve a forgotten wallet, is it not "fair" to require her/him to do so when it is religiously incumbent. Aside from giving the Shammaites the last word, the response introduces into the *sugya* the motif of a valuable object that is found by the party that returns to say grace—here, a wallet; in the next narrative, a wallet of gold (or dinars); and in the third, a golden dove. This recurring object eventually becomes the climactic linchpin of the entire *sugya*, not only unifying the three narrative sections but also giving them a concluding homiletical point, a lesson about the importance of correctly observing the commandments.

The third section (C) of the Gemara recounts a two-part *ma'aseh* about two anonymous students who did not say grace. One of them honestly forgot to say it, acted in accordance with the House of Shammai and returned to where he had eaten, and found a purse of gold. The other student deliberately neglected to say grace, later pretended that he had unintentionally forgotten and (following the revised position of the Hillelites) did not return, and was eaten by a lion.[29]

The poetic justice refracted in the fates of the two students is so hyperbolic it begins to challenge credibility. Yet the force of this *ma'aseh*—and its humor—builds on its hyperbolic rhetoric, and even if the two students' fates are too perfect, too neat, to have happened, the *ma'aseh* is only effective if its claim to have taken place exactly as narrated is accepted by the reader. (If the *ma'aseh* were acknowledged to be a joke, it would have no point.) While the *ma'aseh* does not prove that everyone who follows the House of Shammai will always find a golden purse—though it does follow from the narrative's logic that if a person does *not* go back, s/he will never find one—it does demonstrate that following the more lenient position, particularly under false pretenses, may lead to a fatal punishment, or at least makes one susceptible to that risk. Here, again, the Shammaites' more rigorous position is privileged.

The escalating incredibility of the sequence of narratives—from the "reasonability" of the hypothetical case narratives proposed by the two Houses in section B to the much less credible story of the two students in section C— culminates in the *ma'aseh* in section (D), with its story about the Amora Rabba bar bar Hannah. Rabba was a well-known *naḥota*—a sage who traveled back and forth between Roman Palestine and Babylonia, carrying and transmitting traditions between the two centers—who is also the subject and narrator of a number of tall tales in which he relates various prodigies he witnessed in the desert in the course of his travels—the bones of the ten tribes, the followers of Korah who were swallowed by the earth, a frog the size of a fortress, and so on. Rabba's narrative in this section is not a tall tale, but it approaches that status inasmuch as, like a tall tale, it masks itself as fact while it also points to the existence of the mask, to paraphrase Dan Ben-Amos's definition of a tall tale.[30] (The same is also true, to some extent, of the *ma'aseh* about the two disciples.) On the one hand, the miraculousness of Rabba's discovery of the golden dove (as well as its position as the third in the sequence of three narratives about "found objects") belies its claim to historicity. On the other hand, the psychological verisimilitude of its characterization of Rabba (namely, his fear—or is it embarrassment?—of acknowledging the truth to his fellow caravaneers, who presumably are Gentiles) and the accuracy of his knowledge of what the other caravaneers think and value equally bolster the veracity of the story as a "true" tale. The one thing he does not appear to anticipate is what will happen if he returns without a golden dove, but here, of course, the *incredible* indeed happens.

This *maʿaseh* again affirms the Shammaites' position, but the movement of the passage as a whole exemplifies what we might call the rhetoric of credibility. As increasingly more incredible elements are introduced in the sequence of *maʿasim*—as the purse turns into a golden wallet and then into a golden dove—the claim to historicity is correspondingly intensified, with the effect of repeatedly demonstrating the benefits of following the House of Shammai. This is because the very incredibility of what happens to those who follow the Shammaites' ruling suggests to the reader that the incredible is actually the providential—that is, the workings of a God who appears to be with, or in accord with, the House of Shammai (and more than He is with the House of Hillel).

The final confirmation of the historicity and veracity of the *sugya*'s narratives comes with the question the Gemara asks at its conclusion, "What was the significance of the golden dove?" Why did Rabba happen to find specifically that object, a golden dove (and not, say, a purse)? The Gemara responds by extrapolating the symbolic meaning of the dove from a scriptural verse, Ps 68:14, which shows us that a dove is "saved" through (or protected by) her wings; so too the Jewish people are "saved" by observing the commandments. This answer is a kind of midrash, but its actual effect is to intensify the historicity of Rabba's story by proving that every detail in that story counts, has meaning. Why? Because it actually happened, and the life of Rabba, a sage, is a text like the Torah, possessed of the same historical veracity, every detail of which can be plumbed for meaning. And indeed, the dove literally "saves" Rabba—from the anger the Gentile caravaneers would doubtless have felt if Rabba had returned without the dove, not to mention saving him from the embarrassment of being exposed as a liar. And more importantly the golden dove, which began as his white lie, now becomes Rabba's reward for following the commandment according to the rigorous ruling of the House of Shammai; it gains him a shot at salvation, a life in the world to come. None of these meanings would be plausible, let alone possible, unless Rabba actually found a golden dove.[31]

As this talmudic passage demonstrates, the *ma'aseh* as a literary form, brief as it may be, is capable of extraordinary complexity. That complexity continued to develop in the postclassical Geonic period, when collections of *ma'asim* first began to be compiled.[32] The earliest and most famous of these compilations are two works: the first, Nissim ben Jacob Ibn Shahin's *Sefer Ha-Ma'asiyot*, originally composed in Arabic but translated into Hebrew early on and known (in its Hebrew translation) as *Ḥibur Yafeh me-Ha-Yeshu'a (An Elegant Composition Concerning Relief After Adversity)*; the second, a work of unknown authorship or compilation, *Midrash 'Aseret Ha-Dibrot (The Midrash on the Ten Commandments).*[33] Ibn Shahin's collection was composed in Kairouan, Tunisia, and most scholars agree that *Midrash 'Aseret Ha-Dibrot* was also compiled by an author living in the Islamic realm, probably in either Babylonia or Persia in the late ninth or tenth century.[34] In the case of both compositions, it was both the popularity of the literary genre of the *ma'aseh* in earlier rabbinic literature and the compilation of comparable story collections in the Islamic world that probably inspired their creation.[35] Both works are genuine anthologies that collect and combine exempla, sage stories, ethical exhortations, and midrashic homilies. *Midrash 'Aseret Ha-Dibrot* appears to have been a virtually "open" work, with its various manuscripts and numerous editions each containing different combinations of stories and passages in numbers ranging from thirteen to more than forty; some of the stories and passages are common to all the collections; others are unique to single copies.[36] A good number of the passages have parallels in both Middle Eastern and European folkloric traditions and probably were adapted by Jews in the early Middle Ages and Judaized in the process.[37]

Even though these works represent an essentially new type of composition in early medieval Hebrew literature—a more or less freestanding collection of stories—the individual tales within these collections remain within the generic tradition of the halakhic *ma'aseh* inasmuch as they continue to present themselves as illustrations, exemplifications, or extensions of legal or moral teachings. As its title suggests, the stories in the *Midrash on the Ten Commandments*—the use of the term *midrash* in the title is more honorific than substantive—all exemplify, in different degrees (some stronger, others weaker), the various commandments in the Decalogue. Even so, most of the stories tend to move beyond mere or simple exemplification, and what appears most memorable about them is almost its opposite: the incongruity between the religious lessons they are supposed to communicate, and the utterly profane social and moral universe the stories actually depict.

Consider the following passage from the *Midrash on the Ten Commandments*. To exemplify the first commandment, "I am the Lord Your God," the following story is told:

> It happened that (*maʿaseh be-*) a certain crippled Jew heard of a heathen shrine where any lame person could immediately be made to walk. The Jew said to himself: "I will go there; perhaps I will be cured." He went there and spent the night in the shrine with the other crippled persons. At midnight, when everyone was sleeping, the Jew awoke and saw a demon (*sheid*) come out of the wall with a flask of oil in his hand. He anointed all the sick, but he ignored the Jew. The Jew said to the demon: "Why do you not anoint me?" The demon replied: "Are you not a Jew? Why have you come here? Does a Jew go to idolatrous shrines? Do you not know that heathen rites have nothing in them? It is for this reason that I am misleading the Gentiles, so as to strengthen them in their errors, and so that they will have no portion in the world to come. But you! You are obligated to detest idolatry and to stand and pray to the Holy One, blessed be He, that He heal you. You should know that your time to be healed was to be tomorrow, but because you have done this, you will never find a cure." Therefore, a person should trust only in the Holy One, blessed be He, who lives and exists forever.[38]

The appearance of the demon in this story is not an entirely unexpected feature. In fact, as noted earlier, *sheidim* and other types of demonic figures appear regularly in the Babylonian Talmud (as do other supernatural figures like the prophet Elijah). Widespread popular belief in the existence of *sheidim* is attested not only by literary sources but also by the many Aramaic magic bowls that have been discovered in Babylonia and elsewhere in Mesopotamia dating from the Geonic and early medieval periods, the same period in which *Midrash ʿAseret Ha-Dibrot* was compiled.[39] It is not the mere presence of the demon in the story that is surprising but the role he plays in it—on the one hand, his raison d'être, as it were, to mislead the Gentiles by curing them so that they will never recognize the true God, and, on the other, his function of serving as precisely the figure in the *maʿaseh* to condemn the hapless Jewish cripple who is so desperate to be healed that he is willing even to try a cure in a heathen temple. These anomalies all contribute to a skewed sense of reality that is at odds with the explicitly formulated moral at the conclusion: that a person should trust only in God (a trust that one might expect would exclude belief in the existence of *sheidim*). Nor does this teaching quite prepare the reader for the brutality of the judgment that dooms the poor cripple to remain crippled forever as punishment for not sufficiently trusting in God.[40]

The other stories in the *Midrash on the Ten Commandments*, as in other exempla collections, are often equally at odds with themselves, formally and psychologically. This pervasive incongruity has led some scholars to claim that these stories actually represent the beginning of secular narrative in Jewish literature; though cloaked in the garb of homiletical orthodoxy, possibly in order to facilitate publication, these stories—according to this scholarly view— have already freed themselves from the fetters of enforced religion.[41]

But the moralizing legal framework of these stories is disregarded only at the risk of missing their meaning. Indeed, in some respects, the disparity between the worlds these stories inhabit and their messages seems to be part of their rhetorical strategy. Their function is not to accompany specific laws or rulings, as it is in the Mishnah and even in the Bavli, but to reveal the very nature of the Law, which in these narratives becomes an inescapable presence, reaching out with a long and mighty hand to enforce justice. Thus many of the *maʿasim* in these collections begin with their protagonist fulfilling or trans- gressing a commandment. Which commandment that may be is less signifi- cant than the fact of obedience or disobedience in itself and the ultimate punishment or reward that inevitably follows. The underlying subject of these stories is the logic of justice, which moves these stories at its own pace, inex- orably but often unpredictably. Once again, however, that movement depends upon a claim to historicity, even if that claim has moved from center stage to the peripheries while the narrative itself has taken the central role.

This narrative drive also leads these stories in the direction of the novella, toward lengthier forms of storytelling that can more fully develop the possi- bilities inherent in improbable punishment, excessive reward, and confused human motivation. This tendency can be seen best in a narrative that is, in my view, one of the great masterworks of all Hebrew literature, even though it is hardly known to most scholars. The narrative is called *Maʿaseh Yerushalmi* (or *Maʿaseh Ha-Yerushalmi*), a title that is usually translated as *The Tale of a Jerusalemite*, even though there is no indication in the story that its protagonist was from Jerusalem or that it took place in that city or had any connection to it.[42]

Maʿaseh Yerushalmi was probably first composed to be part of a collection of exemplary stories like the *Midrash on the Ten Commandments*. It was almost certainly compiled somewhere in the Islamic realm between the seventh and eleventh centuries.[43] Its modern editor, J. L. Zlotnick, has even suggested that its title may actually have originally meant "a *maʿaseh* from a Jerusalemite (that is, Palestinian) collection of stories," possibly a Palestinian recension of the Midrash *on the Ten Commandments*.[44] The fact that it probably derived from such a collection is borne out by the moral that comes at its conclusion: "A son should always obey his father's commands and must never break an oath." The story may thus have exemplified either the fifth commandment (to obey one's parents), or the third (never to take a false oath), or possibly both commandments.

Like a number of other *maʿasim*, *Maʿaseh Yerushalmi* begins with a deathbed scene.[45] A wealthy merchant, on the verge of dying, demands that his son take an oath and swear, at the pain of losing his inheritance, that he will never go to sea. The son is named Dihon ben Salmon,[46] and we are told that his father has taught him Torah, Mishnah, and Talmud and that he is married to a woman by whom he has (by the time the narrative begins) children. After his father dies, however, the son is told by sailors that his father has left him a fortune abroad, and he is urged to travel to retrieve it. Initially, Dihon resists their pleas (because of the oath he has taken), but he finally surrenders and goes to sea. This betrayal of his oath, we are told, is a transgression so terrible that it incenses God, and He immediately punishes the young man by wrecking his ship in a storm. Dihon is nearly drowned, but he is miraculously washed ashore on a strange island where he undergoes several more trials. First, he is almost eaten by a lion; then he escapes by climbing up a tree, but once he reaches the tree top, he discovers there a giant monstrous bird, the *kifufa*, which also tries to eat him. Dihon again rescues himself, now by climbing atop the bird's back. This act, in turn, throws the bird into a panic, and it flies off with Dihon on its back, carrying him over seas and foreign lands. Finally, passing low over a certain province, Dihon hears the voices of children studying Torah and, naturally assuming that the inhabitants are Jews, he throws himself to earth, nearly killing himself in the process. Once he recovers, however, Dihon makes his way to the town's synagogue where the rabbi takes him in, but reveals an even more awful truth: the place to which Dihon has come is not a habitation of humans but of *sheidim*, demons. These *sheidim*, the rabbi tells him, hate humans and will kill him as soon as he is discovered.

Ever resourceful, Dihon manages to win the rabbi's pity. When the other demons arrive and discover Dihon and hear his story, they indeed wish to kill him, specifically for transgressing the oath he made to his father, but the rabbi protects him. In the process, the young man also wins the favor of Ashmadai, the king of the demons, who makes him the tutor of his son and, eventually, his top counselor, a Joseph-like figure. Ashmadai even entrusts him with the keys to the entire kingdom—save for those to one room, which Ashmadai makes Dihon swear he will never enter. The young man takes an oath to that effect, but one day, overcome by curiosity, he peers into the forbidden room, sees Ashmadai's daughter sitting inside and, at her invitation, enters. It is a trick; she immediately threatens to tell her father—that he has transgressed his oath—unless the young man agrees to marry her. Dihon consents, and Ashmadai happily agrees to the marriage. Dihon swears everlasting fidelity to Ashamadai's daughter (who is never named). The two wed, and, shortly afterward, the young man and the demon princess have a son whom they name Solomon.[47]

The family lives happily together until, one day, Dihon suddenly remembers his abandoned "human" family and begins to pine for his former life and desires to return to it. He finally confides his desire to his demon wife, and she is furious, accusing him of betraying the oath of fidelity he had made to her. Finally, however, she relents and, with great reluctance, agrees to let Dihon visit his former home—but only on the condition that he swears to her that, after one year, he will return to live with her forever. Predictably, once the Jerusalemite arrives home, he announces that he will never return to the land of demons. After the agreed-upon year passes, Ashmadai's daughter sends a one-eyed, one-legged demon to bring him back—the same demon, in fact, who had transported the Jerusalemite from the demon island to the human realm—but Dihon insults and dismisses him. She then sends other emissaries, but to no avail. He continues to refuse until, finally, Ashmadai's daughter goes herself, with her son, and with an army of demons, to persuade her wayward husband to return, but she has no success. Finally, she goes to the synagogue, interrupts the prayers, and demands that a court adjudicate her case. The court meets, the judges decide in her favor—after all, Dihon had signed a written agreement vowing to return—but even then he refuses to yield to the court's decision. Finally, Ashmadai's daughter, recognizing that the Jerusalemite does not wish to be married to her, gives up and agrees to return home and leave him behind. Before she departs, however, she makes a final request: that she be permitted to kiss him goodbye. The court agrees to her request. She kisses her former husband—and strangles him as they embrace. And then, before returning home to the land of demons, she demands from the community of Jews—threatening them with death and destruction if they do not agree—that they accept Solomon, her son with Dihon, as their ruler. When she departs, she leaves the demon boy as king over the community.[48]

Scholars have shown that the *Tale of a Jerusalemite* is one of the earliest written versions of the tale of a man who marries a demoness.[49] The tale has a lengthy pedigree. Its roots can probably be traced back to biblical references to the enigmatic relations between the "sons of God" (*benei Elohim*) and "daughters of men" described in Gen 6. In early postbiblical literature, in works like Jubilees, the Testaments of the Twelve Tribes, and 1 Enoch, as well as in later medieval works like the Zohar, the theme of demonic sexual seduction appears frequently. The fantasy of sexual couplings between demons and humans—which can be male or female on either side—continued to exert a strong fascination upon Jews through the early modern period. Several different stories dealing with such marriages were composed in Yiddish between the sixteenth and eighteenth centuries, among them the *Mayse fun Vormes* and *Mayse Pozna*.[50] Nor is the theme of sexual relations and marriage between humans and demons the sole folkloric or folk element in *Ma'aseh Yerushalmi*. The fantastic *kifufa*-bird; the angry one-eyed, one-legged demon who can transport Dihon from the land of the demons to the human world in a single day; the forbidden chamber in which Dihon first sees the daughter of Ashmadai and enters, thereby breaking his oath to her father; the kiss of death by which Ashmadai's daughter kills Dihon—all these motifs have parallels in other popular folkloric tales throughout the world.[51]

Ma'aseh Yerushalmi is not, however, a folk tale, nor is it simply the story of a marriage between a human and a demon. In my retelling of the story, I deliberately omitted mentioning two related key details, both of which are tokens of the narrative's extraordinary *literary* sophistication and its much more expansive interpretive possibilities.

The first of these features is the fact that the narrative's language is packed with the language and diction of the talmudic academy, with allusions to rabbinic literature and to the realia of the world of Geonic Judaism, on virtually every page. The narrative brims with recondite allusions to halakhah and rabbinic tradition. Virtually every sentence the demons speak carries a biblical or talmudic reference. After the demons discover Dihon in synagogue and wish to kill him for transgressing the oath he made to his father, they cite the statement in *b. Bava Metzi'a* 33b that even unintentional deeds should be treated as willful acts (*ha-shegagot ne'esu lo zedonot*). And when the one-eyed, crippled demon returns to warn the recalcitrant Dihon that he has vowed to return to Ashmadai's daughter, Dihon insults him by asking him why he is blind. To this the demon retorts by quoting Prov 21:23, and then the talmudic passage in *b. Bava Metzi'a* 59a that states that whoever publicly embarrasses his fellow man loses his place in the world to come. Dihon himself is repeatedly referred to as a *ben torah*, a traditional designation in rabbinic literature for a student of Torah that connotes not only learnedness but also the piety that should come from erudition in Torah.[52] Indeed, the sheer density of the language of *Ma'aseh Yerushalmi*, its naïve narrative voice, and its paratactic sentence structure with its many biblical and rabbinic quotations eerily anticipate the modernist fiction of S. Y. Agnon that similarly harnesses the language of tradition for causes that are often deeply profane.[53]

The second remarkable feature of the story—closely related to the language steeped in rabbinic diction—is that the world of demons in which Dihon finds himself stranded is even more Jewish—that is, rabbinically Jewish—than the world of "human" Jews that he has left behind. As I noted in my plot summary, Dihon initially believes that he has landed among Jews, because he hears children studying verses from the book of Exodus. When the rabbi saves Dihon from the other demons in the synagogue, he hides him under his *tallit* while the other members of the demon congregation recite *pesukei de-zimra*. When Ashmadai hires Dihon to be his son's tutor, it is to teach him Torah, Mishnah, and Gemara. And after his own son Solomon is born, Dihon circumcises him on the eighth day, just like any Jewish child. Ashmadai's daughter herself, at the trial to which she calls the Jerusalemite at the story's conclusion, invokes halakhic precedent on her own behalf. As I have already noted, the story's other demons, too, quote not only Scripture but Talmud.

The idea of Jewish demons is not original to this story. In the Babylonian Talmud (*b. Gittin* 66a), Ashamadai is said to attend the academy (*metivta*) in heaven every day and then to descend and study in the academy on earth.[54] A certain demon named Joseph Sheida (*Yosef sheida*) is said in one passage (*b. Pesahim* 110a) to have conversed with R. Joseph and R. Pappa, and in another passage (*b. 'Eruvin* 43a) to have carried *halakhot*, legal traditions, between the two Babylonian *yeshivot* in Sura and Pumbedita (and thus to have been a kind of *nehota*, like Rabba bar bar Hanna!). Another passage (*b. Gittin* 66a; cf. *b. Yevamot* 122a) mentions a certain Yonathan Sheida who is said to have taught

Torah to R. Ḥanina. The Zohar describes Jewish *sheidim*, Christian *sheidim*, and Muslim *sheidim*—an idea that, as scholars have noted, can be found in the Qurʾan and other early Islamic sources as well.[55]

In no other Jewish source, however, is a world of Jewish demons so fully imagined in such rich detail as it is *Maʿaseh Yerushalmi*, where it becomes a virtual alternate reality, a parallel universe to ours. Moreover, the demons who live in that world, rather than simply being Jewish and possessing fluency in rabbinic tradition, also possess a kind of native piety that even Dihon lacks. The only thing demonic about these demons is that they have a propensity for killing humans, particularly when they break laws and violate oaths. In contrast, Dihon may be learned, but his behavior is, at best, legalistic rather than moral. The repeated invocation of the term *ben torah* as his designation by the demons becomes in the course of the story a virtual rebuke, as the young man proves himself to be anything but a *ben torah*. He repeatedly betrays his promises and oaths: the oath to his father not to go to sea, his promise to Ashmadai not to enter the forbidden chamber, his vow of eternal fidelity to Ashmadai's daughter before they wed, and the agreement to return that he later makes with her; finally, in the story's very last scene, at the trial to which his demon wife brings him, he even tries to renege on the financial promises he made in the *ketubah* he gave her when they married. Each time Dihon pleads extenuating circumstances, but by the tale's end he has lost all credibility in the reader's eye, and his treachery has been confirmed. As the demons repeatedly address him as a *ben torah*, one hears in the honorific designation not only a rebuke of Dihon personally but an implied criticism of the world out of which Dihon has emerged more generally—the Geonic world—and a sharp critique of all types of legalistic shrewdness that disregard the claims of morality.

But *Maʿase Yerushalmi* is not mere social criticism; it is an extraordinary attempt to imagine Otherness. In his study of early modern Yiddish demon stories, Jeremy Dauber perceptively remarks that supernatural fiction "often concerns the establishment and transgression of social mores, codes, and boundaries."[56] The most obvious of such boundaries is the one between the natural and the supernatural—or, as in *Maʿaseh Yerushalmi*, the human and the demonic—but the narrative consistently portrays its protagonist as trespassing all sorts of other borders and as constantly being in places he should not be—the forbidden sea, the top of the tree where the *kifufa* perches, the land of the demons, the demons' synagogue (which is no place for humans to pray), the chamber in Ashmadai's palace he swears never to enter, even, in the final irony of the story, the human world to which he flees from the land of the demons but from which he has promised to return to his demon wife—a place, in other words, he had made forbidden for and to himself through his own oath. It is fitting that just as his life among the demons begins inside their synagogue, so his life among humans ends inside *their* synagogue; in both cases, he never should have gone to *shul*.[57]

What is the meaning of all these transgressed and transgressive spaces? When his father first makes Dihon swear never to go to sea, it is presumably to save his son from endangering his life by seeking out treasures that he, the father, left abroad. But in the course of the narrative, it becomes clear that the real danger in going to sea is not death but the temptation of crossing over to another world. In the imaginative universe of *Maʿaseh Yerushalmi*, that other world is, of course, the land of the demons, but it is important to note that, in this narrative, there exist only Jews and demons. With the exception of one stray *goy* whom Dihon meets when he returns to the land of humans to see his wife and children, there are no human Gentiles in this narrative. And given that fact, the line separating demons from Gentiles becomes blurred. For all practical purposes, the demons play the role of the Gentile in the story, and one is tempted to read Dihon's voyage to the land of the demons allegorically, as the story of a Jew who leaves behind his own world in order to pass over and live among the Others—that is, the Gentiles. To be sure, the precious irony behind Dihon's journey is that this other world in the narrative, a world of true aliens, turns out in practice to be little different from the Jewish world he has left behind. But then, the Jerusalemite himself is no different—no better a person, that is—"there" (in the demon world) than he is "here" (in the human one). In both realms, he shows himself to be a scoundrel, an untrustworthy scamp, a betrayer of others, particularly in comparison to the demons. Indeed, in its empathy for the Other—be it demonic or Gentile—*Maʿaseh Yerushalmi*'s achievement is unparalleled in classical Jewish literature. It enlists imaginative narrative as a medium for exploring the possibility of existence beyond the borders of Jewish reality, an existence that must have been all but unimaginable for an ancient or medieval Jew.

Maʿaseh Yerushalmi does not end, however, in the land of the Other. The narrative concludes in the human—that is, Jewish—world, at the *beit din* in the synagogue where Ashmadai's daughter, after strangling Dihon and before she returns to her native demon land, leaves behind the son she has had by Dihon, Solomon, as the ruler over the Jews. This unexpected conclusion is, I would propose, the ultimate "meaning" of this remarkable narrative. It explains how Jews have come to live under the rule of the Other—be that a demonic or Gentile ruler (if indeed there was a real difference between the two to the author of *Ma'aseh Yerushalmi*). This conclusion does not explain *why* Jews are doomed to live under the rule of the Other; one could extrapolate from the narrative that the reason is punishment for Dihon's sins, thereby making the narrative's conclusion fit the traditional paradigm, but that seems hardly satisfactory as a rationale for the truly unhappy reality of the Diaspora in which the authors of this story lived (and we continue to do so).

Like all great narratives, *Ma'aseh Yerushalmi* was not written to provide an "explanation" for the state of the world; it was composed to tell a compelling story, with a beginning, a middle, and an end. Did the author of *Ma'aseh Yerushalmi* truly believe that the story had taken place exactly as it is narrated or that this story truly explains why Jews live in the Diaspora, under the rule of Gentiles? We will never know, but the *ma'aseh* is sufficiently persuasive in its own narrative terms as to make the question beside the point.

2

THE *ALPHABET OF BEN SIRA* AND THE EARLY HISTORY OF PARODY IN JEWISH LITERATURE

Parody may be the last virgin territory in the study of classical Hebrew literature, one of the few realms in Jewish literary tradition as yet almost unsullied by scholarly hands. Until very recently, the only monograph on the subject was Israel Davidson's 1907 doctoral dissertation, "Parody in Jewish Literature," and while the book is not without value, it hardly scratched the surface of the subject.[1] In the past decade—since the original appearance of this essay in 2004—a number of works on the subject have appeared, but they tend to use the terms "parody," "satire," and "humorous story" more or less synonymously, a practice that does not always help to clarify the passages under discussion.[2] This is especially true when the rabbinic passages are said to be parodies of Christian texts, or when the Jewish text under discussion is *Toledot Yeshu*, the infamous (or celebrated) travesty of Jesus's life and career that circulated in the ancient and medieval periods in several different versions.[3]

In this essay, I will use the term "parody" in an intentionally narrow sense to designate a literary work that "imitates the serious materials and manner of a particular literary work, or the characteristic style of a particular author, or the stylistic and other features of a serious literary form, and applies them to a lowly or comically inappropriate subject."[4] As I will use the term, I mean to distinguish literary parody from a merely "comic" or "humorous" story, on the one hand, and from the highly stereotyped and moralistic narrative discourse that characterizes much other rabbinic writing, on the other. As distinct from these types, a literary parody must be an imitation of an identifiable literary work or genre (whether transmitted in writing or orally) *and* a travesty of that work or genre—that is, a deliberately inappropriate and intentionally outrageous comic imitation—a presentation, for example, in which content and style not only clash but violate the very rules of generic decorum. In this chapter I will explore one famously problematic text, the *Alphabet of Ben Sira*, which, as I intend to show, contains some of our earliest examples of clear-cut literary parody in classical Jewish literature; in the course of discussing the *Alphabet*, I also hope to suggest a few other candidates for the genre.

We do not know where the parodic tradition in classical Jewish literature actually begins. Like most things in classical Judaism and its culture, the roots of parody surely lie in the Bible,[5] but in the case of parody, the route from the biblical to the classical Jewish period is an obscure one. For different reasons, it is difficult to speak about parody in classical rabbinic literature, and the case of rabbinic parodies poses distinct challenges. This is not because the rabbis were humorless or because parody as a genre was considered too sacrilegious to be tolerated or preserved. Rather, the main difficulty we face in identifying literary parody in classical Jewish literature is methodological: on the one hand, parody is inherently a *literary* genre, while so much of rabbinic literature was composed and transmitted *orally*; on the other, what does remain of the earlier oral discourse in the written texts is often both so stereotyped and so fragmentary that it is difficult to identify the background against which the parody is projected.[6] The great Russian literary theorist and still one of the most perceptive writers on parody, Mikhail Bakhtin, once wrote that "in world literature there are probably many works whose parodic nature has not even been suspected."[7] This caveat has special relevance for rabbinic literature.

Even so, one assumes that the rabbis, if they did not actually *write* parodies, certainly engaged in the *activity* of parody. The occasion in the rabbinic calendar most appropriate for indulging in parody was, of course, Purim, and there are, in fact, sections of some midrashim on the book of Esther, like *Midrash Abba Gurion*, that contain identifiably parodic sections.[8] *Amat Di Itztalvu*, the Aramaic lament-parody purportedly recited by Zeresh over Haman, recently published by Yosef Yahalom and Michael Sokoloff, is still another example of the types of parody that would have been traditionally associated with Purim. These surviving texts are undoubtedly only a fraction of what once existed.[9]

As thin and fragmentary as this material may be, it is nonetheless the background against which texts like the *Alphabet of Ben Sira* should be viewed. This text is one of the truly exceptional—that is to say, both unusual and problematic—works in all classical Hebrew literature. Since the beginning of its modern study, scholars have been both scandalized and intrigued by its outrageousness. The seventeenth-century Christian Hebraist Giulio Bartolocci called it a book full of "words of vanity and lies."[10] Jacob Reifmann, one of the first modern Jewish scholars to deal with the text, wrote in 1873 that the work is "full of nonsense and folly . . . and even abomination and disgust" and "warranted being burned even on a Yom Kippur that happened to coincide with the Sabbath."[11] Reifmann's declaration partakes of a hyperbole itself worthy of caricature, and more recent studies have been kinder to the work. Eli Yassif's magisterial edition, published in 1984, has made it possible to resolve some of the difficulties that the text posed to these earlier scholars.[12] My own remarks on the text that follow are deeply indebted to Yassif's extraordinarily thorough and comprehensive study, including both its critical text and introductory monograph. I will begin with a brief introduction to the work, summing up Yassif's discoveries and conclusions in the process, and then follow with my own interpretation of the work's literary character as a parody and its significance.

Yassif has convincingly dated the *Alphabet*—or, more accurately, the different works known collectively by the title of the *Alphabet of Ben Sira*—to eighth- to tenth-century Iraq, the Geonic period in Jewish historiography, named after its spiritual leaders, the Geonim, the heads of the great postclassical Babylonian yeshivot.[13] As Yassif shows, the *Alphabet* is less a single or discrete literary document than a tradition of different texts and stories collected together through association with the character of one Ben Sira. This character takes his name, of course, from the ancient third- to second-century B.C.E. sage Yeshua Ben Sira, the author of the Second Temple–era wisdom book, the book of Ben Sira (a.k.a. Ben Sirach or Ecclesiasticus, "the little Ecclesiastes"), which has been preserved in a Greek translation among the Apocrypha and whose original Hebrew text was famously discovered by Solomon Schechter in the Cairo Geniza.[14]

Aside from his name, however, the *Alphabet*'s Ben Sira has little in common with his austere predecessor. Far from being a venerable moralist and sage, the *Alphabet*'s Ben Sira is the ultimate *yanuka*, a brash and impudent, praeternaturally precocious *wunderkind* who, as the first part of the text tells us, was conceived by the daughter of the prophet Jeremiah from her father's semen (which had been left floating in the waters of the bathhouse after the prophet had been forced to masturbate publicly by the wicked members of the tribe of Ephraim!), and who emerged from his mother's womb with full-grown teeth and eloquent speech. In addition to (1) this initial section of the work that recounts the story of the birth of Ben Sira, the traditions associated with the character include: (2) Ben Sira's "education," in which he first learns the alphabet from a hapless *melamed*, an elderly elementary-school teacher of reading and writing; (3) Ben Sira in the court of Nebuchadnezzar, where he must pass a series of twenty-two tests that include performing seemingly impossible tasks (e.g., shaving a hare's head) and supplying answers to such questions as why dogs hate cats; why mosquitoes, wasps, and spiders were created; and why the donkey urinates in the urine of another donkey and smells its own excrement?; (4) a second alphabet sequence, this one illustrated by alphabetically listed proverbs in Aramaic followed by moralistic homilies and exemplary stories illustrating the proverbs; and finally; (5) a series of "additional" questions posed by Nebuchadnezzar to Ben Sira. In addition, as Yassif notes, much of sections 1 and 2 exist in two versions or recensions that are sufficiently different as to be considered separate and independent works.[15]

What the textual evidence suggests, then, is that the works known as the *Alphabet of Ben Sira* constitute a tradition of many different types of works that are united only by their all being connected to the legendary character of the *wunderkind* Ben Sira, and that even the various texts we possess are themselves composites of separate traditions. Aside from having a common hero/protagonist, the contents of these texts and their traditions are highly varied and span numerous literary genres. These range from the quasi-scatological contents of the initial story of Ben Sira's birth to the many folkloric animal stories and the various pseudoheroic burlesques detailing Ben Sira's exploits (like the story of how he shaved the hare's head or the famous episode relating how he cured Nebuchadnezzar's daughter of a bad case of farts) contained in the sections detailing Nebuchadnezzar's questions. All these traditions and their genres share, however, the feature of being, as it were, *uncanonical.* That is to say, they fall on the margins of the high, serious, and canonical literature of rabbinic tradition, specifically the Talmuds and the classical midrashic collections. Within the confines of this discussion, I cannot deal with the full variety of texts found in the *Alphabet*; the reader should consult Yassif's splendid edition and his notes, particularly in reference to the more folkloric passages and tales in the work's later sections. Here I will limit myself to the first two sections of the *Alphabet*, passages that, I hope to show, directly relate to the genre of literary parody.

The first passage—the story of Ben Sira's conception and birth, to which I have already referred—is probably the single most infamous passage in the *Alphabet of Ben Sira*. Despite its length, I will cite the entire text; the translation is based on version 2 in Yassif's text (although I will add parenthetically a few lines from version 1).[16]

"Who does great things without limit and wonders without number" (Job 9:10). If it is said, "Who does great things without limit," why does [Scripture] say, "and wonders without number"? How did the sages explain "Who does great things"—this refers to all the creatures in the world (*yetzirot*) [who were created or born in normal fashion]. "And wonders without number" refers to the three persons who were born without their mothers having slept with a man. And these were Rav Zeira, Rav Pappa, and Ben Sira.

About Rav Zeira and Rav Pappa, it is said that in their entire lives they never engaged in trivial conversation; that they never slept in the house of study, neither regular sleep nor even a nap; that no one ever arrived at the house of study before them; that no one ever found them sitting in silence, but they were always occupied in study. They never gave a bad name to their fellows; they never failed to perform the sanctification of the Sabbath day; they never honored themselves by disgracing their fellows. They never went to bed cursing their colleagues, and they never looked into the face of a wicked person, so as to fulfill what is said, "I will endow those who love me with substance; I will fill their treasuries" (Prov 8:21) And how did their mothers give birth to them without having [intercourse with] a male? It is said that they went to the bathhouse, Jewish semen[17] entered their vaginas, and they conceived and gave birth.

And Ben Sira—how did his mother become pregnant? It is said about her that she was the daughter of Jeremiah. For once Jeremiah the prophet went to the bathhouse, and he saw that everyone there was masturbating. His initial impulse was to flee, but the people would not leave him; they were all from the tribe of Ephraim during the reign of Zedekiah, and that entire generation—the generation of Zedekiah at that time—was wicked; that is why it is written about them, "And they did evil in the eyes of God" (2 Kgs 24:19). They immediately grabbed him and said, "On account of what you have seen, you will now go [and tell others!] You do the same right now!"[18] He said to them, "I beg you! Leave me, and I swear to you I will never tell anyone." They replied, "Did not Zedekiah see Nebuchadnezzar eating a hare and he swore that he would never tell a person. Yet as soon as he left him, he broke his oath! And you will do the same! If you join us now, fine. And if not, we will do to you what they did in Sodom!" Jeremiah immediately did so [and masturbated], though only of great fear. [Version 1 adds: When he left, he cursed his days, as it said, "Cursed be the day on which I was born" (Jer 20:14).][19] Later he fasted on its account ninety-one fast-days, and the Holy One, blessed be He, preserved his semen until Jeremiah's daughter came [to the bathhouse], and the seed entered her womb, and she conceived.

Seven months later, a son was born, and he was born with teeth and with speech.

But once [Jeremiah's mother] bore [the boy], she became ashamed that people would now say, "The child is a bastard!"

Immediately, the child opened his mouth and said, "Mommy, mommy! Why are you ashamed? The son of Sira am I, the son of Sira!" His mother said to him, "My child, who is this Sira—is he a Gentile or a Jew?" Ben Sira responded, "Mother, Sira is Jeremiah, and he is my father. And why is he called Sira? Because he is the *sar*, the ruling officer, over the officers [of the Gentile nations], and he is destined to make all of them and their kings drink the cup of punishment. Do not be surprised at this. Just add up the numerical equivalents of the letters in the name Jeremiah, which come to 271, and those in the name Sira, which also add up to 271 [thus proving that Jeremiah is the same as Sira]! His mother said to him, "But if this is true, you should have said, 'I am the son of Jeremiah.'" Ben Sira replied, "I wanted to say that, but it was too shameful to suggest that Jeremiah had sex with his daughter!" His mother said, "My child, is it not written, 'That which has been is that which shall be' (Eccl 1:9)? But who has ever seen a daughter giving birth by her father?" Ben Sira replied, "My mother, 'There is nothing new under the sun' (Eccl 1:9). For the daughters of Lot became pregnant through their father, and just as Lot was a perfectly righteous man, so was my father perfectly righteous" [Ben Sira then proceeds to point out all the similarities between Lot and Jeremiah, after which:] His mother said to him, "My son, the only thing that astonishes is how you know how to say all these things." Ben Sira responded, "Mother, do not be astonished! For my father Jeremiah did the same. When his mother was about to give birth, the child opened his mouth from out of his mother's womb and said, 'I will not come out until you tell me my name. [Ben Sira then goes on to list all the equivalences between himself and his father Jeremiah, the last of which is:] Just as Jeremiah composed a book arranged in alphabetic acrostics [namely, the book of Lamentations, each of whose first three chapters have their verses arranged alphabetically], and there were things in it so difficult that people wished to destroy it, so too will I compose a book in alphabetic acrostics, and there will be things in it so difficult that people will wish to destroy it. And in the future I will be revealed to them. So do not be amazed!"

More than any other passage in the *Alphabet*, this long section has aroused the attention—and the ire—of numerous scholars. To be sure, as Yassif points out, in itself the story of an extraordinary birth amid supernatural circumstances is not out of the ordinary for heroes and other legendary figures. In ancient literature it is commonplace for miracles to attend the births of heroic figures; consider the birth stories of Moses, Jesus, Darius, Muhammed, and Zarathustra—the list goes on and on.[20] Even so, the story of Ben Sira's conception, with its account of the near sodomizing of the solemn prophet Jeremiah by the Ephraimites, then the divinely ordained preservation of the prophet's semen in the bathhouse water, the subsequent impregnation of his daughter, and finally the birth of the young *wunderkind* who emerges out of the womb brashly proclaiming his paternity—this birth narrative is literally over-the-top, unparalleled in its improbability and effrontery by any other birth narrative. It is hardly surprising that the story has elicited numerous attempts to explain away its offensiveness, though virtually no one has acknowledged the outrageous humor of the original. Early on scholars like Reifmann proposed that the story was the creation of "forgers"—that is to say, Karaites—who invented it in order to mock rabbinic tradition.[21] Israel Levi proposed in an article in 1891 that the story's motifs were borrowed from early Persian myths about the birth of Zarathustra; as Levi pointed out, both Syrian Christian and some early Muslim traditions assert that Jeremiah was in fact Zarathustra's teacher.[22] Somewhat more obviously, Adolph Jellinek, in his introduction to this work in *Beit Ha-Midrash*, pointed out the parallels between the story of Ben Sira's birth and that of Jesus, and he argued that the *Alphabet's* narrative was in fact composed as a satire or parody of Jesus's "immaculate" conception and virgin birth.[23]

As more recent scholars like Joseph Dan have pointed out, however, these various theories of the text's origins all fail to account for the fact that the text satirizes biblical figures like Jeremiah and Lot as much as Ben Sira or any other unnamed figure from later rabbinic tradition.[24] Furthermore, if the text were indeed a polemic against Karaism, Christianity, or Islam, one would expect to find in it some kind of defense of rabbinic (or Rabbanite) Judaism, which it utterly lacks. According to Dan, the real target of the text's polemics is religious hypocrisy, which he sees as being the butt and moral of many of the text's constituent tales. Yet this "explanation" for the text is also not satisfactory. For one thing, it is far from clear how exactly hypocrisy explains the details of Ben Sira's extraordinary birth; for another, we do not know what Jewish group or sect would create a text like the *Alphabet* to criticize or expose the hypocrisy of the rabbis, a fact that Dan himself acknowledges. Yassif, in turn, has argued that the story of Ben Sira, from his birth on, is meant to be taken entirely seriously as an attempt on the part of its author(s) to create a Jewish mythic hero on the model of other mythic heroes found in national epics. Yassif correctly warns us against applying an anachronistic reading that would impose upon the text modern assumptions about what an ancient or early medieval Jew could take seriously; instead, he argues that the story should be taken more or less at face value, as a work of pure literary art.[25]

The difficulty with Yassif's approach to the passage is that it overlooks the manifestly *low* voice that is evident in both the work's vulgarity and its comedy. To paraphrase Oscar Wilde, one would need to have a sense of humor made of stone not to be entertained by Ben Sira's antics. To be sure, as we have noted, the identification of a parody is always a tricky matter. The late critic Wayne Booth correctly remarked that "the contrasts between an original [work of literature] and a really skillful parody [of it] can be so slight that efforts to explain them can seem even less adequate to the true subtleties than explanations of other ironies."[26] Parody inevitably involves an ironic compact between the author and the reader, whereby the reader is expected to recognize the signals pointing to the "original" text (or genre, if a specific literary work is not involved) being parodied—the "victim," in Booth's felicitous terminology. The irony inherent in parody consists of the reader's recognition of precisely that distance between the *victim text* and the *parody text*, the clash between the victim's decorous combination of style and content with the parody's undecorous combination. This ironic element is also what distinguishes a parody from a mere travesty or a satire.

In the case of our Ben Sira narrative, the victim text is both classical midrash generally and a specific midrashic text with whose traditions we may also assume a reader of the *Alphabet* would have been familiar. Thus to any reader acquainted with midrash, the interpretive conventions and exegetical language of the *Alphabet* passage would have been (and are) immediately recognizable. The opening interpretation of Job 1:10 has countless parallels in classical midrash that frequently plays on the seeming redundancy of parallelistic verses in biblical poetry; see, for one example, *Vayikra Rabbah* 1:1 *ad* Ps 103:20. So, too, the *gematria* (arithmological analogy) between the letters in the name Jeremiah and those in Ben Sira is typically midrashic. The passage in praise of Rav Zeira and Rav Pappa imitates many passages of rabbinic hagiography (although the final citation of Prov 8:21 as a "fulfillment prooftext" seems to be nonsensical, thrown in purely for affect).[27] Similarly, the repartee between Ben Sira and his mother, wherein the mother begins Eccl 1:9 and the boy retorts with the verse's conclusion, also imitates many midrashic stories, most famously the story of R. Joshua ben Hananiah and the Jewish slave boy in Rome recorded in *Eikha Rabbah* 4:1.

Yet beyond all these easily identifiable conventions of classical midrash, the *Alphabet* passage also parodies a specific midrashic text—a famous passage in chapter 26 of *Pesikta Rabbati*, a collection of homilies that was probably edited in fifth- or sixth-century Palestine, though it contains much older material as well.[28] This passage is indeed cited by Yassif, who acknowledges its presence behind the Ben Sira birth narrative, though he treats it purely as a putative source for some of the latter's details.[29]

In fact, its role behind the Ben Sira passage is far more crucial than being merely a source for some details. Knowledge of the *Pesikta Rabbah* passage and of its context is indispensable for appreciating the humor of the *Alphabet's* story.

A few words about that context will be helpful. *Peskita Rabbati*, chapter 26, is an unusual homily in that it does not begin with an explicit citation of the initial verse of the weekly Torah reading or, as would be the case here, the first verse of the week's *haftarah* (the reading from the Prophets that follows the Torah reading in the synagogue). Even so, it is clear that the *haftarah* reading that is the subject of the homily is Jer 1:1 and that the Sabbath for which this homily was composed is the first of the three special Sabbaths preceding Tisha B'Av, the fast day in the Jewish calendar that commemorates the destruction of the temple. Those Sabbaths are known as the *telata de-pur'anuta*, "the three of persecution," and are among the most solemn—literally mournful—periods in the Jewish ritual calendar.

Pesikta Rabbati's homily on Jer 1:1 for the first Sabbath in this period is appropriately grave and serious in tone, and especially so when it describes the singularity of the prophet Jeremiah, Judaism's prophet of doom *par excellence*. Following a short introduction, the chapter opens with an exegetical enumeration (a common midrashic literary form that organizes all instances of a given phenomenon, like the number of people born without their mother having slept with their father). In this case, the reader will immediately recognize the victim text of Ben Sira's enumeration in *Pesikta Rabbati's* enumeration:

> [Jeremiah] was one of four men who were known as *yitzurim* (creatures who were directly created by God). [The passage then goes on to name the other three—Adam, Jacob, and Isaiah—and cites a prooftext for each figure.] And the fourth was Jeremiah, to whom God said, "Before I created you (*etzarkha*) in the womb, I knew you (Jer 1:5)." These are the ones about whom the word *yetzirah* (creature) is employed.

The passage then continues:

> [When he came out of the womb, Jeremiah] cried a great cry as though [he were already] a full-grown youth and exclaimed, "My bowels! My bowels! I writhe in pain! The chambers of my heart are in agony! My limbs are all trembling! Destruction upon destruction! I am the one who will destroy the entire world!"
>
> And how do we know that Jeremiah spoke thus? Because it is written, "Oh, my suffering, my suffering! How I writhe! Oh, the walls of my heart! My heart moans within me, I cannot be silent" (Jer 4:19).
>
> Jeremiah opened his mouth and reprimanded his mother, "My mother, my mother! Is it not true that you did not conceive me in the manner of other women and that you did not give birth to me in the way of other women who give birth? Perhaps your ways were like the ways of unfaithful women? Perhaps you cast your eye upon another man? As one who has been unfaithful to her husband, why have you not drunk the bitter waters? [see Num 5:11] You are brazen!" And how do we know that Jeremiah spoke thus? Because it is written, "You had the forehead [i.e., brazenness] of a woman of the street" (Jer 3:3).
>
> Once his mother heard these things, she said, "What makes this one speak thus? Surely not on account of sins [that I have committed]!"
>
> He opened his mouth and said to her, "Not about you, my mother, do I speak thus. Not about you, my mother, do I prophesy. But to Zion and Jerusalem do I speak. For she adorns her daughters and clothes them with scarlet and crowns them with gold. But the spoilers are coming and will despoil them, "And you, who are doomed to ruin, what do you

accomplish by wearing crimson, by decking yourself in jewels of gold, by enlarging your eyes with kohl?" (Jer 4:30)

The chapter then goes on to describe how God designated Jeremiah to deliver the message of doom to the nation of Israel, first of all nations, after which it concludes, "When Jeremiah heard this command, he opened his mouth and cursed the day of his birth, as it is written, 'Accursed be the day that I was born!'" (Jer 20:14).

The reader familiar with this passage in *Pesikta Rabbati* will easily hear its numerous echoes as travestied in the birth narrative of Ben Sira. These begin with the use of the word *yetzirah* in the opening enumeration that is echoed in the *Alphabet's* playful exegesis of Job 9:10 to relate to all the *yetzirot* (creatures) in the world who are born normally, on the one hand, and those who were created (*notzru*) without their mothers having slept with their father, on the other. The mode of Ben Sira's emergence from his mother's womb—fully grown, with teeth, and talking—clearly imitates Jeremiah's emergence from his mother's womb, with the predictable difference that Jeremiah emerges in character—that is, mournfully—lamenting his fate and the message of doom he must prophesy to Israel, while Ben Sira, too, emerges in character—that is, with the unabashed *sprezaturra* of a young wiseass, shamelessly boasting of his incestuous paternity. So, too, the story of Ben Sira's conception—the entire bathhouse tale that explains how his grandfather became his father—would seem to travesty Jeremiah's remonstration of his mother for having committed adultery (since the identity of his father seems to be clearly unknown, even to Jeremiah), though again with the difference that Jeremiah immediately clarifies the fact that he is speaking only of his allegorical "mother"—Israel—not his biological parent. Ben Sira, in contrast, comes out of the womb boasting of his parentage, telling his mother to be proud of it and not embarrassed, and as "proof" of the legitimacy of his pedigree, he cites Lot as an analogously righteous figure who also had children through incestuous relations with his daughters; as scholars have noted, Lot is not your typical example of a righteous figure in rabbinic lore. And so, as well, at the passage's conclusion, Ben Sira draws an equally outrageous, mocking analogy between his father and himself, citing the fact that both of them will or have composed texts with alphabetic acrostics—the one, the book of Lamentations, certainly the saddest book in all Scripture; the other, Ben Sira's own *Alphabet*, doubtless the least solemn composition in classical Jewish literature.

To be sure, not every detail in Ben Sira's travesty derives from the *Pesikta Rabbati* passage. The notion of a woman becoming pregnant through seed preserved (miraculously or not) in bathhouse waters is drawn from a famous talmudic passage in *Hagigah* 14b–15a. This passage was first pointed out (and dismissed) by Levi, and it is again cited by Yassif, who takes it more seriously as a putative source for the narrative; he does not, however, look at the passage within its talmudic context and thus seems to miss the point.[30] In context, the line about a virgin becoming pregnant through semen left in the waters of a bathhouse is cited in the course of a passage that follows the famous story about "The Four Who Entered Pardes," one of whom, ben Zoma, we are told, "looked and became demented." Following that story, the Talmud records two questions that were said to have been asked of ben Zoma. First: Is it permissible to castrate a dog?[31] And second: Can a virgin who has become pregnant be married to a high priest (who must marry a virgin)? In response to the second question, the Talmud asks whether we need be concerned about the case of someone as skilled as the Babylonian sage Samuel, who boasted that he was so skillful a lover he was able to penetrate virgins without breaking their hymens(!)—in which case the pregnant maiden would not in fact be a virgin (because she had sexual relations and was therefore disqualified to marry a high priest)—but the Talmud dismisses this possibility as unlikely and instead provides an alternative scenario—namely, that the virgin became pregnant through seed preserved in bathwater. (Even so, a student might wonder how many virgins Samuel penetrated this way to justify his boast.)

Given this context for the statement, it is not disrespectful to suggest that the notion of becoming pregnant through seed preserved in bathwater should be taken, even by a serious student of the Talmud, with a grain of salt, as it were.[32] The very fact that the question instigating the scenario is asked of a *demented* sage should minimally indicate to the reader that we may be entering a world of demented questions. At the least, a pregnant virgin is a case of talmudic hyperbole—an *extremely* hypothetical case—and not far from being a kind of rabbinic joke. And the *Alphabet of Ben Sira* merely turns that joke into the premise of a comic narrative.

In short, I am suggesting that the entire passage in the *Alphabet* is a literary parody of the homily in *Pesikta Rabbati* about Jeremiah *and* a pastiche of references to other passages like the Gemara in *Hagigah* as worked into the parodic narrative. Let me emphasize that these other texts—both *Pesikta Rabbati* and the *Hagigah* passage—are not mere literary footnotes to the *Alphabet*; they are the indispensable victim texts to the parodic text of Ben

Sira's conception and birth—passages and traditions that the *Alphabet*'s author expected his reader to know and to recognize. He also expected the reader to recognize the grotesque (and funny) disparity between the somber *Pesikta Rabbati* homily and the low, vulgar style of the *Alphabet*—the parodic irony, in other words. Nor does the *Alphabet*'s irony end here. An even more profound irony lies behind the text, though it is never explicitly mentioned. This is the irony inherent in the reader's knowledge that Ben Sira, the very unexemplary grandson of Jeremiah, the exemplary prophet of doom, will shortly end up in the court of Nebuchadnezzar—Jeremiah's foe, the agent of the temple's destruction—but acting as the latter's Daniel-like interpreter/counselor and performing such feats of wonder as curing Nebuchadnezzar's daughter of her farting. To be sure, the destruction of the temple is never so much as hinted at in the *Alphabet*, but its lachrymose presence hovers over the text, shrouding the entire parody in the gallows humor of Jewish history.

To be sure, the *Alphabet*'s King Nebuchadnezzar is more like Ahasuerus than either the archvillain of later rabbinic aggadah or even the maddened-by-arrogance king of Dan 4:30 who "ate grass like cattle, and his body was drenched with the dew of heaven until his hair grew like eagle's [feathers] and his nails like [the talons of] birds." But it is safe to assume that none of these ironies would not have been lost upon the text's original or intended audience, who would have found this narrative truly entertaining. And who might have been that audience that would have been entertained by a literary parody of this sort? Only a reader who (as I have argued) would have recognized the parodic references to the traditions like those preserved in *Pesikta Rabbati* and *Hagigah*. That is to say, a *talmid hakham*, either a senior scholar or a student of the scholars who filled the courts of the Geonic yeshivot in Babylonia during the ninth and tenth centuries.

Before we explore this last suggestion more fully, let us consider the second text from the *Alphabet* that also possesses clear parodic elements. This second text immediately follows the story of Ben Sira's birth. When Ben Sira is a year old, we are told, he goes to the synagogue, where he finds a teacher of children (*melamed tinokot*) "who has seven daughters," and he commands him to teach him. The teacher refuses, telling the child he is too young to be taught, and citing as his authority *m. Avot* (5:21), which states that a child should begin to study Bible only at the age of five. To this Ben Sira retorts by quoting verbatim the saying of R. Tarfon in *m. Avot* 2:15, "The day is short but the work is great, the workers are lazy and the reward is great," and berating the teacher for not being willing to teach him. The teacher, in turn, reproves Ben Sira for violating the rabbinic prohibition against teaching the law in the presence of one's teacher—a prohibition the rabbis took so seriously that they made its violation a capital offense—to which Ben Sira, ever the smartass, responds by telling the teacher that as yet he has taught him nothing, and so he cannot be considered his teacher. At this point, the *melamed* capitulates and the lesson begins.

The lesson is a lesson in the alphabet—the *aleph-bet*—and it follows a pedagogical method that is attested in the Talmud (*b. Shabbat* 104a), wherein the alphabet is taught by associating each letter with a maxim or proverb whose initial word begins with that letter in the alphabet; this pedagogical method is also attested in Roman sources.[33] Thus the teacher says to Ben Sira, "Aleph," and Ben Sira responds with the saying, "Abstain from worrying in your heart (*al titein deagah be-libekha*), for worry has killed many men who were mighty (*giborim*)." The teacher then says, "Bet," and the child responds, "By a beautiful woman's countenance many have been destroyed, and numerous are all her slain ones." And so on.

In the *Alphabet of Ben Sira*, however, the lesson does not stop with the alphabet. Each maxim that the child Ben Sira quotes in turn elicits a confession from the elderly teacher. Thus in response to Ben Sira's maxim about abstaining from worry (as quoted above), we are told that the teacher immediately "was thrown into a panic and said, 'I do not have a worry in the world—except for the fact that my wife is ugly.'" In response to the maxims for the letters *bet* and *gimmel*, we learn that the elderly man wishes to divorce his wife "on account of an especially beautiful widow who lives in my courtyard." In response to *dalet, heh,* and *zayin,* the teacher reveals that the woman flaunts herself before him every day, that she practiced witchcraft against her first husband, and that he would already have married her if he did not fear that she would bear him more daughters. And as the lessons continue, the maxims themselves become increasingly misogynistic, bewailing the misfortune of a father of daughters (let alone seven daughters!). A daughter, Ben Sira tells us, is only a source of worry—"when she is a child, he fears that she will be molested; when she is a girl, that she will be promiscuous; when she is a young woman, that she will not marry; and when she is old, that she will practice witchcraft." And so, we are told, Ben Sira "traded words with [the teacher] until he had completed all twenty-two 'chapters' in the alphabet."

As Yassif and others have noted, this entire passage is a work of considerable literary craft. The alphabet lesson is joined with the elderly *melamed*'s confession in such a way as to reverse the roles of teacher and student. Each letter that the *melamed* teaches Ben Sira evokes a maxim from the student that in turn draws out of the teacher one more confession that he seems incapable of *not* making to his disciple. And each confession in turn confirms the hapless fate to which the teacher seems doomed, a fate of being victimized by a succession of females—his ugly wife, the beautiful but sorcerous widow, his seven daughters.

In constructing this narrative, its author has drawn, in turn, upon at least three literary traditions and/or texts (in addition to *Shabbat* 104a, mentioned earlier). In the first place, he has drawn upon a widespread tradition that one scholar has recently called "The Wise Child's Alphabet," in which a child prophet, in the course of learning the alphabet, teaches his teacher the true meaning of the letters; the tradition is attested in stories about the Buddha, Jesus, the Shiʿite Fifth Imam, the Sikh Guru Nanak, the Bab of the Baha, and, of course, Ben Sira.[34]

Second, the passage reflects a widespread tradition of insulting tales told about teachers of children that is especially well attested in Near Eastern literature, both Jewish and Arabic. The Jewish sources have been collected by Saul Lieberman as they have been extensively preserved in Yemenite midrashim.[35] The texts abound in insults about elementary teachers, both calling them "the weakest minded of the weak minded" (*kal ha-kalim*) and condemning them as teachers of false teachings; the person who pays them honor, one midrash states, is doomed to hell (*yoreish geihinom le-ʿatzmo*).[36] The Arabic sources, in turn, have been described by Ignaz Goldziher; in his description, he cites one typical epigram: "It is sufficient indication of a man's inferiority— be he never so eminent—to say that he is a teacher of children."[37] Other Arabic texts abound in stories about lecherous schoolteachers. As Lieberman notes, the Jewish texts may well reflect the prejudices of the Arabic sources.

Third and finally, the *Alphabet*'s narrative directly derives from an actual literary text—to use Wayne Booth's terminology once again, a victim text— namely, *b. Sanhedrin* 100b. Again, I am far from being the first to call attention to the relevance of this text but where others have seen it at best as a source from which the *Alphabet* drew its material, I would like to argue that it is in fact the very target of the *Alphabet*'s parody. The Gemara under discussion is a commentary on the mishnaic dictum attributed to Rabbi Akiba: "Even one who reads "outside books" (*sefarim ḥitzoniyim*) has no place in the world to come" (*m. Sanhedrin* 10:1). In response to the question "What are 'outside books'?" the Talmud records two opinions: first, a Tannaitic tradition that interprets the phrase to refer to a Zadokite documents (*sefer tzedukim*) (whatever that may have been); then, in the name of R. Joseph, a fourth-century

Babylonian sage, the book of Ben Sira. The talmudic passage continues with the following discussion: The fifth-century sage Abayye asks, "Why is it forbidden to read from the book of Ben Sira?" and then goes on to quote a verse from Ben Sira—"Do not strip the skin of a fish even from its ear, lest you spoil it"—to show that in fact the Torah states the same idea expressed in the "forbidden" book (whether the latter's verse is understood literally or figuratively). Following this exchange, the Talmud (or Abbaye) goes on to quote several more verses from Ben Sira and to show, again, that either the Bible or the rabbis themselves expressed the same sentiments. The passage concludes with the anonymous editor of the Talmud citing a verse—"A thin-bearded man is very wise; a thick-bearded one is a fool"—that has no biblical or rabbinic parallel and thus may be said to be the reason why the book of Ben Sira may not be read. Following this apparent conclusion, however, R. Joseph is cited as making an exception to his own prohibition and as saying that it is permissible to expound the "profitable verses" (*milei ma'alyata*) in Ben Sira; he then proceeds to list a whole series of such "profitable verses."

Yassif, through an exhaustive inspection of the manuscripts, has shown that the original text of the *Alphabet* contained only the initial eleven maxims with which Ben Sira responds to the first twelve letters in the alphabet (*aleph* through *lamed*; there does not appear to have been an original maxim for the letter *vav*); only a later editor filled in verses for the remaining letters (which lack, however, a corresponding confession from the *melamed*, thus reconfirming Yassif's conclusion that only the first eleven maxims are authentic).[38] As it happens, ten of these eleven maxims are verses drawn from the talmudic passage in *Sanhedrin* as examples of either profitable or unprofitable verses from the book of Ben Sira.[39] In other words, it is clear that the author of the *Alphabet* extracted these ten verses from the Sanhedrin passage, arranged them in alphabetic order, and then inserted them into his narrative of Ben Sira's lesson in the alphabet—and, in the process, used each verse as a building block for his secondary narrative built out of the *melamed*'s confessions.

To this extent, then, the Sanhedrin passage obviously served as a "source" for the *Alphabet*; as M. Z. Segal showed nearly half a century ago, it is nearly certain that the *Alphabet*'s author's knowledge of the book of Ben Sira was not first-hand but derived from citations and quotations in rabbinic (and perhaps early postrabbinic) literature.[40] But the indispensability of the Sanhedrin text for appreciating the *Alphabet* goes beyond this borrowing of verses. The *Alphabet*'s lesson plays upon the very ambivalence toward Ben Sira that is at the very heart of the talmudic passage. The latter is a discussion of the canonicity of the book of Ben Sira—or more accurately, its noncanonicity; indeed, the Sanhedrin passage is perhaps the locus classicus for the rabbis' ambivalence toward Ben Sira, a topic discussed extensively in modern scholarship.[41]

In the *Alphabet*, that very ambivalence is thematized. Ben Sira, the *wunderkind*, quotes the verses back to his teacher, seemingly as authoritative, "canonical" maxims to illustrate the letters of the alphabet. But the actual literary function of these verses in the narrative is to serve as bait for the elderly teacher; the misogynistic warnings immediately become inducements to make the elderly *melamed* confess to his hapless yearnings. By turning the verses into provocations of this sort—provocations that the *melamed* is incapable of ignoring—the narrative registers its ambivalence about their canonical status. Yes, the text seems to be saying, the verses from Ben Sira (never, to be sure, identified as such in the *Alphabet*) *are* authoritative, but their authority seems to work best for a lecherous old *melamed* with an ugly wife, seven daughters, and a bad case of the hots for a beautiful young widow across the courtyard who is probably a witch. Is this the same canonical authority that the talmudic rabbis were disputing?

In contrast to the *Alphabet*'s use of the *Pesikta Rabbati* homily, which it imitated in the form of a burlesque, the *Alphabet* transforms *Sanhedrin*'s lofty discussion of canonicity into a crude and sometimes lewd lesson—or counter-lesson—in which the student instructs the teacher in the perils of women. What purpose does such a parodic displacement serve? Part of the answer may lie in the tradition that mocks teachers of children and that, as we have already noted, is one of the subtexts beneath the *Alphabet*'s narrative. In his discussion of the Yemenite sources for this tradition, Lieberman suggests that these nasty attacks on schoolteachers—teachers of elementary reading and writing, and particularly of Bible (which was the first subject to be taught to children)—were motivated by animus against Karaites; even though these schoolteachers were usually not Karaites, they were sometimes suspected by contemporary rabbis of teaching Bible in such a way as to support Karaite readings.[42] This may be true, but it is equally possible that what motivated rabbinic sages to make scurrilous attacks on schoolteachers may have had less to do with fighting heresy than with expressing insecurities about their own status—specifically, their fear of being mistaken to be schoolteachers, a profession whose status appears to have stirred up considerable anxiety on the part of the rabbis.[43]

This anxiety is already evident in the Babylonian Talmud. A fascinating passage in *b. Bava Metzi'a* 97a records an exchange between the fourth-century sage Rabba and his students, in the course of which Rabba quotes a law concerning the laws of borrowing that equates "a teacher of children (*makrei dardekei*), a gardener, a butcher, a cupper, and a town scribe," all of whom are public servants. Rabba's students respond to him, "O Master, you are in our service!" thereby equating him with a teacher of children.[44] Rabba, the passage continues, "was enraged (*ikpid*)!"[45] He accuses his students of trying to rob him and angrily insists that he is not their employee, not a hired worker like a teacher of children. In his study of this passage, Barry Wimpfheimer has highlighted the unusual emotional register in the verb *ikpid* ("he was enraged"). Why is Rabba so enraged? Clearly because his students equate him with a teacher of children. Rabba's anger seems to stem precisely from an anxiety over being mistaken for a schoolteacher rather than a sage—not an unreasonable anxiety given the fact that the difference between the two, then as now, may not have seemed so enormous to some people.

The *Alphabet* gives expression to this same insecurity and anxiety in its own fashion. Ben Sira, *wunderrabbi*—after all, he knows everything he needs to be taught even before he's taught it!—both appropriates the talmudic passage and its verses and uses the latter to upstage the *melamed* and show the reader who is the real teacher in this lesson. Once again, the question we need to ask ourselves is: Who would have been so concerned with presenting such a narrative? Who would have wished to mock schoolteachers in such a nasty way so as to confirm and bolster their identity (and insecurities about that identity)? The answer, once again, points to the rabbis themselves—that is to say, to Ben Sira's contemporary rabbis, the Geonim and their students in the Babylonian yeshivot who dominated Jewish intellectual life in the period between the eight and the tenth centuries. These figures were both the *Alphabet*'s authors and its intended audience.

Our knowledge of the Geonic period—and, more generally, of the early postrabbinic, premedieval period—particularly in Babylonia and its Near Eastern environs, is far more limited than for many other periods in Jewish history, but it has grown enormously in the last two decades. In the case of the Babylonian Talmud itself, scholars have increasingly come to recognize the formative, indeed creative role of the anonymous sages who edited the Talmud both as halakhists and as storytellers, and of their successors.[46] So, too, has our knowledge of the Geonic yeshivot and of the rich and sometimes turbulent intellectual life of the Geonic period in its many facets been considerably enriched by the work of recent scholars.[47] The picture of that world as it is beginning to emerge is of a rich and complex society—far more culturally open than was previously thought on both the popular and more intellectual levels: intensely dominated by the Geonic yeshivot and their overriding interest in the study of Talmud and Jewish legal tradition, and yet not closed to a willingness to engage in heretofore uncontemplated intellectual and literary pursuits. While the Geonic period has often been characterized in the past as a largely homogenous, somewhat dictatorial culture, concerned mainly with establishing the absolute hegemony of Babylonian spiritual leadership throughout the Jewish world, it now seems that Jewish culture in the Geonic period was both more open to outside influence and more heterogeneous in its internal composition. It maintained, as Robert Brody has written, "an ongoing intellectual discourse."[48]

In the sphere of belles lettres, our knowledge of Geonic culture is even more limited. The best-known literature from the period is halakhic, while the most significant (and probably extensive) non-halakhic corpus of material is that of piyyut, liturgical poetry. If piyyut can serve as an index, the Geonic contribution to literary culture was far from insignificant. As scholars have only begun to recognize, the classical tradition of piyyut was massively, even radically, reshaped in the Geonic period, particularly in Babylonia, where the opposition to Palestinian piyyut had originally been most vehement.[49] Yet Babylonian sages like Saadiah and Hai Gaon reshaped the classical genres. They vastly expanded the scope of Hebrew poetry, wrote poetic compositions that were never intended for the synagogue liturgy including (in Hai's case) some of the earliest Hebrew secular poetry as well as poems that were among the first to use quantitative meter based on Arabic poetry.

My point in offering this brief sketch of Geonic culture is simply to suggest that the composition of a learned parodic work like the *Alphabet* would not have been out of place in Geonic Babylonia. Quite the opposite: it seems very much a product of that world and its culture. As I have already argued, the parodic nature of both passages discussed in this chapter presupposes a deep familiarity with rabbinic literature and its literary and thematic conventions— the kind of deep familiarity that would have been possessed only by a student of the Talmud of the sort that populated the Babylonian yeshivot. Likewise, the anxieties behind those works are the anxieties of scholars. As we know, parodies do not merely entertain; they can also do double duty, simultaneously subverting cultural norms and reinforcing them. The *Alphabet of Ben Sira* does both: it mocks the somber sanctity of rabbinic hagiography as found in *Pesikta*

Rabbati's portrait of Jeremiah by creating a kind of antihagiography for Ben Sira's conception and birth; at the same time, it reinforces rabbinic self-identity by mocking the *melamed* in the lesson.

To be sure, it is very important that scholars be careful not to read ancient texts anachronistically by inserting conventions and predispositions of one's own, later age. In the case of parody, this is an especially challenging task, if only because the very identification of a literary work as a parody is always an extremely subtle matter, a matter of literary discrimination. Alas, we have no external evidence to prove that the *Alphabet* is a parody. On the other hand, we know—if only because they were a little bit like ourselves—that the inhabitants of the Babylonian yeshivot, those ever-serious and grave Talmudists, must have done something in their spare time, must have had some form of entertainment. No less authoritative a figure than Maimonides tells us that even a philosopher engaged in difficult and weighty matters must have some outlet for relaxation, and as a prooftext he quotes an Aramaic saying, "The rabbis, when they tired of their studies (*girsayhu*), used to speak among themselves words of amusement (*milei de-bedihuta*)."[50] The source for this prooftext has never been identified, nor do we know to which specific rabbis Maimonides was referring, but is it too remote to imagine that they may have been Maimonides's own Babylonian predecessors, the Geonim? Yes, scholars must always beware the trap of anachronism, but what greater anachronism can there be than to assume that the ancient rabbis lacked a sense of humor or a gift for parody less literary or sharp than our own?

3

THE HEBREW BIBLE IN EUROPE
IN THE MIDDLE AGES

What did the Hebrew Bible—the book that Jews held in their hands and actually used—look like in the Middle Ages? The answer to this apparently straightforward question is not, in fact, either simple or easy to give. For one thing, there currently exists no census of surviving Jewish Bibles from the period before print, nor, given the geographical dispersion and number of existing volumes, is such a census likely to be produced in the near future. Further, the surviving codices are obviously only a fraction of the Bibles that once existed. Even taking that fact into account, however, the picture that emerges from the existing volumes is, as Michele Dukan has noted, inevitably skewed, since the codices that have survived are, by and large, the more luxurious and valuable books.[1] The more modest, ordinary codices were used and reused until the letters virtually fell off their pages, and then they were buried, placed in *genizot* (dedicated storage spaces for books removed from circulation), or lost in some other way. As a result, the current corpus of medieval Hebrew Bibles is virtually guaranteed to be unrepresentative, inevitably tilted toward the Bibles that were probably *less* ordinary than those Bibles that were *more* regularly and intensively used. Finally, we face the problem that confronts virtually all attempts to create typologies of manuscripts that are not based upon codicological data, which is that nearly every codex is in some sense *sui generis*. Most scribes were not slavish copyists; they regularly exploited the opportunities available to them to express their creativity and originality within generic conventions. As a result, there will always be exceptions to all rules. In the case of Hebrew Bibles, one of the more conventional Hebrew books, there may even be more exceptions than usual.

Even so, it is possible to construct a broad preliminary typology of the different types of Bibles that were in circulation among European Jews in the Middle Ages and to trace the development of each type in the major centers of Sefarad (Spain and Portugal primarily but southern France and sections of North Africa as well), Ashkenaz (Germany, France except for its southern portion, England, and later Poland), and Italy; in another context, I hope to deal with Bibles from Yemen and the Near East.[2] The survey I will present in this chapter is based primarily on the manuscripts described in the published catalogues of the De Rossi Collection in the Parma Palatina Library, the British Library (BL), the Bodleian Library (Bodl.) at Oxford University, the Vatican collections in Rome, the Bibliothèque nationale de France (BnF) in Paris, the Staatsbibliothek in Berlin, the Library of the Jewish Theological Seminary of America in New York, Hebrew manuscripts in Madrid libraries, and the former Sassoon Collection as described in *Ohel Dawid*.[3] Wherever possible, I have tried to consult the online catalogue of the Institute for Microfilmed Hebrew Manuscripts at the Jewish National and University Library in Jerusalem, as well as every possible reproduction that I have been able to find.[4] A full exploration of the topic remains, however, a major desideratum for which the present attempt should be considered a preliminary sketch.[5] Because this preliminary typology is not based on a comprehensive survey of all medieval Hebrew Bibles, I will refrain from offering precise percentages or definitive formulations; as annoying as that may be, my generalizations will by necessity be restricted to impressionistic, vague terms like *many, some, few,* and so on.

I will begin by offering a brief description of my typology's three main types of Hebrew Bibles such as they existed in the Middle Ages—the masoretic Bible, the liturgical Pentateuch, and the study Bible. I will then treat each type in greater detail by charting its development in the main geographical-cultural centers of Sefarad and Ashkenaz. Following the survey of the two centers, I will offer a separate, briefer survey of Italian Bibles.

Before beginning, however, a brief explanation about the principles underlying the typology is in order. The typology is primarily based on the contents of these biblical books and on the way in which those contents are organized on the page. It is not based on the function or purpose that these Bibles served, although, in the cases of the liturgical Pentateuch and the study Bible, as their names suggest, a functional element clearly played a role in determining their contents and organization. In point of fact, we know very little for certain about the precise functions that any of these books served for their owners, and least of all about the masoretic Bible. It is virtually certain that all three types of Bibles served as books for study for some owners; similarly, there are clear indications (e.g., *haftarah* markings) that some masoretic Bibles were used in synagogues in much the same way as liturgical Pentateuchs. So, too, there exist hybrid books that combine features from the different types. In the course of my survey, I will try to present whatever evidence exists for function while noting variations in form and content. As I present them, the categories are probably best treated as heuristic, descriptive devices. Their main utility is in allowing us to categorize the different types of Bibles that Jews actually used in the Middle Ages.

I. Masoretic Bibles: This type tends to comprise either a complete Tanakh or part of a complete Bible with the Masorah. Because some colophons explicitly state that the scribe wrote only this single volume—for example, a Prophets or a Hagiographa—we know that parts of the complete Tanakh were sometimes copied alone, but where there is no colophon with an explicit statement to this effect, it is impossible to determine whether or not an existing volume now containing only the Prophets or the Hagiographa is the survivor of a once-complete set of codices.[6] Similarly, there exist stand-alone masoretic Pentateuchs.

The genre is defined by its contents and format—the vocalized and accentuated biblical text with cantillation marks, typically presented in either two or three columns, and the masoretic annotations, usually both the Masorah parva and Masorah magna written in micrography, the former in the spaces between the text-columns, the latter on the top and bottom page margins. Depending on where they were produced, masoretic codices frequently contain either or both *parashah* and *seder* signs accompanying the text as well as masoretic treatises and lists that either precede or follow the biblical text. Rarely, however, do the Bible pages contain texts other than the Bible and the Masorah. As we will see, the marginal Masorah itself was recorded in different ways depending on the geocultural center in which it was produced. The typical title for these volumes as they are called in their colophons is either *ʿesrim ve-arbaʿ* (if they contain the entire Tanakh) or Torah (Pentateuch), Neviʾim (Prophets, both *Neviʾim Rishonim*, Former Prophets, and *Neviʾim Aḥaronim*, Latter Prophets), or Ketuvim (Hagiographa, the Writings).

It is worth noting, too, that the order of the prophetic books in the Neviʾim, as well as that of the various books in the Ketuvim, and particularly the order of the Five Scrolls, varies considerably in medieval codices.[7]

A subtype of the masoretic Bible is the *sefer mugah* or *tikkun sofrim*, the model book. Unlike the modern *tikkun*, with its double columns of the same text (one presented as it appears in a Torah scroll, the other printed with the vocalization and cantillation marks), which is primarily intended to help its users memorize the proper way to chant aloud from a Torah scroll in the synagogue service, the medieval *tikkun* was a biblical codex written with special care, so as to serve as an exemplar for scribes writing Torah scrolls or other biblical codices.[8] In some cases, like the Aleppo Codex, we know that the codex was definitely used as a model book; in other cases, the books are identified as such in their colophons and sometimes include scribal laws and rules for scribes in their margins.[9] While it was certainly the case that during the Second Temple period Torah scrolls were copied from other scrolls—there are talmudic legends describing special scrolls kept in the temple itself as exemplars (*sifrei mofet*)—in the Middle Ages it appears that Torah scrolls were generally copied from model codices.[10]

II. *Liturgical Pentateuchs*: These codices are Pentateuchs accompanied by the *haftarot* (sing. *haftarah*; readings from the Prophets that are chanted in the synagogue following the weekly Torah reading); the Five Scrolls (Ecclesiastes, Esther, Song of Songs, Lamentations, and Ruth); and usually the Aramaic Targum, typically *Targum Onkelos*, though in a few cases other Aramaic Targums, and in Arabic-speaking locales (like Yemen), Saadiah's *Tafsir*. As we will see, Rashi's commentary is sometimes included in these volumes, at times as a substitute for the Targum, at other times in addition to it. I have called this type "liturgical" because the contents correspond to the sections of the Bible that were read in the synagogue on the Sabbath and holidays; their precise use remains to be discussed. The Aramaic Targum or other translations are sometimes recorded in separate columns; at other times, they are presented in the body of the Torah text itself, alternating verse and translation or commentary. On occasion, these books also include the *Sifrei EMeT* (Job, Proverbs, and Psalms)—on which see below—as well as *Megilat Antiochus*, a medieval account of the Maccabean Revolt that was read in the synagogue on the festival of Hanukkah, and chapters from the prophet Jeremiah that were read on the fast day of Tisha B'Av. Typically, these books are called in their colophons *ḥumashim*.[11]

III. *Study Bibles*: These codices either include at least two separate commentaries on the same page, often with Targum Onkelos or the *Tafsir*, or the commentary occupies so prominent a position that the codex appears to have been deliberately produced for studying the commentary. In the Middle Ages, commentaries were generally not copied on the same page as the biblical text but were recorded and studied from separate books called *quntresim* (just as in the case of the Talmud). As we will see, the intricate page format of these codices derives from the Glossa Ordinaria's page format (as does that of the Talmud).

In addition to these three main types, there are several subtypes of Bibles or portions of the Bible that were also produced as separate books:

(1) *Psalters*: As its name indicates, the Psalter contains the Psalms alone, sometimes with commentary, often that of Abraham Ibn Ezra. The practice of reading Psalms liturgically, as a practice of private devotion, is very ancient and goes back at least to Palestine in Late Antiquity where texts refer to rabbis reading *sefer tilim* (*tehillim*) (from, one assumes, a scroll).[12] In the Middle Ages, these Psalters are sometimes decorated and even illustrated. Those psalters with commentaries must also have been used for study in addition to recitation.

(2) *Sifrei EMeT* containing, as noted above, the three poetic (or wisdom) books—its name an acronym for *Iyov* (Job), *Mishlei* (Proverbs) and *Tehillim* (Psalms).

(3) Separate codices containing the haftarot alone, or the Scrolls, or both.[13]

(4) Booklets containing the Torah portion for a single week along with its *haftarah*.[14]

These three main types of Bibles that I have described are represented in all the major Jewish geocultural centers of the Middle Ages. In each one, however, the various genres assumed a different material character that was at least partly dictated by its local book culture. These differences will become very clear when we consider the shapes of the genres in Sefarad and Ashkenaz.

Masoretic Bibles

In Sefarad

The medieval masoretic Bible in general is the direct heir of the earliest Jewish codices produced in the Near East and North Africa beginning in the tenth century.[15] Virtually all these codices are Bibles with the vocalized and accentuated Hebrew text written in either two or three columns on each folio page, and with the Masorah, a vast system of notes annotating and enumerating every point of significance in the biblical text.[16] Figure 1, a page from

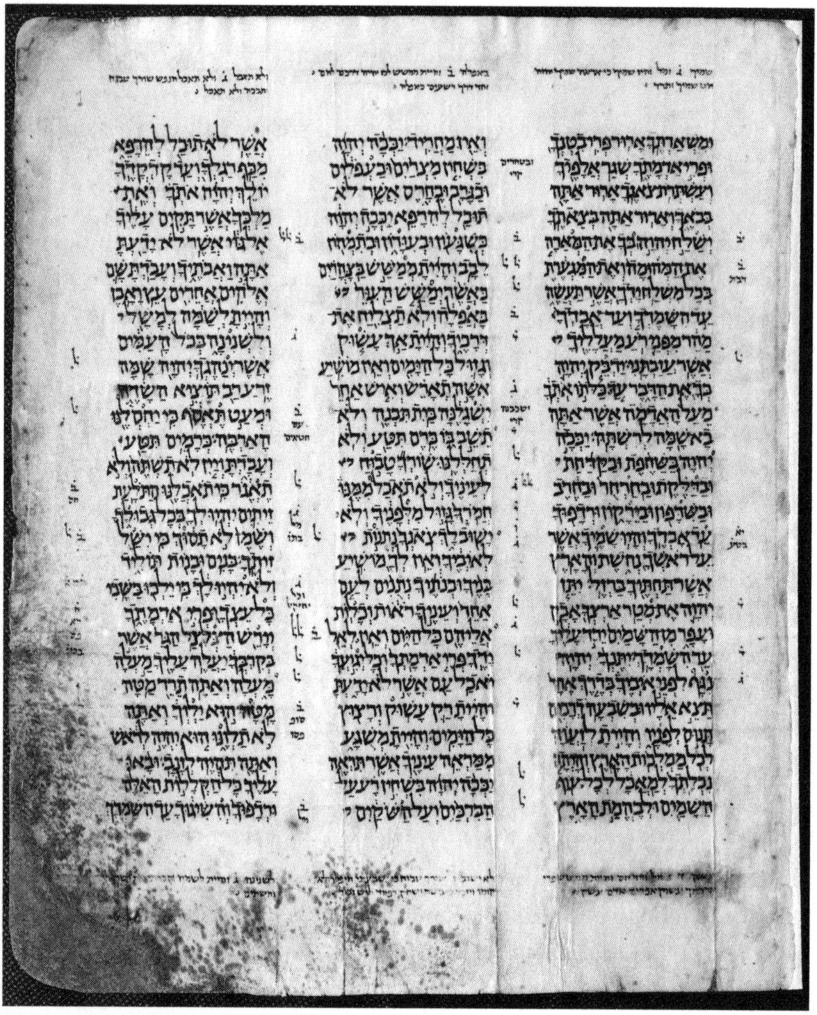

Fig. 1 Hebrew Bible (*Keter Aram Tzova* / Aleppo Codex), Tiberias(?), land of Israel, 920. Jerusalem, Machon Ben-Zvi, Deut 28:18–45. Courtesy of the Ben-Zvi Institute, Jerusalem. Photo: Ardon Bar-Hama.

Keter Aram Tzova, the famous Aleppo Codex (ca. 930), is a typical example of the page layout of the early masoretic codex. The Masorah is written in the margins of the page in two forms: the *mesorah ketanah* (Masorah parva) appears largely in the form of abbreviations on the outer side and intercolumn margins; and the *mesorah gedolah* (Masorah magna), an expansion of the *mesorah ketanah,* in two or three lines across the width of the page on the upper and lower margins. The precise history and nature of these codices has been the subject of considerable discussion over the last century.[17] There existed different masoretic schools, each one with its own scribal traditions, and, as it seems, its own way of transcribing those traditions. The page format of the surviving early masoretic codices seems to have been specific to the Tiberian school; fragments of Bibles with the Babylonian Masorah that were preserved in the Cairo Genizah show that the Babylonian annotations were not written in the margins of the codex but in separate books.[18] When the Tiberian Masorah emerged clearly as the canonical tradition, its page format was also adopted everywhere as the normative page layout for a Bible.

Sefardic masoretic Bibles continue the tradition of those early masoretic Bibles from the Middle East, although it is not clear whether they were direct offshoots or whether the biblical format reached the Iberian peninsula through North Africa (the Maghreb) sometime between the ninth and eleventh centuries.[19] In any case, the connections between these various centers were facilitated by their common location in the greater Islamic empire that covered the entirety of the Near East and North Africa through the Iberian peninsula in southern Europe. The early masoretic Bible already displays the strong impact of the Islamic book, particularly the Qurʾan, especially in the ornamental designs on both its text and carpet pages that replicate well-known Islamic designs; an example of the latter type of page can be seen in plate 1, the famous carpet page in the Leningrad Codex with the colophon of its scribe written, typically, in a micrographic design.[20]

Unhappily, not a single Hebrew Bible survives from the period of Islamic rule in Spain in the eleventh and twelfth centuries—the so-called Andalusian Golden Age—and as a result, we are only able to conjecture about the shape of the Spanish Hebrew Bible in what must have been its most formative period. Even so, the retention of features characteristic of the early Near Eastern Bible—including the aniconism inherited from Islam and the use of carpet pages—remained the single most dominant feature of the Hebrew Bible in Spain even under Christian rule until the expulsion of the Jews at the end of the fifteenth century. This feature is evident in the earliest surviving dated Hebrew Bible from Spain (BnF MS Héb. 105), written in Toledo in 1197.[21] By then, Toledo—one of the great centers of Andalusian Hebrew culture—had been Christian for more than a century (since 1085 C.E.). Even so, the mise-en-page of the 1197 Toledo Bible faithfully replicates that of the early Near

Fig. 2 Hebrew Bible, Toledo, 1232. Paris, Bibliothèque nationale de France MS héb. 25, fol. 125r. Photo: BnF.

Eastern codices with the single exception that the biblical text is written in two rather than three columns.[22]

The same is true of the earliest dated *decorated* masoretic Bible from Sefarad (BnF MS Héb. 25), a relatively small book (185 × 220 cm) written in Toledo in 1232, again in double columns. As can be seen, the Masorah magna appears on double lines at the top and bottom of the folio, while the Masorah parva is

Fig. 3   Hebrew Bible, Toledo, 1232. Paris, Bibliothèque nationale de France MS héb. 25, fols. 40v–41r. Photo: BnF.

in the right and middle margins; on some pages the Masorah magna is written in zigzag patterns, a design also found in the early codices, while on the right-hand page the *seder* (weekly synagogue reading as practiced in the triennial cycle; plural, *sedarim*) is marked by a floral-like decorative medallion above the letter *samekh* (for *seder*); this devise resembles the *ansa* used in Qur'ans to mark *suras*. This custom of marking both the triennial *sedarim* and the weekly *parshiyot* (the weekly Torah reading as practiced in the annual cycle; sing. *parashah*) itself derives from the early masoretic codices, but its persistence in Christian Spain is even more remarkable inasmuch as probably no one in the world by this time still used the triennial cycle. The preservation of the *seder* divisions must have been largely a matter of scribal tradition.[23]

One other decoration in this manuscript is important to note. The magnificent page opening displayed in figure 3 contains the Song at the Sea (Exod 15), which is laid out in the special stichography (dictated by *halakhah*, rabbinic law) called *ʿariyah ʿal gabei leveinah* (a half brick over a full brick), but the most noteworthy feature of the page is certainly the intricate interlaced border created out of micrography that frames the text on the two pages. While the precise origins of this decorative design is unknown, an elaborate micrographic frame for Exod 15 became a staple feature of many subsequent Sefardic masoretic Bibles.[24]

From the evidence of my impressionistic survey, the masoretic Bible appears to have been the most commonly composed type of Bible produced in Spain. Spanish Hebrew Bibles were famous in the Middle Ages for their accuracy, both because their scribes were especially known for their skill as copyists and because of the Spanish proclivity for biblical Hebrew as evidenced in the sophisticated linguistic and philological tradition going back to such figures as Judah Hayyuj and Jonah Ibn Janach in the late tenth and early eleventh centuries.[25] Tenth-century sources already refer to the "accurate and ancient Spanish and Tiberian Bibles," and their excellence was recognized even in Ashkenaz by such figures as R. Meir of Rottenberg (end of the thirteenth century) who mentions "the superior and exact books of Spain."[26] Another thirteenth-century Talmudist, Menahem Meiri (Perpignan, 1249–1316), describes a German rabbi who journeyed to Toledo to acquire a copy of the Pentateuch made from the scroll of R. Meir Halevi Abulafia in Toledo so as to use the Sefardic codex to write Torah scrolls in Ashkenaz![27]

Perhaps the most famous of the Sefardic codices was a model codex known as the Sefer Hilleli, reputed to have been written around the year 600 but more probably written around the year 1000 in the city of Leon.[28] The original was still in existence in 1197 when the Almohades attacked the Jewish communities of Castile and Aragon and carried away at least part of the complete codex. This codex was both consulted and copied; one such partial copy, a Pentateuch, was completed in Toledo in 1241 and survives to this day. As suggested by the large, clear script on the page seen in figure 4, the codex was meant as a model text for scribes and recorded the extraordinary *tagim* (crownlets or ornamental strokes atop letters) as well as certain peculiarly shaped letters.[29] It also contained the text of Aaron b. Asher's *Dikdukei Te'amim*.

The overall development of the masoretic Bible in Sefarad can most visibly be traced through its decorated examples. In her recent monograph on decorated (and illustrated) Hebrew Bibles in Spain, Katrin Kogman-Appel has identified three clear periods in the history of these codices, each period corresponding more or less to one of the centuries between the mid-thirteenth and the late fifteenth.[30] As already noted above, the Bibles of the first period, spanning the second half of the thirteenth century and centered in Castile, Toledo in particular, faithfully continued the presumed tradition of earlier Sefardic Bibles produced during the Islamic period that, in turn, are believed

Fig. 4 Pentateuch (Hilleli Codex), Toledo, 1241. New York, Jewish Theological Seminary of America MS Lutzki 44a, fol. 100v. Courtesy of Library of JTSA.

to have reflected the conventions of the still earlier Near Eastern masoretic Bible. The Castilian Bibles continue to maintain the original masoretic tradition with its aniconicism: the micrographic designs are nearly all geometric or floral, as is the rest of the decoration throughout the carpet pages. Some of the designs also mirror more recent Islamic and Spanish artistic fashions, particularly the new Mudejar designs developed by Muslim artists and artisans living in Christian Spain that drew on the Islamic tradition of the past but enriched it with Andalusian and North African elements.[31]

Fig. 5   Hebrew Bible (Damascus Keter), Burgos, Spain, 1260. Jerusalem, National Library of Israel, Manuscripts Dept., MS Heb. 4°790, fol. 348v. Courtesy of the National Library of Israel.

A premier example of a thirteenth Castilian Bible is the Damascus Keter, written and painted in Burgos in 1260).[32] The opening on display in figure 5 shows the end of the book of Ruth (on the right hand page). On the former page, the Masorah parva is written in its typical style on the right margin and the Masorah magna on the top of the page, but the scribe has filled the space that otherwise would have been occupied by the left text column with an elaborate floral design; next to it, on the right, is an archlike decoration containing the number of verses in the book, again showing Mudejar influence.[33] This influence is discernible, too, in the exquisitely designed carpet page from

Fig. 6   Hebrew Bible (Damascus Keter), Burgos, Spain, 1260. Jerusalem, National Library of Israel, Manuscripts Dept., MS Heb. 4°790, fol. 311r. Courtesy of the National Library of Israel.

the same volume, pictured in figure 6, with its intricate interlace pattern composed of masoretic micrography. This interlace pattern, the inscription of masoretic examples in continuous large square script that serves as the inner frame to the "carpet" inside, and the brocade-like outer frame are all typical examples of Mudejar design.[34] Such inscribed frames anticipate the monumental inscriptions found in fourteenth-century Castilian synagogues, a point to which we shall return.[35]

The Bibles produced in the second period, nearly all in the fourteenth century, are a far more diverse group and difficult to categorize individually even though it was during this century that the vast number of surviving Sefardic Hebrew Bibles were produced, among them some of the most lavish and ambitious volumes. While the textual/scribal side of these codices—the transcription of the biblical text and the Masorah—remains by and large faithful to the heritage of the Islamic past, the art is far more eclectic, showing little continuity with the Castilian Bibles of the preceding century, and drawing upon both Romanesque and Gothic European influences. For example, while masoretic lists at the beginning and end of thirteenth-century codices had often been framed in columns topped by horseshoe shaped arches, which are a typical Islamic/mudejar shape, the columns and arches in these fourteenth-century codices are just as often Romanesque and Gothic in form.[36] At the very beginning of the century, in the region around Tudela in the province of Navarre, the scribe Joshua Ibn Gaon and the illustrator Joseph Ha-Tzarfati collaborated on a number of exceedingly lavish Bibles that include figurative illustrations (like a picture of Jonah being cast into the sea) as well as Masorah in the form of micrographic animals and beasts. All these designs reflect Gothic influence. At the conclusion of this section, I will return to the most lavish of these productions, the Cervera Bible.

The most distinctive feature of the Bibles from this period is found in a group of approximately twenty-five Bibles that were written and produced in the Kingdom of Aragon, particularly in the environs of Barcelona in Catalonia, and in Roussillon, today in southern France, then part of the kingdom of Mallorca, which was, in turn, part of the federation of the Crown of Aragon. All these Bibles share the common feature of having an opening containing (almost always) on two facing pages illustrations of the temple implements— the Menorah (the golden candelabrum with seven branches); the tablets of the Law surmounted by winged cherubim; the showbread table; the jar of manna and Aaron's rod; the golden incense and sacrificial altars; the laver, trumpets, and shofar; and a row of shovels, hooks, and pots used as part of the sacrifical cult. Figure 7 pictures one of the temple implement pages from one of the earliest of these Bibles, composed in Perpignan in 1299.[37] At a somewhat later point, after 1325, an additional element was often added to the ensemble of temple implements—a stylized icon of the Mount of Olives hollowed out with burial caves and topped by a stylized tree.

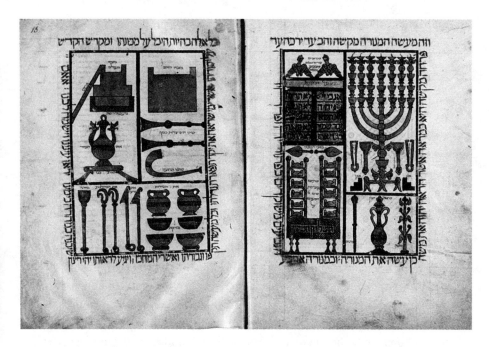

Fig. 7   Hebrew Bible, Perpignan, 1295. Paris, Bibliothèque nationale de France MS héb. 7, fol. 7–8r. Photo: BnF.

These Sefardic codices were not, in fact, the first or last works in Jewish history to contain such illustrations. Ancient synagogue mosaic floors from Byzantine Palestine contain representations of the ark and symbolic icons like the menorah, and one tenth-century fragment, apparently from a masoretic Bible written in 929 C.E. (now in St. Petersburg in the National Library of Russia, Firkovich Collection MS II B17), contains depictions of the temple implements. The earliest Bible produced in Europe containing an illustration of the implements is the Parma Bible (Parma, Bibliotheca Palatina MS Pal. Heb. 2668), written in Toledo in 1276/77, though there is some doubt as to whether the illustrations were originally part of the codex.[38] Around 1300, a number of Bibles that contained pictures of the menorah were also produced in France, Germany, and Italy.[39] Most of the Bibles with the temple illustrations were, however, produced in Sefarad and in Roussillon in the fourteenth century (following the Perpignan Bible of 1299, pictured in fig. 7), but as late as the end of the fifteenth century, an illustration of the temple implements appears in yet another Sefardic Bible, probably in Toledo; this depiction is quite unlike the earlier illustrations and was probably produced in a Christian workshop.[40]

For nearly a half century scholars have debated the relationship between the ancient synagogue mosaics and the illustrations in the medieval codices. Some have used them as evidence for the existence of a continuous line of Jewish art going back to antiquity through the early Near Eastern tradition and continuing into the Middle Ages. Others have pointed out the dissimilarities between the various representations.[41]

For our present concerns, the question of art-historical continuity is less important than the sudden appearance of a large number of codices with temple implement illustrations arranged in so similar a fashion in roughly the same area of Spain at the same time. In her detailed analysis of the iconography and artistic presentation of the illustrations in the different Bibles from the two groups, Kogman-Appel has shown the difficulties involved in tracing the exact lineage and lines of interdependence between the representations, particularly those in the codices from Catalan (those from Roussillon seem to be more of a group), and has specifically remarked upon their diversity, but she has also pointed to the fact that (1) nearly all are found at the beginning of the codices rather than in locations closer to the biblical sections in Exod 25 dealing with the implements; (2) nearly all are based on Maimonides's (and to a far lesser extent, Rashi's) descriptions of the implements rather than those in the Bible itself, either in Exodus or in 2 Kings; and (3) most share a common mode of representation—a flattened, highly stylized and generalized, almost abstracted composition. Whether or not the medieval representations were based upon nonextant models that the artists actually looked at, or whether the illustrations were derived from each other, or whether illustrators drew the pictures from memory, the fact remains that here we have an identifiable group of illustrations whose meaning—and presence *in* these Bibles—demands some kind of explanation. I shall return to this question immediately after completing my survey of Spanish Hebrew Bibles.

The third period of Spanish book production, according to Kogman-Appel, also took place in Castile, but now in the midst of the turbulence of the fifteenth century. This turbulence followed upon the terrible persecutions of the Jews after the Black Plague in 1348–49, and then the anti-Jewish riots in 1391 and the forced conversions that followed the riots. In this troubled period, Jewish book production declined just as did Jewish culture in the Iberian peninsula in general.

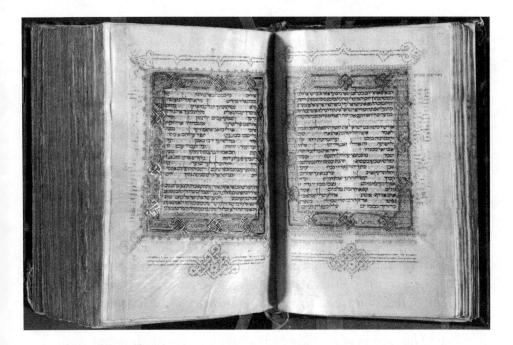

Fig. 8 Hebrew Bible, Lisbon, 1496. Philadelphia, Free Library MS Lewis O 140, fols. 44v–45r. Courtesy of the Free Library of Philadelphia, Rare Book Department.

Around the middle of the fifteenth century, however, from the year 1460 on, in southern Castile—Toledo, Seville, and Cordoba—there was a sudden, unanticipated efflorescence of Bible production that essentially reinvigorated, if not reinvented, the thirteenth-century Castilian tradition. As with their predecessors two centuries earlier, the decoration in these Bibles is largely limited to micrographic Masorah and carpet pages, as well as the use of both *parashah* and *seder* markings (even more anachronistically now than before). In general, the design of the Bibles is almost entirely imbued with the features of Islamic and Mudejar culture and the tradition represented by the masoretic Bibles produced in thirteenth-century Castile. Indeed, if anything, the fifteenth-century Bibles, which usually have smaller formats, are even more exquisitely produced than the earlier Castilian models. Figure 8, a page from one such Bible completed in Lisbon in 1496, with an elaborate, stunning border surrounding the text of the Song at the Sea (Exod 15), is a perfect example of the ornate nature of these books.[42]

One should note here as well a group of extraordinarily lavish Bibles produced in Lisbon, Portugal, in the late fifteenth century, in an atelier apparently specializing in the production of such Bibles (as Gabriella Sed-Rajna has argued).[43] Between 1469 and 1496, the year that King Manuel I issued a decree of expulsion against Portugal's Jews, nearly thirty manuscripts were produced there, all sharing a distinctive style and unusually sophisticated execution. Among the manuscripts are some twelve biblical works, including several liturgical Pentateuchs, a genre that seems to have been especially popular among Portuguese Jews. The most famous and sumptuous of these Bibles is the Lisbon Bible (BL MS Or. 2626), composed in 1482–83.[44] Like the other Bibles, the Lisbon Bible has elaborate floral devices for *parashah* signs and, more strikingly, uses elaborate double-framed pages decorated with floral and bird and animal motifs (particularly on the first pages of biblical books), as well as exquisite filigree-work panels and brilliant characters with much gold leaf. The decoration reflects Mudejar, Italian, Flemish, and Portuguese motifs. The biblical texts inscribed on these pages sometimes look as if they are lying in a paradisial garden bed; on other pages, Scripture appears literally to be framed like a work of art. Figure 9 is a page from the Almanzi Pentateuch, written in Lisbon in the third quarter of the fifteenth century, which contains the opening of the book of Lamentations, and shows how even such a somber text could be rendered into an image of exquisite delicacy and elegance even if drawn solely in ink. Like their Castilian counterparts, these Bibles testify to a burst of creativity at the very brink of one of the most catastrophic moments in medieval Jewish history.

As this brief sketch indicates, the history of the Sefardic masoretic Bible is characterized by two remarkable features—first, its retention of the features characteristic of the early Near Eastern Bible like the aniconism derived from Islam, often at the expense of features perceived to be Christian; second, the temple implement illustrations that appear in so many fourteenth-century Bibles as virtual frontispieces to the text. Both features call for commentary. At the outset it should be said that there is no reason to expect a single explanation, either for both features or for each one separately. Their meaning is most likely to have been overdetermined—that is, replete with different types of significance for different users and audiences. As Eva Frojmovic has lucidly written, it is very possible that "these images were produced with several possible meanings in mind, and received with a wide range of readerly attitudes—from scholarly attention, meditation,

Fig. 9   Pentateuch (Almanzi Pentateuch), Lisbon, ca. 1475.
London, British Library MS Add. 27167, fol. 419v. Courtesy
of the British Library / Granger, NYC.

and devotion to proud conspicuous consumption and the pleasure of gazing
at dazzlingly abundant gold leaf."[45]

Thus it is clear that the temple implement illustrations almost certainly
expressed for many some kind of messianic hope and longing for the restoration of the temple.[46] For others, those features derived from Islam may have
evoked cultural memories of the Golden Age under Muslim rule and thus
reflected the traditionalist inclinations of at least some classes of Sefardic
Jewry, especially the Sefardic elite, who, even in the thirteenth and fourteenth
centuries, still sought to represent the values of Judaeo-Arabic culture.[47]

What, however, do these features tell us about the nature of the Jewish Bible as a material artifact in Spain? And what can these two features tell us about the *meaning* that the Bible held for Spanish Jews and that led them to produce books with these particular features? The answers to these specific questions are, I would like to suggest, related.

We can begin with the tendency in these Bibles to retain the features of the early Near Eastern Bible—particularly the aniconism inherited from Islam and the use of carpet pages—despite the fact that these books were produced in *Christian* Iberia. In fact, the Islamicizing tendency is generally characteristic of contemporary Mudejar culture in the Hispanic kingdoms, particularly in the thirteenth and fourteenth centuries, which was inherently eclectic and hybrid, the culture of *convivencia*, a symbiosis born of the interchange between its Islamic, Christian, and Jewish populations.[48] In fact, Christians also used Mudejar designs, especially in luxury textiles.

Nonetheless, it is noteworthy how consistently the Sefardic Bibles rejected contemporary Christian book culture and—with a few notable exceptions— elements perceived as "Gothic." This tendency in the Jewish sphere to cling to the traditional Islamically derived models and to the influences of contemporary Mudejar style is not unique to the book culture of Sefarad. It also informs the architecture of the synagogues that Jews built in the thirteenth, fourteenth, and fifteenth centuries—buildings like Toledo's Santa María la Blanca, constructed in the thirteenth century; the Cordoba synagogue, erected in the first quarter of the fourteenth century; the synagogue in Segovia (currently Iglesia del Corpus Christi), built in 1419; and the most famous of them all, El Tránsito, erected in Toledo in 1360.[49] The monumental inscriptions in the last synagogue are reminiscent of the inscriptions that frame the carpet pages and temple implement pages in Sefardic masoretic Bibles. All these buildings, constructed in the Mudejar style, depart from the central defining features of contemporary Christian religious architecture. As Jerrilyn Dodds has shown, none of these buildings look at all like contemporary churches built by Christians during the period; they all reflect Islamic or contemporary Mudejar models.[50] Some of the inscriptions are even written in Arabic and include texts from the Qurʾan.[51]

The same "Islamicizing" tendency informs the Sefardic Bibles. None adapt the main stylistic elements found in Christian Bibles produced in Iberia during this period. With a very few exceptions—the illustrations in Joshua Ibn Gaon's and Joseph Ha-Tzarfati's Bibles from the very beginning of the fourteenth century, and such late works as the First Kennicott Bible from the late fifteenth century, and scattered micrographic masoretic grotesques (about which I will speak shortly)—Spanish Bibles resist the kind of representational, narrative illustrations that dominate Christian book art, particularly in the Castilian tradition that John Williams traced nearly a half century ago.[52] The one exception to this rule is the temple implement illustrations, but these are not narrative drawings so much as decorative pages resembling the carpet pages in earlier Castilian or Near Eastern Bibles.

Why did the Jews of Iberia so regularly avoid the features of Christian books in their Bibles and cling to the Islamically derived features of Mudejar style? For one thing, this tendency to avoid contemporary Christian elements violates one of the cardinal rules of Jewish book culture: namely, the tendency for Jewish books to reflect those of the host culture. Part of the answer may lie in viewing the tendency as a reflex of Sefardic traditionality, but it was more than that. The tendency may have served a more contemporary, "politicized" purpose. It may have functioned as a path of resistance to the dominant Christian culture, a way for Jews to identify not only their books but *themselves*, a minority culture, albeit an active one, with the other contemporary minority culture in the Hispanic kingdoms, that of the Mudejars, who, in a similar vein, rejected models that they perceived as Christian. Such a path of resistance would have held special urgency in the thirteenth century, which witnessed the violent dislocations of the Christian conquest of the south and, perhaps even more so at the end of the fourteenth century, with the 1391 persecutions, the forced conversions that followed them, the failure of the apocalyptic expectations predicted for the beginning of the fifteenth century, and the disappointment that must have followed upon the failure of those expectations. Their Mudejar neighbors posed no threat to the Sefardic Jews, and the Jews, by materially identifying their books and synagogue buildings with Mudejar tradition, were able to resist Christian hegemony and to define themselves as a minority culture in a kind of act Eric Lawee has called "counter-acculturation."[53] We know from other cases that the material shape of a canonical text can serve to shape religious identity.[54] Here the material shape of the Hebrew Bible served as a medium of cultural self-definition.[55]

An analogous explanation may lie behind the efflorescence of temple implement illustrations in the Roussillon and Catalan Bibles of the fourteenth century. As both Kogman-Appel and Frojmovic stress, the illustrations should be read not in visual isolation or as mere images, but together with the texts inscribed in monumental frames around them (at least in those cases where such frames exist; not all the Temple implement illustrations have them).

Essentially, there are three separate types of inscriptions: (1) those that quote verses like Exod 25:34 and Num 8:4 that relate directly to the Temple implements, the menorah in particular;[56] (2) those that pray for the rebuilding of the temple;[57] and (3) others that praise Torah and wisdom, usually through a mélange of verses from Proverbs (eg. 2:3–11; 3:1–3; 6:23) and Job (18:16), often using metaphors and similes that liken the commandments to a lamp (*ner*) and Torah to light (*or*) (Prov 6:23 in particular) or that compare the value of wisdom, Torah, and the commandments to silver, gold, onyx, sapphires, and so on.[58] It is not clear why certain verses are chosen for specific pages. In several cases, the different pages that illustrate the implements in the same codex may be framed with combinations of all three types. Still, the overall effect of the inscribed verses is clear: they Judaize the implements illustrated in the picture by explicitly framing them with the words of the Hebrew Bible.

This is not insignificant because the temple implements—the treasured spoils of the destroyed Jerusalem temple—were fiercely contested objects in the religious imaginations of Jews and Christians (and to a lesser extent Muslims). In the Late Antique and early medieval periods, Jewish and Christian traditions explicitly foresaw the restoration of the temple implements as part of their respective apocalyptic scenarios.[59] In Christian Bibles, we find illustrations of the temple implements going back to the seventh-century Codex Amiatinus (which itself derived from the sixth-century Codex Grandior of Cassiodorus), as well as in Spanish Bibles from the tenth through the thirteenth century (though these illustrations picture the consecration of the desert Tabernacle, inside of which the cult objects can be seen). Illustrations bearing even a stronger resemblance to the Jewish ones can be found in a fourteenth-century Spanish manuscript of the *Historia scholastica* of Peter Comestor (d. 1178–80).[60] The contested nature of these cult objects, their association with the apocalyptic scenarios of the rival religious traditions, and the messianic expectations that were current among Catalan and other Spanish Jews following the Barcelona Disputation of 1263 (which itself largely revolved around the messianic doctrines of Christianity and Judaism) and the longings for "end dates" signaling the arrival of the messiah around 1358 and 1403—all these separate elements conjoined to give the Temple implements an especially powerful symbolic force at this particular historical moment.[61]

So, too, in Jewish biblical exegesis of the period, the implements also gained new attention. While the illustrations themselves (as Kogman-Appel and Frojmovic have shown) are closely modeled upon Maimonides's detailed descriptions of the objects, their spiritual significance in thirteenth- and

fourteenth-century Jewish exegesis went far beyond Maimonidean rational-
ism. The key exposition of the implements is found in the popular, quasi-
kabbalistic commentary of Bahya ben Asher (Saragossa, d. 1340), a student of
Nahmanides. In his commentary on the phrase in Exod 25:9, "the pattern of
the Tabernacle and the pattern of its implements (keilav), Bahya begins his
exposition with the statement, "It is known that the Tabernacle and its implements were all material images (tziyurrim gufaniyim) [that were intended]
to make comprehensible the divine ('elyonim) images for which they were
a model."[62] He then proceeds to explicate at length the spiritual meanings of
each of the implements and their respective spiritual powers, and on Exod
26:15, he concludes,

> And it is important to say that even though the Tabernacle and the
> Temple were fated to be destroyed, and the holy material Temple imple-
> ments were fated to be destroyed in the Diaspora (golah), you should
> not imagine that, Heaven forbid!, because they ceased to exist in this
> world (lematah), their forms and models also ceased to exist in the
> higher world (lema'alah). They continue to exist and will exist forever,
> and if they came to an end below, they are destined to be restored as they
> originally were. . . . And lest you say that just as they were destroyed
> below (in this world), their power (sevaran) above was lost; that is to say,
> the power to which they point (mekavim), or lest [you say that] the
> power that we contemplate in them ceased to be, therefore the verse
> teaches: they exist, forever and for all eternity.[63]

What Bahya seems to be pointing to is specifically the image of these implements, something perhaps not all that different from the image that the menorah ultimately takes in the form of the Shiviti (which was typically composed
out of the micrographic rendering of Ps 67)—namely, an iconic image of
devotion.[64] Precisely because the images of these implements—placed at the
very beginning of the codex like carpet pages—were believed to possess such
powers that they were also able to serve as markers of the Jewishness of these
Bibles.

A very similar symbolic meaning for these Bibles is also reflected in the
term mikdashyah, literally "the sanctuary of the Lord," which beginning in the
fourteenth century becomes in Sefarad an honorific title for deluxe masoretic
Bible codices.[65] Some of the codices, though by no means all, contain Temple
implement illustrations, making them virtually self-reflexive books with their

sanctuary-likeness pictured inside them.[66] The use of the term *mikdashyah* was not, however, a fourteenth-century invention and did not derive from the presence within their pages of the Temple implement illustrations. Naphtali Wieder has demonstrated that the use of *mikdashyah* as a term equating the Torah with the Tabernacle goes back to early sectarian circles, as documented in the literature from Qumran, and is later explicated by the Masorite Aaron ben Asher in his *Sefer Dikdukei Ha-Teʿamim* where he analogizes the three courtyards of the Temple to the three divisions of the Bible (with the Penta-teuch equaling the holy of holies, the Prophets the inner courtyard or holy place, and the Hagiographa the outer courtyard).[67] The term was later employed by both Karaites and Rabbinites like Abraham Ibn Ezra. Two masoretic Bibles written in the late fourteenth century—one formerly in the Sassoon Collec-tion, written in the years between 1366 and 1383, the other, the King's Bible (BL MS Kings 1), written in Solsona, Catalonia, in 1384—both describe themselves in their respective colophons as a *mikdashyah*; as Wieder notes, the former manuscript explicitly described the cognomen as one used *be-fi he-hamon*, "by the masses."[68] It was, in other words, a popular designation for a deluxe Bible like other terms such as *taj* and *keter* that were also applied, first, to early Near Eastern masoretic codices (like the Aleppo Codex, *Keter Aram Tzova*) and, later, to Spanish Hebrew Bibles (like the Damascus Keter discussed earlier that was written in Burgos in 1260).[69]

The most extensive explication of the term *mikdashyah* as an epithet for the Bible in a fifteenth-century Sefardic Jewish text is found in the introduction to the grammatical treatise *Maʿaseh ʾEfod*, composed in 1403 by the Catalonian polemicist and grammarian Isaac ben Moses Halevi, better known as Profiat Duran (1360–1412).[70] Duran draws on the analogy between the tripartite divi-sion of the Bible and the spatial structure of the Temple that (as we have seen) was already formulated by the early Masorete Aaron ben Asher. For our con-cerns, however, the real significance of Duran's discussion lies in the special importance he attributes to study of the Bible and in his references to the *actual* Bibles used for study that he uses to support his argument for the importance of Bible study.

Duran's exposition is found in the context of a typology he presents of the three different types of intellectual elites among Jewish scholars of his day; each type is devoted to the acquisition of a different type of knowledge (*hokhmah*) leading to "the ultimate perfection" (*ha-hatzlaha ha-aharonah*)— namely, the fullest realization of Jewish existence. These three elites are the Talmudists, the philosophers, and the kabbalists. While Duran never explicitly rejects any of these types or their respective subjects of knowledge, he proposes a fourth path, Bible study, as the true "worship" (ʿavodah) of God.[71] The term ʿavodah is laden with meaning: originally an epithet for the Temple cult, it was later appropriated by the rabbis as a cognomen for *their* institution of worship, communal prayer, which they called ʿavodah ba-lev, "the worship of the heart." By using this charged designation, Duran effectively attributed to Bible study the same religious efficacy possessed by Temple sacrifice *and* the rabbinic institution of communal prayer.

Another loaded term that Duran uses to describe Torah is *segulah*, a word that means both a "treasured heirloom" and a virtually amuletic source of special power.[72] Thus he writes, "even engagement (ʿeisek), recitation (hagiyah), and reading (keriah) alone [that is, without comprehension] are part of ʿavodah and of that which will help to draw down the divine influence and providence through the *segulah* that adheres in them, because this too is God's will."[73] Indeed, he continues, God specifically prepared the Torah for Israel in its time of exile, so that it could serve as a *mikdash meʾat*, a "small sanctuary," within whose pages God's presence might be found just as it formerly was within the four walls of the Temple; analogously, study of Torah atones for sins just as sacrifices once did.[74] Indeed, the study of Torah is so implicated in the fate of Israel in Duran's view that its neglect by the Jews of Ashkenaz (because of their lamentable concentration upon Talmud study) led to their persecutions in the fourteenth century; so, too, Duran writes, the only reasons Jews of Aragon were spared from destruction was because of their recitation of Psalms, *shimush tehillim*, a kind of devotional reading with theurgic powers.[75] In Duran's view, this powerful *segulah* attaches to any activity related to Scripture, including the compilation of Masorah, the study of biblical grammar, and even the composition of his own grammar in the *Maʿaseh Ephod* that Duran believed would play an active role in the apocalyptic scenario and hasten the Messianic age.[76] Needless to add, the *segulah* of Torah study is efficacious only when the Torah is studied in Hebrew, not in other languages.[77]

For Duran, then, the Bible is more than just a text; it possesses what Kalman Bland has called "artifactual power."[78] This conception gains further depth if it is seen against the background of Duran's time, the years between 1391 and 1415, when the Church in Iberia embarked upon an especially virulous campaign against its Jews. By emphasizing the Bible's artifactual power, Duran was offering his contemporaries an avenue of salvation that was immediately available to them, a sacred shelter inside of which they could occupy themselves in Torah study and thereby protect themselves, spiritually and psychologically, from the hostile world outside. This was the real force of the temple analogy as Duran used it. Strangely, Duran never mentions the temple implement illustrations—a curious omission if he was indeed familiar with them—but it is not difficult to imagine how a fourteenth-century Spanish Jew, looking at those pages, would have felt the palpable connection between the divine presence dwelling in the temple and the material Bible containing those images.

Duran's biblicism should be seen as the culmination of the grammatical tradition going back to the Masoretes and continuing with the work of earlier Andalusian grammarians like Jonah Ibn Janach and exegetes trained in al-Andalus like Abraham Ibn Ezra who stressed the importance of knowledge of Hebrew as a key to interpreting Scripture. But there is something new about Duran's approach. As Irene E. Zwiep has argued, Bible study for Duran is essentially an individualistic activity of studying the written text in order to memorize it.[79] In contrast to the student of Talmud, who is advised to attend a yeshivah, where he will learn to deduce generalized principles from particulars through direct intellectual exchange with his rabbinic teachers, the reader addressed by Duran internalizes his knowledge of Scripture through memorization, an act that is essentially solitary (even though Duran also stresses the importance of studying Bible in study houses with other students).[80]

To facilitate study, Duran provided in the introduction to the *Ma'aseh 'Efod* an entire system of memorization techniques, nearly all of them drawn from known classical and medieval memorial traditions (as Zwiep shows) but adapted to Jewish tradition.[81] A significant number of these techniques relate to the material artifact of the codex. The student should place mnemonic notes (*simanim*), presumably in the margins of the text, so as to facilitate recall from memory (Rule 4).[82] He should always read from the same book, not switch between copies (Rule 5).[83] The text should be written in square, Assyrian letters (*ketav ashuri*), "for because of its beauty the impression of this script remains in the common sense and in the imagination," and these letters should be inscribed in bold and heavy strokes (Rules 9 and 10).[84] And most significant of all, "one should always study from beautifully made books that have elegant script and pages and ornate adornments and bindings, and the places of study—I mean, the study houses (*batei ha-midrash*)—should be beautifully constructed and handsome, for this enhances the love of study and the desire for it. It also improves [the power of] memory, for reading while looking at pleasant forms and beautiful images and drawings quickens and stimulates the soul and strengthens its faculties" (Rule 6).[85] Once again Duran draws upon the Temple analogy, saying that it is only fitting to decorate and beautify "this sanctified book that is a *mikdashyah*" because it was God's will that the sanctuary itself be decorated and ornamented with silver and gold and fine gems.[86] For this reason, he adds, it has always been helpful for learned scholars to be wealthy so as to be able to own their own books and not have to borrow them. And so, too, he comments sarcastically, the wealthy patrons of his day even believe that "possessing these books is sufficient as self-glorification, and they think that storing them in their treasure chests is the same as preserving them in their minds."[87] Duran himself does not believe this, but because he was unable to deny the social power of these wealthy aristocrats, he nonetheless concedes that "there is merit for their actions, since in some way they cause the Torah to be magnified and exalted; and even if they are not worthy of it themselves, they bequeath a blessing to their children and to those who come after them."[88] Therein lies the Bible's artifactual power. It can even help those who do not deserve it!

Duran was not the only figure to level criticism at the wealthy aristocratic classes of the Jewish communities in Aragon and Catalonia in the late fourteenth and early fifteenth centuries for their religious laxity, materialism, and social corruption.[89] As Duran understood, however, these classes constituted the community's leadership, for better or for worse. Duran's discomfort with the values of that aristocratic class, along with the very qualified praise he adds in his closing remarks, epitomizes his ambivalence. He knew that these wealthy patrons were the only ones with the financial means to commission such Temple-like Bibles, and one can see in his remarks something of a defense and even a legitimization of their crucial role despite their failure to exercise proper spiritual and political leadership. While these opulent Bibles should have been used for study, as Duran recommended, he also knew that they were "trophy books," commissioned specifically for the conspicuous display of their owner's wealth. Frojmovic has called attention to the borrowings of ornamental designs for carpet pages in these Bibles from precious Andalusian textiles, wall hangings, and dress. These precious items were signs of nobility and aristocracy (for both Christians and Muslims), and by using them in Bibles, their Jewish owners also signaled their social status. And yet, as Frojmovic also shows, "the Hebrew Bible pages create images of religious contemplation, analogous to the complicated patterns of Islamic textiles that were to be savored slowly in a contemplative fashion."[90] Still, the spiritual profits from showing off should not be lightly dismissed. As I have noted, the production of such books for the wealthy paradoxically spiked in the late fifteenth century, despite the political and religious turbulence of the period. It is almost as though the sheer investment of wealth in such valuable objects of sanctity provided their owners with a kind of spiritual security blanket.

The story of one display Bible of this kind vividly illustrates the circumstances that could lead to the commission of such a book. In 1476, in the town of La Coruña (Corunna) in the far northwestern corner of Spain, the scribe Moses Ibn Zabarah and the illuminator/artist Joseph Ibn Hayyim, working together, completed an opulently illustrated Hebrew Bible.[91] The Bible was written at the commission of a certain Isaac ben Solomon di Braga, an "admirable youth," as he is described in the book's colophon. We have almost no knowledge of the di Braga family's history, but they were probably merchants involved in La Coruña's famous clothing industry. Isaac's father was deceased, so the young man must have been sufficiently wealthy on his own in order to commission the Bible and cover the considerable expenses of production. He may also have had a connection to the Bible's scribe through his father, and the scribe may have felt a paternal obligation toward the youth. The admonition in the codex's colophon, addressed to the book's patron, that "this book of the law shall not depart out of your mouth, but you shall meditate upon it day and night so that you observe and perform all that is written in it" may have been not a cliché but sincere counsel proffered by an elder to a young aristocrat urging him to maintain the traditions of his father's faith.

This Bible is known today as the First Kennicott Bible (Bodl. MS Kenn. 1). It is one of the most extravagantly decorated and illustrated Hebrew manuscripts ever produced. Nearly one quarter of the approximately nine hundred pages in the codex bear some kind of decoration, including arcaded pages at the volume's beginning and end containing David Kimchi's (Radak's) grammatical treatise, *Sefer Mikhlol*; decorative carpet pages at the main divisions of the Bible (between the Pentateuch and the Prophets, where four pages are devoted to the Temple implements, between the Prophets and the Hagiographa, and before Psalms); decorated panels and frames for the beginnings of books, among them Jonah and the Psalms, which themselves contain text illustrations; decorative and narrative motifs for the *parashah* signs throughout; the artist's colophon containing zoo- and anthromorphic letters; and many instances of the Masorah magna written in micrographic designs.

Ibn Hayyim's art drew from eclectic sources—Mudejar motifs, fourteenth-century Catalonian Bibles, Gothic and French figurative illustrations, even contemporary playing cards, whose figures served as models for the depiction of characters like King David as well as for the animals and beasts that populate the marginal *parashah* decorations.[92] The book's main source, however, was an earlier Bible known today as the Cervera Bible (Lisbon, Biblioteca Nacional MS Hebr. 72), which was completed in 1300, nearly a century and a half earlier.[93] This Bible's scribe, Samuel bar Abraham Ibn Nathan, wrote the codex, he tells us in the colophon, while recuperating from a fracture in his leg. Its Masorah, executed in many skillful micrographic designs, was done by the famous scribe and illustrator Joshua Ibn Gaon who, while largely adhering to earlier Castilian Islamicizing tradition, introduced Gothic motifs and themes like playful dragons into the book. Its extensive decorations and lavish illustrations were drawn and painted by Joseph Ha-Tzarfati ("the Frenchman"). Joseph, too, drew on a large repertoire of models for his paintings and drawings—architectural designs, floral patterns, and depictions of animals, many of them Gothic in origin. Most dramatically, he broke with the tradition of Castilian aniconic decoration and drew pictures with human figures that are completely unlike anything in earlier Sefardic Hebrew Bibles.[94]

Both the Cervera Bible and the Kennicott Bible were unique productions. Except for its scribe's fractured leg, we know virtually nothing about the circumstances surrounding the production of the Cervera Bible, but there are some hints to the history behind Isaac di Braga's commissioning of the Kennicott Bible. Marginal notations in the Cervera Bible made by its owner about births in his family indicate that the book was in La Coruña during the first half of the fifteenth century, and it is likely that the book was still there in 1476, when Isaac may have personally seen it. Based on this possibility, the historian Cecil Roth long ago speculated that Isaac not only saw the book but coveted it so much that he wanted to buy it. When its owner refused to sell it, Isaac hired a master scribe and a talented illuminator with orders to produce a Bible modeled upon the Cervera that would surpass it with even more elaborate and beautiful illustrations.[95] Although there is no hard evidence to support Roth's speculation, it has been recognized by Jewish art historians as sufficiently compelling to enter the scholarship. True or not, it offers a captivating story for depicting a wealthy Jew's motive in commissioning a trophy Bible. One can easily imagine how the combination of acquisitive lust *and* spiritual desire could lead a young and wealthy patron to commission such a visually spectacular Bible.

If this were indeed the story behind the creation of the Kennicott Bible, we can understand why the later Bible so obviously copies the earlier one. There can be no question that Ibn Hayyim, the Kennicott's artist, knew the Cervera

Fig. 10   Hebrew Bible (Cervera Bible), Cervera, Spain, 1300. Lisbon, Biblioteca Nacional de Portugal MS IL 72, fol. 449r. Courtesy of the National Library of Portugal.

Fig. 11   Hebrew Bible (Kennicott Bible), La Coruña, Spain, 1476. Oxford, Bodleian Library MS. Kenn. 1, fol. 447r. Courtesy of the Bodleian Libraries, University of Oxford.

Bible, as can be seen by juxtaposing his and Joseph Ha-Tzarfati's colophons, pictured here in figures 10 (the Cervera Bible) and 11 (the Kennicott Bible). In its structure and contents, too, the Kennicott was deliberately modeled upon the Cervera Bible. Both contain grammatical works by Radak at their beginning and end (though they are different works in the two Bibles) as well as similar illustrations, like that of Jonah being thrown off the ship and swallowed by the whale, with the Kennicott clearly taking the idea for its picture from the Cervera.[96]

More than imitating the Cervera Bible, however, the Kennicott seems intentionally to try to exceed it—not only in its sheer calligraphic and decorative beauty and in the opulence and number of its illustrations but in playfulness as well. For all its sublime craftsmanship and its use of Gothic motifs like animals and decorative dragons, the Cervera Bible is, in the end, a fittingly somber and devout Bible. Not so the Kennicott. While Joseph ibn Hayyim's colophon imitates Joseph Ha-Tzarfati's zoo- and anthropomorphic letters, the hollow shapes of the Kennicott's letters are populated with intentionally humorous faces of glaring people, lovable monstrosities, and, even more shockingly, naked men and women. The *parashah* signs—many of them, as noted, based on playing card figures—are similarly inhabited by hybrids and humanoids who point to an imaginative realm literally beyond the edges of the sacred text. Some of the illustrations resort to ironic reversals. Atop the arcades framing *Sefer Mikhlol*, an army of cats with swords besieges a castle of mice. In other pictures, hares attack wolves.[97] In most Hebrew manuscript, wolves represent Gentiles and hares Jews (and the wolves typically chase the Jews). The victory of the hares over the wolves in the Kennicott Bible represents an eschatological fantasy.

In the Ashkenazic Bible we will encounter other examples of humorous (and bizarre) marginal art, but the images in the Kennicott have an irrepressible liveliness that infuses the entire book. Composed only a year or two after the first books printed in Sefarad, and a mere sixteen years before the expulsion of its Jews from the Christian kingdoms, the opulent codex bears witness to a rocket-like burst of creativity at a moment of Jewish history in Sefarad that is usually viewed as the nadir of the rich cultural history that preceded it. It is not to be disregarded that this unexpected creative burst took the shape of a Bible.

In Ashkenaz

The territory called Ashkenaz primarily refers to northwest Europe—Germany, on the one hand, and northern France, on the other—but it also includes other bordering German-speaking lands such as Bohemia, Moravia, and, during a certain period, Poland, as well as England (after the Norman Conquest and before the expulsion of its Jews in 1290). It is often difficult to distinguish between these different areas insofar as manuscript production goes.[98] Even so, it clear that, throughout Ashkenaz, that the masoretic Bible occupied a far less prominent position than it did in Sefarad. According to my preliminary survey, nearly two-thirds of the surviving medieval Bibles in the Iberian peninsula are masoretic; in Ashkenaz, in contrast, they represent no more than a third and, as we shall see, are correspondingly outnumbered by liturgical Bibles.

In terms of its overall contents and page layout, the Ashkenazic masoretic Bible, like its Sefardic counterpart, replicates the early Near Eastern masoretic codices of the tenth and eleventh centuries. The biblical text is generally laid out in three columns (in contrast to Sefarad where two columns increasingly became the norm), and the Masorah magna and parva are written in micrography, the former in two lines in the top margin and three in the bottom, and the latter in the space to the right of each column. Unlike their Sefardiccounterparts, however, the Ashkenazic codices rarely if ever contain at either their beginning or end masoretic treatises like Aaron ben Asher's *Sefer Dikdukei Ha-Te'amim*.

In some codices, however, the biblical text is accompanied by the Aramaic *Targum Onkelos*, which is written *interverse*—that is, the verse in Aramaic literally following the Hebrew original, verse by verse, in each double column. The earliest attestation of the interverse Targum is in Ashkenazic liturgical Pentateuchs, but it is also found in some of the earliest surviving Ashkenazic masoretic Bibles, the three-volume Ambrosian Bible (Milan, Ambrosian Library MS B30–32), probably composed in the region around Würzberg in 1236–38, and in the Wroclaw Bible (Breslau, Universitätsbibliothek Breslau MS M 1106), written in 1238.[99] It is also found in the two "giant" Bibles from Erfurt, to which I shall return shortly.[100]

Jordan S. Penkower has distinguished different geocultural textual and scribal traditions among both Torah scrolls and Bible codices in the Middle Ages, with clear differences between Ashkenaz and Sefarad.[101] Aside from these geocultural textual differences, the main features differentiating the Ashkenazic masoretic Bible from its Sefardic counterpart are material—namely, the book's format, size, and mode of decoration. At times, these differences can be so pronounced they give the Sefardic and Ashkenazic masoretic Bibles entirely distinct characters. Take, for example, the matter of size. In contrast to the Sefardic Bible—whose size usually varies between that of a quarto and a medium-sized folio[102]—the dimensions of the Ashkenazic Bible vary far more extremely, from "giant" Bibles to small, highly portable codices. This large range in size and format mirrors in certain respects the history of the Latin Bible in Western Europe.[103] As scholars have shown, the twelfth century, first in Italy and later through the rest of Europe, witnessed the production of a great number of multivolume Bibles, many of them with enormous, virtually gigantic dimensions.[104] Beginning in the thirteenth century, however, first around Paris and later throughout Europe, the dimensions of the Latin Bible began to diminish, and the large multivolume sets were replaced by single volumes containing the entirety of Scripture, written on thin parchment (itself the product of new technologies), and in tiny but clear handwriting. These literally portable Bibles—frequently referred to as Paris Bibles—were a product of the commercial booktrade in and around Paris and served a large audience—students and masters, members of the court and church hierarchy, lay collectors, and mendicant monks and friars who had to carry them around to use in preaching and teaching Scripture. As these Bibles proliferated, they became available to the entire literate public and were also acquired by individuals for private study.[105]

The changes evident in the Latin Bible are reflected in the history of the Jewish Bible in Ashkenaz, even though the latter did not follow the same neat chronological development and lagged behind its Christian counterpart by about a century in each stage.[106] Between the mid-thirteenth and mid-fourteenth centuries, one finds both "giant" Hebrew Bibles and smaller portable ones. The Ambrosian Bible of 1236–38 and the Wroclaw Bible of 1238 are both decidedly large multivolume codices (453×344 mm = 18×13.5 inches, and 488×360 mm = 19.2×14 inches), but neither of them comes close to Erfurt 1 (Berlin, Staatsbibliothek zu Berlin [SBB] MS Or., fols. 1210–11), completed in 1343, the single largest Jewish Bible in existence with dimensions of 629×470 mm (= 24.7×18.5 inches). There exist approximately fourteen other biblical codices whose height exceeds 500 mm (= 19.7 inches).[107]

The exact purpose of these large-dimensioned Jewish Bibles is unclear. Scholars of the Latin Bible generally agree that the rise of the large-sized volumes in the late eleventh and twelfth centuries was tied to monastic reform and the renewed insistence upon communal reading in monasteries.[108] This is corroborated by their monumental size, which would have facilitated public reading, while their frequent magnificence suggests that they were also intended for public viewing. We know, too, that lavishly decorated Bibles served as gifts from powerful and wealthy individuals to rulers and religious institutions (like monasteries), donated in order to strengthen strategic political relationships.[109] These factors are less relevant to Jewish Bibles. There were no Jewish monasteries, and at least by the thirteenth century, no one in Ashkenaz was using a codex for the weekly public reading of the Torah in the synagogue (as I will discuss below). Furthermore, as Malachi Beit-Arié has shown, virtually all Hebrew manuscripts in the Middle Ages were initially commissioned or produced for individual owners and users even if in some cases those individuals later dedicated the codices to synagogues or other institutions to serve as communal "property."[110] Such a plan may have been behind the commissioning of some of these Bibles. On the other hand, as Beit-Arié has suggested, it may be that the enormous dimensions of these codices simply embodied "the wish of the patron to produce and own an unprecedented book."[111] It may also have been the case that Jews saw Latin giant Bibles owned by Christians and then thought that they, too, should have such books, if only as a reflex of cultural competition. In fact, we know nothing specific about the history or intended use of the Erfurt Bible (or of others like it) before the expulsion of the Jews from Thuringia in 1349.

Beginning around 1300, however, the dimensions of the Hebrew Bible began to shrink, albeit gradually. A particularly striking example of such a portable Hebrew Bible with much smaller dimensions is the Schocken Bible, produced around the year 1300 in the Lake Constance region in southern Germany.[112] The same smaller dimensions characterize several liturgical Pentateuchs also produced in Germany from that period on.[113] An even more remarkable text is a complete Hebrew Bible, undated but apparently composed around the same time as the Schocken Bible, with 408 folios of such thin fine parchment that all the folios together are only a little more than three quarters of an inch thick while the folios themselves measure a mere 100 × 75 mm (3.9 × 2.95 inches).[114] In the later fourteenth and fifteenth centuries, particularly in Italy that absorbed many Jewish scribes expelled from Ashkenaz, complete Bibles in single volumes regularly possess small, portable dimensions of this order. We shall return to these Italian Bibles at the conclusion of this survey.

In addition to reflecting the physical dimensions of the Latin Bible in the West, the Ashkenazic Bible is also imbued with its decorative and illustrative features. For obvious reasons, the Islamic-derived features of the Sefardic masoretic Bible—the aniconism and carpet pages, the colonnaded masoretic pages with lists at the beginning and end of the book—are absent from the Ashkenazic codices. (There are some Ashkenazic liturgical Pentateuchs with pictures of the menorah, but, unlike their Sefardic counterparts, these typically contain narrative illustrations of biblical scenes surrounding the menorah and only rarely include the other Temple implements.)[115] While decoration in Ashkenazic Bibles often has a functional purpose, as it does in Sefardic ones, the devices are very different. In Sefardic Bibles, for example, *ansa*-like signs drawn in the margins mark the beginnings of *parashiyot*. In contrast, Ashkenazic Bibles use enlarged initial words and, in more deluxe codices, initials enclosed in decorated panels to highlight for the reader the beginnings of biblical books and sometimes *parashiyot*.[116] This, too, parallels developments in thirteenth-century Paris Bibles, where initials (usually letters, not words) also begin to serve as the primary spaces for illustration.[117]

Fig. 12   Hebrew Bible, Lorraine, Franche Comte, 1286.
Paris, Bibliothèque nationale de France MS héb. 4, fol. 249v.
Photo: BnF.

An especially lavish example of such an initial-word panel is found in a
French Bible (BnF MS Héb. 4, fol. 249v) composed in Lorraine, Franche
Comte, in 1286, here pictured in figure 12. This page, the beginning of 1 Kings,
has its initial word, *ve-ha-melekh* ("And the king [David])," empanelled against
a blue and red checkered background and enclosed in a colonnade complete
with watchtowers and a howling gargoyle on its right side, while the colonnade's two columns rest on figures of jousting knights labeled in the text as,
respectively, "This is David" and "This is Adoniyahu." The latter is a reference

to the coup attempted by Adoniyahu, David's son, agains his father, as narrated in the accompanying chapter. (The spears held by the knights themselves meet in two shields in the space between the columns from which rises the tail of a dragon whose head reaches the very top beneath the initial word panel.) Not surprisingly, the iconography of the jousting knights has many parallels in contemporary Latin manuscripts.[118]

Even more common in Ashkenazic Bibles are initial word panels and other decorations written in pen in micrography containing the Masorah. Figure 13, from the famous giant Bible known as Erfurt 2, composed in Ashkenaz (Germany) in the late thirteenth century, is an especially intricate example of such a page. Here the initial word of the book of Genesis, *be-reishit*, written in large Gothic-like Ashkenazic square letters, is enclosed within an arch whose tympanum is filled with various grotesques—dragons, griffins, camel-like hybrids—and other mythical beasts are found in the roundels at the bottom of the page. Like the painted figures discussed in the last paragraph, these grotesques mirror very similar marginal figures in contemporary Gothic codices, particularly in missals and liturgical books.[119] It is not clear whether the grotesques are meant to be mainly decorative or whether they are intended to signal to the reader a kind of *tohu va-vohu* lying beyond the edges of the orderly universe (whose creation begins to be narrated on that page). To be sure, not all micrographic illustrations in Ashkenazic Bibles are of such monstrous creatures. A Pentateuch written in Germany, possibly in the Rhineland, in 1286, contains a micrographic depiction of the red heifer that directly illustrates the text on the page, Num 19, as seen in figure 14 and figure 15 (detail); the heifer seems to be pulling a cart on two wheels, though, if one looks closely, there is actually no line or yoke connecting the heifer and the cart, possibly an illustration of the scriptural requirement that the red heifer be one "on which *no* yoke has been laid" (my italics) (Lev 19:2).[120]

Still, the vast number of micrographic figures are grotesques. The hybrids are invariably eye-catching, occasionally charming, and, especially to a modern eye, bizarre. Figure 16, a detail from another page in Erfurt 2 (see fig. 13), shows two rather harried-looking hybrids, one of them disarmingly swallowing or spewing forth a one-eyed snake-like creature, possibly a tongue with an arrow-headed tip. The page on which these hybrids appear records Lev 35, a chapter dealing with the laws of the sabbatical and Jubilee years. There is no clear connection between the image and the content of the text on the page

Fig. 13   Hebrew Bible (Erfurt 2), Germany, late thirteenth century. Berlin, Staatsbibliothek zu Berlin MS Or. Fol. 1212, fol. 1b. Photo: bpk Bildagentur / Staatsbibliothek zu Berlin / Art Resource, New York.

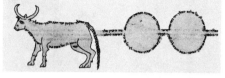

Fig. 15 Pentateuch, Germany (Rhineland?), 1286. Paris, Bibliothèque nationale de France MS héb. 1, fol. 104v, detail. Photo: BnF.

Fig. 14 Pentateuch, Germany (Rhineland?), 1286. Paris, Bibliothèque nationale de France MS héb. 1, fol. 104v. Photo: BnF.

that I can discover. Indeed, within this literary context, the two hybrids look like aliens who just landed from outer space.

These micrographic illustrations did not pass unnoticed by rabbinic authorities. In the influential pietistic manual *Sefer Ḥasidim* (Book of the Righteous), ascribed to Rabbi Judah He-Ḥasid (d. 1217), the author instructs his reader that "one who hires a scribe to write the masorah for the Twenty-Four Books (ie. the Bible) should make a condition with the scribe that he should not make the masorah into drawings of birds or beasts or a tree,[121] or into any other illustration . . . , for how will he be able to see [and read the Masorah]?"[122] This injunction predates any surviving Bible from Ashkenaz, so it is clear that the practice of writing the Masorah in designs had a lengthy history in earlier Ashkenazic codices. But whether or not Judah was the first to oppose the practice, it is clear that his and any other sage's objections were ignored by Ashkenazic scribes and masoretes. There is hardly anything more common in Ashkenazic books than micrographic illustration.

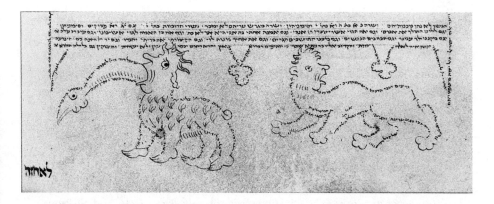

Fig. 16　Hebrew Bible (Erfurt 2), Germany, late thirteenth century. Berlin, Staatsbibliothek zu Berlin MS Or. Fol. 1212, fol. 146b, detail. Photo: bpk Bildagentur / Staatsbibliothek zu Berlin / Art Resource, New York.

Still, the question posed in *Sefer Ḥasidim* is telling: How *will* the reader be able to read the Masorah if it is recorded in the shape of these designs? In fact, it may be that the Masorah was recorded in these Bibles for a purpose other than being read or studied; rather, the Masorah seems to have been more like a necessary, conventional presence, a signature of traditionality. As we have seen, this is also true of the Masorah as recorded in medieval Sefardic Bibles, where its presentation in the form of micrographic geometric, floral, or abstract designs rendered it equally difficult to read. This very fact has led one scholar to suggest that the very purpose of the illustrations was to force the reader to concentrate upon reading the Masorah in these decorative designs. The concentration required to decipher the text may also have been intended to facilitate its memorization.[123] As Mary Carruthers has shown, the association of ideas and texts with specific images was commonly used by medieval scribes as a memory device.[124] Another scholar has suggested, less convincingly, that the Sefardic designs may have had kabbalistic significance.[125] Given their aniconism, the micrographic designs may also have been ornamental in the sense that Oleg Grabar has used this term in writing about similar designs in Qurʾans—namely, as affective in purpose, intended to create in the reader certain feelings of awe and respect for the text, and for the scribe's virtuousity.[126] And, of course, some scribes probably did use especially intricate or grotesque designs to flaunt their virtuousity.

Still, the very grotesqueness of the marginal hybrids and monsters in the Ashkenazic Bibles raises the question as to whether they are expressing more than scribal virtuousity. Some creatures doubtless carried symbolic meanings independent of the text on the page. Dragons, for example, possessed multivalent meanings in medieval culture (Jewish and Gentile) as forces of darkness and evil, or as symbols of fate.[127] But what does one make of the baboons and the snake-eating hybrid in the Erfurt Bible in figure 17?

To be sure, as marginal images (and even in the initial panels, the grotesques frequently inhabit the panel's own margins), these figures are almost by definition figures of ambiguity, inhabitants of a liminal space, who "elude or slip through the network of classifications that normally locate states and positions in cultural space," in the words of the anthropologist Arnold Van Gennep.[128] Here, again, comparison with contemporary Latin manuscripts of the period may be helpful. Recent art historical scholarship has focused extensively on marginal art, particularly as found in Books of Hours, and on the ways in which these marginal images in Christian books challenge and undermine the structured order embodied in the hegemonic, hierarchical texts on the page. Now, in comparison with the Christian books, whose marginal images are sometimes truly outrageous and obscene—"lascivious apes, autophagic dragons, pot-bellied heads, harp-playing asses, arse-kissing priests, and somersaulting jongleurs," in the memorable words of Michael Camille—the images in Jewish books are virtually models of restraint and modesty.[129] Nonetheless, in their own way the Jewish images similarly confront, if not challenge, the textual structure they surround. After all, there is no Jewish text whose structure is more controlled, regulated, and hierarchical than the Bible. Of all types of Jewish scribal activity, copying a Bible, either in a scroll or a codex, is the one that most requires the scribe to be a pure *copyist*, leaving almost no room for innovation or personal creativity, precisely because the whole point of copying a Torah is to reproduce the original as exactly as possible. One of the purposes of the masoretic notes was, as we have seen, to guarantee its textual accuracy and its faithfulness to scribal tradition, to ensure the *exact* reproduction of the original. It is telling that while the hybrids and other playful marginal illustrations are sometimes painted in the margins, the most striking ones are those written out in the shapes of masoretic micrography, the very stuff of Jewish biblical traditionality. By turning those annotations into fanciful, hybrid, Masorah-eating (or spewing) creatures, might the scribe himself have been using them—very "playfully"—as small rebellious figures to challenge his own proscribed "traditional" identity as a "mere" scribe?

In whatever way we interpret the "meaning" of these images, there is no question that they mirror Christian book art of the period. Rather than viewing them as mere "borrowings," however, it might be more correct to characterize them, along with the other material features of the Ashkenazic Bible, as deliberate appropriations of Gentile culture on the part of Jewish scribes—that is to say, as active efforts to Judaize the imagery of their surrounding Gentile culture. While the iconography of the marginal illustrations may have derived from Gentile sources, the scribes or masoretes who designed these illustrations imbued them with an indelible Jewishness by literally making the iconography out of Masorah. These decorations are a perfect example of what Ivan Marcus has called "inward acculturation," whereby Jews adapted Christian themes and practices and reworked and fused them with native Jewish traditions and then, having absorbed them in this reconstituted fashion, "understood them to be part and parcel of their Judaism."[130]

In the past, medieval Ashkenazic culture has frequently been portrayed as living in relative isolation from, if not in active hostility with, its Christian surroundings. Recent scholarship has radically revised that picture by showing that encounters between the two communities, fraught as they often were by theological conflict and physical violence, were still intensely productive with demonstrable borrowings and appropriations in both directions.[131] The appropriative stance toward Christian culture embodied in these Ashkenazic Bibles stands in sharp contrast to the very different strategy that scribes in Sefarad took by Islamicizing their Bibles as a way of resisting the dominant Christian culture.[132] They are two very different responses. It is significant, however, that both responses came in the material form of recording the Masorah. What began as a textual apparatus had now become, in the hands of scribes, a creative tool for negotiating difference and exchange between the Jews of a particular community and the Christian host culture in which they lived.

Liturgical Pentateuchs

In Ashkenaz

The dominant position that the masoretic Bible held in Sefardic book culture was occupied in Ashkenaz by the second type of Bible in our typology, the liturgical Pentateuch or *ḥumash*. According to my preliminary survey, roughly two-thirds of the surviving Hebrew Bibles written in Germany, northern

France, and England in the thirteenth and fourteenth centuries fall under this rubric.

The most prominent feature of the liturgical Pentateuch is its overall organization. Rather than presenting the biblical text in its canonical order, the liturgical Pentateuch organizes its contents to follow the synagogal practice of reading the Torah in weekly divisions according to an annual cycle; the Pentateuchal readings are accompanied by *haftarot* or prophetic readings. The volumes typically (though not always) include as well the Five Scrolls, which are read on various holidays and fast days in the Jewish calendar, and sometimes the chapters of "doom" from the prophet Jeremiah and the book of Job, both of which were recited on the fast day of Tisha B'Av.

This way of organizing and presenting Scripture has no precedent in the early Near Eastern tradition represented by the masoretic codices. As noted earlier, some Spanish masoretic Bibles continued to mark in their margins the *sedarim*, the weekly readings as read in the early Palestinian triennial cycle, but the division in all liturgical Pentateuchs follows the Babylonian practice of an annual cycle. The earliest dated example of an Ashkenazic liturgical Pentateuch is the famous Anglo-Norman Pentateuch written in England in 1189 (making it the earliest datable and localizable Hebrew manuscript to have been written in England), pictured in figure 17.[133]

The Anglo-Norman Pentateuch also displays what is probably the most striking *material* feature of the *text* in the Ashkenazic Bibles—namely, the interverse presentation of the Targum, with each biblical verse followed immediately by its Aramaic translation written in the same square letters and size in (usually two) columns on each folio; in this mode of presentation, Bible and Targum are visually indistinguishable. As noted earlier, the interverse Targum for the Pentateuch is found in another early Ashkenazic masoretic Bible, the Ambrosian Bible, as well as in a fragmentary Pentateuch (Vatican Library MS Vat. ebr. 448) in which the Targum's (Tiberian) vocalization signs are written supralinearly—above rather than below the consonants—which is a typical feature of early Babylonian texts; this manuscript probably dates from the late eleventh century.[134] The path that led this type of Bible from Babylonia to Ashkenaz is not known. The Parma Palatina library contains a Pentateuch with interverse Targum whose colophon states that it was copied from an earlier Pentateuch brought from Babylonia that also contained supralinear vowel points—apparently very much like Vatican 448—and that it was "corrected" to conform to the normative Tiberian sublinear vocalization by a R. Nathan bar Makhir bar Menahem from Ancona, the son of R. Samuel bar Makhir from the

Fig. 17 Pentateuch, England, 1189. London, Valmadonna Trust MS 1, fols. 59b–60a (Exod 40–Lev 1). Courtesy of Museum of the Bible. All rights reserved. © Museum of the Bible, 2018.

province of Oria.[135] This R. Nathan bar Makhir may have been the ancestor of the great sage Gershom ben Judah (ca. 960–1028) known as Rabbeinu Gershom Meir Ha-Golah, "Our teacher Gershom, the Light of the Exile," who was possibly born in Ancona but later settled in Mainz, where he made that community the earliest center of Ashkenazic Jewry. Gershom, it is worth adding, was also a scholar of Masorah, and he wrote his own masoretic notes.[136] Gershom's journey from Italy to Germany was a typical one for early Ashkenazic Jews, and the Bible may have passed through communities like Bari and Otranto on its way to Germany. As we know, these communities were also instrumental in conveying Palestinian traditions to Ashkenaz.[137] In this regard, it is worth noting that the earliest Hebrew manuscripts containing interverse Targum are Cairo Geniza fragments of *Palestinian* Targumim (which are different from the *Targum Onkelos* preserved in all the medieval biblical codices).[138] The origins of the interverse practice may thus have originated in Palestine, and then traveled to Babylonia, where it was applied to *Targum Onkelos*. Whatever its origins, the scribal practice attests to the likelihood that the Targum was intended to be read *alongside* the Hebrew original, not to substitute for it.[139]

In general, the features of the liturgical Pentateuch in Ashkenaz are more variable than those of the masoretic Bible. Some French liturgical Pentateuchs either omit the Targum altogether or, somewhat more tellingly, substitute Rashi for the Targum. In those cases, Rashi is sometimes written in a second column next to the scriptural text.[140] The De Castro Pentateuch, completed in 1344, has both Targum and Rashi, each verse followed by Targum that is, in turn, followed by Rashi; the scriptural text is in a darker square Ashkenazic hand, the Targum and Rashi in a slightly less dark and smaller semicursive script. Figure 18 is the very opening of Genesis. Above the initial word *be-reishit* (in super-large letters), Adam and Eve appear to be portrayed twice: once (inside the roundels) before they ate of the fruit, the other time after eating.[141] Similarly, some liturgical Pentateuchs record the Masorah (and sometimes in micrographic decorations or figures), while others do not.[142]

The origins of the liturgical Pentateuch are not known. The genre has parallels in different types of Bible books that were developed in the Latin West for biblical readings during the Mass.[143] One system was to list *capitula*, or chapter cues, which identified the order and location of readings from the Pauline epistles and the gospels so that readers could find them in complete copies of those books. Similar notations and lists are found in masoretic Bibles. Another genre was devised by scribes who began to collect the readings in separate books where they were arranged in liturgical order—epistolaries for readings from the Pauline and Catholic Epistles and Acts, evangelistaries for readings from the Gospels, and larger Mass lectionaries that contained both the epistle and gospel readings. All these types—lists of capitula, epistolaries, evangelistaries—appear to have been in use simultaneously going back to the eighth century although they reached the height of their use during the thirteenth and fourteenth centuries. The resemblance between liturgical Pentateuchs and epistolaries, evangelistaries, and Mass lectionaries is obvious. There is, however, no evidence to suggest that one religious tradition borrowed the genre from the other. Christian *and* Jewish scribes could easily have come up with the similar types of Bibles that would be equally convenient to use in their respective liturgies.

For the Christian biblical books of this sort, there is hard evidence confirming their use in the Mass, the Divine Office, and other liturgical services.[144] For the Jewish Bibles, in contrast, we have little explicit information upon which to rely. Their overall organization obviously suggests a connection with the synagogue and the weekly Torah reading in the synagogue. But precisely how were these Bibles used in the synagogue? Were they ever read from in place of a Torah scroll?

Fig. 18 Pentateuch (De Castro Pentateuch), Germany (Ashkenaz), 1344. Jerusalem, Israel Museum MS 180/94 (formerly Sassoon 506), fol. 1v. Photo © The Israel Museum, Jerusalem / Ardon Bar-Hama.

There is some evidence indicating that some rabbinic authorities beginning with the Geonim of Babylonia and continuing with their successors in the Iberian peninsula, Provence, and even northern France permitted communities that did not own a Torah scroll to read the weekly lection from a codex in a synagogue.[145] In contrast, the rabbinic authorities in Palestine, Germany, and Italy absolutely forbade the practice; by the end of the twelfth century, sages in northern France, and, by the end of the thirteenth century, in Sefarad as well, all joined in the prohibition. Since the liturgical Pentateuch first became a widespread book in Ashkenaz only in the thirteenth century, it is virtually certain, then, that the surviving codices were never used as a surrogate for Torah scrolls. Another possibility is that Bibles with Targum and (even more obviously) those with Rashi's commentary in them, served as study texts for the weekly *parashah*.[146] It is also possible that the profusion of these books in Ashkenaz in the thirteenth and especially fourteenth centuries points less to study *per se* than to a new way of "reading" the Bible in the synagogue. I am referring to a developing and attested practice among Jews—certainly among sages but also among individuals wealthy enough to own their own liturgical Pentateuch—not simply to listen silently to the public chanting of the Torah but to follow along with the public reader and read the text for themselves, twice in Scripture and once in the Targum (or through Rashi's commentary), in fulfillment of the talmudic injunction attributed to the fourth-century Amora R. Huna bar Judah (who himself repeated it in the name of his predecessor R. Ammi): "Every person is obligated to complete the weekly lectionary readings (*parshiyotav*) with the congregation [by reciting] Hebrew Scripture (*Mikra*) twice and the Targum once" (*b. Berakhot* 8a–b). Seven centuries later, Isaac bar Moses of Vienna (1189–1250), the author of the influential *Sefer Or Zaruʿa*, described personally seeing his teachers, R. Judah Heḥasid and R. Abraham ben R. Moshe, reading the weekly *parashah* in precisely this way—twice in Hebrew, once in Targum—while listening to the Torah reader publicly read the Sefer Torah in the synagogue.[147]

Such private reading in a communal context would have satisfied a religious need felt by these individuals that was not being fulfilled by passively listening to the Torah chanted aloud by another person. Bible reading of this sort by individuals is also reflected in a more general trend that had independently spread throughout the academic and book culture of Western Europe during the thirteenth century. For example, we know that, in 1259, students at the University of Paris were formally required to bring their own copies to the public lectures in which the texts were explained and taught.[148] Around the same time,

Fig. 19 Pentateuch (North French Hebrew Miscellany),
northern France, 1280. London, British Library MS Add.
11639, fol. 51v. Courtesy of the British Library / Granger, NYC.

Humbert of Romans (ca. 1194–1277) is quoted to have said that collective
prayer was only "enriched by individuals gazing on the text of a written prayer
as it was collectively pronounced."[149] The profusion of liturgical Pentateuchs
in Ashkenaz is best explained as part of this larger change in reading practice
wherein individual members of the audience became active participants in
communal events of reading.

Here, again, one exceptional manuscript may prove the rule. The so-called
North French Hebrew Miscellany, composed around the year 1280, is an exquisitely decorated book.[150] Figure 19 is a typical page, containing playfully decorated
panels (like the one for the end of Exodus on the lower right-hand column, with
the number of verses in the book and a mnemonic for the number; the panel
on the upper left-hand column contains the initial word of the book of Leviticus). Even though it is called a "miscellany," the volume is actually a liturgical

Pentateuch accompanied by a host of other texts including a complete prayer-book for the entire year with a large number of additional legal, calendrical, homiletical and literary texts appended to it, all written in the margins of the liturgical Pentateuch or in separate sections of the volume; many of these texts have some connection to either the liturgy or the liturgical year. A genuinely small book—with dimensions of 5 × 6.5 inches (127 × 165 mm)—this book is not so much an individual's personal library (like the famous late fifteenth-century [ca. 1479] Italian Rothschild Miscellany) as it is a book testifying to its owner's desire to have the entire synagogue service literally at his fingertips, ready for personal use. The codex may have been commissioned as a "trophy" book, but it clearly held a religious meaning for its author. It testifies not only to his wish to "glorify" the liturgical service through its beauty but also to his own desire to be able to fully participate in all parts of the service. I have observed elsewhere that most figurative and representational art in Jewish books is found in litur-gical contexts, either in the form of synagogue decoration (as in mosaic floors) or in prayerbook art.[151] As a *liturgical* Pentateuch, the art in this Bible truly confirms my observation.

In Sefarad

The earliest dated surviving liturgical Pentateuch from Sefarad was composed in 1318 (Bodl. MS Kenn. 4, Cat. 2326), but most examples of the genre in Spain come from the late fourteenth and fifteenth centuries, the latter especially. While their basic contents and organization are identical to their Ashkenazic counterpart—the weekly *parshiyot* of the Torah, the *haftarot*, and the scrolls—many of the Sefardic examples also contain the Masorah, reflecting no doubt the prominent position that the Masorah held in all Bibles in Spain. In the more elaborate codices, like the late fourteenth-century London Catalan Pentateuch, pictured in figure 20, the Masorah is written in the same micro-graphic geometrical designs that one finds in Spanish masoretic Bibles. On this page containing Exod 15, the Masorah is written in a typical double wall around the text with wave-like semicircles between the two walls.

A number of liturgical Pentateuchs were also created in the Lisbon work-shop in the eighties and nineties of the fifteenth century, including one truly remarkable codex, the Duke of Sussex's Portuguese Pentateuch, a folio of which is pictured in figure 21. As the page shows, with the exception of the heading *Vayiqra* (the first word of Leviticus, which this page begins), the

Fig. 20   Pentateuch (London Catalan Pentateuch), Catalonia, late
fourteenth century. London, British Library MS Harley 5773, fol. 56r.
Courtesy of the British Library / Granger, NYC.

biblical text is written in an elegant semicursive North African hand rather
than in the square script in which the Bible is otherwise nearly always written
in Sefarad.[152] The use of the North African semicursive hand appears to be a
concession to its actual use by a Jewish patron who must have been more
comfortable with that script.

In comparison to Ashkenazic Pentateuchs, the Aramaic Targum was less
frequently copied in Spanish *ḥumashim*, a fact that may be partly explained
by a preference to study the Bible with the Judeo-Arabic translation or *tafsir*
of Saadiah Gaon.[153] This practice is famously attested in the ethical will that

Fig. 21   Pentateuch (Duke of Sussex's Portuguese Pentateuch), Lisbon, late fifteenth century. London, British Library MS Add. 15283, fol. 88r. Courtesy of the British Library / Granger, NYC.

the great translator Judah Ibn Tibbon (1120–ca. 1190) wrote to his son Samuel (who grew up to become as great a translator as his father) and in which he admonished him, "Read every week the Pentateuchal section in Arabic. This will improve thine Arabic vocabulary, and will be of use in translating, if thou shouldst feel inclined to translate."[154] A century later, the Tosafist R. Asher ben Yehiel (ca. 1250–1327), who moved from Germany to Spain in 1303, began to encourage Spanish Jews to recite Rashi in place of the Targum.[155] Asher was followed by his son, Jacob, the author of the important early legal code, the *Arba'ah Turim*, in which he explicitly ruled that reading Rashi was equivalent to reading the Targum because it, too, "explained" the meaning of the Torah.[156] Rashi's preeminence may have been owed less to his more contextual (*peshat*) interpretations than to the fact that he presented rabbinic tradition in an accessible, carefully abridged, reader-friendly style.[157]

Study Bibles

The possible use of the masoretic Bible and the liturgical Pentateuch as study texts has already been mentioned in the course of our survey. In this section, I want to describe those Bibles that seems to have been intentionally designed for study—that is, either codices with more than one commentary on the page or those in which the commentary occupies so prominent a position that it is fair to assume that the Bible was produced specifically for studying that commentary. As previously noted, the genre of the study Bible overlaps with the other genres. One of the earliest examples of a study Bible, the manuscript known as Leipzig 1 (Leipzig Universitéitsbibliothek MS B.H.1), composed in France probably in the early thirteenth century, which contains what many scholars believe to be the earliest evidence for the original text of Rashi's commentary, is a liturgical Pentateuch with the *haftarot* and Five Scrolls. Figure 22 is a typical page from the codex. In its various columns and windows, the Bible also includes the masoretic notes of earlier Ashkenazic sages as well as many comments upon and additions to Rashi's commentary.[158] The presence of all these texts in the codex would seem to testify to the scribe or patron's original intention that the manuscript be used for study, not simply for synagogue use, and the many annotations in the book attest to its very active reading.

The history of the study Bible is closely intertwined with the history of medieval Jewish biblical exegesis. As I have argued elsewhere, the initial adaptation by Jews of the codex along with the creation of the masoretic Bible in the ninth and tenth centuries had a revolutionary impact on Jewish reading practice and how the Bible subsequently came to be studied and interpreted.[159] The various material shapes that the Hebrew Bible later took in the Middle Ages were partly the result of these new reading practices and types of exegesis. It is beyond the range of this survey to describe these new practices in any detail, but a few words can help us appreciate the development of the study Bible as a subgenre.

The first thing to note is the difference in attitudes toward Bible study that obtained in Sefarad, on the one hand, and Ashkenaz, on the other. These differences have sometimes been exaggerated in past scholarship, but they

Fig. 22   Pentateuch with commentary of Rashi and Masoretic notes, France, early thirteenth century(?). Leipzig, Universitätsbibliothek MS B.H. 1, fol. 204v. Reproduced with permission from the Universitäts-bibliothek Leipzig.

were significant.[160] Spanish Jewish biblical exegesis, the direct heir of the nascent grammatical tradition pioneered by the Masoretes, was further enriched by the exposure of Jews living within the Islamic orbit to the developing sciences of philology and philosophy, all of which came to inform their reading of the Bible. This process began with the Babylonian Saadiah Gaon and continued with his successor Samuel ben Ḥofni, and, even more so, with later Andalusian grammarians like Jonah Ibn Janach and Andalusi-trained exegetes like Abraham Ibn Ezra. The attention to Bible study as a primary discipline continued into the period of Christian kingdoms in Iberia and in related areas like Provence, with such commentators as Naḥmanides (1194–270) and Radak (ca. 1160–ca. 1235). Despite the complaints of figures like Duran over the waning of Bible study, it is possible to speak of a continuous history of biblical commentary in Sefarad until the time of the expulsion. The Pentateuch remained the main focus of elementary education; the Prophets and the Writings were considered texts for more advanced study.[161] Plate 2 is from a volume of Former Prophets copied in Segovia in 1487 that contains on its pages the Targum and the commentaries of Rashi, Radak, and Levi b. Gershon.[162] Proverbs, Job, and Ecclesiastes in particular were studied intensively as ethical tracts, as evidenced by the number of manuscripts of these books with commentaries on their pages.[163]

In Ashkenaz, in contrast to Sefarad, the attitude toward study of the Bible was more complicated. In northern France, through the eleventh and the twelfth centuries, there was a distinguished line of biblical exegetes beginning with the eleventh-century sage Jacob b. Yakar, "a teacher of Gemarah and Scripture" who was also the teacher of Rashi, and then continuing with Rashi himself and his disciples and successors, Joseph Kara, Joseph Bekhor Shor, Samuel ben Meir, and Eliezer of Beaugency, among others. These exegetes drew on the late midrashic tradition even though they famously eschewed midrash for what they called *peshat*; this term is difficult to translate, and it clearly meant different things to different exegetes, but it is probably best understood as the (more or less) literary-contextual sense of Scripture. Following the period of the Crusades, however, the independent study of Scripture waned and was overshadowed by the study of Talmud even though the talmudic corpus, as Talmudists argued in their own defense, included within itself an enormous amount of biblical exegesis.[164] Still, Bible study remained a staple of elementary education in Ashkenaz, and German pietists (*ḥasidei Ashkenaz*) continued to stress the importance of Bible study as part of their critique of the dialectical study of the Talmud championed by the Tosafists.[165]

The difference between biblical commentaries produced in Spain and in Ashkenaz is reflected in their literary form. Beginning with Saadiah's Commentary on the Bible, Sefardic commentaries were self-consciously written *ḥibburim*, literary compositions, and regularly included programmatic introductions and sometimes virtually essayistic explorations of problems raised by a verse.[166] In contrast, Ashkenazic commentaries tended to be purely lemmatic—that is, written as brief comments on specific words or phrases. We do not know how the Ashkenazic commentaries were originally written—whether they were composed as commentaries, or whether (as some scholars have suggested) they originated as notes written in the margins of Bibles or as responses to earlier commentators like Rashi that were later collected by disciples and copied by scribes into separate books of their own so as to create continuous commentaries.[167] The case of Rashi himself is especially complicated because it is clear that Rashi's commentary was edited, added to, and glossed by his students as well as by later scribes—indeed, so much so that it may be impossible today to determine exactly what Rashi's commentary originally looked like.[168] On the other hand, all these later interventions in Rashi's text also testify to the intensivity with which his commentary was copied and studied.

Most biblical commentaries in the Middle Ages circulated in separate books, sometimes (and in the case of Rashi, nearly always) called *quntrasim* (sing. *quntres*, from the Latin *quinterion*, a quire of five sheets).[169] Figure 23 is a remarkable example of a Rashi *quntres* written in France in the early thirteenth century. The page contains Rashi's commentary on Exod 25, the biblical passage describing the Temple implements, and incorporates within its page design an illustration of the menorah. If one compares this illustration with the depiction of the menorah in the Sefardic Temple implement carpet page from the Perpignan Bible (see fig. 7) one can easily see the difference between Rashi's conception of the menorah's shape and that of Maimonides, which served as the basis for the Spanish image. The fact that the illustration in the Rashi *quntres* is so clearly integrated into the page's format suggests that it was part of the original commentary and conceptually part of Rashi's interpretation.[170] Like this text, most *quntresim* were typically written in a semicursive, so-called rabbinic script, with their comments often separated by a lemma—that is, a word or short phrase from the Bible that keyed the reader to the comment's scriptural occasion.

A *quntres* could also be a truly deluxe codex. Indeed, our earliest illustrations in any medieval Hebrew book are found in a folio-sized *quntres* containing the commentaries of Rashi and other French exegetes from his school that was written in the vicinity of the German town of Würzberg in 1232/33. The illustrations that serve as initial panels for the different biblical books were drawn by a Christian artist who received instructions from the codex's Jewish scribe as to what to draw; we know the artist was a Christian because a recent study of the manuscript has revealed that the directions written in the margins were in Latin.[171] Figure 24 is the beginning of the section *Vayishlaḥ* (beginning with Gen 32:4). The historiated initial on the page shown in figure 25 depicts Jacob prostrating himself before his brother Esau.

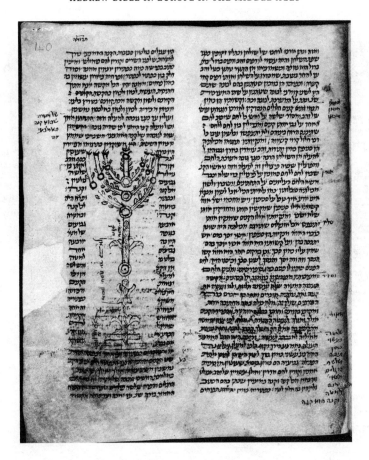

Fig. 23   Rashi Commentary (Quntres), France, early thirteenth century. Oxford, Bodleian Library MS Opp. Add. Fol. 69, fol. 40v. Courtesy of the Bodleian Libraries, University of Oxford.

Here, again, we do not know exactly how these *quntresim* were used. While it is possible that they were studied alongside biblical codices, some readers may have used them alone, the Bible presumably being known by heart, with the lemmata serving merely as verse reminders. The dangers of studying this way were apparently sufficiently well-known that the twelfth-century exegete from Narbonne, Joseph Ibn Kimchi, the father of David Kimchi (Radak), had to warn his reader always to have a Torah in front of him, "and then everything will be in the right place."[172]

At some point, however, scribes began to copy Bibles with the commentaries on the same page. Leipzig 1 (fig. 23) is one such text. Unfortunately, the

Fig. 25 Rashi and School of Rashi Commentary (Quntres), Würzberg, Germany, 1232/33. Munich, Bayerische Staatsbibliothek Cod. Hebr. 5(1), fol. 29v, detail. Courtesy of Bayerische Staatsbibliothek / Bildarchiv.

Fig. 24 Rashi and School of Rashi Commentary (Quntres), Würzberg, Germany, 1232/33. Munich, Bayerische Staatsbibliothek Cod. Hebr. 5(1), fol. 29v. Courtesy of Bayerische Staatsbibliothek / Bildarchiv.

manuscript has no colophon, and scholars have debated its dating, some arguing that it was produced in the first half of the thirteenth century (that is, within a little more than a century of Rashi's death), others pushing its date into the fourteenth century. As one can see from the illustration, the scribe appropriated a page format—best known today from the format of the talmudic page—that derived from the glossed page format developed by Christian scribes in the twelfth and thirteenth centuries for the Christian Bible with the collected patristic commentaries known as the Glossa Ordinaria.[173] This page format first appeared in France, around the university community of Paris. If Leipzig 1 indeed originated in France in the early thirteenth century, as some believe, it would be about a hundred years earlier than the earliest tractate of

Fig. 26 Five Scrolls (Song of Songs 4:4–8) with Targum and commentaries of Rashi and Abraham Ibn Ezra. Italy(?), 1327. Oxford, Bodleian Library MS Digby Or. 34, fol. 17v. Courtesy of the Bodleian Libraries, University of Oxford.

the Talmud with the same format.[174] By the fourteenth and fifteenth centuries, the page layout had spread to Jewish communities in Germany, Spain, and Italy, and was used for almost any text with commentaries.[175]

Figure 26 is a page from such a codex, written in 1327, probably in Italy. The codex contains the Five Scrolls with the Targum and the commentaries of Rashi and Abraham Ibn Ezra; the page in the illustration has the text of Song 4:4–8. The biblical text and the Targum are written respectively in larger and smaller Ashkenazic scripts, while the commentaries are in an Italian semi-cursive hand, making the page's textual hierarchy transparent to the reader.[176]

The glossed format with the biblical text and commentaries on the same page was obviously a more convenient text for a student. But more than being convenient, it was transformative. It changed the very nature of Bible study. First, by placing the Bible with its commentary on the same page, it made studying Bible with a commentary normative. Second, with the commentary on the page, the student was less likely to read the biblical text sequentially; rather, he (or she) now read it verse by verse with the commentary intervening wherever it existed. The biblical text was thus atomized into small lexical and semantic units that combined verse and exegesis. In this way, as Colette Sirat has noted, the glossed page forced the text and commentary constantly to confront each other, and out of that confrontation, the very habit of always reading the Bible with commentary also became regularized.[177] Furthermore, multiple commentaries on the same page encouraged comparative study of commentaries. This process led as well to the composition of supercommen-taries, commentaries upon commentaries. The profusion of these supercom-mentaries eventually led scribes to appropriate the form of the glossed *biblical* page so as to make a glossed *commentary* page, with a "core" commentary like Ibn Ezra in the center of the page (that is, where the biblical text would normally have been) and surrounded in the margins by a supercommentary on Ibn Ezra's commentary.[178] Such supercommentaries regularly compare one commentator to another.

As with the Talmud, this glossed format was not easy for scribes to produce by hand, and the number of manuscripts with the format are small compared to the other types. And as with the Talmud, it was only with printing that this format became widespread and, over time, virtually canonical.[179]

The Bible in Italy

As the site of the earliest dated European Jewish manuscript, Italian Jewish book culture has exhibited distinctive and independent characteristics since its beginnings.[180] Southern Italy in the Byzantine period was one of the original fonts of early Ashkenaz and in its earliest phases, Italian Hebrew book culture exhibited strong connections with early French and German Jewish book culture.[181] From the middle of the fourteenth century, Italy became a haven for refugees, first for Jews expelled from Ashkenaz, and then, after 1391, for some émigrés from Sefarad.[182] Both groups of immigrants included scribes who continued to write in their native scripts and according to their native scribal practices as well as in the distinctive script and formats of Italian Jewish book culture. Nearly one third of all surviving dated Hebrew manuscripts were written in Italy between 1350 and 1550.

All three types of Bibles I have surveyed thus far—the masoretic Bible, the liturgical Pentateuch, and the study Bible—are represented among Italian Bibles, but each of these genres assume a number of distinctive features in Italy.

(1) Perhaps the most striking characteristic of Italian Bibles in general is their relative disregard for the Masorah. This tendency can be observed even in some codices containing the entire Bible—which look as though they were intended to be masoretic codices except that they lack the Masorah—but it is especially evident in liturgical Pentateuchs.[183]

(2) A large number of liturgical Pentateuchs also lack the Targum or Rashi. There is also, it seems, a more frequent tendency to have *either* the Five Scrolls or the *haftarot* rather than both, in contrast to liturgical Pentateuchs in Ashkenaz or Sefarad. Both this feature and the preceding one—the infrequent presence of the Masorah as a defining feature of these Bibles—seem to indicate a less rigorous attitude toward the distinctiveness of the biblical book genres in Italy than in either Ashkenaz or Sefarad.

(3) From the year 1375 on, there are a significant number of codices in which the biblical text is written in a single page-wide column (and, again, without the Masorah or other texts like Targum or commentaries on the page).[184] The page-wide, single-column format is not unique to Italy—there are specimens of this format in Ashkenaz and Sefarad, as well as in early Oriental (Near Eastern) codices and in Yemenite Bibles until the fifteenth century—but in proportion to all the biblical manuscripts produced in each geocultural area, those written in Italy (including those in Ashkenazic and Sefardic script that were most likely written by émigré scribes) are most prominent. A number of these "plain" Bibles are also beautifully illustrated.

One of the more striking examples of such a Bible is the Duke of Sussex's Italian Pentateuch, written in Italy in the fourteenth or fifteenth century. Figure 27, containing the beginning of the book of Deuteronomy, displays characteristically Italian floral decorations and initial *letter* panels, the latter a relatively rarity in Hebrew manuscripts, which tend to have initial *word* panels. Initial letter panels, in contrast, are very typical of Christian Latin manuscripts from the Carolingian period on, and in late medieval manuscripts those panels are the most frequent sites for illustrations in Christian books.

Fig. 27   Pentateuch (Duke of Sussex's Italian Pentateuch), Italy,
fourteenth–fifteenth century. London, British Library MS Add.
15423, fol. 117r. Courtesy of the British Library / Granger, NYC.

It is very likely that the Italian plain Hebrew Bibles reflect the larger
humanist culture in Italy at the time. This culture was shared by contemporary Jews as well as Christians. As scholars have noted, in the fifteenth and
early sixteenth centuries humanist Italian Bibles also began to be written with
the biblical text alone on the page, without commentaries or other accompanying "mediators."[185] These volumes represent a kind of return *ad fontes* in
respect to reading. The humanist reader, Christian or Jew, is seen as returning
to the original core text to enjoy its wisdom directly without intermediaries.

The same approach may lie behind the Hebrew plain Bibles. The significance of these Italian plain Bibles, then, may represent something very different than other such Hebrew Bibles like those noted above from Yemen and the Near East.

(4) The page from the Duke of Sussex's Italian Pentateuch (fig. 27) also illustrates another distinctive trait of Italian Bibles—namely, their use of the semicursive rather than the square letters that, in Ashkenaz and Sefarad, are almost invariably used for the biblical text, be it in a scroll or in a codex.[186] The difference between the two scripts is especially evident on this page because the initial letter *aleph* is written in the square script.

These plain Bibles were not the first to use the semicursive letters.[187] In the second half of the fifteenth century, however, the practice became more common in liturgical Pentateuchs copied in glossed formats in northern Italy. Figure 28 shows a page from one such book. Indeed, as this page indicates, the biblical text in the center surrounded by the delicate floral decoration is almost a replica in miniature of the plain Bible page with no other texts on it and with the biblical demarcated by the colorful floral border around it. In the case of this Pentateuch, however, the scribe has framed the biblical text in the page's center, with the Targum on the inner margin outside the floral border, and with Rashi in the even smaller semicursive in the outer margins. (On a typical glossed page, the secondary texts, the commentaries, are part of the writing grid and are not marginal; in contrast, this page begins to blur the line separating writing grid from margin.) As noted earlier, a Bible with the Targum *and* Rashi is a rarity in Italy.

The growing preference for the semicursive mode of script can be seen also in Ashkenazic and Sefardic manuscripts in the late medieval period, but only in Italy is the semicursive used so widely for biblical manuscripts. Given the traditional mandate and virtually universal practice to write the biblical text exclusively in square letters, the shift to the semicursive is both dramatic and perplexing. There do not appear to have been economic reasons for the switch, nor does it appear to have been motivated by factors like legibility. Rather, as Beit-Arié has suggested, the most likely motive was aesthetic, with the semicursive mode being "regarded by medieval scribes and owners of books as more beautiful and elegant than the various square modes."[188] This preference in Italy for beauty over halakhic traditionality represents a remarkable sea change in Jewish cultural sensibility.

(5) Along with the use of the semicursive script, the other truly distinctive feature of these Italian Bibles is their small size. Many are of quarto and

Fig. 28 Pentateuch with Targum and Rashi, northern Italy, second
half of fifteenth century. London, British Library MS Harley 7621,
fol. 254v. Courtesy of the British Library / Granger, NYC.

octavo-like dimensions, but some are virtual miniatures, as small as 8.5 × 5.8
cm (3.4 × 2.3 inches).[189]

Both the use of the semicursive script and the small, very portable sizes of
these Bibles, as well as the growing preponderance of plain Bibles, albeit
sometimes lavishly illustrated ones, seems to point to the increasing popularity of the Bible as a book sought out by individual, not necessarily scholarly,
owners, whether for use in the synagogue or for private reading and study.

The Bible was not the only book to gain such popularity among Jews in Renaissance Italy; prayerbooks also became far more common. The increased proliferation of these books reflects, as Robert G. Calkins has written in regard to Christian books of the period, "profound changes in the role of books in society and in the nature of religious worship."[190] As Calkins elaborates, these changes included the growth of literacy generally (which in turn increased demand for such books not only among the intellectual elite but also among the growing mercantile class), and "the pervasive need for more immediate, personal, and meaningful religious experience through private devotions."[191] The latter need led, in turn, to increased individual ownership and use of these books.

The impact of both changes can also be seen in the increased popularity in Italy of two special subgenres of biblical books, the Psalter and what are called *Sifrei EMeT*, codices consisting of the three poetic texts, Job, Proverbs, and Psalms.[192] While both types of books have antecedents in earlier Sefardic and especially in Ashkenazic book traditions, where the books are generally of large format, the Italian codices are distinguished (again) by their numerousness, by their use of semicursive script, and their small format.[193] Psalters and *Sifrei EMeT* similarly bridge the liturgical and the biblical genres. The Psalter was used as a book of private prayer *and* as an object of study; numerous commentaries were written on it, some polemical, others more philosophical, and they were sometimes recorded with the biblical text in a glossed format. The *Sifrei EMeT*, in turn, became in Renaissance Italy objects of rich intellectual discussion and exchange between Jewish and Christian humanist scholars.[194] The book of Job in particular was interpreted by both circles of *eruditi* as a source of the *prisca theologica*, the original, pristine truth from which later theological traditions and philosophical systems were believed to have devolved. Job, Solomon, and even David could all be seen as types of the *priscus philosophus*, the "ancient wise man who, after attaining universal knowledge, transcended human reason in order to reach the ultimate happiness of the religious philosopher who finds in God all responses to his intellectual curiosity."[195]

The same culture of Renaissance humanism that fostered the cultivation of a *prisca theologica* inevitably fostered and encouraged other forms of intellectual exchange between Jews and Christians. Foremost among these was the emergence of Christian Hebraism with its new interests in classical Jewish texts. The intellectual exchanges between Jewish and Christian humanists also anticipated the social and economic interactions that would later take place between Jews and Christians in the great printing houses of Venice in the sixteenth century that were owned by Christians who employed Jews as editors and printers. These Christian Hebrew publishing houses dominated the field of Jewish book culture for more than a century and produced the definitive editions of most of the Jewish classics including the Rabbinic Bible. As noted frequently, a significant number of Jews involved in these presses either already or later converted to Christianity, a darker dimension of the Jewish-Christian encounter.

The work of one scribe in particular—a convert, as we shall see—epitomizes the complexity of such collaborations, not to mention the many unanswered questions that these odd conjunctions raise. Isaac ben Ovadiah of Forli, working mainly in Florence in the mid-fifteenth century, produced at least twenty-five extant manuscripts between 1427 and 1467, a remarkable number of productions even in comparison to Christian humanist scribes of the period. Even more remarkable than the quantity of his production was its quality. As Nurit Pasternak has noted, Isaac was "a paragon of the Florentine '*bel-libro*' among Jewish scribes of his day."[196] His work was characterized both by its high-level material and execution, which drew upon the new technology of the day as well as traditional Hebrew book practices. Isaac appears to have worked closely with local book traders, and his manuscripts were decorated and illuminated in Christian ateliers by some of the best local artists including Fra Angelico. A number of his manuscripts were commissioned by Christians, including one manuscript, a *Sefer EMeT* (Jerusalem, Israel Museum MS 180/55), that bears the device of Lorenzo il Magnifico di Medici.

Isaac eventually converted to Christianity. On the final folio of a Bible manuscript (Florence, Biblioteca Medicea Laurenziana MS Plut. 1.31), he proclaimed his faith in Christ by writing: "For the honour and glory of Joshua Nazarenus our Lord King of the Jews."[197] We do not know what motivated Isaac to convert, whether it was the climate of syncretism encouraged by the culture of *prisca theologica*, or the outcome of a sincere religious experience of his own, or reasons of convenience to advance his career. Whatever led him to Christianity, his conversion led to the production of some of the most unusual biblical manuscripts in all of medieval Hebrew book culture.[198]

Plate 3, from another Bible by Isaac, is the opening of Genesis. Its two columns, written in an Italian semicursive hand, replicate what we have seen is a typical Italian Hebrew biblical format. The colorful floral design framing the page is also reminiscent of other Italian biblical manuscripts, even if its scrolling vines are especially elaborate. What transports the page to another realm, however, is the large initial letter *bet* (of *be-reishit*) that occupies nearly half the folio and that frames a scene of the crucifixion with Saint Dominic and a Carmelite saint kneeling at Christ's feet, and with Mary, the mother of Jesus, and the apostle John standing beside them. At the bottom of the page, a roundel pictures the *imago pietatus*, an iconic image of the dead Jesus standing in his sarcophagus.[199] Incongruous as this page may appear to us, its almost indefinable hybridity vividly epitomizes the main question that will dominate the subsequent history of the Hebrew Bible: Is it Jewish or not?[200]

4

THE MAKING OF THE RABBINIC BIBLE

Since the publication nearly forty years ago of Elizabeth Eisenstein's *The Printing Press as an Agent of Change*, the revolutionary impact of printing has been the subject of considerable scholarly debate.[1] There is little question that the invention of print touched every aspect of Western culture, but historians continue to debate whether or not printing constituted an authentic revolution. Did print in fact initiate an unprecedented era and radically change the nature of book production and distribution and reading practices in ways that manuscript culture never approached? Or was the invention of print actually the culmination of a series of processes and developments that had already begun in the late Middle Ages with gradual changes in the way manuscripts were copied, sold, bought, and read, and did the invention of print only intensify, quicken, and expand those changes? In either case, there is no disagreement that by the time of its wide adaptation, print set in motion a vast array of effects. These range from the growing standardization, fixation, and preservation of texts to the exponential increase in their diffusion and circulation. That diffusion resulted, in turn, in the eventual reorganization of knowledge and an enlarged readership. The demystification of textual mastery and the new forms of access to knowledge available to anyone able to acquire a printed book fairly quickly disrupted the social, religious, and intellectual hierarchies that had governed much of Western culture up until the age of print.

Print is often conceived as a collaborative effort—between authors, publishers, and binders, to mention only a few of the major actors involved in the production of a printed book—but even in the manuscript age, book production had been a collaboration between scribes, patrons, illustrators, binders, and still other figures. The new technology of print did, however, create a new social institution: the print shop. The social space of the print shop brought together different professionals and persons from the world of the book— authors, printers, translators, typefounders, correctors, artists, engravers, booksellers, censors, clients, and book buyers—and not infrequently, these figures were from entirely different cultural and religious worlds; they included Catholics and Protestants, faithful Jews, Jewish converts to Christianity, and Greek-speaking emigrants from Byzantium following the Ottoman conquest. Because of the particular complications of the technology of printing, the cooperation of all these different artisans and professionals became an absolute necessity, and the degree of their collaboration grew ever more complex. The print shop became their meeting place, their common space.[2] And within its walls a new persona also emerged: the editor. Indeed, by the mid-sixteenth century, the editor had begun to eclipse the author as the central figure in book production.[3] The rise of the editor was also accompanied by the invention of what were effectively unprecedented types of books. As Eisenstein and others have shown, a new type of scientific literature emerged after print.[4] So, too, were new genres of books, most famously perhaps the polyglot Bible, enabled by print.[5] The eye-catching format of the polyglot, with its array of columns of parallel texts in different scripts laid out next to each other across the full width of a page (and in some polyglots, across a double page opening), may not have been literally impossible in a manuscript, but the massive editing and expert labor in multiple languages required to produce these pages was virtu- ally inconceivable before the development of the new technology.

For the Jewish book, the effects of print were manifested in all the ways just mentioned, but its impact—particularly after the year 1500—was even more radical in still another way: it changed the very nature of the *Jewishness* of the Jewish book. Before the sixteenth century—whether in the age of manuscripts or in the fifty-year incunable period of early Jewish printing—the Jewish book was essentially a text created by a Jewish author written in Hebrew script (whether the language was Hebrew or one of the Jewish languages like Judeo- Arabic or Yiddish) and produced by a Jewish scribe or printer for a Jewish reader. Beginning in the sixteenth century, particularly in Italy, and specifically in Venice, the city that dominated the Jewish book market for the first half of the century, none of these verities could be taken for granted any longer. Gen- tiles regularly owned the printing houses that produced books for Jews, Christians (who were sometimes but not always apostates—that is, former Jews) wrote books in Hebrew, Christian Hebraists were avid readers of Jewish books, and not all Jewish readers (like conversos who had returned to Judaism) could be assumed to know Hebrew, with the result that books for Jews were now produced in languages other than Hebrew or one of the Jewish languages. The very character of the Jewish book thereby changed; indeed, the "Jewishness" of the Jewish book was itself called into question as a given and now had to be asserted and demonstrated.[6] And no book illustrates this radical shift in the Jewishness of the Jewish book more vividly than that most "Jewish" of Jewish books, the Biblia Rabbinica, or Rabbinic Bible (RB), eventually known as the Mikra'ot Gedolot, which appeared in two formative editions in Venice: the first in 1517 and the even more famous second in 1524–25.[7]

Both of these editions, as well as later editions of the Rabbinic Bible, have been treated extensively in past scholarship. Especially noteworthy among recent works are those by Jordan S. Penkower and B. Barry Levy.[8] My intention in this chapter is to build upon and enrich this earlier scholarship by situating the production of these Bibles and their publication within the larger history of the Jewish Bible as a material object going back to the Middle Ages, and within the changes that Jewish book culture underwent in the course of the sixteenth century. I will begin by summarizing the contributions of past scholars and the discoveries they have made about the publication histories of the two Rabbinic Bible editions.[9]

These histories begin sometime before 1515, with the arrival in Venice of a scion of a wealthy family of merchants from Antwerp, a man named Daniel Bomberg (1483–ca. 1549).[10] Bomberg was probably sent to Italy to represent his family's export-import business, but shortly after arriving in Venice, he set up a publishing house with the intention of printing Hebrew books. Bomberg's partner in publishing was a Jewish convert who had become an Augustinian monk; he is known today only by his Christian name Fra Felice de Prato (Felix of Prato) or Felix Pratensis. Little is known about Pratensis except that he was very learned, both in Hebrew and in classical Jewish sources, as well as being truly gifted as a textual scholar.[11] We do not know how Pratensis and Bomberg met. Pratensis had previously been the Hebrew teacher of the famous early Orientalist Cardinal Egidio da Viterbo in Rome, and he may have first met Bomberg, who was a devout Christian with an interest in becoming a Hebraist, in the same role.[12] The first book that Bomberg and Pratensis produced together—not in their own publishing house but in that of Peter (Pierro) Lichtenstein—was a *Psalterium*, a translation of the Psalms into Latin done by Pratensis, which appeared in September 1515. The very next month, Bomberg, Pratensis, and Lichtenstein jointly applied to the Venetian Senate for a privilege, or exclusive right, to publish three additional Latin translations of Hebrew books—a grammar with a dictionary, and two kabbalistic treatises—as well as "a Hebrew Bible, in Hebrew letters, both with and without the Aramaic Targum, and with Hebrew commentaries."[13] As Penkower has shown, the latter request was for what eventually became the two editions of the Hebrew Bible that Bomberg and Pratensis published in Bomberg's own publishing house in Venice in 1517.[14] (Lichtenstein appears to have dropped out of their partnership.) The first of these Bibles, in folio size, and with the Targum and commentary, came to be known eventually as the first Rabbinic Bible. The second was a Hebrew Bible, in quarto and without Targum or commentary, printed sheet by sheet on the press immediately after the Rabbinic Bible's sheets and after the type had been rearranged for the smaller format.

Before Bomberg and Pratensis applied for the Venetian privilege, Pratensis had already applied for and been granted a ten-year papal *approbatio* and a comparable *privilegio* by Pope Leo X in Rome, but he evidently wished to publish in Venice, probably because he felt that his rights would be better protected there. Shortly after receiving the Venetian privilege to publish the three Latin translations and the Hebrew Bible editions, Bomberg himself applied for an exclusive patent for the use of Hebrew cuneate type that, he argued, he deserved because of the great expense he had incurred by having the Hebrew type cast specially for his press. When his petition was granted, Bomberg effectively won for himself a monopoly on all Hebrew printing in Venice.[15] Indeed, the right to publish Hebrew books in Venice was not something to be taken for granted. Gershom Soncino, the greatest of all Jewish early printers of Hebrew books, had tried unsuccessfully to receive a privilege to publish in Venice; it is not known for certain whether his failure to receive the privilege was due to Christian suspicions about the contents of Jewish books and their threat to Christian faith, or whether his request was blocked by Aldus Manutius, the leading printer in Venice at the time, who also aspired to print Hebrew books (in addition to the Greek texts for which he became famous).[16] In any case, there can be little question that Bomberg owed his success in gaining the Venetian privilege and patent to his being both a Christian *and* a wealthy businessman with capital to spend in Venice. Even more important, and especially so for marketing the book, he had the support and imprimatur of Pope Leo X who had openly vouched for the value of Hebrew works for the Christian religion.[17] Still, even Bomberg's own privileges were not guaranteed. In 1525, when his first *privilegio* expired, he applied to the Venetian Senate for a renewal, but his application was turned down four times—apparently out of fear of complications with Christian authorities who objected to the books' Jewish subject matter.[18] Bomberg finally received the renewal, but only after he agreed to pay five hundred ducats, a sufficiently weighty sum to overcome the Venetians' religious scruples.[19]

The importance of Pope Leo X's approbation for the success of Bomberg and Pratensis's publishing project cannot be underestimated. Its significance was more than merely financial. This Hebrew Bible actually came out in two separate versions, one intended for Christian readers, the other for Jews. The first volume of the version for Jews, the Pentateuch volume, has an elaborate title page in an architectural frame—indeed, it is the first Hebrew book to use such a frame—with a lengthy description in Hebrew of its contents, as can be seen in figure 29.[20] The version for Christians, however, also contains, on the verso of the title page, a dedication in Latin to Leo X, reproduced in figure 30, in which Pratensis wrote that, in addition to the Hebrew biblical text, he had included the "Chaldee scholia, to wit the common Targum and that of Jerusalem," which "contain many obscure and recondite mysteries (*multa . . . arcana et recondita mysteria*), not only useful, but necessary to the devout Christian."[21]

This last statement was not a mere aside. As I have already noted, before coming to Venice, Felix Pratensis had been Egidio da Viterbo's Hebrew tutor. In addition to being a close compatriot of Leo X, Egidio was a Christian kabbalist; his major work, *Libellus de litteris sanctis* is based upon the kabbalistic text *Sefer Ha-Temunah* (which Egidio translated, possibly with the help of Pratensis). Along with other Catholic Hebraists and Orientalists of the period, the cardinal believed that the letters of both Hebrew and Syriac (including Chaldean or Aramaic) contained mystical secrets in their very shapes.[22] In 1505, Egidio commissioned the copying of the Aramaic Targum known today as Targum Neofiti, and marginal marks on the surviving manuscript (Vatican Library MS Neofiti 1) suggest that he may have searched the Aramaic text for kabbalistic secrets.[23] Pratensis's statement in his dedication to the pope referred, in other words, to a very specific audience of Christian readers. This was also the likely reason why Pratensis emphasized to the pope that his edition included (for the first time) not only the common *Targum of Onkelos* but also the Jerusalem Targum.

Aside from the Latin dedication, however, the Christian edition was essentially identical to the Jewish one. They both contained the same biblical text, as well as the same accompanying texts of the Targum and commentaries. The

Fig. 29   Arba'ah ve-'Esrim (First Rabbinic Bible) (Venice: Daniel Bomberg, 1517), title page. From the collection of David and Jemima Jeselsohn, Zurich.

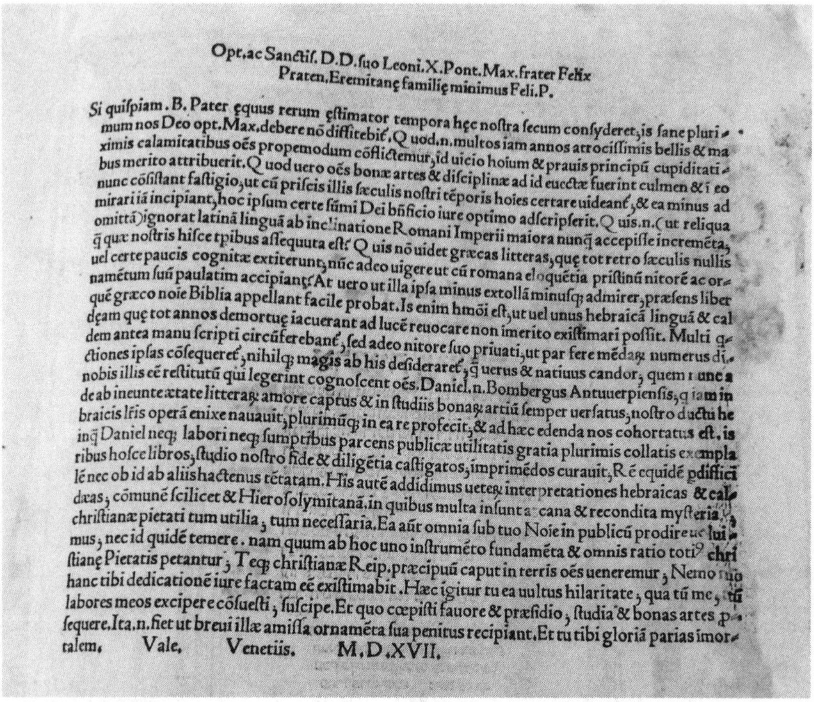

Opt.ac Sanctif. D.D.suo Leoni.X.Pont.Max.frater Felix
Praten.Eremitanę familię minimus Feli.P.

Si quispiam.B.Pater equus rerum ęstimator tempora hęc nostra secum consyderet,is sane pluri-
mum nos Deo opt.Max.debere nõ diffitebif.Q uod,n.multos iam annos atrocissimis bellis & ma
ximis calamitatibus oēs propemodum cōflictemur,id uicio hoium & prauis principũ cupiditati-
bus merito attribuerit.Q uod uero oēs bonæ artes & disciplinæ ad id euectę fuerint culmen & i eo
nunc cōsistant fastigio,ut cũ priscis illis sęculis nostri tēporis hoies certare uideant,& ea minus ad
mirari iã incipiant,hoc ipsum certe sũmi Dei bñficio iure optimo adscripserit.Q uis.n.(ut reliqua
omittã)ignorat latinã linguã ab inclinatione Romani Imperii maiora nunq accepisse incremēta,
q quæ nostris hisce tpibus assequuta est(Q uis nõ uidet gręcas litteras,quę tot retro sęculis nullis
uel certe paucis cognitæ extiterunt,nũc adeo uigere ut cũ romana eloquētia pristinũ nitorē ac or-
namētum suũ paulatim accipiant(At uero ut illa ipsa minus extollã minusq admirer,præsens liber
quē gręco noie Biblia appellant facile probat.Is enim hmōi est,ut uel unus hebraicã linguã & cal
dęam quę tot annos demortuę iacuerant ad lucē reuocare non imerito existimari possit. Multi q-
dem antea manu scripti circũferebant,sed adeo nitore suo priuati,ut par fere mēdaq numerus di-
ctiones ipsas cōsequeret̃,nihilq magis ab his desideraret,q uerus & natiuus candor, quem i unc a
nobis illis eē restitutũ qui legerint cognoscent oēs.Daniel.n.Bombergus Antuuerpiensis,q iam in
de ab ineunte ætate litterag amore captus & in studiis bonaq artiũ semper uersatus,nostro dučtu he
braicis lris operã enixe nauauit,plurimũq in ea re profecit,& ad hæc edenda nos cohortatus est, is
inq Daniel neq labori neq sumptibus parcens publicæ utilitatis gratia plurimis collatis exempla
ribus hosce libros,studio nostro fide & diligētia castigatos,imprimēdos curauit,R ē equidé pdiffici
lē nec ob id ab aliis hactenus tētatam.His autē addidimus uetex interpretationes hebraicas & cal
dæas, cōmunē scilicet & Hierosolymitanã.in quibus multa insunt a-cana & recondita mysteria,
christianæ pietati tum utilia, tum necessaria.Ea aũt omnia sub tuo Noie in publicũ prodire uc lui-
mus, nec id quidé temere. nam quum ab hoc uno instrumēto fundamēta & omnis ratio toti chri
stianę Pietatis petantur, Teq christianæ Reip.præcipuũ caput in terris oēs ueneremur, Nemo tũ
hanc tibi dedicatione iure factam eē existimabit.Hæc igitur tu ea uultus hilaritate, qua tũ me, tũ
labores meos excipere cōsuesti, suscipe.Et quo cœpisti fauore & præsidio, studia & bonas artes p-
sequere.Ita.n.fiet ut breui illæ amissa ornamēta sua penitus recipiant.Et tu tibi gloriã parias imor-
talem.   Vale.   Venetiis.   M.D.XVII.

Fig. 30 *Arba'ah ve-'Esrim* (First Rabbinic Bible) (Venice: Daniel Bomberg, 1517), 2 (papal approbation). From the collection of David and Jemima Jeselsohn, Zurich.

page layout displayed in figure 31, the first page of Genesis, was not a recog-
nizably Jewish format; the Targum was printed in a column of nearly the same
width as the biblical text in the adjacent column, and in a font that was only
slightly smaller than that used for the Bible, and Rashi's commentary was laid
out in a block beneath the Bible and Targum columns. Pratensis's biblical text
in particular was a major achievement in the history of the Bible. As Penkower
has shown, it was the first critical *edition* of the Hebrew text. Pratensis did not
simply copy a single manuscript or previously printed edition of the Bible, but
with Bomberg's financial assistance, he collected manuscripts (mainly Sefardic,
as Penkower has shown, but some Ashkenazic as well), and produced, in good
humanist fashion, what he believed to be the most accurate text of the Bible;
indeed, in his Latin prologue, he claimed to the pope that all previous manuscripts in circulation have "almost as many errors as words in them" and that
"no one has attempted [an edition comparable to his] before."[24] For the first

Fig. 31 *Arbaʻah ve-ʻEsrim* (First Rabbinic Bible) (Venice: Daniel Bomberg, 1517), 1 (Genesis 1). From the collection of David and Jemima Jeselsohn, Zurich.

time in a printed Bible, he also noted variants in the margins (including plene and defective spellings) as well as the *qere* in the margins (while keeping the *ketiv* in the text), unlike earlier editions that had printed the *ketiv* with the pronunciation of the *qere* in the text itself. No less important, the 1517 Rabbinic Bible (RB 1517) was the first complete edition of the Bible to contain an Aramaic Targum (with the exception of the books of Daniel, Ezra-Nehemiah, and Chronicles) *and* a medieval Jewish commentary on every book of the Bible (Rashi on the Pentateuch, David Kimchi [Radak] on the Prophets, and various others on the Hagiographa).[25] In apparent deference to Christian readers,

Fig. 32 *Arbaʿah ve-ʿEsrim* (First Rabbinic Bible) (Venice: Daniel
Bomberg, 1517), inserted page with Kimḥi's refutations of Christian
interpretations of various Psalms verses. From the collection of
David and Jemima Jeselsohn, Zurich.

however, several passages in Radak's commentary on Psalms that refuted
Christological interpretations of certain verses were censored.[26] In some copies, most likely intended for the Jewish edition, a separate single folio containing the censored sections was inserted in the Hagiographa volume immediately
after Psalms, as can be seen in figure 32.[27] In addition to the Jerusalem Targum
to the Pentateuch, RB 1517 also included the Second Targum to Esther, Aaron
ben Asher's *Shaʿar Dikdukei Ha-Teʿim*, and other masoretic treatises, as well
as the list of differences between the Ben Asher and Ben Naftali traditions of
the Masorah in the Pentateuch and the Five Scrolls. RB 1517 was also the first

Hebrew Bible to use chapter numbers, which were indirectly taken from Christian Bibles, as well as the first to divide the books of Samuel, Kings, and Chronicles into two books each, with marginal comments at the point of division such as "Here non-Jews (ha-lo'azim) begin the second book of Samuel, which is the second book of Kings to them."[28]

RB 1517, then, addressed itself to both Jewish and Christian markets, but in distinct editions. We do not know how commercially successful these editions were. The average print run of an edition of a complicated folio-sized book like RB 1517—in which Bomberg had invested considerable sums in gathering manuscripts, commissioning Hebrew type, and production work—was probably around one thousand copies.[29] If Jewish readers knew that its editor was an apostate Jew, its marketability, at least among Jews, may have been diminished. What is known is that RB 1517 *quarto* edition, which lacks any reference to Pratensis or to the papal dedication, was probably intended primarily for a Christian audience unable to read the Hebrew commentaries and was so successful that Bomberg reprinted it in 1521.[30]

This was not the case with RB 1517. The question of its commercial success aside, barely eight years after publishing RB 1517, Bomberg did publish another edition of the Rabbinic Bible, but this second edition, RB 1525, was a new book, and it advertised itself as such. While (as I have noted) RB 1517 had been the first Hebrew book to use an architectural frame on its title page—the Hebrew *sha'ar* being the name for both a gate or entranceway *and* a title page—this second edition of the Rabbinic Bible signaled its difference to the reader with a distinctively new *sha'ar* (fig. 33)—indeed, a panel in the typanum was inscribed with the phrase *sha'ar adonai he-hadash*, "the new gate of the Lord." And in nearly all respects, it was indeed a new gateway. In the first place, the edition had a new editor, Jacob ben Ḥayyim Ibn Adoniyahu, a known Jewish scholar with wide learning and expertise in the full range of classical Jewish literature from Bible and Rabbinics to Kabbalah; indeed, as Penkower has shown, Ibn Adoniyahu was a full-fledged kabbalist.[31] Ibn Adoniyahu had come to Venice from Tunis, and prior to working on RB 1525, he had edited several other books for Bomberg, including two kabbalistic commentaries on the Bible and, most probably, *Meir Netiv*, the biblical concordance of Isaac Nathan b. Kalonymus (Venice, 1523), a book that would prove indispensable to his edition of the Rabbinic Bible.[32]

As an editor, Ibn Adoniyahu was more consistent than Pratensis. In his detailed comparative study of the 1517 and 1525 editions, Penkower has shown that Ibn Adoniyahu improved upon Pratensis's text by relying almost

Fig. 33 *Torah, Nevi'im, Ketuvim* (Second Rabbinic Bible) (Venice: Daniel Bomberg, 1524–25), title page. Courtesy of the Library at the Herbert D. Katz Center for Advanced Judaic Studies, Kislak Center for Special Collections, Rare Books and Manuscripts, University of Pennsylvania.

exclusively on Sefardic manuscripts that were closest to the Tiberian tradition (in contrast to Pratensis, who had partly used Ashkenazic sources).[33] In addition to the Targum (*Onkelos* on the Pentateuch; Pseudo-Jonathan on the Prophets, and others on the Hagiographa) and Rashi (on the entirety of the Bible, with the exception of Proverbs, Job, and Daniel), Ibn Adoniyahu also included a second commentary, that of Abraham Ibn Ezra on the Pentateuch, Isaiah, Minor Prophets, Psalms, Daniel, and the Five Scrolls, as well as other commentators on other books of the Prophets (Radak and Gersonides on the Former Prophets; Radak on Jeremiah and Ezekiel) and Hagiographa (Gersonides on Proverbs and Job; Saadiah Gaon on Daniel, and Moshe Radak on Proverbs and Ezra-Nehemiah).[34]

Most important, Ibn Adoniyahu, for the first time, also edited the Masorah from manuscripts and, in a revised form, published it for the first time on the page with the Targum and the commentaries. Even more important, those sections of the expanded Masorah, a vast corpus including all the lists and annotations Ibn Adoniyahu found discovered in different manuscripts, and that he could not fit onto the biblical text page, he placed at the end of the final volume in what has come to be known as the *Masorah finalis*. Organized alphabetically, so that a reader could easily search it for entries in the *Masorah magna* on the biblical page, this Masorah finalis, as Penkower has noted, actually functioned as a kind of masoretic lexicon/concordance.[35] Ibn Adoniyahu also wrote a lengthy introduction that includes an autobiographical account and history of the book's publication along with a powerful defense of the Masorah and its importance—the first such treatise to appear in print. This second edition of Rabbinic Bible was published in 1524–25 and reprinted in 1546–48. With its commentaries and supplementary texts, RB 1524–25 quickly established itself for Jews as the model for most subsequent editions of the Bible through the next three centuries. For nearly all students of the Hebrew Bible, Jew and Christian alike, Ibn Adoniyahu's biblical text became the undisputed *textus receptus* for nearly the next four hundred years.[36]

Why did Bomberg, barely eight years after publishing RB 1517 edited by Felix Pratensis, decide in 1525 to publish this new second edition? It is possible that Bomberg wished to exploit his ten-year *privilegia* before it ran out, and because of legal strictures limiting *privilegia* to new works alone, perhaps he felt that he could not simply reprint Pratensis's RB 1517.[37] It is possible that he believed that a new edition produced by a recognized Jewish scholar like Ibn Adoniyahu would be more commercially successful than the earlier 1517 edition.[38] The page format of the new edition (fig. 34) also returned to a traditional

Fig. 34 Torah, Nevi'im, Ketuvim (Second Rabbinic Bible) (Venice: Daniel Bomberg, 1524–25), 1 (Gen 1). Courtesy of the Library at the Herbert D. Katz Center for Advanced Judaic Studies, Kislak Center for Special Collections, Rare Books and Manuscripts, University of Pennsylvania.

Jewish page layout—the layout of the study Bible with the biblical text literally surrounded like an island by an ocean of commentaries—a format that eventually comes to be associated with the Babylonian Talmud in particular but that had already appeared in Bibles, Talmuds, and other books in manuscript.[39] (In figure 34, the first page of Genesis, the biblical text, which begins with the word *be-reishit* in the elaborate large panel, continues for a single line beneath it, with the Targum [in a single line] next to it, the Masorah in the block beneath it, and the commentaries of Rashi and Ibn Ezra on the two side columns.) A Jew looking at this page would have found it familiar, something that was not true of RB 1517.

The most plausible set of reasons for Bomberg's decision have been advanced by Penkower, who has proposed two major arguments for a new edition that Ibn Adoniyahu may have made to Bomberg. First, Penkower argues, Ibn Adoniyah u probably persuaded Bomberg that Pratensis's 1517 edition had not, in fact, succeeded in its aim to restore the biblical text to its true and genuine purity (*verus et nativus candor*), as Pratensis had claimed; aside from the textual corruptions introduced by the Ashkenazic manuscripts and non-Tiberian manuscripts, there were other deficiencies in the markings of unusual letters, in *qere/ketiv* annotations, and in accentuation and punctuation.[40] Second, and possibly even more significantly in Penkower's view, Ibn Adoniyahu convinced Bomberg that the Hebrew Bible was incomplete without the full Masorah. Not only was the Masorah indispensable for establishing the accurate biblical text, but it also contained its own teachings—homilies (*derashot*), laws (*halakhot*), and, most important, kabbalistic secrets (*sodot*), particularly in the *qere/ketiv* annotations.[41] Ibn Adoniyahu knew that Bomberg was interested in Kabbalah. In fact, in his Latin introduction to the edition of R. Abraham de Balmes's *Mikneh Avram* (1523), Bomberg had expressed his intention to publish kabbalistic works, if only because he knew there was a demand for such books from other Christian Hebraists.[42]

Penkower's two suggestions for how Ibn Adoniyah convinced Bomberg—an improved biblical text and the Masorah's value for kabbalistic study—are persuasive even though he never explicitly states them. The general importance of the Masorah as the raison d'être for the new edition is, however, explicitly cited by Ibn Adoniyahu at the end of the introduction where he describes how he persuaded Bomberg to undertake the new publication.

> And when I saw the great benefit[43] that is to be derived from the Masorah magna, the Masorah parva, and the Masorah finalis, I informed Seignior

Daniel Bomberg, may his Rock and Redeemer protect him, and showed him the benefit to be derived from [the Masorah]. Whereupon he did all in his power to send into all the countries in order to search after whatever may be found of the Masorah, and praised be the Lord, we obtained as many of the masoretic books as could possibly be got. The previously mentioned Seignor [Bomberg] never proved indolent, his hand was not closed, nor did he draw back his right hand from producing gold out of his purse to pay the expenses of buying the books and the messengers who were engaged to search for them in the most remote corners (lit. "holes and cracks") and in every other place they might possibly be.[44]

As this passage clearly states, it was Ibn Adoniyahu who initiated the project and convinced Bomberg to publish it. At the very beginning of his lengthy introduction, however, Ibn Adoniyahu relates a somewhat different, far more elaborate narrative to explain the project's genesis. The introduction itself begins with a passage of florid praise of God for endowing mankind with language and his chosen nation, the Jews, with the holy language of the Torah "so that all the nations of the world may know that there is nothing like this holy language." Even so, he continues, God gave the Torah to the Jews alone, and only they know its mysteries (*sodeiha*), its grammar, and rules, and the men of the Great Assembly (*anshei ha-kenissiya* [sic] *ha-gedolah*) "have set up marks, and built a wall around it, and made ditches between its walls and bars and gates to preserve the citadel in its splendor and brightness . . . [s]o that no other hand might touch it and desecrate it. . . . And the spirit (*ha-ruah*) rested upon them, and they were of those of whom it is written 'and they prophesied but did not continue.'"[45] These last statements certainly refer to the Masoretes and their annotations; in rabbinic tradition, the Masorah was known as a "fence around the Torah" (*mesoret seyag le-torah*).[46] As we shall see, however, Ibn Adoniyahu's suggestion that the masoretic annotations were divinely inspired may not have been purely rhetorical.

Immediately after concluding this opening section, Ibn Adoniyahu relates the following biographical account. Because of its importance, I will cite large sections of the passage (though not its entirety). The narrator relates (*amar ha-magid*):

I was at ease at home, flourishing in my abode, diligently pursuing my studies in the province of Tunis, which is on the borders of ancient

Carthage, when Time (*ha-zeman*) carried me off to the lands of the West and did not take away its hand from consuming me, nor did it reconsider and relent, and it pushed me here to Venice, this chief and great city. And here I did nothing, for the hand of Time was still high and mighty, and its troubles and cares found me in the city, smote me, wounded and crushed me. And it was after about three months of suffering its blows that I left the furnace of my affliction for a short period, for I was in a thirsty land. I said to myself: Let us get up, walk about the city, through the market and the streets. And as I went out in the city, silently marveling, suddenly coming towards me—for God had summoned him before me—[was] one of the righteous Christians (*mi-ḥasidei ha-notzrim*), a highly distinguished person, by the name of Seignor Daniel Bomberg, may his Rock and Redeemer protect him. This came about through the efforts of a Jewish man (*ish ʿivri*), who bestowed great kindness upon me; his name is R. Chaim Alton, son of the distinguished R. Moses Alton, may his Rock and Redeemer protect him.[47]

[Bomberg] brought me to his printing house and showed me his entire house of treasures and said, "Turn in, abide with me, for here you shall find rest for your soul, and balm for your wound. I want you to correct (*she tagiha*) the books that I print, remove the stumbling blocks of error, purify and refine them in the furnace of examination, and weigh them on the scales of correctness, until they emerge fine as refined silver and pure as purified gold.

Although I saw that his desire was greater than my ability, yet I thought to myself: One should not refuse a superior.[48] Even so, I told him I did not know so much, not nearly as much, as we learn in the Talmud of Jerusalem. [Ibn Adonyiahu continues with a number of statements that contrast the modesty of his abilities with the importance of the work he was asked to undertake, as well as others that emphasize the care he felt he must accordingly take in his work, not relying upon his judgment but always inspecting multiple books and evaluating them so as not to make emendations based upon conjecture.]

And it came to pass, after I had remained there for some time, doing my work, the work of heaven, that the Lord, may He be blessed, roused the spirit of the noble man (*heiʿir ruaḥ ha-sar*) for whom I worked and encouraged his heart to publish the Twenty-Four books (i.e., the Hebrew Bible). He said to me, "Now gird your loins like a man, for it is my desire to publish the Twenty-Four, in such a way that they will be accompanied by the commentaries, the Targum, the Masorah magna and the Masorah parva, those [words] that are read as they are written and those that are written but are not read, and those that are full or defective, and all the glosses of the scribes, and following all this, the Masorah magna according to the alphabetical order of the *Arukh*, so that the reader can run through it to find what he wants." Like a bear robbed [of her young], he did not delay his work, for he desired the daughter of Jacob. He summoned artisans expert in printing, and each one with his club in his hand[49] [took] himself to work. And when I saw that the work was urgent and [that it would be] a benefit and a glory for Israel to show the nations and princes the beauty and excellence of our holy Torah—for since the day it has been put in a book (*sefer*), it has not been done in its proper way (*ke-matkonetah*)—and since its excellence has grown in the eyes of the builders (*ha-bonim*), becoming the capstone, I made it my goal to fulfill his desire.[50]

Unlike the account discussed earlier that is found near the conclusion of the introduction, this passage at the introduction's beginning clearly describes Bomberg as the one who initiated the project to publish the Bible with the Masorah. The reason, Jacob tells us, was that Bomberg "desired the daughter of Jacob"—a quotation lifted from Gen 34:18 referring to Shechem, who also desired one of Jacob's daughters, Dinah, and lost no time in circumcising himself in order to become an Israelite (an act that was already understood by the rabbis as part of the conversion process) so as to be able to marry her. To be sure, Bomberg does not act entirely on his own. Behind Bomberg there stands the figure of God, who sends Bomberg—"May *his* Rock and Redeemer protect him!" (emphasis added)—to meet Ibn Adoniyahu as he wanders aimlessly around Venice. It is also God who "roused the spirit of the noble man (*hei'ir ruah ha-sar*) . . . and encouraged his heart to publish the Twenty-Four books" of the Bible with its full array of accompanying texts. The phrase *hei'ir ruah ha-sar* directly alludes to the beginning of the book of Ezra (1:1), where we are told that "the Lord roused the spirit of King Cyrus of Persia to issue a proclamation" that allows the Israelites to return to Jerusalem and rebuild their Temple.[51] Just as Cyrus is God's agent, so is the Gentile Bomberg; further, both are God's agents in parallel projects of restoration—the first to restore Israel to its homeland, the second to restore the Hebrew Bible to its original glory. In this construction, the Jew Ibn Adoniyahu is merely Bomberg's servant, who fulfills his master's desire. (We might say that Ibn Adoniyahu stands in the same relationship to Bomberg as did the scribe Ezra to Artaxexes, Cyrus's successor; both figures restored the Torah to Israel.) Indeed, only after seeing Bomberg's printers immediately begin their work, and after he realizes that the new edition will redound to the glory of Israel, inasmuch as "it will show the nations and princes the beauty and excellence of our holy Torah," does Jacob ben Ḥayyim himself set to work on the Bible.

The factual discrepancies between this account and the one found at the introduction's end are not its only unusual features. For one thing, the biographical detail of the narrative is itself remarkable; while other early printed Hebrew books—both in the fifteenth and sixteenth centuries—often contain autobiographical details and publishing histories on their title pages and in their colophons, it is rare to find so extensive an account as this one.[52] The Hebrew text is also more exceptional than it appears in English translation. Like much medieval Hebrew prose and poetry, Ibn Adoniyahu's text is dense with recondite biblical allusions and rare scriptural phraseologies.[53] What the translation does not convey at all, however, is that large portions of the Hebrew text are written in rhymed prose—that is to say, virtually in the form of a *maqama*, the literary genre of rhymed-prose narrative that was immensely popular among Spanish Hebrew poets in the thirteenth and fourteenth centuries and that was adapted in turn by Immanuel ben Solomon ben Yekutiel of Rome (1261–1328), the author of *Maḥberot Immanuel*, a collection of *maqama* narratives that remains among the most celebrated medieval Italian Hebrew literary compositions. Ibn Adoniyahu was certainly familiar with the *Maḥberot*, which was first published by Gershom Soncino in Brescia in 1491.[54]

Indeed, the resemblance to Immanuel's work goes far beyond the rhymed prose. Jacob ben Ḥayyim's autobiography has many of the literary conventions of Immanuel's narratives. In the first place, Ibn Adoniyahu casts himself—as was the custom of most authors of *maqama*—in the role of the rhymed-prose narrative's protagonist, who is typically a fictional representation of the poet himself. Ibn Adoniyahu's autobiographical narrative opens with the phrase *amar ha-magid*, a formulaic expression used in *maqama* to punctuate the narrative; the phrase is probably best translated as "the narrator relates," even if it is not always clear to what extent medieval authors distinguished between the historical author and the literary persona of the narrator.[55] For example, Immanuel's *Maḥberot* regularly begins *amar Immanuel ha-meḥaber* ("Immanuel the author/compiler related"). Even more significantly, the "plot" of Ibn Adoniyahu's autobiographical account appears to be based on a model taken from Immanuel. As Ibn Adoniyahu tells his reader, his happy, comfortable existence is suddenly uprooted by *ha-zeman*, literally Time or Fate (though a better translation might be "Fickle Fortune"), and then he is tossed to and fro in his wandering until suddenly, walking down the street, he is miraculously saved by a stranger—in this case, the Gentile Daniel Bomberg, who takes him home, employs him, and effectively gives him back his life. Immanuel's first *maḥberet* begins in a strikingly similar way.[56] Fate (*ha-zeman*) sends out a royal decree to upset the poet's life; he is thrust into exile, wandering aimlessly, until he meets his savior, the *sar*, in whose eyes he finds favor, and who brings him to his home There is no indication in the first chapter of the *Maḥberot* as to whether the *sar* is Jewish or Gentile, but the third *maḥberet*, which relates the story of how the *sar* introduces Immanuel to a nun, with whom he falls madly in love, raises the possibility that the *sar*, too, was a Gentile.[57]

Ibn Adoniyahu's explicit use of the conventions of *maqama* poetry in general, and those of Immanuel's *Maḥberot* in particular, may also be a key to reconciling the factual discrepancies between this opening account of the history of the Rabbinic Bible's inception and the second account at the end of the introduction. There can be little question that the latter is far closer to what actually must have transpired and that it was Ibn Adoniyahu who initiated the project and persuaded Bomberg to publish this new edition of the Rabbinic Bible. Why, then, did Ibn Adoniyahu open his introduction with this narrative of salvation (for lack of a better term) in which Bomberg is cast as the project's initiator? In part it may have been a rhetorical strategy for Ibn Adoniyahu to praise his patron. It may also have been partly a way of exonerating Bomberg in the eyes of Jewish readers so as to convince them that, far from having ulterior (conversionary) motives in publishing the Hebrew Bible (as his previous association with Pratensis would have suggested), he was, rather, truly like Shechem, in love with the "daughter of Jacob," virtually willing to convert to Judaism.

The literary form of the passage, however, was probably more than a mere rhetorical medium for an encomium to his patron. By casting this narrative in the shape of a fictional *maqama* or an Immanuelesque *maḥberet*, Ibn Adoniyahu may have been signaling to his reader that his account, too, was a fiction but that it also was—as David Malkiel has recently argued in regard to Immanuel's *maḥberot* and the poetics behind those compositions—a fiction with a didactic lesson.[58] Precisely what lesson Ibn Adoniyahu wished his reader to derive from his narrative may be inferred from the paragraph that follows the narrative, a passage that rather abruptly shifts the argument of the treatise-like introduction away from the story of his life and the history of the Rabbinic Bible's inception:

> And when I saw that many of the masses, and among them even many groups of sages in our time, in our own generation, value in their hearts neither the Masorah nor any of the methods of the Masorah—as when they ask, "What profit can be derived from it for themselves?"—and that it [the Masorah] has been nearly forgotten and lost, I bestirred myself[59]—on account of it being "a time to act for the Lord" (Ps 119:126)—to show the nations and the princes the value of the Masorah and that, without it, it is impossible to copy biblical books correctly and properly, not to mention Torah scrolls.[60]

The masses of people and sages to whom Ibn Adoniyahu refers in this passage are all Jews, none of whom, he complains, value the Masorah as it should be appreciated. And it is precisely for this reason—so one must understand—that God chose the Christian Bomberg both to save Ibn Adoniyahu and to restore the Masorah to its rightful place in the Bible. The lesson of the narrative, in other words, is that, because of the Jews' own failure to appreciate the Masorah properly, it could only fall to a Christian to print such a Bible with the Masorah correctly and properly. Indeed, God Himself must have arranged this fortuitous marriage between a Jew and a Gentile in order to "save" the Torah.

If nothing else, this remarkable narrative, in which a Christian printer rescues a Jewish scholar by enlisting him to restore the Jewish Bible to its full glory, points to the unusual historical circumstances in which RB 1524–25 was produced, and in particular to the complicated relationships between Jews and Christians in Venice in the early sixteenth century. The complications in these relationships were epitomized by the movement of figures from one world to the other. As we now know, Ibn Adoniyahu eventually—sometime after 1538—converted to Christianity.[61] There is no indication whatsoever in his introduction to RB 1524–25 that thoughts of conversion were in his mind at the time, nor is there in the text so much as a hint that he had theological or religious sympathies toward Christianity at the time of his work on the edition. Nor was Ibn Adoniyahu the only one of Bomberg's Jewish employees to praise the printer for his exceptional generosity and native piety even though he was a Christian and, in the words of the historian Joseph Ha-Kohen (1496–1578), did not have "a drop of Jewish seed" in him.[62] Nonetheless, Ibn Adoniyahu's narrative of salvation maps out the routes by which an intellectual figure could move from one religious culture to another. Ibn Adoniyahu was not the only one of Bomberg's editors and printers to apostasize (nor was Bomberg the only Gentile Venetian printer of Hebrew books to employ apostates), and there has been some scholarly speculation that Bomberg himself was motivated by missionary impulses to publish Hebrew books.[63] While Ibn Adoniyahu's introduction does not cast any direct light on these questions, the very fact that he could narrate such a narrative of salvation in which a Jew is saved by a Christian, "may *his* [my emphasis] Rock and Redeemer protect him," points to a new kind of Jewish self-perception *and* perception of Christians. However porous or fluid were the actual lines of communication between Jewish and Christian society in early sixteenth-century Venice, there is something unprecedented about a cultural environment in which a pious Jew could imagine a Christian as the divinely inspired initiator of a Hebrew Bible with the Masorah.[64]

The exceptionality of Ibn Adoniyahu's narrative is complemented by the singularity of RB 1524–25 as a book. This edition of the Bible is different in its contents and structure from any previous Bible manuscript produced by Jews in the Middle Ages or printed Bible during the incunable period in the fifteenth century. Does understanding the singularity of the cultural environment that produced this Bible help us appreciate the Bible's own singular features? We can begin to answer this question by briefly reviewing the history of the Jewish Bible as a book before the sixteenth century.[65]

During the Middle Ages in Europe, there existed basically three different subgenres of Bibles, each of which had somewhat different shapes in Ashkenaz (Franco-Germany, with some more subtle differences between French and German books), Sefarad, and Italy.

(1) *Masoretic Bibles*: This type tends to comprise the complete Tanakh or a part of the complete Tanakh—the Prophets or the Hagiographa alone—with, as its name indicates, the Masorah. The format of these Bible derives directly from that of the earliest Jewish codices produced in the Near East and in North Africa in the ninth through the eleventh century. The biblical text is laid out in two or three columns, almost always written in large square letters, while between the columns are the abbreviated annotations of the Masora parva (*mesorah ketanah*), and on the top two lines and the bottom three are the lengthier notes of the Masorah magna (*mesorah gedolah*), typically written in a semicursive hand in micrography, and often in various designs or figures—in

Sefarad, the designs tend to be floral or geometric and reflect Islamic influence; in Ashkenaz, they are frequently in grotesque human or animal shapes that show Gothic influence. Depending on whether the codices were produced in Spain or in Ashkenaz, they are also generally marked by *parashah* and/or *seder* signs. In Spain, the masoretic codices frequently contain at their beginning and end masoretic lists and treatises like Aaron Ben Asher's *Sefer Dikdukei Te'amim*. In Ashkenaz, the biblical text is sometimes interversed with the Aramaic *Targum Onkelos*—that is, each verse of Scripture is followed by the Targum, verse by verse. But aside from these two types of texts—the masoretic treatises found at the codex's beginning or end and the interverse Targum—the masoretic Bible lacks any other sort of text on its pages.

These Bibles probably served multiple purposes for different owners (or even the same one). Some copies were used as model books or *tikkunim* for scribes wishing to copy Torah scrolls. It is even possible that in some areas, in small towns or villages that did not own a Torah scroll, these codices were used for the liturgical reading of the Bible in the synagogue, at least in the early Middle Ages.[66] In Spain, the masoretic Bible was the most commonly produced type of Bible, and it was probably the type a Jew wishing to own his own Bible would have commissioned for himself.

(2) *Liturgical Pentateuchs*: As its name indicates, the volumes in this subtype are not complete Hebrew Bibles but Pentateuchs accompanied by the *haftarot* (prophetic readings) and the Five Scrolls as well as other texts that were sometimes read communally like the *Book of Antiochus* (recited on Hanukkah) or chapters from Jeremiah and Job (read on the fast day of Tisha B'av). Because of their contents, these codices were clearly intended to accompany, in one way or another, the reading of the Pentateuch and related biblical texts in the synagogue as part of the liturgy, though exactly how they were used is still not certain. Some participants in the synagogue service undoubtedly used them to read along with and follow the public chanting of the weekly reading from a Torah scroll and thus to fulfill the talmudic injunction that "every person is obligated to complete the weekly lectionary readings (*parashiyotav*) with the congregation [by reciting] Hebrew Scripture (*Mikra*) twice and the Targum once" (*b. Berakhot* 8a–b). Whether this repeated reading constituted actual study of the Bible or a more ritualistic recitation of the text is a subject deserving more exploration than is possible here. In either case, many of these liturgical Pentateuchs contain the Aramaic Targum that is written sometimes in the interverse fashion and sometimes in a separate column. Some French liturgical Pentateuchs leave out the Targum and substitute the

commentary of Rashi (Rabbi Shlomo bar Yitzḥaki, 1040–1105) in its place, others have both Rashi and the Targum; in Spain, the Aramaic Targum was copied far less frequently, and Rashi was sometimes substituted for it.[67] Some liturgical Pentateuchs in turn have the Masorah, while others do not. In either case, the Masorah is not the normative feature in the liturgical Pentateuch that it is in the masoretic Bible. When it is found in a liturgical Pentateuch, however, it is written in the same traditional manner as in a masoretic Bible—in micrography, often in decorative patterns or in figurative representations.

(3) *Study Bibles*: Under this subtype, I group those biblical codices that appear to have been produced specifically for the purposes of study. As noted above, some masoretic codices and some liturgical Pentateuchs were probably used for study, as the presence of Rashi and/or the Targum on their pages suggests. In the case of the study Bible, however, study appears to have been their paramount purpose, inasmuch as these codices contain either multiple commentaries on the page or the commentary occupies so prominent a position on the page that it is fair to say that the codex was produced specifically with the commentary in mind as its main object of study, not the biblical text per se.[68] Even so, this subtype overlaps with the other genres. One of its earliest examples, Leipzig 1, probably composed in France in the early thirteenth century, which contains both masoretic notes of early Ashkenazic sages as well as Rashi's commentary with comments and additions to his commentary made by later students, is also a liturgical Pentateuch.[69] The dating of this volume has been the subject of considerable discussion, but it is worth noting that its pages use a page format that is similar to the one later used for the Babylonian Talmud, with the separate components on the page—for example, the biblical text, Rashi, and the Targum—recorded in what appear to be interlocking blocks. In fact, this page format goes back to the glossed Christian Bible format of the Middle Ages, from which it was adapted by Jewish scribes for Hebrew texts with commentaries.[70]

This type of format, however, is relatively uncommon. Most biblical commentaries in the Middle Ages were transmitted and preserved not on the pages of biblical codices themselves but in separate volumes called *quntrasim* in which the commentary was written in a semicursive, so-called rabbbinic script with only lemmata, short phrases from the Bible, intended to key the reader to the comment's scriptural occasion.[71] Exactly how these *quntrasim* were studied is also unknown: Did students use them with a biblical codex on the table next to them? Or was the Bible presumed to be known by heart? In any case, the utility and advantage of a page with both the biblical text and the commentary on it—and even more so, multiple commentaries—is obvious. On the other hand, the format is far more difficult to reproduce by hand in a manuscript than either a masoretic or liturgical Bible, and as a result, the number of such Bibles is far smaller than either of the other two subgenres.

All three subtypes that I have just described are found in Italy as well as in Ashkenaz and Sefarad, but, especially from the late thirteenth century on, Italian Bibles exhibit a few distinctive features that may be relevant for the early printed Hebrew Bible. First, the Hebrew Bible in Italy undergoes a certain process of paring down, for lack of a better term. For example, in contrast to both Ashkenaz and Sefarad, there is a recognizable disregard for the Masorah; even two-column Bibles that look as though they were written to be masoretic Bibles lack the masoretic annotations. Similarly, a significant number of liturgical Pentateuchs lack either the Targum or Rashi, and there is a discernible tendency among them to have *either* the Scrolls or the *haftarot* but not both. From the later fourteenth century on, one also finds a growing number of codices in which the biblical text is written in a single page-wide column without either the Masorah or the Targum or commentaries on the page. These plain Bibles appear to reflect contemporary Italian humanist manuscripts, particularly of classical ancient texts, that emphasize the unadorned core text on the page.[72] Finally, Italian Bibles increasingly become smaller in size and more portable, again a sign of the times and the growing popularity of books whose owners wished to use them as an article of daily life. These developments anticipate, to one degree or another, some of the changes that come to the Bible with the advent of print.

Nonetheless, it is significant that the early printed Bibles of the fifteenth and early sixteenth centuries (before 1517) essentially follow the basic subgenres of the medieval Bible with a few major qualifications.[73] First, as Herbert Zafren noted, early Jewish printers most often printed biblical commentaries rather than Bibles themselves.[74] Why this was so is not clear. It may have been that a sufficient number of Bibles in manuscript form were still in circulation and that there was simply less commercial demand for Bibles than for commentaries.[75] It may also have been that printers hesitated to publish Bibles because of the technical difficulty they faced in setting the type for both the consonantal letters and the vowels in their correct positions.[76] In either case, as Herbert Zafren has noted, among the approximately fifty editions of complete Bibles, Pentateuchs, Former and Latter Prophets, and Hagiographa[77]—many of the latter two types published separately—there are several Pentateuchs with Targum and Rashi (e.g., Bologna 1482, Lisbon 1491) *or* with the *haftarot* and

Megillot (e.g., Hijar 1487–88, Brescia 1492–93).[78] (There are a few editions that have the Scrolls, *haftarot, and* Targum or Rashi).[79] These Bibles appear to reflect the subgenre of the liturgical Pentateuch. Beginning with the Bologna 1482 Pentateuch, these editions not infrequently use the talmudic page format that, as I remarked earlier, goes back to the manuscript age. Print, however, made this format far more feasible to produce than it had been in the manuscript age, and, as a result, it became standard only with printing.

In addition, beginning with Joshua Soncino's 1488 *editio princeps* of the complete Bible, there are also a number of later editions published in two-column pages that copy the two column format found in handwritten masoretic Bibles even though they lack the Masorah. The absence of the Masorah may have been due to the technical difficulties of printing in miniscule type that would resemble micrography, which is how the Masorah had always been written in Hebrew Bibles; equally so, it may have been a reflection of the general disregard for the Masorah, about which Ibn Adoniyahu complained in his introduction, as we saw earlier. This may have been especially the case with the Italian editions. The second of the two editions of the complete Bible printed by Gershom Soncino in several volumes in Brescia, between 1492–94, is in octavo, in a single column on the page, and, as Soncino himself writes in a colophon, was designed to be a portable Bible, clearly mirroring the contemporary Italian manuscript tradition that also regularly produced small, portable Bibles with a single, page-wide column and no other text on the page. While there are numerous editions of biblical books or sections like the Prophets or Hagiographa with a single commentary, there are only two editions with two commentaries, both of them published by Don Samuel D'Ortas in Leiria, Portugal.[80]

Viewed, then, from the perspective of the medieval and early printed Bibles, the 1517 edition, with its Targum and single commentary on the entirety of the Bible (and two commentaries without Targum on one or two books), was unprecedented, but it was not entirely a newly conceived book. Essentially, it took the basic structure of the liturgical Pentateuch with Targum and Rashi (or another commentary on the later sections of the Bible) and now provided these ancillaries to the biblical text for the entirety of the Bible (albeit stripped of the *haftarot* and the utility of having everything requisite for synagogue use present in a single volume).[81]

In contrast, RB 1524–25 was a truly new book inasmuch as it is virtually a composite of all three earlier subtypes—the masoretic Bible (with the biblical text and Masorah), the liturgical Pentateuch (with the Targum and Rashi), and the study Bible (with the additional second commentary of Abraham Ibn Ezra on the Pentateuch and other commentators on other biblical books).[82] In that sense, it was a kind of "whole" book that attempted to do everything in one volume. It was, in short, a kind of anthology that brought together into a new composition all the previous components and subtypes of the Hebrew Bible and thereby appealed to diverse Jewish audiences.

That appeal is most visible in Ibn Adoniyahu's decision to print two commentaries on each biblical book and, even more so, in his choices for the second commentaries. By the early sixteenth century, Rashi's commentary on the Pentateuch had become a kind of universal presence in a Jewish Bible; even if originally Rashi was principally an Ashkenazic authority, his commentaries had attained equally authoritative status in Sefarad as early as the fourteenth century.[83] It is therefore no surprise that he is printed in Spanish and Portuguese imprints like Toledano's 1491 Lisbon Pentateuch, not to mention Italian editions like the 1482 Bologna Pentateuch, or either the 1517 or the 1524–25 Venice editions. The addition, however, of the commentary of Ibn Ezra on the Pentateuch and of Ibn Ezra, Radak, and Gersonides—all of them classical commentators deriving from the Sefardic tradition in its larger sense (including, that is, figures from Provence, like Radak, or Languedoc, like Gersonides)—on books in the Prophets and Hagiographa would have directly appealed to a Sefardic audience of readers, either in Italy itself (including Sefardic refugees in Italy following the Spanish Expulsion in 1492) or, more likely perhaps, for export to the larger postexpulsion Sefardic communities in places like Salonica and Constantinople in the Ottoman empire.[84] This—along with the fact that Ibn Adoniyahu himself was descended from Sefardic Jews— may have been the reason that led him to add these specific commentators rather than their Ashkenazic counterparts like R. Shlomo ben Aderet (known as Rashba) or Joseph Kara or Joseph Bekhor Shor or even more contemporary exegetes, most prominently the Italian Obadiah Seforno (Bologna, ca. 1475– 1550).[85] Exactly why Ibn Adoniyahu decided to substitute Ibn Ezra in a number of cases for Radak (who had been the main commentator included in the 1517 edition for the Prophets and many of the books of the Hagiographa) is not clear; as I noted earlier, Radak's commentary on Psalms had been partially censored, and Ibn Adoniyahu may not have wanted to print it for that reason. In general, Ibn Adoniyahu appears to have wished to produce a classicizing edition, and Ibn Ezra was probably the most classical of all Sefardic commentaries. Yet the addition of Ibn Ezra (and the other Sefardic or Provençal commentators) was attractive not only because it added a second commentary to the page. By including the Sefardic exegetes in his Rabbinic Bible, Ibn Adon-iyahu's edition joined the Sefardic and Ashkenazic communities of readers into a single audience and effectively produced a new canon of classical Jewish exegesis. Even if this was not Ibn Adoniyahu's intention, his inclusion of the more grammatically and philosophically oriented Sefardic commentators had perceptible repercussions in contemporary Ashkenaz. Indeed, as Elhanan Reiner has suggested, the inclusion of the Sefardic exegetes in the Rabbinic Bible seriously challenged the traditional Ashkenazic canon and even aroused the ire and opposition of some Polish Ashkenazic rabbinic authorities who were not inclined to approve of these rationalistic Spanish exegetes and admit them into their curriculum of permitted study.[86]

As we have already noted, RB 1517 appealed to both Jewish and Christian audiences, albeit (it seems) in slightly different editions. RB 1524–25 also appealed to audiences of both faiths, but now in a single edition. Indeed, it is possible that Ibn Adoniyahu included Ibn Ezra and the other Sefardic com-mentators with an eye to Christian readers. As one scholar has noted, between the years 500 and 1500 C.E., there may have been no more than a few dozen Christians who could read Hebrew, even the Hebrew text of the Bible, let alone postbiblical writings, with any real facility.[87] In the first half of the sixteenth century, however, there appears to have been a dramatic increase in Hebraic literacy among Christians, largely due to the visible rise of Christian Hebraism in all its varieties. Even though most of these Hebraists before the seventeenth century had only a smattering of Hebrew, there were a select few—particularly those with an interest in biblical grammar and philology like Sanctes Pagninus (1470–1541), Conrad Pellican (1478–1556), and Sebastian Muenster (1488–1552)—who read Hebrew with enough facility to control rabbinic biblical exegetes like Rashi, Radak, and Ibn Ezra.[88] In the Latin general introduction to his translation of the Pentateuch, *Mikdash Adonai* (Basel, 1534–34), Muen-ster not only cited the three Jewish commentators (and still others) as sources but even quoted verbatim (in the original Hebrew and in Latin translation) from Ibn Adoniyahu's introduction to RB 1524–25 regarding the origins of the Masorah.[89] However limited an audience of readers there were like Muenster Bomberg must have been alert to its existence and would have wished to target it even if he knew that the Bible's principal audience was inevitably going to be Jewish. Among the surviving evidence to corroborate this point is the correspondence between Bomberg and the great Christian Hebraist and kab-balist Johannes Reuchlin that took place in the years between 1519 and 1521 and that began with a request by Reuchlin to Bomberg to send him a copy of Psalms, Proverbs, and Ecclesiastes.[90]

Historically, the presence of multiple commentaries on the page eventually became the distinguishing feature of the Rabbinic Bible.[91] Indeed, the impact of this feature of the book on the history of Jewish reading—with its implicit invitation to comparative exegetical study—remains a subject yet to be explored in the depth it deserves. For Ibn Adoniyahu himself, however, it was less the presence of multiple commentaries on the page than that of the Masorah in its corrected, edited version that was his proudest achievement, what he saw as his edition's most important element. As Penkower has demonstrated, Ibn Adoniyahu understood the Masorah's importance on multiple levels—homiletical, halakhic, and, most importantly, kabbalistic. But there was an additional feature that Ibn Adoniyahu attributed to the Masorah that went beyond its cognitive contributions to all these levels of knowledge, an intrinsic importance that was, arguably, unprecedented in the entire history of the Jewish Bible. Whether Ibn Adoniyahu himself fully appreciated the novelty of this significance of this feature is unclear, but it was, in many respects, one of RB 1524–25's most important legacies to the subsequent history of the Jewish Bible—that is, the Bible as claimed by Jews to be their own.

The status of the Masorah—by this term, I am referring to the entire system of masoretic annotations that go back to the early biblical codices of the ninth through the eleventh century, including both the Masorah magna (*mesorah gedolah*) and the Masora parva (*mesorah ketanah*)—during the Middle Ages was distinctly ambiguous. On the one hand, as we have seen, the presence of the Masorah—whether written in straight lines or in decorative or figurative patterns—on the pages of biblical codices, particularly masoretic codices, was a conventional, virtually necessary presence. Furthermore, such masoretic codices, particularly model books (*sefarim mugahim*) or *tikkunim* were used by scribes to copy Torah scrolls for liturgical use.[92] On the other hand, classical rabbinic literature—the Babylonian Talmud in particular—contains a number of biblical quotations and citations that differ from the masoretic text, and in their discourse *about* the biblical text, rabbinic sages throughout the Middle Ages (and even into the modern period) evinced a distinct ambivalence toward the Masorah as the definitive authority for deciding upon the correct biblical text. In rabbinic discourse, this ambivalence extended toward the Masorah in general.

Most articulations of this ambivalence are recorded either in collections of rabbinic responsa or in scribal manuals, largely because the question of the Masorah's authority tended to come up less as a theoretical or ideological topic than as a matter of practical import every time a questionable detail of orthography or pronunciation or spacing was found in a Torah scroll and needed to be approved or corrected. The basic problem was as follows: According to rabbinic halakhah, a single mistaken or incorrectly written letter or orthographic detail invalidates a Torah scroll for liturgical use.[93] On the other hand, there were different traditions of orthography, particularly in regard to plene and defective spellings in the consonantal text.[94] To add to the complications in making a decision as to *the* correct form, there were competing sources of halakhic authority and differing procedures for arriving at a decision: (1) following the majority of existing Torah scrolls, a practice in line with the general rabbinic doctrine to follow the majority in cases of halakhic doubt (cf. Exod 23:2);[95] (2) following the readings found in model biblical codices (*sefarim mugahim*) and *tikkunim* (scribal exemplars), as well as masoretic codices with the masoretic annotations (*sifrei masoret*); (3) following stated attestations in the Babylonian Talmud to correct readings, particularly in cases where those readings involve the determination of *halakhot* (legal rulings); (4) or following *midreshei aggadot* (rabbinic homiletical interpretations that, in the Middle Ages, included those found in the Zohar, the thirteenth-century mystical treatise that was believed to be of classical rabbinic authorship) that were based on specific textual readings.[96]

In his comprehensive survey of the different medieval (and postmedieval) rabbinic views on the question of "fixing" the Torah text, B. Barry Levy has shown that while following the Masorah was not a neglected procedure, it was by no means privileged or even a primary source of authority in deciding upon the correct consonantal text. In fact, there existed a spectrum of varying attitudes toward its relative importance.[97] For example, Abraham Ibn Ezra (1098–1164), in the introduction to his Pentateuch commentary, announced that he would ignore the explanations (*ta'ameihem*) of the Masoretes (specifically toward plene and defective readings) and was even more dismissive about homilies based on such masoretic distinctions, which, he wrote, "are good only for children."[98] In contrast, Meir Ha-Levi Abulafia (1165–244, known as the Ramah), the author of *Masoret Seyag la-Torah* (1227), one of the earliest systematic attempts to fix the definitive text of the Torah on the basis of corrected scrolls [or model books] (*ha-sefarim ha-mugahim*) and *masorot*, relied upon the Masorah when it was clear, but in cases of doubt he followed the majority; it is not entirely clear if that was a majority of Torah scrolls or codices.[99] Ramah's attitude to the Masorah was one of the more positive ones. Rashba (ca. 1235–1310), the Spanish rabbinic authority whose responsum on the subject became the most widely circulated and frequently cited source, emphatically stated that in all cases involving a halakhic decision, one follows the Babylonian Talmud; in all other cases, including those involving plene and defective spellings, one follows the majority of readings in scrolls.[100] Similarly, the Provençal sage Menahem Meiri (ca. 1249–1316) noted the uncertainty and unreliability of both scribal exemplars (*tikkunim*) as well as of masoretic treatises and midrashim, and he followed Rashba in stating a strong preference for the talmudic reading in all textual points used for halakhic decisions.[101]

The position that the Masorah held in Jewish halakhic circles before the early sixteenth century was, then, far from unanimous, and certainly not the absolute, unquestioned one it ultimately came to possess.[102] Ibn Adoniyahu's complaint about the neglect of the Masorah and the ambivalence some of his contemporaries showed it, in the passage quoted earlier in this chapter, was a realistic description of the state of masoretic affairs at the time. Indeed, it is precisely in light of that state that we can appreciate the importance Ibn Adoniyahu attached to the Masorah.

We can begin by noting the rhetorical strategy Ibn Adoniyahu adopted in introducing his position. He did *not* begin by reviewing the halakhic positions I have just reviewed (most of which centered around questions of the consonantal text). Instead, he approached the topic *historically*, by presenting and refuting the views of three scholars who, if not his contemporaries, lived "nearer our time" and who—either in their biblical commentaries or biblical grammatical treatises (but not halakhic documents like that of responsa literature)—had proposed historicizing theories regarding the origins of the *qere* and *ketiv* pattern (which Ibn Adoniyahu took as emblematic, *pars pro toto*, for the Masorah in its entirety). By the very act of couching his views within this historicizing, if exegetical, frame, rather than a halakhic one, Ibn Adoniyahu was already making a significant departure from previous rabbinic reflection upon the Masorah. At the same time, his decision also reflected the new humanistic, virtually historical approach that was beginning at that time to characterize the study of the Bible—even if, as we shall see, the solution he offered was radically ahistoricizing in other respects.

The three scholars Ibn Adoniyahu challenged were David Kimḥi (Radak, 1160–1235), Profiat Duran (1350–1415), and Isaac Abravanel (1437–1508).[103] Both Radak and Duran had proposed, in slightly different versions, the idea that the *qere/ketiv* systems originated either during or shortly after the Babylonian exile (in the sixth century B.C.E.) "when the sacred books were lost and scattered about, and those wise men who were skilled in the Scriptures were dead, the men of the Great Synagogue [*anshei keneset ha-gedolah*) found different readings in the sacred books; and in every place where they met with a doubtful and perplexing case they wrote down a word in the text, but did not put the vowels to it, or wrote it in the margin and left it out in the text, not being sure as to what they found."[104] In other words, the *qere/ketiv* annotations were evidence of a state of unresolvable confusion into which the biblical text had fallen due to historical catastrophe.

Abravenal rejected the views of Radak and Duran on both logical and theological grounds while offering his own solution. Ibn Adoniyahu, in turn, essentially adapted Abravenal's refutation of the two earlier scholars, but he argued that Abravanel's own solution to the *qere/ketiv* problem was even more problematic. While Abravanel believed that the Torah text of Ezra was "perfect," he had conceded that some of the "anomalous expressions," including some instances of *qere/ketiv*, were the result of "carelessness on the part of the sacred speaker or writer." Abravanel was referring here specifically to the text of Jeremiah, which indeed has more instances of *qere/ketiv* than almost every other book in the Bible; the reason for this, according to Abravanel, was that Jeremiah the prophet had been imperfectly schooled in the details of Hebrew grammar.

Abravanel's willingness to consider this very human possibility was itself an indication of the new perspective he brought to his reading of the Bible, if not also of humanistic influence upon his work.[105] Nonetheless, for Ibn Adoniyahu, this idea—that a prophet could be either careless or grammatically deficient—was so unacceptable as to be virtually scandalous. Instead, Ibn Adoniyahu proposed a radically rehistoricizing view: the Masorah was not a late phenomenon in any way; it was Sinatic in origin. The basis for his argument was an oft-cited talmudic passage in *b. Nedarim* 37b in which, in the course of interpreting Neh 8:8, R. Isaac stated that "the pronunciation of certain words according to the scribes (*mikra sofrim*), the removal of [the letter] *vav* by the Scribes (*'ittur sofrim*), the *qere ve-lo ketiv* (where a word is read even though it is not written) and the *ketiv ve-lo qere* (where a word is written but not read) are laws of Moses given from Mount Sinai (*halakhah le-mosheh mi-sinai*)."[106] The phrase refers to a special legal category used in early rabbinic literature—and increasingly so, in the Babylonian Talmud—to legitimate various rabbinic enactments that appear to have little biblical corroboration.[107] While the *Nedarim* passage mentions only four types of textual phenomena, Ibn Adoniyahu extrapolated from the four to all of the Masorah and extended Sinaitic authority to its entirety (citing, as support, a responsum of Rashba!). In this way, he not only defended the integrity of the Masorah. He made it the original, exclusive determinant of the biblical text, locating the Masorah's origins in the same revelatory moment as that of the Bible itself.[108]

As Penkower has demonstrated in his meticulous study of Ibn Adoniyahu's editorial techniques, Ibn Adoniyahu believed that there existed a single original text of the Torah as well as a single original text of the Masorah that had "safeguarded" the biblical text.[109] He did not presume to have direct access to the original text of the Torah, or to possess a trustworthy copy of it, but he did believe he could reconstruct it on the basis of the "accurate manuscripts" that he was able to collect; the same belief and approach characterized his reconstruction of the original Masorah. Like other humanist scholars, the text he reconstructed was an eclectic one, but Ibn Adoniyahu was an extremely responsible and conservative textual critic, particularly when it came to emendation; as a matter of principle, he refused to emend the text on the basis of conjecture (*sevara*) and sought sources in earlier manuscripts.[110] According to Penkower's analyses, it does not seem that Ibn Adoniyahu had a fixed or systematic method of emendation or of deciding between conflicting readings (whether between biblical mss; between a biblical ms. and a Masoretic note; or between contradictory Masoretic notes), but it is remarkable how few instances there are in which Penkower cannot identify Ibn Adoniyahu's ad hoc reasoning for each specific case.

As Ibn Adoniyahu reconstructed it, the Masorah—in its three forms (Masorah magna, Masorah parva, and Masorah finalis), all of them represented in the Rabbinic Bible—was both a critical apparatus to the biblical text *and* a lexicon and concordance. Yet by ascribing a Sinaitic origin to the Masorah, Ibn Adoniyahu also transformed the Masorah into a text in its own right, with a meaning of its own, as a source (like the Bible itself) for interpretations, homilies, and even legal deductions. As Ibn Adoniyahu argued in his introduction, the Masorah had already been used as a source for halakhhic explanations by Mordechai b. Hillel (d. 1310) in his *Sefer Mordechai* and by the Maharam, Meir b. Baruch (1230–1293), in his responsa.[111] But Ibn Adoniyahu not only breathed new life into this idea; his Sinaitic ascription also provided a textual rationale for this use of the Masorah, which was also, of course, perfectly in accord with his belief in its kabbalistic significance. Every masoretic enumeration was written, he wrote, "for some great purpose (*le-tzorekh gadol*), and not for nothing (*le-ḥinam*), and this proves the sanctity of our sacred Torah, and that [these signs] were not designated for nothing (*ve-lo nismenu le-ḥinam*).[112] In the century following the Rabbinic Bible's publication, as Penkower shows, Ibn Adoniyahu's claim was corroborated by a marked increase in sermons and homilies delivered in synagogues and in the number of books published that were specifically devoted to interpretations of the Masorah.[113] Within those hundred years, Ibn Adoniyahu's edition was itself republished twice, in 1546–48 and in 1568–69, a clear indication of its popularity and wide acceptance.[114] By the early seventeenth century, Ibn Adoniyahu's edition of the biblical text had clearly come to be accepted in the Jewish world as the universal standard.[115] It is obvious, but nonetheless worth repeating, that only a *printed* book of this kind—namely, a single definitively edited text of a book like the Bible that had previously circulated in so many manuscript copies, all of them slightly different, and with an equally definitively edited apparatus that also had previously circulated with many variants—could ever have attained such standard acceptance and wide circulation so as to become the *fixed* text. Finally, as Penkower has also noted, by virtue of its authoritative *printed* status, RB 1524–25 also marked the triumph of the Sefardic text type of the Bible over the Ashkenazic text type. Such an unambiguous triumph of one biblical textual tradition over all its rivals could never have occurred in the centuries of handwritten transmission of the biblical text.[116]

The greatest impact of Ibn Adoniyahu's edition upon the Jewish Bible—in particular, upon the *Jewishness* of the Jewish Bible—came, however, indirectly—that is, through the Rabbinic Bible's impact upon Christian attitudes to the Hebrew Bible and the Jewish response that followed upon those Christian attitudes. The full story of this chapter in the history of the Bible is too lengthy and complicated to repeat in detail here, and it has been extensively traced in several articles by Moshe Goshen-Gottstein, and more recently by others.[117] In the early and late sixteenth century, Catholics and Protestants heatedly disputed the antiquity of what was essentially known as "the masoretic Bible" and its relation to the Latin Vulgate (and the Septuagint) and their respective authenticity and originality.[118] While the Council of Trent (1545–63) affirmed the absolute authority of the Vulgate, Protestants supported both the antiquity of the Hebraica Veritas (in its masoretic form) and the *sensus litteralis* of the Hebrew Bible, for which they found support and elucidation in classical and medieval Jewish literature. By the end of the seventeenth century, however, most sophisticated Christian biblical scholars, even in Protestant Germany, had become biblical philologists, for whom the masoretic text was essentially a veil to see through so as to discover behind it the "original" biblical text, typically by means of comparative study with the other versions, including the Samaritan Pentateuch (which had been first introduced to European readers in 1616). A major issue animating this new philology was the character of biblical vocalization and accentuation, a topic that took on special urgency as Christians realized that many of the differences between the traditional (or masoretic) Hebrew text and the Latin or Greek versions could be understood as simple differences of vowelization. By vocalizing the Hebrew text differently, its meaning could also be radically emended and thereby brought into line either with the Vulgate or, more commonly, with more contemporary theological and ideological beliefs. These emendations, which proliferated exponentially as the scholarship grew, stood behind the new critical editions being produced by figures like the Benjamin Kennicott (1718–83) and J. G. Eichhorn (1752–1827) as well as the many new translations into the modern European languages.

It was against this background of theologically motivated Christian biblical scholarship and vernacular translation that the Masorah reemerged as a "Jewish issue" in eighteenth-century Germany as one of the motivating concerns of the early Haskalah or Jewish Enlightenment. Moses Mendelssohn (1729–1786) and Solomon Dubno (1738–1813) were appalled by what they saw as the capricious liberties that Christian scholars were taking with the traditional Hebrew text in both their critical and philological works and their sophisticated new translations; at the same time, they were equally embarrassed by the impoverished state of contemporary Jewish biblical scholarship (and well aware of the attractiveness of the new translations by Christians to theologically naïve Jewish readers). In 1778, in response to both feelings, the two Jewish "enlighteners" undertook a new edition of the Pentateuch in which they planned to include a German translation of the highest literary order as well as a Hebrew commentary and a separate set of notes concerning the masoretic text. As scholars have shown, this new edition, eventually published under the title of *Sefer Netivot Ha-Shalom* (1780–83), was intended to serve multiple purposes, but foremost among them was the intent to defend the precise lettering and vocalization of the traditional Jewish text as determined by the Masorah and explicated by rabbinic interpretation.[119] Mendelssohn wrote, "For us, the Torah is an inheritance. . . . Our Sages decreed for us the Masorah and erected a fence for the Torah and for the commandments. . . . We should not move from their straight path . . . [to follow] the conjectures and deliberations of a grammarian or editor drawn from his own mind. We do not live from the mouth [of such an emendator], but from that which our trustworthy masters of the Masorah transmitted to us."[120]

Mendelssohn's statement brings us full circle from the historical moment that led to Ibn Adoniyahu's edition of the accurate Hebrew biblical text according to the Masorah. Whatever may have been the Masorah's "original" purpose or function when it was first compiled by the Masoretes in the seventh through tenth centuries, by the Middle Ages it had acquired an assured place as an integral part of the biblical page as inscribed by Jews in their various types of biblical codices. Ibn Adoniyahu, for the first time, made the Masorah the unconditional and absolute determinant of the biblical text's accuracy and endowed it with an authority and significance that was borrowed from that of the Bible: namely, Sinaitic sanctity. If the Hebrew language and the Torah written in its words was the visible sign of God's love for the Jews, Ibn Adoniyahu saw it as his mission "to repair (*le-takein*) the Masorah so that it remain (*le-hash'irah*) pure and bright, and to show the nations and the princes her beauty, for she is fair in appearance."[121] He could not have foreseen the consequences of his achievement. In an age when Jews and Christians would compete over ownership of the correct biblical text, the Masorah would indeed become the literal embodiment for Jews of the purity and brightness of the Hebrew Bible, its beauty, its Jewishness.

5

THE TOPOGRAPHY OF THE TALMUDIC PAGE

The iconic visual image in classical Jewish literary culture is the image of a page, and no page is more iconic than that of the Babylonian Talmud, the Talmud Bavli (fig. 35). This page is the final literary crystallization of the Oral Torah (Law), a term that in classical Judaism designates the entirety of post-biblical and premedieval exegetical, legal, narrative, and homiletical tradition (which is to say, everything that constitutes classical Jewish culture). The Oral Torah came into existence and was formulated and transmitted—mainly orally, as its name indicates—between the second and sixth centuries C.E. The Babylonian Talmud—so called because it was compiled and edited in Babylonia between the sixth and eighth centuries—records the traditions of the rabbinic sages of Late Antiquity. It existed as a written document consisting of some two and a half million words by the late eighth or early ninth century. There also exists a parallel Palestinian Talmud (also known as the Talmud of Jerusalem, or Talmud Yerushalmi), compiled and edited in Byzantine Palestine about a hundred years before its Babylonian counterpart, but from the early Middle Ages until the dawn of modernity, the Babylonian Talmud was the main subject of the classical Jewish curriculum. Indeed, the study of Talmud, eventually assumed in traditional Jewish culture the importance of a supreme religious activity in its own right.

Within rabbinic tradition, the Talmud is often referred to as *yam ha-talmud*, "the sea of the Talmud," a cognomen that is visually represented on this page with its central block of text, the Talmud proper, afloat like an island in an ocean of commentary in the surrounding columns.[1] The page pictured in figure 35 is from the last great edition of the Babylonian Talmud published by

Fig. 35 Babylonian Talmud with Rashi and Tosafot, Tractate *Berakhot* 2a (Vilna: The Widow of Romm and His Brothers, 1880–86). Courtesy of Van Pelt-Dietrich Library, University of Pennsylvania.

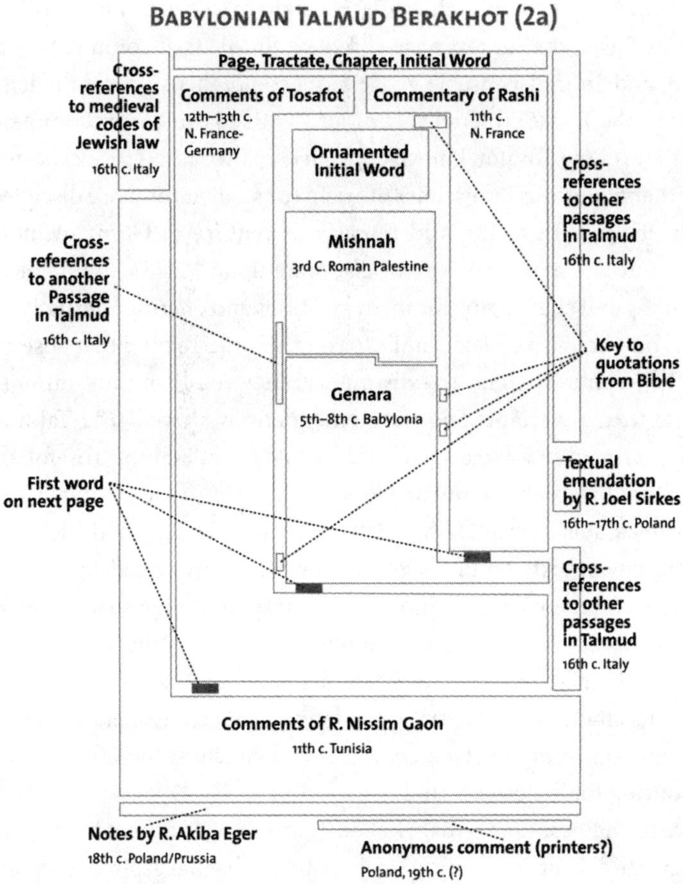

BABYLONIAN TALMUD BERAKHOT (2a)

Fig. 36   Outline of talmudic page.

the Vilna press of the Widow of Romm and His Brothers in 1880. Figure 36 is a diagram that outlines the page's contents. The block in the center of the page, beneath the ornamental initial word panel, contains the Talmud itself—first, the Mishnah, the third-century law code, and beneath it, the Gemara, edited in Babylonia between the late fifth and eighth centuries. The latter, the bulk of the Talmud, presents itself as something between a commentary on the Mishnah and a seemingly unedited transcript of a study session in a rabbinic academy in the course of which the sages debate and explicate the law, often digressing to discuss related (and not so related) topics. Surrounding the talmudic text are the commentaries—on the right-hand inner side of the page, the commentary of Rabbi Shlomo Yitzḥaki (1040–1105, northern France), known as Rashi, the earliest near-complete full-fledged commentary on the Talmud, and an indispensable guide to its comprehension; on the left-hand outer side, the Tosafot (literally, "additions"—that is, to Rashi's commentary). The authors of the Tosafot, known collectively as Tosafists (baʿalei ha-tosafot), were either grandsons or disciples of Rashi (or students of those disciples) and lived in the twelfth to the mid-fourteenth century in Germany, northern France, and England. The Tosafot elaborate upon Rashi's comments, often questioning and challenging his interpretations and offering alternative explanations, but they also collate parallel passages in the Talmud that pose explicit or implicit contradictions and distinguish between them; not infrequently, they cite textual variants and offer emendations as well. The Talmud text proper is printed in a large square font while Rashi and the Tosafot are in a smaller font based on a semicursive Sefardic script (that eventually came to be known as "Rashi script"); the differing scripts and sizes of the letters make the hierarchy of texts on the page—the primary core text as opposed to the secondary commentaries and novellae—transparent even to a reader who is unable to read Hebrew. And on the outer margins on the sides and on the bottom of the page lie still more commentators and notes as well as cross-referencing citations and textual emendations. Taken together, the contents of this page span some fourteen centuries and much of the inhabited Jewish world during this lengthy period.

Since its publication, the Babylonian Talmud's page format has become the paradigmatic layout for nearly every Jewish text that has aspired to the authority and status of the Talmud.[2] The precise contours of its pages derive from the earliest printed editions of the Talmud, specifically the *editio princeps* of the entire Talmud printed by the Christian publisher Daniel Bomberg in Venice in 1520–23. Bomberg did not invent the format. He borrowed it from earlier Jewish printers who, in turn, adapted it from late medieval models used by Jewish scribes. And even these Jewish scribes did not invent the page format, though, as I will argue, they radically transformed its function and meaning. How they did this and to what effect—that is, how the page format shaped the study of the Talmud (and, to a lesser extent, the Hebrew Bible)—are the linked subjects of this chapter.

The talmudic page's format derives from the page layout of the Glossa Ordinaria.[3] The Glossa Ordinaria is the name of a specific genre of the medieval Latin Bible that first emerged in the early twelfth century and continued to develop through the mid-thirteenth century, first in northern France and later throughout Europe; indeed, in the course of those centuries, the glossed Bible became the most common type of Christian Bible.[4] Its invention is conventionally attributed to Anselm of Laon (d. 1117), one of the great teachers of his time.[5] In fact, Anselm himself composed only the Glossa on Psalms and the Pauline Epistles (and possibly the Gospel of John), but his work was continued and completed by his brother, Ralph of Laon, his disciple Gilbert of Auxere, and several others. Anselm and Ralph both taught (and first used the Glossa) in the Cathedral School of Laon. After Anselm's death, the work was carried to the various schools of Paris, and from Paris, the work spread through France and eventually throughout Europe, reaching its heyday around 1250.

The Glossa Ordinaria presents the Vulgate text of the Christian Bible along with the "standard" (*ordinaria*) commentary (*glossa*), both laid out on the page in a specific format that I will describe shortly. Anselm and his successors created both the text of the Glossa and the work's page format, and it is the combination of the two that give the Glossa Ordinaria its singular identity. The contents of the Glossa are essentially an abridgment of interpretations drawn from the church fathers, particularly Jerome, Ambrose, and Augustine, as well as other early Christian commentators like Bede and Cassiodorus, and some later Carolingians, Hrabanus Maurus in particular (most of whose commentaries also abridged earlier patristic exegesis). As noted earlier, the Glossa on different books of the Old and New Testaments were compiled at separate times by different figures. Following the initial consolidation of the standard Glossa, the project was taken up by two twelfth-century Paris masters, Gilbert of Poitiers (d. 1154) and Peter Lombard (d. 1160), each of whom wrote expanded commentaries that were then incorporated into the Glossa Ordinaria; Peter's work is known as the *Magna glosatura*, Gilbert's as the *Media glosatura*. Scholars are still not entirely certain as to how completely the text of the Glossa was ever fully stabilized, but there is no question that it reached a sufficient degree of stability to give it a recognizable identity as its own literary document.

The page layout of the Glossa Ordinaria essentially consists of a page with three vertical columns of unequal width. The central column, usually the narrowest, contains the Vulgate, written in a larger script in lines spaced generously enough so that there is room between them for brief interlinear comments. On both sides of the Vulgate column are two additional columns, also of unequal width (though both are usually wider than the Vulgate column), each of which is dedicated to the Glossa itself; these lines are spaced roughly twice as closely together as those in the Vulgate column. Before the invention of the Glossa format, commentaries were written in their own separate volumes with scriptural lemmata—phrases or words—placed as headings to individual comments in order to key the reader to the biblical text being expounded. In addition, as might be expected, students and readers frequently wrote random notes in the margins of scriptural books (which is where one expects to find such notes). Before the Glossa Ordinaria, however, the Vulgate and the commentaries were never both integral parts of the writing grid of the same page, ruled and planned in tandem by the master scribe. Indeed, this was the great programmatic innovation of the Glossa—to place Scripture *and* commentary literally on the same page and thereby demand that the reader study both. Previously, Scripture did not need to be consulted in order to read a commentary that, whether the scriptural text was present or not, told the reader what Scripture *meant*, the most important thing the reader needed to know.

Christopher de Hamel and Lesley Smith have both tracked the development of this format, and they have identified two basic forms for the page that appear to have developed chronologically in stages.[6] Figure 37, a leaf from a glossed Psalter written sometime between 1150 and 1175, pictures an example of the earlier page format. This page essentially conforms to the format described in the preceding paragraph, with three columns of unequal width, and with interlinear comments between the generously spaced lines of the Vulgate. In the side columns containing the Glossa, each comment is its own separate unit. At least in these earlier volumes, there are no symbols or keys connecting the gloss to its prooftext, and the same glosses are sometimes copied in different manuscript in different orders; in some cases, the interlinear comments move into the margins, and vice versa.[7] It does not seem to have mattered whether the note was in the right or left column. Moreover, as is evident in the left-hand column, if there was no gloss on a passage, the space in the side column was left empty (a waste of parchment space, which was not ideal). Most copies of the Glossa before 1170 have this format.

After 1160, a more complex variation of the format developed. Figure 38 illustrates a page from a Gospel of John written in France, probably in Paris, around the year 1300. In this version, the columns no longer remain static shapes but become dynamic entities, with the middle text column invading one of the Glossa columns on either side of the page, or the reverse, with the Glossa columns protruding into the Vulgate text. The main rationale for this change was probably the scribe's desire to use up all the available parchment space.[8] Thus if he saw as he was writing that he did not have enough gloss to

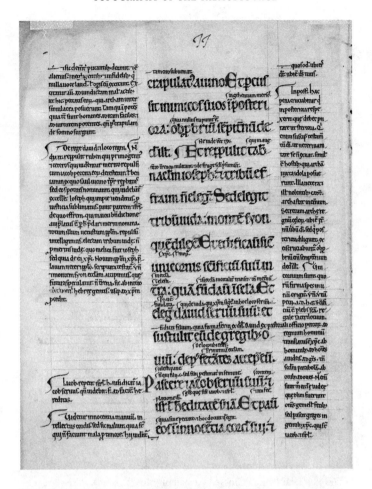

Fig. 37 Leaf from a Glossed Psalter (77.59–72), France, 1150–1175. Philadelphia, University of Pennsylvania, Rare Book and Manuscript Library MS Coll. 591, folder 31, fol. 1v. Courtesy of Kislak Center for Special Collections, Rare Books and Manuscripts, University of Pennsylvania.

fill the right or left column, he simply extended the middle column to either the right or left margins of the writing grid (or he did the same with the Glossa if he saw he had too much commentary to fit on the page) until the balance between core text (the Vulgate) and the secondary text (the Glossa) resumed, at which point he returned to the original design of parallel columns. This format was obviously much more challenging for a scribe to produce. In the first place, it necessitated a new schedule of production. In the earlier, simpler

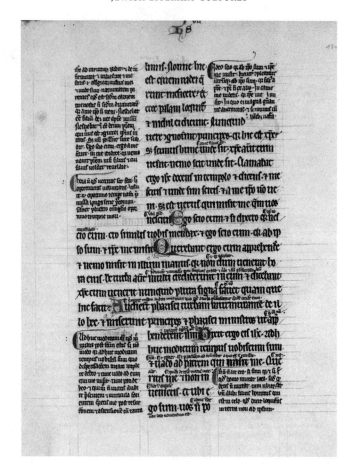

Fig. 38   Leaf from a Glossed Gospel of John (7.25–39), Paris?, ca. 1300. Philadelphia, University of Pennsylvania, Rare Book and Manuscript Library MS Coll. 591, folder 18, fol. 120r. Courtesy of Kislak Center for Special Collections, Rare Books and Manuscripts, University of Pennsylvania.

format, the scribe wrote the central column of Scripture throughout the manuscript continuously and then added the glosses in the side columns as he wished, ruling the different columns in separate stages. With the more dynamic layout, the scribe had to write all three columns simultaneously, and the Vulgate and Glossa columns had to be ruled together with their respective line heights geared to the changing size of the script: generally, the biblical text takes two lines for every line of gloss. To create a legible page, the scribe essentially had to prophesy the proportion of text to commentary before he could actually see them—an almost unimaginable feat. Given this challenge, one might imagine that once a scribe had worked out the complex ratios between Scripture and commentary for a page, other scribes would have copied at least its approximate shape in their own manuscripts. But, as Smith writes, this is not the case.[9] Each page of every manuscript appears to have been produced independently, an extraordinary achievement of scribal virtuousity.

Undoubtedly, there must have been an aesthetic as well as a pragmatic motive to the more complex format. There is no question that its pages are much more interesting visually than the simpler format's. In addition, the complex format also opened the path to still more variations on the basic Glossa format. For example, if there were not enough comments to justify its presence, the third column of gloss might be completely eliminated; alternatively, if there was too much commentary, the glossa columns might take over nearly the entire writing space of the page.[10] Indeed, this is what eventually happened in some manuscripts of Peter Lombard's *Magna glosatura*, like the one pictured in figure 39, from a thirteenth-century, probably English copy of his *Magna glosatura* on the Pauline Epistles (here, Rom 1:5–6). On the left-hand side of the page, a thin scriptural column remains as a token presence, but the commentary itself actually provides the full Vulgate text and essentially returns to the lemmatic format.[11] (The column on the right side of the page, in rubrics in the original, is neither Scripture nor gloss, but simply a list of citations and cross-references.) In the case of the Talmud, we will also see comparable variations on the standard Glossa form.

Anselm himself did not invent the simple version of the Glossa format. Psalters and some other biblical books with commentaries as well as classical texts like Boethius's *Consolation of Philosophy* were composed as early as the ninth century in monastic scriptoria at Fulda and Saint Gall using the basic principles of the Glossa format; even though these texts did not have a standard commentary, side columns with a commentary were an integral part of the page layout and its writing grid.[12] Indeed, it was probably from these books that Anselm, who was originally a teacher of the Arts, learned how to use the format, which he then adapted to Scripture. Not coincidentally, it was precisely at this time that the Latin Bible also began to replace antique manuals and classical authors as the basic educational texts for teaching the Arts.[13] By placing Scripture at the center of the page, flanked by commentary on its two sides, the Glossa format made Scripture the primary subject of education. The

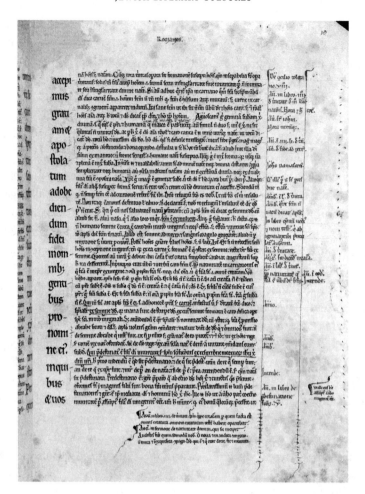

Fig. 39 Peter Lombard, *Magna Glosatura on the Roman Epistles*
(Romans 1:5–6), Exeter Castle, England, twelfth century. Oxford,
Bodleian Library MS Bodl. 725, fol. 10r. Courtesy of the Bodleian
Libraries, University of Oxford.

teacher could move from expounding the literal or historical sense of the text
to the spiritual meaning revealed by the church fathers. This use of a page
format for pedagogical purposes was also part of a more general shift from
teaching theological topics orally to using scholastic and academic texts as the
basis of lectures. Glossing was widely practiced by teachers and students alike
almost as "second nature," to use Beryl Smalley's phrase.[14]

The early format of the Glossa was designed specifically so that the master, while teaching the scriptural text, could easily locate the relevant commentary and expound it. The whole point was to have the commentary in proximity to the prooftext. In contrast, the complex page was much less suitable for live teaching in the classroom; the format is too complicated, the text too dense, and with its different elements "interwoven" on the page, it was a challenge for a teacher to locate the correct glossa to the scriptural text being taught. As Smith notes, this format is more suited "to private consultation," for use as a kind of reference book.[15] In fact, for a student using the Glossa as a book for consultation, the complex format is more useful inasmuch as it packs more material onto the page. Furthermore, the development of the complex page format was accompanied by the addition to the page of such reading aids as "tie marks" that connected comments to their scriptural prooftexts as well as chapter numbers and other helpful paratextual elements, all of which made the book easier to use. These features were all missing from manuscripts with the earlier, simpler format.[16] While the simple format did not cease to be produced after its more complex sibling emerged, it was in the format of the latter that, in the late twelfth and early thirteenth centuries, the Glossa spread throughout Europe, into monasteries, cathedral schools, and universities.

Manuscripts of the Glossa Ordinaria continued to be copied through the fourteenth and fifteenth centuries, with the first printed edition appearing in 1481 (Strassburg, Adolph Rusch). Much earlier, however, around the end of the thirteenth century, the life of the Glossa had essentially reached its term. For all its utility as a teaching or reference tool in presenting Scripture and commentary on the same page, this very fact—the requirement that the space of the page contain both elements—necessarily limited the amount of commentary that could fit on the page. As lengthier and more ambitious commentaries like those of Hugh of Saint Cher or Nicholas de Lyra were composed, new page formats were invented to contain them.[17]

It is only slightly ironic that just as Latin scribes were giving up on the Glossa as the cutting-edge page format for a Bible, Jews took up the layout as a way to copy their own texts, particularly the classical texts of Jewish literature. Colette Sirat and Joseph Shatzmiller have outlined the social and financial routes through which Jewish scribes became aware of the Glossa page format and adapted it to their own books, albeit around a hundred years after the format had passed from Christian scribal culture. As Sirat and Shatzmiller have shown, Jewish moneylenders took Latin manuscripts, among other objects both religious and secular, as security for loans; the terms of the transactions are often spelled out in Hebrew (and occasionally Latin) inscriptions inside the Latin manuscripts.[18] While most Jews did not read Latin, it was not difficult for them to see the architecture of the pages, the dense black letters, the complex Gothic decorations, and the interplay of text and image. If they were curious about any of these material features or their meaning, they doubtless were able to ask their Christian clients about them. There was in any case nothing to stop them from adopting these features to their own books with the eventual effect that, as Sirat has written, "the traditional Hebrew text acquired the mantle of the Latin book."[19] As we will see, however, that mantle was effectively transformed into a *tallit*.

The first Jewish books to adapt the page layout of the Glossa Ordinaria appear to have been Bibles. Figure 40 shows a page from a Pentateuch, a *ḥumash*, composed in France in the first half of the fourteenth century, sometime before 1348.[20] The basic three-column format has been retained, but with significant variations from the Glossa's layout. The middle column, with the biblical text in large vocalized square letters, is wider than either of the side columns, the opposite to what we saw in the Glossa Ordinaria. The inner, somewhat truncated column contains the Targum, the Aramaic translation of the Bible that was read along with the weekly scriptural reading, while the outer column, which extends across the top and bottom of the page because of its length, contains Rashi's commentary. The micrographic writing in the spaces between the biblical text and the Targum and Rashi columns reproduces, in the side margin, the Masorah parva and, in the three and four line blocks above and below the Bible, the Masorah magna; the masoretic annotations are holdovers from the earliest Near Eastern biblical codices of the tenth and eleventh centuries and became normative elements in Jewish Bibles throughout the Middle Ages.[21] Even though the format of this page basically follows the earlier of the two Glossa formats, the size of the script and the density of writing in the side columns, not to mention the tininess of the masoretic notes, make it very unlikely that this page was intended for a teacher to use in the classroom; most likely this was a reference book that was read privately. We know independently that early on Rashi's commentary served as a genuine commentary—that is, as a text individual students studied alongside the Bible both privately and in the synagogue during the liturgical reading of the Torah in order to learn Scripture's meaning.[22] This is one clear difference between the Jewish use of the early Glossa format from that of its Christian model.

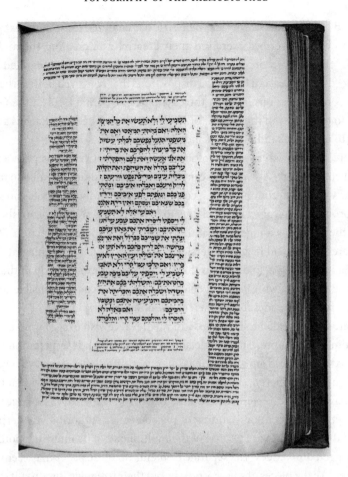

Fig. 40   Pentateuch with Targum and Rashi (Leviticus 26:14–23),
France, before 1348. Vienna, Österreichische Nationalbibliothek Cod.
Hebr. 28, fol. 182v. Courtesy of Österreichische Nationalbibliothek.

Compare, however, the orderliness of the page in figure 40 to the page in
plate 2, from a volume of Former Prophets (Judg 4:21–5:6) written in Segovia,
Spain, in 1476. The latter page maintains the rudiments of three columns but
in a kind of deconstructed, almost cubist rendering of the Glossa format. There
are five separate texts on the page—the biblical text (Judg 4:21– 5:6), the Aramaic Targum, and three commentaries, Rashi, David Kimchi (Radak), and
Levi ben Gershom, each of which the scribe has differentiated for the reader
by placing it in its own asymmetrical geometric shape, in a different script and

size, and in different ink. Malachi Beit-Arié has analyzed these multitext pages and shown how scribes exercised their creativity in creating them. As he writes, "the need to deploy a flexible layout in producing integrated texts produced decorated and figurative dispositions that conveyed both verbal and visual communications."[23] As in the case of the dynamic form of the Glossa page, no two pages in this codex (or in others like it) are alike. Each is a testimony to its scribe's individuality and virtuousity.

There is, however, a more profound difference between this page and its Glossa counterpart. As we have seen, the Glossa is a compendium of patristic and early medieval commentaries, compressed into individual notes on scriptural prooftexts. While it never claims to be a summa of earlier patristic exegesis, the Glossa is a digest, an authoritative and coherent selection. While there are shorter and lengthier versions of the text, each is an integral document in its own right, and even in the case of the dynamic version of the page layout, the format with its three columns remains a comprehensible format that the reader searches for a coherent meaning to Scripture.

There is no parallel to the Glossa in medieval Jewish exegesis, no attempt to summarize and present a single authoritative Jewish interpretation of the Bible. As the page from the Segovia manuscript testifies, Jewish exegetical tradition is not coherent. Each commentator maintains his individuality, his distinctiveness and separateness on the page. The reader of these pages does not emerge with an understanding of the correct or authoritative interpretation of the Bible but with a sense of the multiplicity of its interpretations and their jagged differences. The separate elements on these pages may seem to fit together like the pieces of a jigsaw puzzle, but their irregular, discordant shapes actually have the effect of forcing the reader to compare, contrast, and recognize the disparities between the various commentaries, each of which has its own unmistakable identity that will never be confused with another's. This is a page that invites not harmonization or systematization but the acknowledgment of irreconcilable differences. Those differences point to the richness of Scripture's meaning, its multiple meanings, not to a single correct or authoritative interpretation.

In the case of the Talmud, the adaption of the Glossa format took a different direction. Before describing that direction, however, it is important to acknowledge how few complete (or near-complete) manuscripts of individual tractates of the Talmud survive from the entire Middle Ages: sixty-three manuscripts in all.[24] Most of these manuscripts contain one or two tractates (of the thirty-seven tractates in the complete Babylonian Talmud); in general, only the tractates studied in the yeshivot (talmudic academies) were copied during the medieval period. With a single exception, every tractate in the Talmud is preserved in at least one manuscript, but there survives only a single codex—the famous Munich, Bayerische Staatsbibliothek (BSB) Cod. Hebr. 95 (often cited as Munich 95), written in France in 1342—that contains the entire Talmud in one volume.[25] (As we will see shortly, Munich 95 also displays a unique page format.) In any case, as a result of the sparsity of manuscript witnesses, all generalizations on their basis must be provisional.

Aside from Munich 95, medieval Talmud codices display three different page formats. The two most common of these are pictured in figures 41 and 42.[26] In figure 41, picturing a page from the Florence Talmud written in Germany or Italy sometime before 1250, the text is laid out in two columns, much like biblical codices of the same period. In figure 42, the thirteenth-century Hamburg codex, the text is written out across the width of the entire page. In both types, the Mishnah for each chapter in the tractate is usually copied in full at the beginning of the chapter, although there are a smaller number of Talmud manuscripts in which the Mishnah is broken up into separate paragraphs that are interspersed in the Gemara (as they are in printed editions). In either case, both the Mishnah and the Gemara are typically written in so-called square letters, the same formal script used in a Torah scroll. Neither format contains any commentaries on its pages. (The notes in the margins in both images are those of private readers.)

The third and least common format for medieval Talmud manuscripts derives from the Glossa Ordinaria and records commentaries along with the Talmud text. Three manuscripts, to which we will turn shortly, have both Rashi and Tosafot.[27] In addition, four manuscripts survive that have Rashi alone and use the "late" Glossa format developed for lengthy commentaries (like that of Peter Lombard's *Glosa magnatura*, in which the commentary overwhelms and subsumes, as it were, the core text); all four of the latter manuscripts were written in Ashkenaz in the fourteenth century.[28] Finally, Munich 95, the unique codex containing the entirety of the Talmud in a single volume, also uses the "late" Glossa format even though it has *no* commentaries on the page. Figure 43 pictures the beginning of the tractate *Berakhot*.[29] The Mishnah is written in large square letters inside the block inset on the left-hand side of the page, while the rest of the page, written in the much tinier hand, is the Gemara. As noted earlier, the Gemara presents itself in the Talmud *as though* it were a kind

Fig. 41 Babylonian Talmud, Tractate *Sanhedrin* 45b–47a, Italy-Ashkenaz, before 1250. Florence, Biblioteca Nazionale Centrale MS II 1 9, pp. 174–75. Courtesy of Biblioteca Nazionale Centrale di Firenze.

Fig. 42 Babylonian Talmud, Tractate *Baba Kamma* 63b–64b, Spain(?), thirteenth century(?). Hamburg, Staats- und Universitätsbibliothek Hamburg Cod. Hebr. 19, fols. 38v–39r. Courtesy of Staats- und Universitätsbibliothek Hamburg.

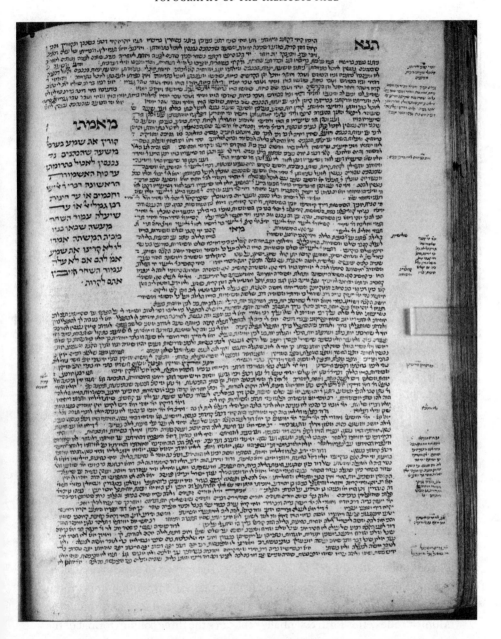

Fig. 43 Babylonian Talmud, Tractate *Berakhot* 2a, France, 1342. Munich, Bayerische Staatsbibliothek, Cod. Hebr. 95, fol. 139v. Courtesy of Bayerische Staatsbibliothek / Bildarchiv.

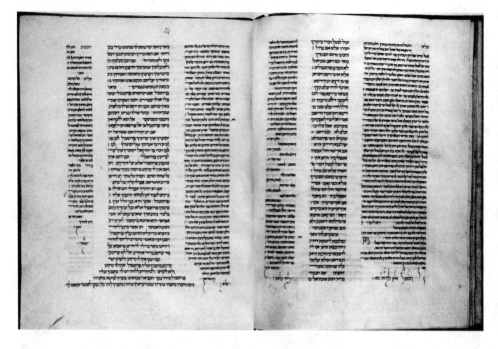

Fig. 44 Babylonian Talmud with Rashi and Tosafot, Tractate *Gittin* 36b–37a, northern France, second half of the fourteenth century. Arras, Bibliothèque municipale MS 889 (969), fols. 23v–24r. Photo: Médiathèque.

of commentary on the Mishnah, and here the scribe has indeed copied the Gemara exactly as he would have copied a commentary—in a smaller semi-cursive script around its core text, the Mishnah!

The three remaining Talmud manuscripts with both Rashi and the Tosafot, taken together, effectively chart the transformation of the Glossa format by Jewish scribes from the simple three-column page to a complex format that directly anticipates the printed Talmud page. The earliest of these manuscripts, pictured in figure 44, is an opening from a manuscript written in northern France in the latter half of the fourteenth century, around the same time as the Munich codex. This form essentially replicates the three column format of the early Glossa page, with the Talmud text in the middle column while the two side columns on both pages contain, respectively, Rashi in the innermost column, and the Tosafot on the outer side.[30]

In contrast, figure 45, from a Talmud written in northern Italy in the first third of the fifteenth century, represents a more complex form of the page

Fig. 45   Babylonian Talmud with Rashi and Tosafot, Tractate *Yeba-mot* 101a–12b, northern Italy, after 1429. Oxford, Bodleian Library MS Opp. 248 (MS Neubauer 367), fol. 204v. Courtesy of the Bodleian Libraries, University of Oxford.

layout, very possibly influenced by the more dynamic version of the Glossa format. The wide inner column is the Gemara, the thin column to its left is the Mishnah, Rashi is in the left outer column (near the gutter), and the Tosafot are opposite them on the right side.[31] Finally, figure 46, a page from a Talmud written in Spain in 1440, pictures a page format almost identical to the one familiar to us as the printed "talmudic page," with its columns virtually wrapping around and embracing each other.[32] (Unlike the glossed Bible page, which stresses the irreconcilable differences between its elements, the Talmud page invites the reader to reconcile and harmonize its contents.) There is something

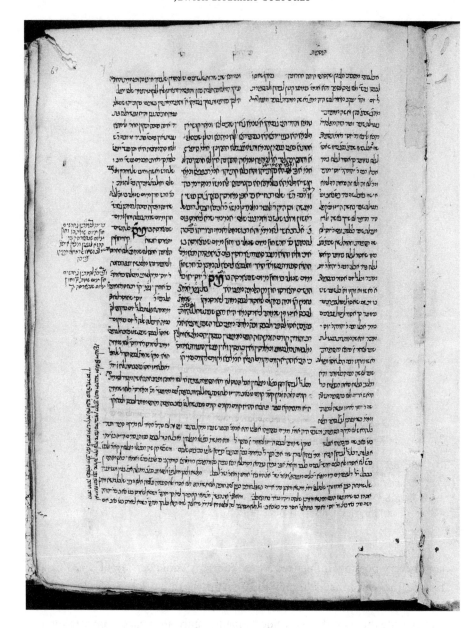

Fig. 46 Babylonian Talmud with Rashi and Tosafot Ro"sh, Tractate *Yebamot* 20b–21a, Spain, 1440. Moscow, Lenin Library Cod. 594, fol. 69a.

else noteworthy about this page. As I mentioned earlier, the glossed page format was especially challenging for a scribe inasmuch as he virtually had to prophesy the exact proportion of text and commentary in order to get it all on the same page and without wasting precious parchment space. This page graphically illustrates what happened when a scribe miscalculated. In this case, he had too much commentary, and the poor guy had to write the last lines of the Tosafot along the outside margin, climbing up the side of the page like a gecko on a windowsill.

As we have seen, the glossed format is the rarest of the three page layouts; the three surviving manuscripts with both Rashi and Tosafot on the page represent four percent of the surviving Talmud manuscripts from Europe.[33] (If one includes the manuscripts with only Rashi using the "late" Glossa format, the percentage rises to about fourteen percent.) And yet, despite its rarity *and* the challenges of producing a glossed page, that format was the one adopted by the earliest printers of the Talmud in Italy—specifically, the Soncino family, first Joshua Solomon Soncino (active 1483–92) and then his nephew, Gershon ben Moses Soncino (active 1488–1534).[34] The Soncinos may have had three reasons for adopting this format. First, a Talmud with Rashi and the Tosafot on the same page was clearly a more marketable book than one with only the Talmud (which would require a student who wished to study a commentary to acquire an additional volume). Second, and perhaps even more important, it was far easier to produce this format in print than in manuscript because, before beginning the printing process, the editor (*ha-magihah*) prepared a model book (*sefer ha-ʿatakah*), a manuscript copy of the book with its layout exactly as it was to be printed, page after page, so that the typesetters could directly copy it. If the editor realized, in producing the model book, that he had to alter the layout of the lines to improve the ratio of core text and commentary and accommodate more or less text, he could easily make the alteration in the model book before the labor of typesetting had begun, and he could then print an edition of two hundred to three hundred copies.[35] Print, in other words, was a much more efficient technology for producing the glossed page.

The third reason that may have motivated Joshua Solomon Soncino's original decision to use the Glossa format may have been a matter of familial familiarity. As we have seen, the earliest manuscripts with the format come from either northern France or elsewhere in Ashkenaz, in the very areas in which the Tosafists themselves lived, albeit only near the end of the Tosafist period. As we know, the Soncinos themselves were originally from the

Rhineland and traced their ancestry back to a thirteenth-century Tosafist named Moses of Speyer.[36] (The family moved to Italy in the beginning of the fourteenth century and eventually settled in the small town of Soncino in Lombardy, from which they took their last name.) Most likely the Soncino family members were educated in Tosafist-affiliated rabbinic academies. While there is no evidence that they themselves studied Talmud from glossed manuscripts, it is not impossible that they did so; in any event, because of their family history, they would certainly have been inclined to use the glossed format if only because it placed their ancestors on the same page with the Talmud and Rashi.

In the course of three generations of publishing Hebrew books, the Soncinos printed twenty-three editions of various tractates of the Talmud.[37] Gershon Soncino *wished* to print an edition of the entire Talmud, but he could not receive a privilege and rights from the city of Venice. The *editio princeps* of the complete Babylonian Talmud had to wait until a Christian printer from Antwerp, Daniel Bomberg (ca. 1483–1549), arrived in Venice in 1515 and received the municipal privilege from the city of Venice and approval from the pope to print with Hebrew type, thereby gaining a monopoly over Hebrew printing in Venice. In the succeeding decades, Bomberg printed definitive editions (for centuries) of many classical Jewish texts including, in the years between 1519/20 and 1523, an edition of the entire Talmud. Figure 47 is the first page of the tractate *Berakhot*.

In printing his Talmud, Bomberg borrowed liberally from the Soncino editions—so liberally, in fact, that Gershon Soncino complained loudly about it[38]—and followed the page format they had established. He also relied heavily on the Soncino editions in selecting the specific collections of Tosafot to publish.[39] Most important, for the first time in the history of the Talmud, Bomberg foliated his editions, thereby creating the possibility of cross-referencing sections and pages in separate tractates or in different books far more easily and conveniently than previously had been possible.[40] The foliation was a boon especially for Christian Hebraists (like Bomberg himself) who wished to study the Talmud. Jews had studied the Talmud for centuries without page numbers; they referred to sections by tractate and chapter or by their location in specific chapters.[41] For Gentiles lacking familiarity with the vast talmudic corpus, however, such a referencing practice was of little use. Foliation helped make the Talmud as accessible for them as other books. In figure 47, the foliation (with the letter *bet*, two) is on the upper left corner. (Only the rectos of the folios were marked.)

Fig. 47 Babylonian Talmud with Rashi and Tosafot, Tractate *Berakhot* 2a (Venice: Daniel Bomberg, 1520). Courtesy of the Library at the Herbert D. Katz Center for Advanced Judaic Studies, Kislak Center for Special Collections, Rare Books and Manuscripts, University of Pennsylvania.

During the incunable period, Jewish printers in Iberia, in both Spain and in Portugal, published several editions of talmudic tractates, some with no commentary on the page, others with Rashi alone (using, again, the "late" Glossa format).[42] These editions (and their presumed successors) would have competed with the Italian editions had Iberian Hebrew printing not come to an abrupt end with the Spanish expulsion in 1492 and the forced conversion and compulsory exodus of Jews from Portugal in 1496. This happenstance coincidence—that the end of Iberian Jewry happened in the early fifteenth century at the same time as the formative period of printing—had a decisive impact on the history of the Talmud. While Sefardic printing resumed on a limited scale in Ottoman Turkey, Greece, and Morocco in the early fifteenth century, the hiatus in time allowed Italian printers of Hebrew books to take over the world market of Hebrew printing for nearly two decades. In the case of the Talmud, the hiatus was especially crucial because it enabled Bomberg's edition to become for all time the universal printed edition of the Talmud. Aside from the fact that, after the demise of Iberian Hebrew printing, Bomberg's Talmud edition did not have any serious competitors, no printer after Bomberg wished to invest the substantial sum of money the Christian publisher had spent in preparing model books for the entire Talmud.[43] As a result, virtually every Talmud since Bomberg's has followed his page layout, beginning and ending each page with the same word, with Rashi and the Tosafot occupying the almost identical spaces on the page. Figure 35, the page from the Widow Romm's 1880 edition, is the direct descendant of Bomberg's 1519/20–23 edition in figure 13.[44] Unlike Hebrew study Bibles using the Glossa format, each of which is basically different in its details, even in printed editions, there is only a single format for the Babylonian Talmud.

Indeed, Bomberg's page not only effectively set the talmudic text in stone; it also became an object of interpretation and study in its own right, with homiletical interpretations invented to explain every material detail on the page. For example, it was said that the reason that Rashi and Tosafot occupy the first four lines at the top of every page is to teach the Talmud's students that they have not even begun to understand the text until they have reviewed it at least four times! Or another: the reason every Talmud begins with folio 2a (recto) is because the Talmud has no beginning or end. (The more prosaic reason is that in early printed books, the title page is fol. 1a.) Many other such homilies exist.[45]

Recent scholarship on book history has demonstrated that the material shape of a book—its page layout, among other features—informs and shapes the reading and reception of the text on its pages.[46] What impact did the glossed talmudic page have on its study? Did the page format change the history of the Talmud?

Because of the paucity of manuscripts with the glossed format and the absence of any documentation of reading practices associated with it, we will limit our investigation to the printed Talmud, particularly after the Bomberg edition. The most obvious effect of the page format was that, by placing the Tosafot opposite Rashi, the glossed page decisively altered the status of the Tosafists and elevated their novellae—or that selection of the Tosafot that ended up in print—to a "canonical" position within Talmud study. (It also doomed the Tosafot that were not printed to oblivion, at least until they were rediscovered in manuscript in the twentieth century.) The canonical status now attained by the Tosafot also made the Talmud an Ashkenazic document. To be sure, the commentary of Rashi—the foremost Ashkenazic sage of the Middle Ages—had been an indispensable part of Talmud study in Sefarad long before print. More than a hundred years earlier, the Sefardic sage Menahem ben Aaron Ibn Zeraḥ (died 1385) acknowledged that "if not for [Rashi], the path of the Talmud would have been forgotten among the people of Israel," obviously including himself and every other Sefardic Talmudist among the latter.[47] Before print, however, study of the Tosafot was almost entirely limited to Ashkenazic rabbinic culture, and even there, the specific collections of Tosafot studied varied in different yeshivot. In contrast, in Sefarad, Talmud was typically studied with (in addition to Rashi) the novellae of Nahmanides (1194–1270). Once the Bomberg edition became the definitive and universal Talmud, however, the Tosafists of northern France and Germany attained a position almost equal to Rashi's wherever Talmud was studied.

To appreciate fully the difference made by the presence of the Tosafot on the page, another comparison with the Glossa Ordinaria may be helpful. As noted earlier, the right and left columns on either side of the Vulgate text, along with the interlinear glosses between its lines, are all part of a single composition, the Glossa Ordinaria. Where a comment ended up being placed—in the right or in the left column—was mainly determined by its proximity to its scriptural prooftext. In contrast, the columns on the two sides of the talmudic text contain two separate, distinct compositions, the commentary of Rashi and the novellae of the Tosafists, and the two are frequently at variance, in conflict. One might even say that the two columns, if not actually disputing each other, are engaged in constant, contentious debate.

The talmudic page, in short, turned the Glossa format into a site of dialog-ical combat. The writing grid was no longer merely a literary space for inscrib-ing Scripture next to its interpretation. It became a scene for conflict and resolution. This new function of the page format elicited a completely different strategy of reading the texts on the page. The student of the Talmud begins by studying the core text in the page's center; s/he then moves to the right column and to Rashi's explicatory commentary to understand the Talmud's argument, and s/he then skips over the core text to the column on its other side, to the Tosafot, which (as noted) often contest Rashi's interpretations by raising ques-tions or offering alternative explanations. The student then attempts to resolve the disagreements between Rashi and the Tosafot (or at least understand the basis of their disagreement) and finally returns to the core text with the new understanding that s/he has acquired in the course of their journey across the columns of the page. In provoking this dialogical reading experience, the talmudic page format goes from being, in the words of Johanna Drucker, a "representation of knowledge" to becoming a "generator of knowledge."[48]

To be sure, this dialectical strategy, with its focus upon identifying and resolving contradictions and inconsistencies in the text, was not new to the history of the Talmud. The very text of the Gemara—the literary record of the talmudic sages' discussions and their analyses of the Mishnah—largely consists of the collation and juxtaposition of parallel or associated early, orally trans-mitted rabbinic traditions (baraitot in particular) that either contradict each other or offer variant legal decisions to the Mishnah's. The sugya, the primary literary unit of talmudic discourse, incorporates various rhetorical and logical strategies for reconciling and harmonizing these inconsistent or contradictory legal traditions.[49] Behind these strategies lie the same textual assumptions about the Oral Torah that the rabbis brought to their study of the Written Torah (as they called the Hebrew Bible)—namely, its omnisignificance (the meaningfulness of every detail) and perfectness (the impossibility of contra-dictions or inconsistencies).[50] By applying these axioms to the Mishnah and the baraitot, the rabbis sought to prove that the Oral Torah was Torah just like the Written Torah. The strategies for harmonizing discrepancies and demon-strating omnisignificance are, in turn, constructed in the sugya typically in the form of dialogue, with the voice of either the anonymous editor (the so-called Stam) or a named sage posing a question or presenting a conflicting tradition, and another voice responding to it. Not coincidentally, the development of the sugya as this type of literary-rhetorical unit probably began to take shape while the Talmud was itself still in the oral stage of its transmission (as early as the sixth or seventh century) and continued even after the text was committed to writing. It was obviously an attempt to reproduce in writing the atmosphere of an oral environment.

Beginning in the twelfth century, the Tosafists extended this project of collation and harmonization to the inscribed, *written* corpus of the Talmud in its entirety, collating disparate, sometimes seemingly unrelated passages throughout the full breadth of the Talmud that they saw as being either inconsistent or implicitly contradictory and then resolving those inconsistencies and contradictions by systematically distinguishing between them (by showing, for example, that the apparently contradictory rulings actually referred to very different cases or circumstances).[51] The Tosafists also extended their dialectical scholasticism to the adjudication of law (and especially with resolving contradictions between the Talmud and local practice or *minhag*).[52] In pursuing both projects of collation and harmonization, the Tosafists, as I have noted, also frequently proposed alternative or different interpretations of passages than those of Rashi and not infrequently disagreed with him and with each other. In either case, by applying similar axioms of omnisignificance and perfectness to the entirety of the Babylonian Talmud, they were able to prove the meaningfulness, coherence, and unity of the written text as a whole (thereby continuing, in effect, the project begun by the Talmud's earliest editors/compilers, the Stam, in the Talmud's oral stage of transmission).

Some two centuries later, in the second half of the fourteenth century, still another, even more intense mode of dialectical Talmud study began to develop in Ashkenazic yeshivot.[53] This new mode of study eventually came to be known as *pilpul*, a term originally used in the Talmud itself to designate "casuistic analysis."[54] Now, however, the term came to possess a more technical meaning for a specific method of Talmud study.[55] In contrast to the Tosafist project to harmonize conflicting or contradictory passages spread throughout the talmudic corpus—a project the Tosafists had more or less completed—pilpul took dialectical analysis in a new direction and emphasized the individual *sugya*, the talmudic passage recorded on a specific page (or pages) virtually in isolation, and sought to analyze it in its own terms. Pilpulistic analysis involved a number of different techniques.[56] These included dissolving the *sugya* into its various components and subarguments, then explaining each section alone as an independent unit, as well as assuming a kind of absolute omnisignificance to every detail in the *sugya* (including even the sequence and order of its various arguments, challenges, and resolutions). The latter assumption proceeded upon the further assumption that every argument and explanation entailed the exclusion of every other conceivable argument and explanation. For our present purposes, this last technique is the most relevant because, as we will see, it was eventually applied not only to views expressed within the *sugya* but also to those offered by talmudic commentators like Rashi and the Tosafot.[57] The student was required to explain not only why the commentator explained the passage as he did but also why he did not accept any other possible explanation (all of which he was assumed to have known). In effect, then, the Tosafist project to identify and harmonize all contradictions and inconsistencies in the talmudic corpus as a whole was now extended in pilpul to include even the differences and conflicts in explanation between Rashi and the Tosafists in regard to specific *sugyot*.

As Elhanan Reiner has shown, in its earliest formative stages, pilpul was intended to be solely an exercise in sharpening and refining the analytical abilities of students.[58] It was limited to a specified period of time in the yeshiva curriculum (a period that was called, revealingly, *zman tosfos*, "the Tosafot period," which could be either an allotted time in the day or in the week, or a specified semester-like block of time). It was deliberately not intended to encroach upon the main focus of yeshiva study, which was expertise (*beki'ut*) in study of the Talmud according to its plain sense (i.e., Rashi) and of the legal codes and other relevant texts as a source of halakhah, practical rabbinic law, and its adjudication. Only over time, as pilpul became increasingly popular among students and teachers in the yeshivot because of its intellectual challenges, did it begin to challenge the traditional curriculum and threaten to subvert the adjudicatory focus of yeshiva study (as well as the traditional hierarchy of communal leadership in Eastern European Jewry). At this point, in the seventeenth century, pilpul became a source of major controversy, the famous *Vikuah Ha-Pilpul* (the Pilpul Controversy). That later development is not relevant to the present study. Our single concern is with the question: Did the glossed talmudic page play any role in the rise of pilpul and its subsequent history?

The first thing to state is that the glossed page did not create this new form of study. Pilpul emerged in the fourteenth century (if not somewhat earlier). The earliest forms of the glossed Talmud page may have emerged in the fourteenth century in circles associated with the Tosafists (and near the close of the Tosafist period), but even so, the small number of surviving manuscripts with the format suggests that the format did not play a significant role in Talmud study *before* print.

Our earliest description of pilpul study *after* print is found in a work entitled *Seder Eliyahu Zuta*, a history of the Jews in the Ottoman empire written by the Cretan rabbi Eliyahu Capsali (1420–1495) and first published in 1523.[59] Capsali himself had studied in the yeshiva of R. Judah Mintz in Padua, one of the first yeshivot in which pilpul played a major part, and while the printed Hebrew book had just begun to appear during the last decade of his life—Joshua Solomon Soncino published his edition of *Berakhot* in 1483/84—his description of Mintz's yeshiva suggests the impact that the material book, if not the glossed page, had on Talmud study.

> And those students who lived with the Rav were also taught by him. And this is the order of their studies. . . . [He then describes the daily order in which the Rav taught individuals and different groups of students depending on how advanced they were.] On the next day, after prayers, the Rav went with those students who lived with him, as we have written, to a small house that was in the courtyard of the Great Synagogue of Padua, and it was called a *yeshivah*, and around the house there were wooden seats, and there they sat for the judgment of the Talmud (*mishpat ha-talmud*). And the other rabbis and teachers with their students also gathered there, and the Rav began to ask questions, and each one answered according to his ability. And after this, each one of them asked and answered and brought obscure matters to light, and this is called the *pilpul ha-yeshivah*. And each one of the participants would be *mefalpeil* [do *pilpul*] with his partner, the elder according to his seniority, the younger according to his youth. This *pilpul* was done "outside," by which I mean without opening a book, because the law was fluent in the mouths of all, and they had no [other book] than the Gemara of the Rav who showed them the *halakhah* (section of Talmud) for the day. And they gave voice with the noise of mighty waters. . . .
>
> And they used to sit there in the yeshivah for more or less an hour, as much as the *pilpul* and the *halakhah* required, and at the end, the Rav of the yeshivah, R. Judah Mintz (1408–1508), our great teacher, would open his book and show them until where they should study the law [for the next day], and they should neither add to or diminish from what he showed them.[60]

Capsali does not say what the page in these Talmuds looked like. (Obliviousness to the material shape of the book is typical of most Jewish writing until recently.) Because of the early date of the passage, it is unlikely that the Talmud described in it was glossed; it is not even clear if the book was a manuscript or printed. Even so, the physical book is a palpable presence in the passage. It is present even when it is physically absent. On the one hand, Capsali emphasizes that the activity of pilpul is conducted *without* a book—that is, "outside." But Capsali also tells us that the text to be studied through pilpul is rigorously demarcated by the page Mintz shows the students before he dismisses them and that the assignment, the *halakhah*, is not to be added to or diminished from. The student prepared for the pilpul session by studying the allotted Talmud section from a codex and, in effect, memorizing it, and he then conducted the pilpul on the passage from memory. And most strikingly, the pilpul itself is done in pairs, *be-ḥevruta*, out loud, "with the noise of mighty waters," as Capsali writes. The practice of studying in pairs as a normative way to study Talmud also developed in this period; indeed, this text is one of our earliest witnesses to it. Another author of the period describes the study practice as follows: "One [student] engages another. This one speaks, the other responds. This one leads, the other repeats. This one tears down, the other builds up. The sound of battle is in the camp."[61] The last line in the passage is a playful citation of Exod 32:17, Joshua's portentous remark to Moses as he began to descend from Mount Sinai with the Decalogue in his hands and heard the roar of the Israelites as they worshipped the Golden Calf. In our context, the citation captures the combative nature of pilpul study and *its* "roar." The dialogical element implicit within the *sugya*'s text, presented in the form of a dialogue between sages disputing and debating each other, is now dramatized—performed aloud—in the act of study by the two study partners, as they recite the talmudic passage to one another, from memory, without the book. The memorized text of the Talmud has become a kind of script as the process of study moves from the written page to oral enactment.

Approximately one hundred fifty years later, a second description of pilpul was recorded by Natan ben Moses Hannover (d. 1663) at the conclusion of *Yeven Metzulah*, an account of the massacres of Polish and Lithuanian Jewry during the Chmelnitzki Uprising in 1648.[62] In the final chapter, Hannover describes Polish Jewry at the outbreak of the uprising and paints a vivid picture of a session in a Polish yeshiva devoted to pilpul. While Hannover's description of the pilpul session superficially resembles Capsali's, Elhanan Reiner has pointed out important differences between the two accounts.[63] As Capsali described it, the pilpul session in Judah Mintz's yeshiva was a pedagogical exercise of intentionally limited scope, designed to train the students and to sharpen their abilities in dialectical analysis of the *sugya*. The head of the yeshiva oversaw the students as they practiced pilpul, participating in the questioning and debate, but there was no formal lecture at its conclusion. The provisional character of the pilpul time, the *zman tosfos*, is reemphasized at the passage's conclusion when he tells us that after "more or less an hour," the students returned to their main subject, the study of Talmud and other legal works as a source of law and its adjudication.

In contrast, in Hannover's account, pilpul has become the dominant subject of the yeshiva's curriculum during the main semesters (*zemanim*). It has effectively replaced the study of halakhah and adjudication. The pilpul session lasts well into the afternoon. At its conclusion, the head of the yeshiva delivers a formal pilpul lecture, the *ḥiluk*, which produces an integrated and legitimate interpretive analysis of the talmudic passage under review.[64] Furthermore, Hannover tells us, at the conclusion of the semesters, the Rosh Yeshivah, the head of the yeshiva, "honors" the students by inviting them to deliver their own *ḥilukim* before the yeshivah, and then he, too, did pilpul with them. The fact that the Rosh Yeshiva extends this invitation to the students to present their own *ḥilukim*—a privilege that previously belonged exclusively to the Rosh Yeshivah—did not only signal a certain democratizing of the academy; as Reiner notes, it also indicated the collapse of the traditional hierarchical order that had governed the traditional structures of Eastern European Judaism.[65]

For our concerns, however, Hannover's account is important for another reason. Like Capsali, he makes no mention of the material form of the Talmud being studied, but he also makes no mention of the pilpul session being conducted "outside," that is, without a book.[66] Instead, he describes the head of the Yeshiva's main lecture, the *ḥiluk*, as a series of questions about "the Gemara or Rashi or the Tosafot where their words contradict each other, or he asks about superfluous arguments or internal inconsistencies[67] between the Gemarah, Rashi, and the Tosafot. He then resolves the problems, but the resolutions themselves contradict each other. He answers one question with a second answer, and so on, until the *halakhah* (the talmudic passage) is fully clarified."[68] As Reiner emphasizes, the *ḥiluk* is an actual composition with a beginning, middle, and end.[69] Pilpul is no longer merely an exercise in dialectical analysis. It has become a mode of composition of a literature of its own, a harmonization not only of the contradictions in the text but those on the *page* itself—that is, the Gemara, Rashi, and Tosafot.

By the mid-seventeenth century, there is no question that the copies of the Talmud used in the Polish yeshivot were printed editions, either those printed by Bomberg himself or by one of his successors, with the glossed form—that is, with Rashi and Tosafot on the page. The glossed talmudic page did not create pilpul, but it also appears to have guided its development, transforming it from an exercise in analytic skills to a work of harmonizing the various texts printed on the page in adjacent columns. The page now has become the true focus of study, not just the talmudic text. This subtle but significant shift could not have taken place without the impact of the printed glossed Talmud page.

The Talmud began in Late Antiquity as a corpus of orally transmitted traditions that was by definition fragmentary, inconsistent, and unsystematic. After those oral traditions were gradually committed to writing in a composition that mimicked an oral environment and yet sought to overcome the tradition's fragmentation by shaping it into coherent literary forms, the Talmud also began to be taught and studied orally and by memory from a written text, first in manuscript, later in print. And as that text became increasingly inscribed, and fixed, culminating in its printed edition, its study became increasingly more oral, more vociferous. This process became fully manifested once the glossed format emerged as the definitive talmudic page. The page itself took on the Talmud's dialogical character, with its readers, its students, voicing the words of the sages as they argue and dispute and resolve their disagreements with each other in the columns across the page. The reader cannot *hear* the noise of debating sages on the talmudic page, but s/he can see it.

6

"JEWISH" ART AND THE MAKING
OF THE MEDIEVAL PRAYERBOOK

The past several decades have witnessed a dramatic resurgence of interest in Jewish art, and with it, a revival of the old questions: What is Jewish about Jewish art? Is it a matter of a consciously chosen subject, or of the identity of the artist, or of the connection of the work of art to the Jewish experience?[1] Even if these questions remain open, there exists today a greater appreciation of the fact that Jewish art is not, and never was, an impossibility. The view that the second commandment prohibits all figurative representation—thereby making it forbidden for good Jews to engage in any sort of image-making—is now understood to be a misconception; the commandment explicitly prohibits only the worship of images, and at the very most, the making of engraved or three-dimensional representations.[2] Furthermore, even this prohibition and others like it that discouraged (if not proscribed) the making of art by Jews were never universally obeyed or followed. When rabbinic authorities over the centuries sought to prohibit the making of images, neither Jewish artists nor Jewish patrons always listened to them.[3]

There is, however, another more revealing feature of Jewish art that has rarely been noted. Not only was representational Jewish art *not* prohibited out of a fear that images would be worshipped, but, to the contrary, most Jewish art in the ancient and medieval periods happens to be found precisely *within* contexts of worship—that is, in synagogues (such as on the mosaic floors found in many ancient Palestinian synagogues) or in prayerbooks or paraliturgical texts like the haggadah.[4] Consider figure 48, a page from a thirteenth-century South German prayerbook known as the Worms Maḥzor. This page contains the beginning of a liturgical poem *Iti mi-Levanon* whose first words

בלבנון כלה מראש אמנה תשגורי בטוהר שדרי לובש ההב
התכהבי ויהתפארי בישב ריקוח התכשימי מור ולבנה התנקטרי
כי בא עתי והגיעה שעה אשר למלך השורדי
שדי לין אשכל הכופר צבצפת ואמת כלה כאמורי
שפר כעז ממון זבוליו רוחשיב בלי חפר וק כר דרשתו
נעריז תכפר במעלה התקדש ובבטחה יכתלכל תמיד
ליל וצפר קדוש

גזנעיל קראני דודי חמיק עבר ושוכיריכ נשאוי את רידיד
הלפה ישע תרסה כזכר שתני וכירודי דירהוי אהבת חשק התאות
חז כלא לב ולב ובנפש הפיצה דהן מתנרב
וכלה רו עד זה מה זה מתאחר רין העליזה

Fig. 48 Illustration to the piyyut *Iti mi-Levanon*, Worms Maḥzor, Würzburg, 1272. Jerusalem, National Library of Israel MS Heb 4°781/1, fol. 34v. Courtesy of the National Library of Israel.

are *"Iti mi-Levanon kalah"*: "Look out with me from Lebanon,[5] O bride[6] / from the summit of our union.[7] . . . Perfume yourself in redolent scent, make yourself fragrant with the incense of myrrh and levanah, / For the time is coming, the hour is near, when you will behold the king."[8]

The poem was composed by the eleventh-century poet Benjamin ben Zeraḥ to be recited on Shabbat Ha-Gadol, "The Great Sabbath" that immediately precedes Passover, the holiday in the Jewish liturgical calendar during which it is customary to read the Song of Songs in the synagogue. Not surprisingly, the poem draws on the traditional interpretation of the Song of Songs as an allegory of God's love for Israel, and the few lines quoted above draw repeatedly upon that exegetical tradition, as my notes to the translation indicate. The "bride" is Israel (or the congregation addressed by the poet/prayer leader); the "king" is God, and He is drawing near to His beloved in order to consummate their union, the covenant on Sinai. The lines quoted above are not exceptional. The poem's language and imagery repeatedly alludes to the Song of Songs— indeed, it is suffused with the biblical text.

The illustration at the top of the page is also related to the piyyut and to the Song of Songs. The initial word, *iti*, is flanked on the left by a couple about to be married under the *tallit*, or prayer shawl, which here serves as the *ḥuppah*, the traditional bridal canopy. The groom, in the view of most scholars, is the blond-tressed figure on the right, an identification made mainly on the basis of the fact that he is wearing the *pileus cornutus*, the pointed Jew's hat that by the thirteenth century was a conventional attribute of representations of Jews in medieval Christian art, while the bride, the figure next to him, is very modestly covered from head to toe in a brown mantle.[9] On the far right stands the officiant—possibly but not necessarily a rabbi—who is about to perform the marriage by bringing the couple the traditional cup of wine for the wedding blessing. As the reader will note, this figure, in addition to wearing the pointed Jews' hat, also has a bird's head, a piece of grotesquerie characteristic of thirteenth-century Ashkenazic illuminated manuscripts whose rationale or meaning still has not been settled definitively.[10]

As its details indicate, this drawing seems to be a realistic depiction of a wedding ceremony as such a ritual would have actually been celebrated in thirteenth-century Ashkenaz.[11] That is not, however, the reason the picture is on the page. It is there because of Benjamin ben Zeraḥ's liturgical poem, and that poem, based as it is on the allegorical interpretation of the Song of Songs, suggests that the groom and the bride depicted in the picture symbolically represent God and Israel. The illustration, in other words, is both highly realistic and profoundly allegorical: it depicts both a thirteenth-century Ashkenazic wedding and the timeless union of God and Israel.

What is the function of such an illustration? How are we to explain the existence and significance of such an illustration, which is at once symbolic *and* realistic, in the medieval prayerbook? What can such an illustration tell us about the subject of "Jewish" art and its connection to the prayerbook, or to Jewish book culture more generally? Before turning to these questions, a brief introduction to the history of the Jewish liturgy and the maḥzor is necessary.

The first thing to be noted is that, in general, we know little for certain about the early history of Jewish prayer.[12] Scholars dispute the question of whether the classical Jewish liturgy—that is, the institution of set, obligatory prayers with fixed wording that must be prayed within a quorum, or *minyan*, of ten men at set times every day—was created de novo by the rabbinic sages following the destruction of the temple in 70 C.E., or whether the sages merely consolidated and formalized an already existing tradition of prayer worship that had developed out of its own imminent logic during the Second Temple period.[13] In either case, early Jewish prayer was essentially an activity conducted orally. For virtually all its early history, the prayers in the Jewish liturgy were recited from memory, without written texts. Not only were there no prayerbooks, but the very idea of reading one's prayers from a written text most likely was considered inappropriate, perhaps partly for theurgic reasons and partly because it was viewed as disrespectful to the majesty of God (just as it would have been considered disrespectful for a rhetor to read a speech before the Roman emperor).[14]

Despite its orality—or perhaps because of it—the institution of Jewish prayer was initially informed by two divergent tendencies that both proved crucial to its later historical development. On the one hand, the rabbinic establishment, first in Roman Palestine, and even more so later in Babylonia, consistently sought to standardize prayer and thus to establish a uniform text and service for all Jewish communities with set words and rules of order. On the other hand, individuals and communities regularly displayed resistance to such standardization, along with a desire to imbue the fixed prayers with more innovative and spontaneous features.[15] Not surprisingly, these two tendencies frequently conflicted with each other, and that conflict decisively shaped the early history of the liturgy. The conflict was only intensified by the rabbinic requirement that prayer be recited in a *minyan*. By requiring Jews to pray together, the early rabbis made obligatory prayer communal, and particular communities inevitably developed their own distinctive communal liturgical conventions and traditions. The sum result of these developments was to make the liturgy and its setting a locus for the literary expression of communal identity.[16]

The conflict between standardization and innovation also helps to explain the next major development in the early history of Jewish prayer. By the sixth century at the latest, the texts of the main prayers in the liturgy, the Shema with its surrounding blessings and the ʿamidah, had become more or less fixed. Partly in reaction to this stabilization of the liturgy, and in part because of its own communal character, in Byzantine Palestine a new kind of liturgical poetry called *piyyut* (from the Greek *poiētēs*, poetry) appeared. The emergence of piyyut was, in many ways, the most radical development in the entire history of Jewish prayer.[17] As it originally developed, piyyut was not just a poetic embellishment for the liturgy, but rather poetry that was specifically intended to replace the standard, fixed version of the prayers, indeed to provide an alternative to the standardized prayers, whose repeated recital seems to have become too familiar and habitual, even tedious, to some Palestinian Jews, especially those of a more scholarly bent. In its original manifestation, a piyyut was an occasional composition, written in order to be recited by the prayer leader—who was, one imagines, often the *paytan* (composer of liturgical poems) himself—at a specific service on a specific day. Because of its functional setting, from its beginnings piyyut also worked to tailor the synagogue service to its communal context and its location in the Jewish calendar.

As an example of the mechanics of piyyut, consider the following poem composed for the blessing that immediately precedes the Shema, the so-called *birkat ahavah* (after its concluding words "*oheiv 'amo yisrael*"—"Who loves His nation, Israel"); the text quoted is the one that appears in the current Ashkenazic daily evening service:

> You have loved the house of Israel, your people, with everlasting love. You have taught us Torah and precepts, laws and judgments. And so, Lord our God, when we lie down and when we arise, we will speak of Your laws. We will rejoice in the words of Your Torah and in your precepts forevermore. Indeed, they are our life and the length of our days; we will meditate upon them day and night. And do not ever take Your love away from us.
>
> Blessed are You, O Lord, Who loves His nation, Israel.

This blessing essentially praises God for loving His nation Israel, with the sign of His love being the Torah that He has given to Israel and in whose study Israel both rejoices and immerses itself.

That is the standard blessing. The following is an early Palestinian piyyut that was composed to be recited in its place:

> A vine from Egypt our God has brought up.
> He drove out nations and planted it.
> From Sinai He gave it water to drink,
> Yea, running waters from Horeb.[18]

Then, like the standard version, the piyyut concludes with the same closing blessing or "signature" (*ḥatimah*), "Blessed are You, O Lord, Who loves His nation Israel." The piyyut, in other words, replaces what is called the *guf ha-berakhah*, "the body of the blessing." In both the standard blessing and the piyyut, the *ḥatimah* remains the same.

The piyyut, as a replacement for the body of the standard blessing, essentially expresses the same idea of God's love for Israel. It does so, however, *poetically*, in a far more allusive and intellectually demanding fashion than does the standard version. In the piyyut, the nation of Israel is figured as a vine sapling carried from Egypt, planted in Israel, and watered by Torah. These are all biblically derived images, and like the use of the place-names of Horeb and Sinai, they point to the likelihood that the piyyut may have been originally composed to be recited precisely on a Sabbath in which the Torah reading included the famous section about the waters of Horeb (Exod 17:6).[19] By making such references, the piyyut would have tailored the liturgy to the specific occasion of a particular service.

As this example demonstates, piyyut was a powerful expression of both the felt need to introduce innovation into the routine of the standard liturgy and the desire to make prayer speak to the requirements of a community's liturgical needs. Yet even with these good intentions, its ambition to displace the standard liturgy conflicted with the halakhic requirement for standardization. Piyyut inevitably aroused opposition from the rabbinic establishment, specifically in Babylonia where some sages actually prohibited its recitation.[20] Babylonian opposition to piyyut was exacerbated, in turn, by the fact that the liturgical phenomenon of piyyut was originally an almost exclusively Palestinian phenomenon, a fact that, along with its halakhic irregularity, only added to its objectionableness in the eyes of the Babylonians. The opposition to piyyut, in other words, was not solely halakhic. It also expressed the competition between the two centers, a rivalry that was especially fierce on the Babylonian side (with its imperial ambitions to establish its liturgical practices as the universal standard).

The intrarabbinic conflict was eventually resolved, though not entirely predictably. Because piyyut was so popular—on account of answering to a genuine religious desire on the part of its audience—it proved impossible for the Babylonian authorities to uproot it completely from the liturgy. Instead, they effectively domesticated and blunted its most halakhically problematic features by turning piyyut into *mere* poetry—that is, into an elaboration of the regular prayers that was recited *in addition* to the standard liturgy rather than in its place.[21] Piyyut thus survived shorn of its subversive features, as an ancillary to the standard liturgy. Because of its popularity, however, piyyut still became part of the rites of virtually every Jewish community.

Piyyut's impact upon the liturgy went beyond its original function. For one thing, piyyut introduced poetry into the liturgy—that is to say, language meant not merely to communicate a message to God but language that demanded, like all poetry, to be savored and appreciated and read in its own right. Indeed, piyyut demanded its audience's full attention; early on, it developed a rigorous aesthetic that prided itself on its enigmatic allusiveness and its virtually riddle-like features, such as neologisms and learned references to recondite aggadic and exegetical traditions. At the same time, the presence of piyyut in the liturgy vastly expanded its scope. It allowed the prayer service to embrace aspects of daily Jewish existence to which the standard prayers did not even allude as well as references to the weekly Torah reading and related *midrashim*, legal topics of import, mystical beliefs and allusions—that is to say, to the entire textual universe of the ancient and medieval Jew, which now could be encompassed within the prayer service. So, too, specific historical events that had befallen a community, such as a catastrophe, an earthquake, or a massacre, or a happier event like a wedding or circumcision, could all be commemorated or celebrated in the synagogue through the composition of special occasional piyyutim.[22]

In this way, piyyut made prayer not only a medium for worshipping God but also a vehicle for expressing the communal life of the worshippers. It thereby *localized* the liturgy, enabling each community to stamp its signature upon the standardized universal prayer service and thus to create its own rite, one that was similar and yet different from those of other communities. The prayer service became, in the course of the Middle Ages, the primary forum in Jewish religious culture for expressing distinct communal identity as well as for worshipping God. (This feature of prayer remains true even today, the only difference being that our communities are no longer specific geocultural sites but ideological homes—for example, Orthodoxy, Conservative and Reform Judaism, Reconstructionism.) Different communities had their own *paytanim*, and even though the piyyutim of the classical *paytanim* of the sixth and seventh centuries—Eliezar ben Kalir in particular—came to be increasingly accepted as virtually canonical parts of the liturgy, each rite also contained the compositions of its local *paytanim* as well as the specific piyyutim that had come to be venerated and were regularly recited as distinguishing parts of its service.[23] Through piyyut, in short, the standard liturgy became a possession of the local community, a monument in words to the world in which the Jews of a particular place not only prayed but actually lived.

As anyone at all familiar with piyyut knows, it is also a literally *literary* genre—that is, one based on written texts. It is virtually impossible to imagine a piyyut not composed in writing or not transmitted by means of written copies. The short and relatively simple piyyut for the Shema quoted above is, in fact, thoroughly *un*representative of piyyut in general. The typical classical piyyut is a lengthy, near-epic composition. The authors of this poetry had to have composed it in writing, and we know that piyyutim circulated among *ḥazzanim* (prayer leaders) and between communities in written copies or texts—at first, one imagines, as single compositions, and then as collections in the form of codices. Indeed, these collections may have been among our earliest types of liturgical books.

One such collection, originally consisting of some two hundred folio pages, was compiled in the land of Israel around the year 900 and has recently been reconstructed and published by Yosef Yahalom of the Hebrew University from single folio pages now scattered in libraries throughout the world.[24] One such folio is reproduced in figure 49. Called *maḥzorim*, from the term *maḥzor*, "a cycle," these collections contain the piyyutim and special prayers for the holidays and special Sabbaths in the yearly liturgical cycle. These early maḥzorim, however, are different from today's "maḥzor," which contains the complete prayers for each holiday, the high holidays in particular. The early maḥzorim generally did not contain the regularly recited texts of the standard prayers that, it was assumed, every prayer leader, if not every congregant, knew by heart. A book like the maḥzor was composed specifically of those prayers that a *ḥazzan* would *not* have memorized—namely, the piyyutim.

In contrast, the origins of the daily prayerbook, the *siddur* (which does contain the regular prayers), were very different. The earliest siddur-like book was not a a book meant to be prayed from but a composition *about* the daily standardized liturgy. In the year 856 C.E., a community of Jews living in Spain—which was then close to being the last frontier of Jewish civilization— wrote to Amram ben Sheshna of Sura, asking him for guidance in reciting the one hundred daily blessings that the talmudic sage R. Meir had deemed obligatory (*b. Menahot* 43b). In response, Amram wrote a treatise, subsequently known as *Seder (the order of) Rav Amram Gaon*, the first work to contain the full wording of all the prayers, along with the laws governing their recitation. This work quickly established itself as the definitive legal authority on the liturgy, and it ultimately became the model for the siddur, or daily prayerbook.[25] Largely because of its influence, most subsequent prayerbooks also contain at least some halakhic directions.[26]

Amram's epistle eventually acquired so much authority as a liturgical standard that scribes, especially in communities in Europe where local practices differed significantly from those in the original *Seder Rav Amram*, regularly

Fig. 49 Maḥzor Eretz Yisrael. Oxford, Bodleian Library MS
Heb. D 41, fol. 1r. Courtesy of the Bodleian Libraries, University
of Oxford.

revised and modified Amram's text in order to bring it into accord with the
local practice. Ultimately, these modifications were so extensive that today, in
the absence of an independent, trustworthy manuscript tradition, it is impossible to reconstruct what Amram himself wrote.[27] The transmission history of
Seder Rav Amram itself proves the power of local practice and communal
self-confidence to rewrite (literally) legal tradition.

The drive for communal self-identification informs the composition of
subsequent prayerbooks. The first actual prayer*book*—that is, a book meant
to be prayed from—was composed approximately a hundred years later at the
beginning of the eleventh century by the great Babylonian sage Saadiah Gaon
(with, incidentally, legal instructions in Judeo-Arabic), again with the

intention of establishing a standardized liturgy in the face of the multiplicity of local customs in the Jewish world (although Saadiah did not necessarily prohibit all divergences from what he called "the essential tradition").[28] Following Saadiah, numerous prayerbooks were composed in short order throughout the Jewish world, each of which reflected its local rites—for example, the rites of the School of Rashi in the Ashkenazic world and that of Maimonides in Spain and Egypt.[29]

Figure 50 charts, in vastly simplified form, the relationship of the many different rites that developed through the Middle Ages from the earliest practices in Palestine and Babylonia. As the diagram shows, the Babylonian rite all but subsumed its Palestinian predecessor and then itself branched off into what ultimately became the Ashkenazic and Sefardic traditions. Each of these larger rites, or *nushaot*, in turn, contained numerous variant subrites that reflected local practices of specific communities; the diagram does not even attempt to reflect the diversity of subrites that existed in Ashkenaz throughout the Middle Ages. Admittedly, the differences between these subrites in purely liturgical terms were often minor, but what may appear to us to be the smallest of differences could nonetheless seem substantial to members of a community.

The full distinctiveness of these local rites can be seen most vividly in the prayerbooks themselves as they were produced in the scribal culture of medieval Judaism. Thanks largely to the pioneering work of Malachi Beit-Arié, Colette Sirat, and their colleagues in the Sfar Data project over the last two decades, we have learned much about the history and nature of that scribal culture.[30] Perhaps the most important lesson these scholars have taught us is that the single most significant criterion in describing the nature of a medieval Hebrew manuscript is the specific place in which the manuscript was produced, or, at the least, its main geocultural location—whether it was Ashkenaz (northern Germany and France), Italy, Byzantium (Greece and Turkey), Sefarad (Spain), or the Orient (the Near East and North Africa). In each of these areas, Jewish scribes wrote in scripts distinctive to the location, used materials like parchment or paper specific to the region, and employed scribal techniques such as ruling and devices for line and page management that invariably reflect the conventions and practices of the larger Gentile scribal culture of the host country.

As a consequence, a Jewish book will invariably mirror in material terms the Gentile books produced in its country or region with the important exception that the Jewish text will almost always be in Hebrew script. (At the

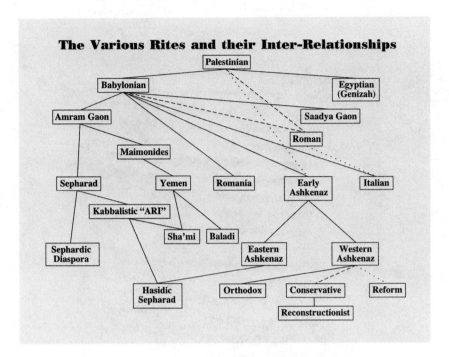

Fig. 50   Diagram of prayer rites: the various rites and their interrelationships.

same time, it is important to remember that Hebrew script itself varies from one historical geocultural area to another and, like the other material features of the Jewish book, tends to mimic the native Gentile script of its region and time—for example, thirteenth-century Ashkenazic script looks like Latin Gothic of that period; twelfth-century Sefardic script mirrors types of Arabic script.)

And what is true of Jewish manuscripts generally is even truer of prayer-books. As Beit-Arié has remarked, the medieval prayerbook was virtually the creation of Jewish scribes.[31] In this respect, the prayerbook is almost a microcosm of the typical medieval Jewish manuscript, with the impact of its geocultural context evident not only in its codicological features but extending even beyond that to its makeup and contents. The early prayerbook was generally a modest codex, as the folio pictured in figure 51 illustrates. This is a page from an eleventh-century Egyptian prayerbook containing the Sabbath morning liturgy, written on paper, which seems to follow Siddur

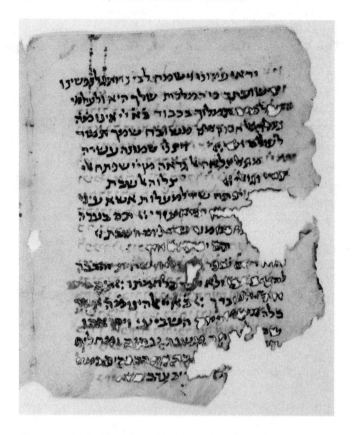

Fig. 51   Prayerbook, Egypt, eleventh century. Philadelphia, University of Pennsylvania, Center for Advanced Judaic Studies Library MS Halper 182. Courtesy of the Library at the Herbert D. Katz Center for Advanced Judaic Studies, Kislak Center for Special Collections, Rare Books and Manuscripts, University of Pennsylvania.

Saadiah. Like the Gaon's prayerbook, this codex also has instructions in Judeo-Arabic.

Not long after these early prayerbooks, however, liturgical codices grew more elaborate, sometimes even ornate, and eventually took on characteristic shapes and material forms that were regional as well as traditional. For example, although only a few Spanish prayerbooks survived the expulsion, those that remain consist mainly of prayers and piyyutim, with minimal halakhic instructions, as illustrated by the page in figure 52, taken from a Spanish

Fig. 52   Spanish Maḥzor for Yom Kippur. New York, Jewish Theology Seminary of America MS 8251, fol. 1. Courtesy of Library of JTSA.

maḥzor for Yom Kippur composed around 1480; the oblong shape of the book is characteristic of Arabic books of the period.

In Italy, in contrast, it was common for prayerbooks to contain extensive halakhic instructions (often subtitled with the term *'inyan*) as well as virtual treatises on topics like the laws of ritual slaughtering or the calendar, which were placed at the siddur's conclusion. Plate 4 is a page from such a siddur, composed in northern Italy in 1441; the halakhic comments are on the upper right and lower left hand columns in the smaller rabbinic script.[32] Finally, in Ashkenaz, there was a clear preference for prayerbooks with glosses and commentaries, such as the opening of two pages from a fourteenth-century Ashkenazic siddur with a commentary on its piyyutim. The page in figure 53 has a format roughly corresponding to the layout of the talmudic page.[33]

The impact of geocultural context on medieval Jewish book culture is most evident, however, in prayerbook illustration. As noted earlier, the belief that the second commandment prohibits representational or figurative illustration is a misconception; indeed, there is a venerable tradition of representational Jewish book art in Ashkenaz that can be documented as early as first third of

Fig. 53   Siddur with piyyut commentary, Ashkenaz, fourteenth century. Jerusalem, National Library of Israel MS Heb 8°3037, fols. 8v–9r. Courtesy of the National Library of Israel.

the thirteenth century and perhaps even earlier.[34] On the other hand, it is also clear that Jewish book art—and prayerbook art in particular—is not a universal phenomenon characteristic of all Jewish books in every period and in all places. Like the other codicological features of the medieval Jewish book, such as techniques of ruling and line justification, the use of figurative illustration seems to have been a function of geocultural location and historical context. Thus one finds figurative illustrations in Jewish liturgical books in essentially four periods and places: (1) in thirteenth- and fourteenth-century Ashkenaz, primarily western and southern Germany (in both maḥzorim and haggadot); (2) in northern/Christian Spain in the mid-fourteenth century (almost exclusively haggadot); (3) in fifteenth-century Ashkenaz and Italy (haggadot, some siddurim); and in sixteenth-century Renaissance Italy (maḥzorim, haggadot, and miscellanies). This particular essay will address the prayerbooks of the first period, the maḥzorim of thirteenth-century Ashkenaz, and specifically the Worms Maḥzor, but the overall argument can easily be extended to other periods.[35]

The starting-place for any discussion of the Maḥzor Worms's history is its colophon:

> I, Simḥah b. Judah the scribe, have written the maḥzor for my uncle R. Barukh b. Isaac in forty-four weeks, setting and arranging from beginning to end every prayer read by the *ḥazzan*, and I have completed it, with the Almighty's help, on the 28th of Tevet in the 32nd year of the era [1272 C.E.]. May the Lord privilege him [R. Barukh] to use it to thank, to praise, to chant, to laud the creator of his soul and to bequeath it, as intended, as an act of piety, for his soul, for he means well; may his righteousness endure forever. And I, Simḥah the Copyist [*ha-lavlar*], will give praise, thanks, and glory to my Rock through my majestic labor, which is beautiful and bright, which I have executed in faith and purity. May He grant me the privilege of seeing children and grandchildren busying themselves with the study of the Torah, and may He save me from all anguish and trouble, amen and amen speedily. (fol. 217v)

As this colophon tells us, the maḥzor was written in the year 1272 in a little over ten months by the scribe Simḥah b. Judah for his uncle R. Barukh, a prayer leader, or *ḥazzan*, who had commissioned it for two reasons: first, so that he could "use it to thank, to praise, to chant, to laud the Creator of his soul"—that is, lead the prayers in the synagogue—and, second, so that, after his death, he could bequeath the volume to the community "as an act of piety for his soul" (*le-sheim mitzvah baʿavur yeḥidato*). Simḥah himself then tells the reader that he, too, the scribe, will offer praise and gratitude to God through the maḥzor he has been privileged to write. Now, in most colophons at this point, the scribe typically offers blessings for the children of the patron or commissioner who has paid for the production of the book. The reader of this colophon will note, however, that Simḥah does not offer prayers for Barukh's progeny but for his *own* children and grandchildren. On account of this striking discrepancy, Beit-Arié has speculated that Baruch was in fact childless and that the very reason he commissioned his nephew to write the maḥzor was for the book to take the place of the son he never had. By serving as his memorial, the maḥzor would literally perpetuate its patron's name in the community for, as the colophon tells us, Barukh had decided, even before the book was written, to bequeath the maḥzor to his community after his death.[36]

As we now know, the maḥzor's original home—the community in which Barukh lived and to which he bequeathed the maḥzor after his death—was Würzburg, a small Jewish center in Franconia in northern Bavaria. By the end of the fifteenth century, however, the maḥzor had landed in Worms, one of the major centers of Ashkenazic Jewish culture in the Rhineland, where it was housed in the town's great synagogue, the famous Rashi Shul. The maḥzor was used continuously in that synagogue (as the signatures of the *ḥazzanim* of Worms on the maḥzor's back pages attest)[37] from 1565 until November 9, 1938, the infamous night known as Kristallnacht, when the building was torched and the maḥzor disappeared. After the war, it miraculously reappeared, and it was then revealed that it had been saved and hidden by the non-Jewish archivist of Worms, Friedrich M. Illert, of blessed memory.[38] Barukh's name thus came to be immortalized in a book whose own fate—a story of displacement and wandering, near destruction, and unforeseen salvation—is the virtual embodiment of a medieval Ashkenazic Jewish life, like that of Barukh himself, though not all such lives ended so fortunately.

In addition to its own history, the maḥzor's pages are filled with other historical traces. As the prayerbook moved from Würzburg to Worms, the prayer rite of the community shifted slightly, and the maḥzor's contents had to be adjusted accordingly.[39] Figure 54 is a detail of the page reproduced in figure 48 (with the allegorical poem *Iti mi-Levanon*). In its far right margin, one can make out a pair of alephs, an abbreviation for the phrase *ein omrim*— "we do not say," or more colloquially, "skip this"—meaning, in other words, that at some point the congregation in Worms had ceased to recite this piyyut.[40] In another instance, several folios (221r–24r) were inserted into the codex with a new piyyut to replace another that was no longer recited in Worms.[41] In still other maḥzorim, later users of the book—prayer leaders or rabbis—simply drew lines through piyyutim that were no longer recited, and wrote others that were recited in its place in the margins.[42] In the last section of Worms Maḥzor (fol. 209v), a marginal note calls attention to a liturgical idiosyncrasy observed in Worms on the fast day of Tisha B'Av. That unusual practice can still be seen on other pages devoted to the laments for the fast day where it is still possible to make out drippings from wax on the parchment—our earliest material evidence, as it happens, for the custom of reading the scroll of Lamentations and reciting the *kinnot* (poems of lament) by candlelight. This custom, which

Fig. 54   Illustration to the piyyut *Iti mi-Levanon*, Worms Maḥzor, Würzburg, 1272. Jerusalem, National Library of Israel MS Heb 4°781/1, fol. 34v, detail. Courtesy of the National Library of Israel.

is now almost universally observed by Jewish communities throughout the world, originated in northwestern Ashkenaz.[43]

Most remarkable of all, on folio 54r, pictured in figure 55, inside the hollow letters of the initial word of the piyyut "Be-daʿato" of the piyyut *Be-daʿato Abiʿah Ḥiddot*, in now-faint rubrics (red lettering), Simḥah wrote out a short rhyming poem in Yiddish: "*Gut tak im betage / she vayr dis maḥzor in beis hakneseth trage*," which can be loosely translated as "May he be granted a good day / who this maḥzor to synagogue does convey."[44] As the historian of Yiddish literature Chone Shmeruk has conjectured, Barukh the Ḥazzan probably kept the maḥzor at home (since it was a very valuable possession) and had it carried for him to synagogue on the days in which he led the prayers—not a light feat, given the codex's size. This poem was a blessing for the servant who carried the heavy maḥzor for Barukh, and it was written in Yiddish because, as Shmeruk argues, the servant was undoubtedly a member of the common folk and Yiddish was probably the only language he knew. In this covert way, Shmeruk writes, Yiddish, the lingua franca of Ashkenaz, along with a vernacular prayer for its speakers, also found a home within the community's maḥzor, inside the hollow sacred letters of Hebrew.

Fig. 55 Initial word of the piyyut *Be-Da'ato Abi'a Hiddot,* with Yiddish poem in
rubrics, Worms Maḥzor, Würzburg, 1272. Jerusalem, National Library of Israel MS
Heb 4°781/1, fol. 54r, detail. Courtesy of the National Library of Israel.

All these instances reflect the maḥzor's literal encasing of its community's
identity. So, too, the maḥzor was a site of communal memory. As already
noted, the final folio of the codex is filled with the signatures of the *ḥazzanim*
of Worms who used the book from the time it arrived in that great center until
Kristallnacht; in this way, the maḥzor recorded its own use. These pages anticipate the custom observed by many Jews of using the family prayerbook or
Bible as a ledger for family records. In some cases the back of the book contained much more than a list of watershed dates and events. For example, one
sometimes finds bound into some medieval prayerbooks, though not in the
Worms Maḥzor, other texts important to the life of the community—calendars, legal treatises, and records of local rituals. The National Library of Israel
in Jerusalem owns a very interesting siddur containing the Roman rite from
1391, into which, in addition to its prayers, several supplementary documents
are bound, including a chronicle of an earthquake that befell the city of Norcia;
the special prayers recited by a legation of Jews from the community to Rome,
where they met with the Pope; and finally, a library list of one of the more
distinguished members of the community.[45]

Plate 1 Hebrew Bible (Leningrad Codex), Cairo, 1008. St. Petersburg, Oriental MSS, National Library of Russia, MS EBP IB 19A, fol. 474r. Courtesy of National Library of Russia.

Plate 2   First Prophets, with Targum and commentaries of Rashi, David Kimchi, and Levi b. Gershon, Segovia, 1487. Oxford, Bodleian Library MS Kenn. 5, fol. 46v. Courtesy of the Bodleian Libraries, University of Oxford.

Plate 3 Hebrew Bible, Florence, Italy, 1427–67. Florence, Biblioteca Medicea Laurenziana Conv. Soppr. 268, fol. 1r. By permission of MiBACT. Any further reproduction by any means is prohibited.

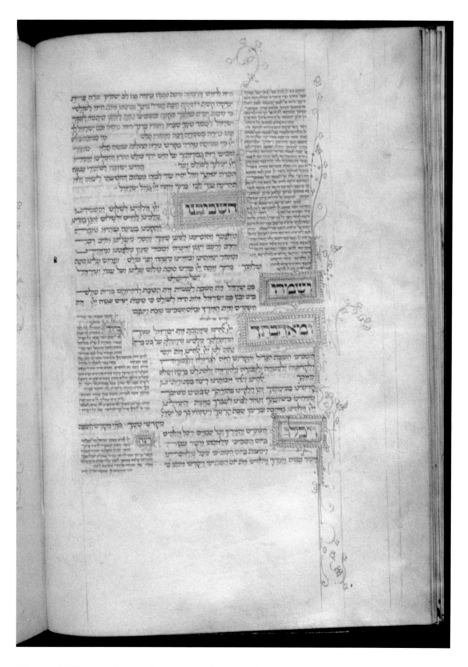

Plate 4   Siddur, northern Italy, 1441. London, British Library MS Add. 19944, fol. 29v. Courtesy of the Bodleian Libraries, University of Oxford, and the British Library / Granger, NYC.

Fig. 56 Zodiac, Worms Maḥzor, Würzburg, 1272. Jerusalem, National Library of Israel MS Heb 4°781/1, fols. 58v–59r. Courtesy of the National Library of Israel.

Through its very materiality, the prayerbook, as well as the liturgy, became a site for expressing communal identity. Nowhere is this function more visible than in the maḥzor's illustrations. We have already seen one such illustration on the *Iti mi-Levanon* page with its depiction of a wedding ceremony that, as suggested, was keyed specifically to the piyyut on the same folio page and that possessed both symbolic and realistic dimensions, simultaneously representing a thirteenth-century Ashkenazic wedding service and the union of God and Israel. Another example in the Worms Maḥzor can be found in figure 56, an opening of two facing pages that are part of the liturgy for the *Musaf* service for the first day of Passover, when *Tefillat Tal*, the annual prayer for dew, is recited. This particular prayer includes the piyyut, *Elim be-Yom Meḥusan* which in eleven double strophes enumerates the twelve signs of the zodiac in relation to the twelve lunar months of the Jewish calendar year from Nissan through Adar; the two months Tevet and Shevat are described in a single strope. In the left margin on both folios, alongside the text, round medallions alternately depict the signs of the zodiac *and* the twelve corresponding labors of the months. This sequence of illustrations, it should be added, is not unique to our maḥzor; it is found in other thirteenth- and fourteenth-century Ashkenazic maḥzorim, including the Leipzig Maḥzor, the Budapest volume of the Tripartite Maḥzor, and the Passover Maḥzor in the Library of the Jewish Theological Seminary of America.[46]

The zodiac, a well-known pagan symbol from the time of antiquity, is probably the most unlikely picture to find in a Jewish book, let alone a prayerbook. But, in fact, use of the zodiac by Jews as a representation in liturgical contexts is a very ancient practice, going back at least to the Byzantine period and to mosaic floors in Palestinian synagogues that have been dated by contemporary archaeologists to the fifth through seventh centuries.[47] The meaning and function of these mosaic floors is still a subject of considerable scholarly debate; different scholars think they alluded to theological mysteries or truths, or that they expressed a messianic hope, or that they served as calendars.[48] Whatever their meaning, however, it seems likely that the synagogue floors were direct sources of inspiration for early *paytanim*, including Eleazar ben-Rabbi Qilir, the seventh-century author of *Elim be-Yom Meḥusan*. Indeed, Qilir might even have composed his piyyut for a synagogue with such a mosaic floor (at whose medallions the *paytan*, while he recited his poem, could have actually pointed).[49]

The direct inspiration for the illustrations in our maḥzor was not, however, an ancient synagogue floor, nor the piyyut, but contemporary thirteenth-century Latin calendars found in Christian psalters and breviaries. The art historians Gabrielle Sed-Rajna and Bezalel Narkiss have done comparative studies of the iconography and sequence of the zodiac illustrations as well as those of the labors of the months in our maḥzor and in the other Ashkenazic texts, and they have shown that, while none of the Jewish series are exactly identical either to each other or to those in contemporary thirteenth-century Christian books (particularly from Franconia), there can be little question that the illustrator of our maḥzor, Shemaiah the Frenchman—as his name indicates, he was unquestionably a Jew—was familiar in some way with the Christian iconographical tradition. Whether that familiarity derived from direct knowledge of a Christian model, or whether Shemaiah used as his model a zodiac sequence from another Jewish book that in some way relied upon the non-Jewish models, is not known. In either case, it seems fair to say that Shemaiah inserted these illustrations in the maḥzor (almost certainly at Simḥah's direction) so as to provide Barukh the Ḥazzan and other Jewish readers with a counterpart to what their Christians neighbors looked at in their own liturgical books. At the same time, Shemaiah (and Simḥah) transformed the non-Jewish zodiac and Judaized it in several clear ways. First, he attached the sequence to the piyyut (which is what it illustrates, rather than the calendar itself, as in Christian codices); second, he gave the signs Hebrew months as indexes and followed the sequence of the Jewish year (beginning with Nisan, the biblical first month); and third, he changed some of the signs themselves according to what seems to have been a native Jewish tradition of iconography.[50]

This example demonstrates that even when a Jewish artist like Shemaiah (or Gentile artists illustrating Jewish books under a Jewish scribe's direction) used the iconographical motifs and illustrational conventions of contemporary Christian culture, they did so with a difference.[51] Nonetheless, the almost certain, though somewhat nebulous, relationship—I hesitate to use the word "dependence"—of the Jewish zodiac illustrations to their Gentile counterparts again raises the question of the Jewishness of the art. What, in the end, makes this cycle of illustrations "Jewish"? Perhaps there *is* only the fact of context—a picture found placed in a Jewish book becomes Jewish as opposed to one found in a Christian book.[52] But if that is the case, was there any explicitly Jewish motivation that drove an artist like Shemaiah to paint this cycle in the maḥzor? Did these pictures serve any specifically Jewish function within the books for which they were composed that differs from the role that equivalent illustrations served in Christian books?

In point of fact, illustrations served several different functions in the maḥzor (just as they did in Christian books of the period).[53] The first and most obvious purpose was aesthetic: the illustrations beautified the book, and that beauty was meant to add to the book's value, both as a sacred object and as a material possession in its own right. Second, the illustrations served a very clear structural function; they "organized" the maḥzor by marking its separate sections; for example, full page illustrations, often in the form of a gate or *shaʿar*, tend to frame the initial pages that open the prayer services for the different holidays.[54] Third, and finally, the pictures also played a didactic or pedagogical role in the book. To use the phrase most commonly associated with medieval illustrations, visual images were *laicorum litteratura*, "the literature of the laity," and they conveyed messages to their readers just as did the texts in words in the book.[55]

In the past, the phrase *laicorum litteratura* has often been taken to mean that pictures were designed as substitutes for the written word for the vast majority of persons who could not read and therefore had no other access to the content of texts like the Bible. According to this view, the pictures were "letters for the illiterate," as the Latin phrase is sometimes loosely translated. Recent scholarship has seriously revised, if not discarded, this assumption. For one thing, the notion of illiteracy among the widespread populace in the Middle Ages, has been seriously questioned, and literacy among Jews has always been believed to have been greater than among their Gentile neighbors. Further, books like a maḥzor were obviously not intended for users who could not read! Moreover, the notion that illustrations are no more than surrogates for texts disregards the fact that illustrations themselves *are* "texts" in their own right, insofar as they function in the same way as the written word, by making "something present to the mind by acting on memory."[56] As Mary Carruthers has shown, medievals—including Gregory the Great—understood the phrase "the literature of the laity" to mean that visual images were "literature" no less than letters and demanded to be "read" as much as any written text. The illustrations were not transparent signs—*mere* illustrations; rather, they tend to be complex, often symbolic, code-like representations that require active interpretation on the part of their viewer/readers. Even in cases like the *Iti mi-Levanon* page or the zodiac images, the illustrations provide the reader with information or messages that may overlap with but do not simply repeat the information conveyed in the text. The pedagogical and didactic role of the maḥzor illustrations cannot therefore simply be dismissed as a secondary supplement to the texts that they accompany.

In the case of Jewish book art, the illustrations, particularly biblical illustrations (which are most frequently found in prayerbooks, not Bibles), have often been treated in past scholarship as visual interpretations, as *midrashim* in image form—that is, interpretations along the lines of classical rabbinic exegeses of the Bible.[57] This interpretive model has been one of the main rubrics under which the pedagogical, didactic role of the illustrations has been understood. And certainly, many illustrations with biblical content reflect ancient and medieval interpretive traditions. It is less clear, however, what exactly in the text the biblical illustrations actually interpret or explain; in the case of nonbiblical illustrations, the midrashic model is even less satisfactory in explaining the role of those illustrations.

Rather than serve as visual *midrashim*, I would like to suggest that the illustrations in these prayerbooks function as visual piyyutim. To appreciate this model, consider one final image. Figure 57 pictures the first folio of the Worms Maḥzor. The illustration on this page literally opens the codex with an elaborately decorated, monumental Romanesque portal, inside of which an obviously symbolic scene appears to be transpiring. In the center, within the gate,

Fig. 57   "El Mitnase," Worms Maḥzor, Würzburg, 1272. Jerusalem, National Library of Israel MS Heb 4°781/1, fol. 1v. Courtesy of the National Library of Israel.

an erect, bird-headed male figure in a red robe holds scales; each pan of the scale has a single word inscribed on it—on the right, *shekel* (or *shakal*); and on the left, *Yisrael*—and the latter pan is filled with either loaves or coins, with the scale clearly tipped in its favor. On the right side next to the scale, a fierce animal stands with an outstretched paw threatening the scale; on the lower left-hand side, a virtually identical beast is climbing up the *aleph*, the last letter of the black initial word *mitnasei*. Art historians take both animals to represent demonic forces seeking to tip the scales in their favor. Above the scale-holding figure in the middle, within the tympanum of the gate, there is a giant ligature for the word El—namely, God. The *aleph* is most prominent; the *lamed* is visible only as a black line that forms a fleur-de-lis above it. This ligature, however, does not only name "God." It is there, actually, to signify His presence, and the symbolic letter is flanked on its two sides by highly stylized emblems, one for the sun, the other for a crescent-shaped moon. Finally, within the empty space of the *aleph* of El, in faint rubrics, the scribe has written the words, "*sheli ben Yitzḥak z"l* [*zikhrono li-vrakhah*]": "this is mine, Baruch bar Isaac of blessed memory." As the reader will recall, Baruch the Ḥazzan was the owner of the maḥzor, who had commissioned his nephew, the scribe Simḥah, to write the codex. The inscription is, one might say, Barukh's ex libris.

What is the meaning of this elaborate picture? As my description has suggested, the illustration seems to depict a heavenly day of judgment; the bird-headed man might be an archangel, the round objects in the scale the souls of the righteous. It is an illustration one would expect to accompany a prayer for Rosh Hashanah or Yom Kippur. But that is not, in fact, its context. The prayers on this page are for a special Sabbath, the Sabbath preceding Purim, known as Shabbat Shekalim, named after the Torah portion read on that day—namely, Exod 30:11–16, which deals with the obligation of every Israelite male to contribute a half-shekel to the Lord and to His sanctuary. During the temple period, this half-shekel was the national tax that every Jew paid to the temple, and according to the art historian Rachel Wischnitzer, the picture's subject is not a scene of heavenly judgment but one of the moneychangers in the Temple who provided the actual coins, the shekels, for making this national contribution.[58] The root of the word *shekel* is a verb meaning "to weigh"—hence the scale in the picture. According to this interpretation, the portal is not a heavenly gate but the idealized entrance to the temple, God's earthly abode, in whose tympanum He dwells, as evidenced by the ligature for His name.

Wischnitzer's interpretation is unquestionably correct. But the illustration may *also* be a depiction of a day of judgment. After all, Exod 30:12, the biblical verse enjoining every Israelite to make the shekel contribution, describes it as a *kofer nafsho*, "a ransom for his person," a phrase that is interpreted in the piyyut accompanying this picture as signifying a ransom for one's soul—namely, a *kapparah* or atonement for one's sins.[59] This notion of atonement money would certainly have evoked in the mind of a medieval Jew an image of the final day of judgment. Like the wedding scene on the *Iti mi-Levanon* page, this illustration operates on two levels, with a double allegorical meaning: the picture illustrates the money changers in the temple who weighed and provided the shekels for all who needed them, *and* it depicts the day of judgment, when every person's life is weighed on the scales of justice. Hence the demonic beasts and hence the inscription on the pans, "Israel is weighed"—that is, in judgment. The scene of judgment is both personal and communal.

But why did Simḥah inscribe Barukh the Ḥazzan's name on *this* page, right in the center of the tympanum? The answer to this question is, I would propose, the key to the page's meaning as a whole, and it relates to both levels of the illustration's signification. This book, the maḥzor, was, in fact, Barukh's contribution to the community of Würzburg—it was his symbolic shekel, which he had already decided (as we know from the colophon) to donate to his personal temple, the synagogue in Würzburg in which he served as cantor. And he wanted everyone in Würzburg to know it, and to remember him by it, forever. Indeed, he doubtless wanted God as well to remember it in his favor on the final day of judgment. Barukh, as the reader will recall, was very probably childless. This book was to be not only his shekel but his figurative child as well, the ransom for his soul, the heritage he would leave after him, his main chance for immortality. Barukh had his name written on the maḥzor's opening page so that, whenever a *ḥazzan* would open the codex to pray from it, God could look down from the heavens and behold the childless cantor's name inscribed before His eyes and remember his merit. And so, too, would the members of the community worshipping out of the maḥzor—first in Würzberg, later in Worms.

The complexity of this page, with its multiple levels of meaning and intricate interplay between text and image, points, I believe, to the deeper function that these illustrations serve within the maḥzor. These illustrations are visual piyyutim. They stand in the same relation to the text on the page as the verbal piyyutim stand in relation to the standard prayers—that is, they are meant to elaborate upon the text by widening its scope of allusions and references, and they do this by contextualizing and individualizing the prayers. Most of all, like the piyyut, the illustrations localize the liturgy and make it specific to the community of worshippers using the maḥzor. The relationship of picture to text is contrapuntal in the same way that piyyut relates to the normative liturgy—at once reexpressing its message, albeit innovatively, and expanding its range, often by reformulating the message in language and motifs specific to a particular community and its occasions. And like piyyut, with its highly allusive and enigmatic aesthetic, each of these pages of illustrations plays on the distance between the literal and the symbolic, and in that play of signification enriches prayer, so as to make it speak not only to God but to the congregation of worshippers as well.

This piyyut-like function of maḥzor illustration is, I would suggest, what ultimately marks these pictures as "Jewish." In comparison to this function, the other factors that have traditionally figured in the discussion of the "Jewishness" of Jewish art seem to me to pale. As I have already remarked, the artist of the Worms Maḥzor was a Jew, Shemaiah the Frenchman. Even if the artists of some of the other maḥzorim and books were Gentiles, they received instructions as to what to draw from Jews.[60] Those instructions were often related, as we have seen, to contemporary Christian and European iconographical traditions, but within the maḥzor, those motifs were Judaized and turned into visual piyyutim, a species of poetic illustration that is distinctively Jewish in its function within the prayerbook, and whose development transpired wholly within the logic of Jewish liturgical tradition. The piyyut-like character of these illustrations is, I would argue, the essence of their Jewishness as Jewish art.[61]

7

MAPPING THE REDEMPTION

Messianic Cartography in the 1695 Amsterdam Haggadah

The Passover Haggadah published by Moses Wiesel in Amsterdam in 1695 is justly famous for several reasons. For one thing, it was the last of the four great printings of the Passover Haggadah between the sixteenth century and the end of the seventeenth, and even more than its predecessors—the 1525 Prague edition, the 1560 Mantua, and the 1609 Venice editions—it was reprinted countless times in the eighteenth and nineteenth centuries.[1] This edition of a major Jewish classic text was also the first of its type to have been produced—almost singlehandedly, so far as we know—by a proselyte, a former Christian preacher from the Rhineland who came to Amsterdam, converted, and took the name of Abraham bar Jacob; in addition to the haggadah, bar Jacob is known to have done copper-engraved title pages for several other books and a ketubah, and to have worked in Amsterdam at least until 1720.[2]

In terms of the technology of its production, the haggadah also represented a watershed moment in the history of the printed haggadah. It was the first to use copper engravings for its illustrations rather than woodcuts, thus setting a new standard of graphic excellence. With its text, including the abridged version of Abravanel's commentary, *Ḥukkat Ha-Pesaḥ*, it became in many ways the standard for all subsequent haggadahs.

The Amsterdam Haggadah may also be called the first modern haggadah. For one thing, it was modern in the sense that it broke with the most basic pictorial conventions that had defined its three printed illustrated predecessors. While each one of these editions was different from the other, they all derived from the basic model of the illustrated haggadah as it developed in the late fourteenth and early fifteenth centuries in southern Germany and northern Italy, in the books produced by such scribes and illustrators as Joel ben Simeon Ashkenazi and Meir ben Israel Jaffe of Ulm.[3] These illustrations (unlike those in fourteenth-century Sefardic haggadot) were nearly all in the margins of the text (and sometimes, as in the case of the early printed haggadot, in historiated initials) and illustrate both biblical scenes mentioned in the haggadah's text (like the ten plagues or the Jews slaving away in Egypt) as well as the signal ritual moments in the *seder*—for example, the head of the household holding a goblet of wine for the kiddush, or lifting the matzah and the bitter herbs (or pictures of the symbolic foods themselves); along with standard illustrations of passages in the haggadah text itself like the Four Sons and the Five Rabbis in Bnei Brak.[4] In nearly all these haggadot, however, the most striking illustration was of an event implied but never explicitly mentioned in the haggadah: the arrival of the messiah on a white donkey, often accompanied by the prophet Elijah blowing a shofar. In the fifteenth-century manuscript haggadot as well as in the Prague and Mantua editions, this illustration is found on the *Shefokh Ha-Matekha* (Pour out your rage) page (possibly because true vengeance against the Gentiles could only be imagined taking place in the messianic era!), but in the 1609 Venice edition, the picture was transplanted from the *Shefokh Ha-Matekha* page to the penultimate one in the haggadah, which records the song "Adir Hu" and where the messiah and Elijah are pictured as arriving at the rebuilt Jerusalem Temple (which, in turn, is pictured in the image of the Mosque of the Dome of the Rock).[5] More than any other image, this illustration typifies the Italo-Ashkenazic haggadah tradition and its particular messianic imagination. Unlike Sefardic haggadot, which tended to picture redemption in nationalistic terms, the Italo-Ashkenazic haggadot envision the messianic moment as a far more familial, even personal, experience, with the messiah literally arriving at the doorstep of the Jewish homes.

The copper-engraved illustrations in the Amsterdam Haggadah entirely break with this pictorial tradition. With one exception (that I will discuss shortly), there are no illustrations depicting *seder* rituals or scenes, nor any of the traditional biblical pictures (including the Israelites slaving in Egypt), nor the illustration of the messiah's arrival. In their place are a series of new illustrations almost entirely of biblical scenes that are never or barely mentioned in the haggadah—for example, Abraham smashing the idols of his father Teraḥ, Abraham greeting the three angels at Eilon Mamrei (Gen 15), Moses slaying the Egyptian overseer (Exod 2:11–12), the discovery of the infant Moses in the Nile by Pharoah's daughter, the Israelites journeying through the desert, and the revelation at Mount Sinai.

In a seminal article published in 1931, the pioneering Jewish art historian Rachel Wischnitzer-Bernstein demonstrated that Abraham bar Jacob had borrowed or copied nearly all of his illustrations from the engravings that Matthaeus Merian the Elder of Basel (1593–1650), one of the most famous illustrators in the early sixteenth century, had made for his highly popular *Icones biblicae, historiae sacrae Veteris et Novi Testamenti* (Frankfurt and Strasbourg, 1625–30) and for his world history, the *Historische Chronica* (Frankfurt, 1630–57) Merian even led to somewhat incongruous images. For example, the picture of the Passover meal, meant to illustrate a Jewish *seder*, is a direct copy of an original in Merian and has its participants *standing* before the table rather than sitting at it.[6] In the second half of the haggadah, accompanying the concluding section of the Hallel service (which consists of selections from the book of Psalms), Abraham provided an illustration depicting King David composing Psalms under the direct inspiration of the Holy Spirit (fig. 58). I will discuss this illustration's composite features shortly, but the reader will note that David's position—kneeling with clasped hands before the Holy Spirit—makes the picture seem, as Cecil Roth noted, "wholly Christian in conception."[7] No matter how sincere a convert Abraham may have been, it appears that, at some deep level, he could not entirely escape viewing the world through the prism of Christianity.

For all his reliance on Merian's engravings, however, bar Jacob did not merely copy them. As Wischnitzer showed, he sometimes altered the originals, changed their direction or orientation, or combined images from different contexts in their original sources in order to make them fit the haggadah and his particular needs. The most famous example of this is the panel of "The Four Sons" (fig. 59)—the first time the four sons had appeared together in a single panel—in which he combined figures from diverse (and somewhat unlikely) sources: the Wise Son was a reverse of the figure in a scene from his *Historical Chronicle* in which Hannibal swears enmity against Rome; the Wicked Son was a soldier from one of Merian's battle-scenes; the Simple Son was taken from the *Icones* from a reverse of a figure of Samuel as he anoints Saul; and the Son Who Does Not to Ask was again taken from the Hannibal scene.[8] Equally interesting as a pastiche is the picture of David composing Psalms mentioned in the previous paragraph. Bar Jacob could not find an exact model for this picture in Merian, so he took an engraving from the New Testament section

Fig. 58 Illustration of David composing Psalms from *Pass-over Haggadah* (Amsterdam: Moses Wiesel, 1695). Courtesy of the Gross Family Collection.

of the *Icones* illustrating the parable of the Pharisee and the Publican (Luke 18), removed the two figures, and replaced the figure of the Publican with another one modeled on King Solomon at prayer that goes back at least to the De Keyser Bibles of 1530 and 1532.[9] Finally, the upper left-hand corner, which in Merian's original picture of the Lukan parable had been filled by drapery, bar Jacob now filled with a flaming circular cloud in which he inscribed the words *Ruaḥ Ha-Kodesh*, "The Holy Spirit," while the open book of Psalms lies before him on what looks like a prayer table. These last two details are based on still another source Abraham appears to have used, the first complete edition of the Lutheran Bible (1534).[10]

Fig. 59   Panel with four sons from *Passover Haggadah* (Amsterdam: Moses Wiesel,1695). Courtesy of the Gross Family Collection.

Wischnitzer's article was a watershed study in Jewish art history, but since its publication, Falk Wiesemann and others have shown that Abraham bar Jacob's *modus operandi* was neither unusual nor new.[11] Merian himself had borrowed heavily from the biblical woodcuts of Hans Holbein the Younger (1497/98–1543), and such "borrowings" were in fact a staple of early printings of illustrated Bibles in Northern Europe, particularly in the Netherlands, since the early sixteenth century.[12] Already in the Yiddish edition of *Sefer Yossipon* (Zurich, 1546), the Christian publisher had also copied Holbein's woodcuts to illustrate his history. Similarly, the first folio edition of the *Tzene u-Rene* (Sultzbach, 1692) borrowed from Holbein, while later editions from Frankfurt and Amsterdam used Merian as the models for their woodcuts. In all these cases, the publishers of the Jewish books had removed features from the original illustrations that Jewish readers would have found unacceptable or offensive— images of Christ, full depictions of God, typological intimations of the cross— but the origins of the illustrations, whether Jewish readers recognized them or not, were Christian pictorial traditions.[13]

To be sure, virtually all Jewish book art, since the beginning of the Middle Ages, has been strongly informed and influenced by the Gentile book art of the host cultures in which the Jewish producers of the books lived, a feature

Fig. 60   Detail showing the messiah and the prophet Elijah in the illustration of David composing Psalms from *Passover Haggadah* (Amsterdam: Moses Wiesel, 1695). Courtesy of the Gross Family Collection.

of Jewish book culture only intensified in Europe, where in many cases the artists themselves were Christians. Furthermore, all pictorial traditions through the early modern period, Jewish and Gentile, are heavily conventional, with artists generally basing their work on model books and earlier iconographic traditions if not specific pictures. What distinguishes Abraham bar Jacob is not the derivative nature of his copper engravings but the original manner in which he sometimes created new images out of separate distinct models—as in the panel of the "Four Sons"—or in the way he was able to Judaize images that previously were not Jewish and give them new meanings, even sometimes cryptic, if not esoteric, Jewish ones.

There is no better illustration of this last feature of bar Jacob's work than the way he treated the messianic dimension of the haggadah in pictorial representation. As I have already noted, the Amsterdam Haggadah lacks the picture of the Messiah arriving on a donkey and led by the prophet Elihan on the *Shefokh Ha-Matekha* page. But the illustration is not entirely lacking from the haggadah. Figure 60 enlarges the picture of David kneeling before the Holy Spirit that we have already discussed (fig. 58), and one can make out in the distance to the right of the column next to David the figures of the Messiah on a donkey and behind him the prophet Elijah blowing a shofar (which looks more like a tuba!).[14] The detail is a certain allusion to the traditional image, and its peculiar placement on this page can only be explained by the messiah's genealogical descent from David, but it is a barely visible allusion to the Messiah.[15]

In contrast, the haggadah has two other illustrations that are more explicitly messianic. The first of these is a large depiction of the temple based on Merian's engraving of Solomon's Temple that is placed on the page next to the hymn "Adir Hu" ("Mighty One, build Your house soon, in our days"), found at the book's conclusion. This illustration gives visual expression to the hope that the Temple will be rebuilt by the Messiah.[16] This picture was not entirely unprecedented. As noted earlier, in the Venice 1609 edition, a picture of the Temple was also placed beneath "Adir Hu" and served as a backdrop to the figures of the Messiah on a white donkey and the prophet Elijah. Bar Jacob, however, left the Messiah and Elijah out of his engraving, and where the 1609 haggadah had pictured the Temple in the image of the Dome of the Rock, bar Jacob's Temple is a grandiose seventeenth-century palace with massive courtyards and looming towers at the four corners of its brick walls.

The second messianic picture in the haggadah, however, was entirely unprecedented—a complete foldout Hebrew map, printed on the back flyleaf of the book, showing the exodus from Egypt, the route along which the children of Israel wandered through the desert, and the land of Israel divided into tribal territories (fig. 61). This was not the earliest printed Hebrew map, but it was the first to be printed in a book, and it has remained one of the Amsterdam Haggadah's most famous features.[17]

Like Bar Jacob's other engravings, the map drew on an earlier model with established iconography, the map of the Holy Land found in the *Theatrum terrae sanctae* (1590) of the important Dutch mapmaker and historian Christian von Adrichem (1533–1585) (fig. 62).[18] Adrichem's own map ultimately goes back to a cartographic plan first developed by the Italians Marino Sanuto (ca. 1260–1338) and Petrus Vesconte (d. ca. 1350), but his extensive delineation— including ships with billowing sails in the Mediterranean, whales and sea monsters, and Jonah being tossed overboard into the mouth of a waiting whale—had become the near universal standard by the late seventeenth century. Not surprisingly, it served as the model for the earliest known map in Hebrew (Amsterdam, 1621) which was commissioned by Jacob ben Abraham Zaddik (Justo) (fl. ca. 1620) from Abraham Goos, one of the finest engravers

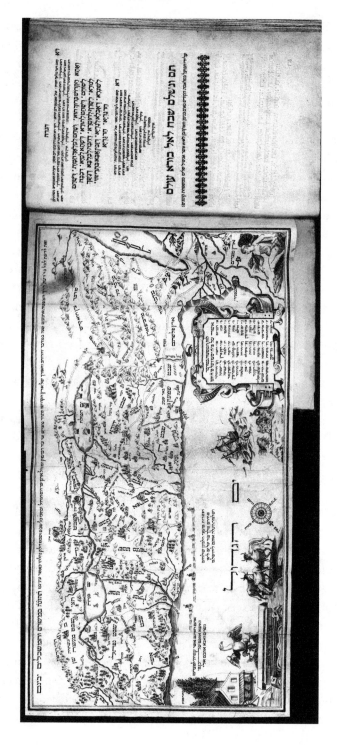

Fig. 61   Map of the Holy Land from *Passover Haggadah* (Amsterdam: Moses Wiesel, 1695). Courtesy of the Gross Family Collection.

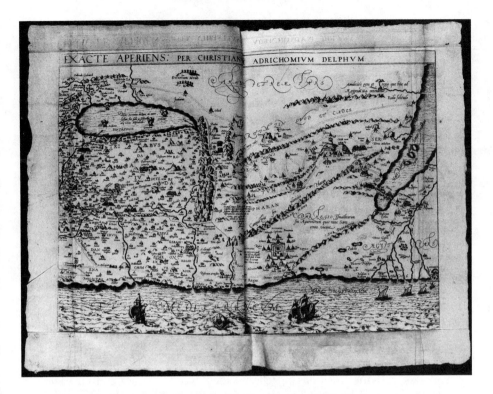

Fig. 62   Map of the Holy Land from Christian van Adrichem, *Theatrum terrae sanctae* (Amsterdam, 1590). Courtesy of the Gross Family Collection.

in Amsterdam in that period. Zaddik's map is also not a slavish copy of Adrichem. It lacks Adrichem's picture of Jonah being tossed from the ship and it replaces the southern section of Adrichem's key map with a detailed rendition of the desert of Paran that emphasizes the exodus and its stations.[19] Extensively coded and marked, it was later annotated by a guidebook to the biblical sites on the map that Zaddik published in 1633. This guide was, in fact, a part of the larger plan for which Zaddik intended his map. In a square text panel on the map (next to his engraved portrait), he explained the map's—and later guidebook's—purpose: that they might inspire people through their depiction of the Holy Land to visit or even move to "Eretz Yisrael."[20]

We do not know if Abraham bar Jacob was familiar with Zaddik's map, but his clear model was Adrichem. Like his source, Abraham's map was oriented eastward, with the Mediterranean coast forming the bottom horizon of the page, the city of Damascus at the far left, and Egypt at the far bottom right of the page. The land of Israel itself was divided into the tribal portions, and the names of famous biblical cities and towns and other sites (like *ma'arat ha-makhpelah*, the burial cave of Abraham and other patriarchs) were carefully marked—all in Hebrew. The main difference in Abraham's map was that he left a relatively larger portion of the bottom of the page empty for the Mediterranean Ocean and filled the space with various illustrations and devices. Thus on the bottom far right, the goddess of the Nile rides on a crocodile. To her left is a table within a scrolled frame listing the forty-one stations through which the Israelites journeyed on their forty-year march through the desert; in the desert on the map itself, on the upper right-hand side, each station is marked by its letter on the table.[21] To the left of the table is a depiction of a storm-tossed ship with two figures at the stern throwing a third, Jonah, into the mouth of a surfacing whale; beneath the sea scene, immediately to the left of the table, is the crouching figure of Jonah who has miraculously been saved on land. This image was, again, a complex borrowing: the model for the ship from which Jonah is thrown came from Adrichem's map, but the figure of Jonah, as Rachel Wischnitzer already showed, was borrowed from Merian.[22] Finally, moving toward the left-hand side of the page, one finds a circular compass (with the directions in Hebrew), then a group of cows, a proud eagle perched on a masonry bench that serves (as the Hebrew inscription across its bottom indicates) as a distance scale for the map in Persian parasangs,[23] and, on the far left, a house whose porch is filled with beehives. The beehives are labeled as *devash*, "honey," and the cows as *ḥalav*—together signifying, obviously, the "land of milk and honey" (Exod 3:8) Finally, above the cows and the large superscription (*yam ha-gadol*, "the Great Sea," i.e., the Mediterranean), there is a string of four ships, each towing three or forge barges, and beneath them the inscription "Rafts of cedars of Lebanon sent by Hiram, king of Tyre, on their way to Jaffa, from whence Solomon brought them to Jerusalem" (1 Kgs 5:21–25). Like the device of Jonah being tossed from the ship into the whale's mouth, the image of the ships and barges carrying the cedars of Lebanon had been used in previous Christian maps, but here, as we shall see, they formed an integral part of a larger conception.[24]

What led Abraham bar Jacob to include the map in his haggadah? In part, his decision was probably a commercial ploy to make his edition not only distinctive and unlike all its competitors but also more marketable. Bar Jacob was certainly aware of the popularity that maps had enjoyed among the general reading public since the middle of the sixteenth century and the publication of Abraham Ortelius's *Theatrum orbis terrarum* (Antwerp, 1570), the first collection of maps that could be called an atlas (even though he did not use the term). With its prominent foregrounding of the "Great Sea," it is possible that Abraham wished the map to reflect not only the biblical history of Israel but also the Netherlands's new self-image, and growing self-importance, as an international mercantile sea power. To be sure, inasmuch as the map visually describes the Israelite's exodus from Egypt and journey to the land of Canaan, it clearly possessed a thematic connection to the story of the haggadah. Indeed, this was the reason Abraham himself stated for including the map. In the superscription stretching across the top of the map page, just inside the borders, the text in smaller letters—I will return shortly to the conclusion written in larger letters—reads: "This is to make known to every understanding person the route of the of the forty-years journey in the desert, and the breadth and length of the Holy Land[25] from the River of Egypt to the City of Damascus and from the Valley of Arnon to the Great Sea, and within it the territory of each and every tribe."[26]

Still, no previous haggadah illustrator had ever felt it important to depict the exact stages of the Israelites' journey as bar Jacob did in his map. Nor is their journey described in detail anywhere in the haggadah's text. The material shape of most classical texts of Jewish books, including its illustrative dimension, has always been inherently conservative, and the haggadah is no exception: witness the three previous printed editions of the haggadah and their fundamental similarity to each other (as well as to the Italo-Ashkenazic manuscript haggadot). Even with his own explanation in the superscription, Abraham bar Jacob's decision to include the map in his haggadah warrants further explication.[27] And most important of all, it seems likely that Abraham bar Jacob himself supplied hints in the map that he included it for reasons other than those he explicitly stated.

These hints are contained in two superscriptions on the map. The first of these is the conclusion of the superscription stretching across the top of the page, the beginning of which I cited in the paragraph before the last. The conclusion of the superscription, written in larger black letters, is a combination of two scriptural quotations; "so that your eyes will behold (*ve-tehezenah*) those things properly" (Ps 17:2) and "the knowledgeable will understand them (*ve-ha-maskilim yevinan*)" (Dan 12:10). The section from Ps 17:2 was selected for two reasons: first, its words contained the thought Bar Jacob needed at that point in his superscription, and second, three of the word *ve-tehezenah*'s five letters (marked with dots above them) spelled out the numerical equivalent of the Hebrew year 5455 (= 1695), the year of the book's publication, a typical technique in Jewish book culture of using a biblical word or verse to date a book. The quote from the second verse is more revealing, as one can tell by looking at its context in Dan 12: "What will be the outcome of these things?," the bewildered prophet Daniel asks the angelic figure after he has just been shown the harrowing vision of the end of days. To which the mysterious angel replies: "Go, Daniel, for these words are secret and sealed to the time of the end. Many will be purified and purged and refined; the wicked will act wickedly and none of the wicked will understand; but *the knowledgeable will understand* (Heb: *ha-maskilim yavinu*)" (Dan 12:9–10, my emphasis).[28] What they will understand is the secret of the end-time.

The second superscription that offers a clue to ben Jacob's motivation in including the map is the verse quoted above the eagle perched on the masonry table. This verse presumably explains the eagle's presence. As it appears in the Bible, Exod 19:4 reads: "You have seen what I did to the Egyptians, and how I bore (*va-esa*) you on eagles' wings and brought you (*va-avi*) to Me." In context, the construction of the verb forms *va-esa* and *va-avi* are typical of the Bible's use of the *vav*-conversive, which changes the future form of *esa* and *avi* into the past tense. The *vav*, however, could be read, with only a little exegetical liberty, in its usual form as the conjunction "and." In this case, the verse would read, "You have seen what I did to the Egyptians, and how I *will* bear (*ve-esa*) you on eagles' wings, and *will* bring you to Me." In other words, by literally seeing—on the map—the miracles that God wrought for the Israelites in bringing them out of Egypt, the viewer will merit the divine promise that He will redeem them again.

This rationale, I would propose, is the more cryptic reason for why Abraham bar Jacob placed the map in his haggadah. The map is an eschatological chart. It is not just a map of the Israelites' journey through the desert in the past; it is also a mapping of the messianic journey of the future. This interpretation of the Israelite's journey and its stations as written in the Bible in Num 33 was not bar Jacob's invention. Don Isaac Abravanel (Lisbon, 1437–Venice, 1508), in his commentary on the Pentateuch, had already proposed that the reason why, in Num 33, God repeated the list of the stations through which the Israelites journeyed in the desert was to make them refer to the future redemption and the stations in the (figurative) wilderness (*midbar*) of the Gentile nations—their *galut*, their exile—from which the Jews would be redeemed.[29] Similarly, Abraham Saba (Castile, 1440–Fez, 1508), an exile from Spain and the author of a famous quasi-mystical commentary on the

Pentateuch, *Tzeror Ha-Mor* (A bundle of myrrh), also interpreted the purpose of Num 33 as being intended to strengthen faith in the redemption to come and even contrasted the forty-two stations in the desert with the forced migrations that the Iberian Jewish community endured in their expulsions from Spain and Portugal.[30] While Saba expected the redemption to arrive in 1647–48, his interpretation of the lengthy passage in Numbers, like Abravanel's, certainly points to a widespread exegetical outlook.[31]

There were additional, more immediate reasons why bar Jacob may very plausibly have believed that the redemption was to take place imminently, even in his own time. As recent scholarship has shown, the period following the apostasy of the false messiah Sabbatai Zevi in 1666 was one of intense messianic turmoil and millenarian expectation among both Jews and Christians.[32] While Sabbatai's movement originated in Turkey, Amsterdam soon became one of the northern European centers for both his followers and opponents, as is attested by the very fact that the first actual history of Sabbatianism, the Yiddish text called *Beshreibung fun Shabbesai Tzvi*, was written by the beadle of the Amsterdam community, R. Leib b.R. Oizer, in 1707–8.[33] In the year 1700, a group called the "holy society of Rabbi Judah Ḥasid," emigrated en masse from Poland to the land of Israel (many of them Sabbatians awaiting Sabbatai Zevi's second manifestation). Although the society disintegrated after they arrived in the Holy Land, their pilgrimage created a vast stir in Europe, including Amsterdam.[34] For Christians, too, the years around 1700 were also the focus of interpretations of the prophetic passages of the apocalypse in works like Dan 12 and the book of Revelation.[35]

It is unfortunate that we have virtually no biographical information about Abraham bar Jacob, and no insight into why he converted to Judaism or came to Amsterdam. While there is no indication that he had Sabbatian leanings, it is difficult to imagine that he was not caught up in the general fervor, in the messianic and milleniarian excitement that possessed both Jewish and Christian communities. This excitement was not limited to sectarian or esoteric circles, as demonstrated by the case of the Amsterdam-based scholar Jacob Judah Leon (Templo) (1602–1675) and the popular model of the Temple that he constructed from wood for public viewing and study, and which he took on tour throughout Europe to great acclaim until the model eventually disappeared in England.[36] As A. K. Offenberg has remarked, Leon's models provided "a kind of blueprint" for the reconstruction of the temple in the forthcoming end of days.[37] Even certain conventional features of the map like the division of the promised land into its patrimonial, tribal portions, which actually goes back to Sanuto and Vesconte,[38] may have taken on new meaning in the second half of the seventeenth century. While bar Jacob copied the cartographic divisions from Adrichem, their *meaning* must have taken on new import in the wake of the publication in 1650 of Manasseh ben Israel's *Esperança de Israel* (The Hope of Israel) with its vision of the rediscovery and restoration of the ten lost tribes of Israel as a prelude to a universal messianic age.[39]

Historians of Dutch culture in the Golden Age have long recognized the degree to which the exodus story became a common reference for "godly nationalism"—"a source book of analogues for their own contemporary history," as Simon Schama has written.[40] Indeed, Christian Dutch maps represent the Holy Land along precisely these lines—as a site to be associated with their own current history as viewed through the prism of the biblical history of redemption narrated in Exodus.[41] Whether Abraham bar Jacob, the former pastor, carried the baggage of such a sensibility from his Christian past into his newly espoused Jewish identity, or whether he used the Bible's own geographical information and its Jewish interpretation as a source for his map for the approaching messianic age, he infused his haggadah with the stamp of a distinctively Dutch Golden Age sensibility. The map became a new element in the history of the haggadah as a book, and through the wide influence of the Amsterdam edition, a staple for many haggadot in subsequent centuries. And by reinscribing the messianic scenario into its pages, Abraham bar Jacob gave Jews still another way to fulfill the haggadah's injunction that everyone is required to see themselves as having gone out of Egypt.

NOTES

CHAPTER 1

1. David Stern, *Parables in Midrash: Narrative and Exegesis in Rabbinic Literature* (Cambridge: Harvard University Press, 1991), 9–13.

2. As my colleague Dan Ben-Amos has pointed out to me, these three generic categories are not entirely equivalent. The sages themselves use the terms *mashal* and *ma'aseh*. The term *sippur darshani* is a modern term invented by scholars.

3. Stern, *Parables in Midrash*, 63–71.

4. The text translated here is based upon *Midrash Rabbah Shir Ha-Shirim: Midrash Ḥazit*, ed. Shimshon Dunsky (Jerusalem: Dvir, 1980), 6. The translation is mine.

5. The most recent consideration of this question is Chaim Milikowsky, "Midrash as Fiction and Midrash as History: What Did the Rabbis Mean?," in *Ancient Fiction: The Matrix of Early Christian and Jewish Narrative*, ed. Jo-Ann A. Brant, Charles W. Hedrick, and Chris Shea (Leiden: Brill, 2005), 117–28; as Milikowsky's title indicates, he juxtaposes "fiction" and "history" as opposites, but he never inspects or justifies that opposition, which, in fact, may not be a helpful categorization of the alternatives in play. See also my comments on the question in *Midrash and Theory: Ancient Jewish Exegesis and Contemporary Literary Studies* (Evanston: Northwestern University Press, 1996), 91–93.

6. Paul Veyne, *Did the Greeks Believe in Their Myths? An Essay on the Constitutive Imagination*, trans. Paula Wissing (Chicago: University of Chicago Press, 1988).

7. For the closest thing to a catalogue of the *ma'asim* in the Mishnah, see Shaye J. D, Cohen, "The Rabbi in Second-Century Jewish Society, Appendix 29:2, Interaction Between Rabbis and Jews: The Tannaitic Evidence," in *The Cambridge History of Judaism*, vol. 3: *The Early Roman Period*, ed. by William Horbury, W. D. Davies, and John Sturdy (Cambridge: Cambridge University Press, 1999), 980–90. As noted, not every *ma'aseh* begins with the formulaic *ma'aseh be-*. Some are first-person narratives; others simply begin with the narration of the event.

8. Moshe Simon-Shoshan, *Stories of the Law: Narrative Discourse and the Construction of Authority in the Mishnah* (New York: Oxford University Press, 2012); on case stories, see, in particular, 130–66; on exempla, see 167–93.

9. See Simon-Shoshan, *Stories*, 80–83.

10. On the *chreia*, see the classic article of Henry A. Fischel, "Story and History: Observations on Greco-Roman Rhetoric and Pharisaism," *American Oriental Society Middle West Branch Semi-Centennial Volume*, ed. D. Sinor (Bloomington: Indiana University Press, 1969), 59–88.

11. Probably the best-known *ma'aseh* of this sort is the one about the sons of Rabban Gamliel in *m. Berakhot* 1:1. On the structure of this Mishnah, see Burton L. Visotzky, "So Why Did the Sages Say, 'Until Midnight'? On M. Berakhot 1:1," in *Tiferet le-Yisrael: Jubilee Volume in Honor of Israel Francus*, ed. Joel Roth, Menahem Schmelzer, and Yaacov Francus (New York: Jewish Theological Seminary, 2010). This *ma'aseh* is also a good example of the kinds of

problems raised by many *maʿasim* in the Mishnah—described in the next paragraph—inasmuch as it supplies too much information and thereby raises questions that go far beyond the task of exemplification for which the anecdote is presumably cited. For example: What were Rabban Gamliel's sons doing before they came home? Why had they not said the Shema at a more reasonable hour? What was the tone of Rabban Gamliel's directive to his sons?

12. See Simon-Shoshan, *Stories*, 225–31, where he also uses the term "undermine" to describe the relationship of some *maʿasim* to their "normative" contexts.

13. Ḥoni's story has been discussed extensively in scholarship over the last century. For a summary and bibliography, see ibid., 149–66.

14. On rabbinic beliefs in supernatural creatures, see Joshua Trachtenberg, *Jewish Magic and Superstition* (1939; repr., New York: Atheneum, 1970), 15–44 in particular and passim, and see now Gideon Bohak, *Ancient Jewish Magic: A History* (Cambridge: Cambridge University Press, 2008), 143–226 and 351–425. For readings of many texts dealing with magic, see Daniel Sperber, *Magic and Folklore in Rabbinic Literature* (Ramat Gan: Bar Ilan University Press, 1994).

15. My translation is based on the text in the *editio princeps* (Soncino, 1484); all significant variants will be noted.

16. Munich 95: R. Yehuda bar Avin; Florence II-I-7, Paris 671, Oxford, Bodleian Library Opp. Add. Fol. 23: Rav Zvid, and some say R. Idi bar Avin.

17. Oxford: "to his place" (*li-mkomo*).

18. Oxford: "on top of a mountain" (*rosh he-har*).

19. Oxford: "for the honor of his Creator" (*li-khvod kono*).

20. Munich 95 has "on account of an accident" (*mi-shum ones*).

21. Oxford: "of dinars" (*de-dinarii*).

22. Paris 671 and Opp. Add. Fol. 23 lack *be-meizid*.

23. Oxford: "was traveling on the road" (*have kaʾazil be-urḥa*).

24. Oxford: "and forgot" (*inshei*).

25. Munich 95 lacks this line. Florence II-1-7 places this line after the midrash on Ps 68:14 and adds (as do Paris 671 and Oxford Opp. Add. Fol. 23): "and a miracle happened, and he found a golden dove."

26. Florence II-1-7 adds: "Just as the wings of a dove protect, so do the commandments protect Israel."

27. See *b. ʿEruvin* 13b.

28. Simon-Shoshan, *Stories*, 16–22.

29. According to those manuscripts that omit *be-meizid*, the incrimination behind the second student's fate is even more extreme. He does not return and is eaten by a lion, even if it was a case where he honestly forgot to say grace.

30. Dan Ben-Amos, "Talmudic Tall Tales," in *Folklore Today: A Festschrift for Richard M. Dorson*, ed. Linda Dégh, Henry Glassie, and Felix J. Oinas (Bloomington: Indiana University Press, 1976), 25–43, 28 in particular. Rabba's tall tales, as well as those of other rabbis, are collected in a long section in *b. Bava Batra* 73a–74b. These stories have long fascinated students of Talmud, but in the recent past there has been an explosion of scholarship on them. In addition to Ben-Amos's seminal article, "Talmudic Tall Tales"—which still remains, in my view, the best treatment of these stories and the complex negotiations through which they engage their audiences—see Günter Stemberger, "Münchhausen und die Apokalyptik: Baba Batra 73a–75b als literarische Einheit," *JSJ* 20 (1989): 61–83; Dina Stein, *Textual Mirrors: Reflexivity, Midrash, and the Rabbinic Self* (Philadelphia: University of Pennsylvania Press, 2012), 58–83; Stein, "Believing is Seeing: A Reading of Bava Batra 73a–75b" [in Hebrew], *Jerusalem Studies in Hebrew Literature* 17 (1999): 9–32; Reuven Kiperwasser, "Rabbah bar bar Ḥana's Voyages" [in Hebrew], *Jerusalem Studies in Hebrew Literature* 22 (2008): 215–41; Joshua Schwartz, "Sinai—Mountain and Desert: The Desert Geography and Theology of the Rabbis

and Desert Fathers," in *"Follow the Wise": Studies in Jewish History and Culture in Honor of Lee I. Levine*, ed. Zeev Weiss, Oded Irshai, Jodi Magness, and Seth Schwartz (Winona Lake: Eisenbraums, 2010), 355–74; Reuven Kiperwasser and Dan D. Y. Shapira, "Irano-Talmudica II: Leviathan, Behemoth, and the 'Domestication' of Iranian Mythological Creatures in Eschatological Narratives of the Babylonian Talmud," in *Shoshannat Yaakov: Jewish and Iranian Studies on Honor of Yaakov Elman*, ed. Shai Secunda and Steven Fine (Leiden: Brill, 2012), 203–35; and, most recently, an impressive Harvard College honors thesis by Daniel J. Frim, "'Those Who Descend upon the Sea Told Me . . .': Myth and Tall Tale in Baba Batra 73a–74b"; I want to thank Mr. Frim for allowing me to read his thesis. Because these stories are not halakhic narratives, they fall beyond the purview of this project, but it should be said that they directly raise the issue of credibility and historicity of the *ma'aseh*, albeit in an inverted fashion. As Ben-Amos shows, these stories use various techniques to validate their veracity—the first person narratives, the citations of verses as prooftexts, the invocations of other sages who confirm the veracity of the reports or who accept them even when they make fun of Rabba bar bar Hannah (see, for example, the response of the rabbis to Rabba's story about having seen the Israelites who died in the desert and having failed to steal a corner of their talitot, presumably to count the number of fringes; they do not challenge Rabba, they simply make fun of him for not counting them on the spot!) As Dan Ben-Amos has pointed out to me, our story in *Berakhot* is unique inasmuch as it is not a first-person report, as are nearly all the other Rabba bar bar Hanna traditions, but a narrative *about* him. The exact purpose of these stories, and particularly the collection in *Bava Batra*, remains somewhat unclear, but one possibility (in my view) is that they were collected in order to parody the very process of rabbinic transmission of tradition: as noted above, Rabba was a well-known *nahota*, and therefore an all-too-appropriate target for a parody about transmitters of tradition. As literary parodies, they certainly would have drawn upon popular traditions of tall-tale telling; they also served to rabbinize various Iranian myths and folk traditions (as Kiperwasser and others have demonstrated), and they entertained Talmudists by demonstrating the gullibility of rabbis to believe *any* tradition just as long as it carried the marks of authority. As parodies of the process of transmission, these stories provide a remarkable reflection of the rabbis' self-awareness, and insofar as they revolve around the rhetoric of credibility, they also serve to confirm the claim to historicity and authenticity that typical *ma'asim* make.

31. This final midrash also seems to explain and justify why the Gemara here privileges the House of Shammai's position over the House of Hillel's.

32. On the many different types of narrative that begin to appear in the Geonic period and continue through the Middle Ages, see Eli Yassif, *The Hebrew Folktale: History, Genre, Meaning*, trans. Jacqueline S. Teitelbaum (Bloomington: Indiana University Press, 1999), 245–370.

33. For the first composition, as called by its Hebrew title, *Hibur Yafeh Me-Ha-Yeshu'a*, see the English translation, Nissim ben Jacob Ibn Shāhīn, *An Elegant Composition Concerning Relief After Adversity*, , translated from the Arabic with introduction and notes by William M. Brinner (New Haven: Yale University Press, 1977). For the *Midrash on the Ten Commandments*, see now the critical edition Anat Shapira, ed., *Midrash Aseret Ha-Dibrot (A Midrash on the Ten Commandments): Texts, Sources, and Interpretation* [in Hebrew] (Jerusalem: Mosad Bialik, 2005). The other Geonic-period work that is usually mentioned with these two collections of stories is the *Alphabet of Ben Sira*, about which, see chapter 2 in this volume.

34. Shapira, *Midrash Aseret Ha-Dibrot*, 182–86.

35. Eli Yassif, "Hebrew Prose in the East: Its Formation in the Middle Ages and Transition to Modern Times" [in Hebrew], *Pe'amim* 26 (1986): 53–70; cf. the methodological reservations raised by Galit Hasan-Rokem in her response immediately following Yassif's article, 71–74. See also Joseph Dan, *The Hebrew Story in the Middle Ages* [in Hebrew] (Jerusalem: Keter, 1974), 13–32.

36. See Shapira, *Midrash Aseret Ha-Dibrot*, 159–86 and 193–245; M. B. Lerner, "On the Midrashim to the Ten Commandments" [in Hebrew], in *Meḥkerei Talmud (Talmudic Studies Dedicated to the Memory of Professor Ephraim E. Urbach)*, ed. Yaakov Sussman and David Rosenthal (Jerusalem: Magnes, 1990), 1:217–36, and Lerner, "Fragmentary *Maʿasiyot*: A Reconstruction of a Fragmentary Story in a Geniza Remnant from the Midrash Aseret Ha-Devarim and Its Earliest Version in the Bavli," in *Higayon L'Yona: New Aspects in the Study of Midrash, Aggadah, and Piyut*, ed. Joshua Levinson, Jacob Elbaum, and Galit Hasan-Rokem (Jerusalem: Magnes, 2006), 377–402. I have borrowed the term "open work" from Israel M. Ta-Shma, "The 'Open' Book in Medieval Hebrew Literature: The Problem of Authorized Editions," in *Bulletin of the John Rylands University Library of Manchester* 75 (1993): 17–24.

37. For cross-cultural parallels and its collorary, Judaization, see Yassif, *Hebrew Folktale*, 265–82.

38. The translation is based on the text of Paris, Bibliotheque nationale de France MS Heb. 716, transcribed in Shapira, *Midrash Aseret Ha-Dibrot*, 47–48. In the Verona 1647 edition the last line reads: "Therefore do not trust in any mortal being, but rather in the Holy One, blessed be He. For He, this kingly God, is a physician who heals for free!" Could this be a jibe at high-charging Italian Jewish physicians?

39. For a general introduction to Jewish demonology, see Trachtenberg, *Jewish Magic*, 25–54; Bohak, *Ancient Jewish Magic*, 480, s.v. demons, and Dan Ben-Amos, "On Demons," in *Creation and Re-Creation in Jewish Thought: Festschrift in Honor of Joseph Dan on the Occasion of His Seventieth Birthday*, ed. Rachel Elior and Peter Schäfer (Tübingin: Mohr Siebeck, 2005), 27–37. On the magic bowls, see Joseph Naveh and Shaul Shaked., *Amulets and Magic Bowls: Aramaic Incantations of Late Antiquity*, 2nd ed. (Jerusalem: Magnes, 1987).

40. As Michal Bar-Asher has pointed out to me, this story is especially remarkable because it illustrates knowledge of incubation practice in contemporaneous Greco-Roman temples (like those of Asclepius). The irony behind the story is that it does not deny the efficacy of the pagan practice; Jews simply are not allowed to use it. Compare the story in *t. Ḥullin* 2:22–23.

41. The most vocal and explicit proponent of this view is Joseph Dan; see *Hebrew Story*, 19–20. See also Yassif, "Hebrew Prose in the East," 54–55, who proposes a modified version of Dan's stance, characterizing works like the *Midrash on the Ten Commandments* as "transitional."

42. For the text and its background, see Jehuda L. Zlotnick, ed., *Maʿase Yerushalmi (The Story of the Jerusalemite), Attributed to R. Abraham b. Maimon*, with a bibliography and an Arabic version by Nehemia Allony, and a preface by Raphael Patai (Jerusalem: Palestine Institute of Folklore and Ethnology, 1946). Zlotnick's edition contains two synoptic versions of the story, the *editio princeps* as it appeared in *Sefer Divrei Yamim she Moshe*, Constantinople 1517/18 (?), and that found in an undated Yemenite manuscript owned by Zlotnick. The latter text was translated by David Stern and Avi Weinstein as "The Story of the Jerusalemite," in *Rabbinic Fantasies: Imaginative Narratives from Classical Hebrew Literature*, ed. David Stern and Mark J. Mirsky (1990; repr., New Haven: Yale University Press, 1998), 143–66. In its various manuscripts and printed editions, the work has different titles: Zlotnick's Yemenite manuscript and other manuscript have *Maʿase Yerushalmi*; both the Constantinople 1517/18 and Venice 1544 editions call it *Maʿaseh shel Yerushalmi*. See Zlotnick, *Maʿase Yerushalmi*, 17–19, and Nehemia Allony's bibliography in that volume, 92–96. Zlotnick's edition of the text was also republished in Hayyim Pesach and Eli Yassif, eds., *The Knight, the Demon, and the Virgin: An Anthology of Hebrew Stories from the Middle Ages* [in Hebrew] (Jerusalem: Keter, 1998), 155–73, under the title *Maʿaseh bi-Rushalmi*; on what basis, I have not been able to discover. The precise significance of the attribution to Abraham b. Maimon is unclear; he definitely did not compose it, but see Zlotnick's introduction (17–18), where he suggests that Abraham may have retranslated the story either from Arabic or Aramaic back into Hebrew.

43. Thus Zlotnick, *Ma'ase Yerushalmi*, 37, who dates it sometime between the Arab conquest of the Middle East in the mid-seventh century and the time of Sherira Gaon (d. 1006). In both "Five Versions of the Story of the Jerusalemite," *PAAJR* 35 (1967): 99–111, and in *Hebrew Story*, 96, Joseph Dan argues on the basis of other stories about sexual relations between human males and demonesses (succubi) (recorded in *Sefer Ḥasidim* and in the *Dialogue of Miracles* by the thirteenth-century German preacher Caesarius of Heisterbach) that the story originated in Christian Europe, probably in the early thirteenth century, but other than the fact that all the stories share the motif of demon-human sexual relations, the other parallels he draws between the stories are not convincing. The controversy of dating the story to the Islamic realm in the Geonic period partly revolves around an episode at the end of *Ma'aseh Yerushalmi*, where Ashmadai's daughter stops prayers in the synagogue in order to demand that her recalcitrant husband be put on trial to force him to return to her and its relation to *'ikuv tefillah*, the practice of a plaintiff stopping prayer in the synagogue in order to demand that a recalcitrant offender be brought to justice. Zlotnick and other scholars have debated whether or not *'ikuv tefillah* was considered permissible and practiced in Geonic Babylonia. Zlotnick (36–37) claims that it was a living custom in Babylonia; Simḥah Assaf, in an appendix to Zlotnick's edition (105–6, and in other works noted in his bibliography), argues that it was not. On the practice in Ashkenaz (and implicitly supporting Assaf's position), see the classic study of Abraham Grossman, "The Origins and Essence of the Customs of 'Stopping-the-Service'" [in Hebrew], in *Milet* 1 (1983): 199–219. More recently, however, Menahem Ben-Sasson, in "Public Outcrying in the Synagogue in Islamic Lands in the Early Middle Ages" [in Hebrew], in *Knesset Ezra: Literature and Life in the Synagogue: Studies Presented to Ezra Fleischer*, ed. Shlomit Elitzur, Moshe-David Herr, Gershon Shaked, and Avigdor Shinan (Jerusalem: Magnes, 1994), 327–50, has shown that publically crying out in the synagogue, if not actually to her and its relation to *'ikuv tefillah* (which involved the threat of stopping synagogue services entirely until the plaintiff's demands were met), was widely practiced throughout the Islamic realm in the early and later Middle Ages.

44. Zlotnick, *Ma'ase Yerushalmi*, 19–20.

45. For other *ma'asim* that begin with a deathbed scene, see those in Shapira, *Midrash Aseret Ha-Dibrot*, 54 and 64; see also Yassif, "Hebrew Prose in the East," 59–60.

46. This name appears only once in the story near its conclusion (Zlotnick, *Ma'ase Yerushalmi*, 65), and scholars have debated its significance inconclusively. M. Grunwald, in a note in Zlotnick (104), suggests (among various possibilities) that the word might be derived from the Arabic *dihkhan*, "a man from a city," perhaps a reference to Jerusalem. The name Salmon is mentioned in Ruth 4:21 as the father of Boaz, but it might also be understood as cognate to Solomon, the name Dihon gives to his son by Ashmadai's daughter, who would then be named after his grandfather.

47. Why they choose this name is unclear. Perhaps it is simply the Hebrew equivalent of Salmon, Dihon's late father, whom the child may have been named after.

48. Technically speaking, the child is half human and half demon, but according to S. Buber, ed., *Tanhuma* (1885; repr., Jerusalem: Ortsel, 1963–64), *Bereishit* 17, p. 12, a child born from a union between a human and a *sheidah* is a full-fledged *sheid*.

49. For another early reference, see ibid. For general discussion, see Trachtenberg, *Jewish Magic*, 51–56. Moses Gaster, in "An Ancient Fairy-Tale Translated from the Hebrew," *Folklore* 42 (1931): 156–78, claimed that the story was the oldest known fairy-tale, but that claim has by now been widely refuted. For an overview of the genre, see Margaretha Folmer, "On Marrying and Divorcing a Demon: Marriage and Divorce Themes in the Jewish, Christian, and Pagan World," in *Religious Stories in Transformation: Conflict, Revision and Reception*, ed. Alberdina Houtman, Tamar Kadari, Marcel Poorthuis, and Vered Tohar (Leiden: Brill, 2016), 275–99.

50. On the latter, see Sara Zfatman, *The Marriage of a Mortal Man and a She-Demon* [in Hebrew] (Jerusalem: Akademon, 1987), and Jeremy Dauber, *In the Demon's Bedroom: Yiddish Literature and the Early Modern* (New Haven: Yale, 2010), 140–71.

51. On these motifs, see Zlotnick, *Ma'ase Yerushalmi*, 34–42, and his references to Stith Thompson, *Motif Index of Folk-Literature*, for which, see now the revised and enlarged electronic edition (Bloomington: Indiana University Press, 1993).

52. Curiously, according to the Bar-Ilan Responsa Project database, all fifty-four occurences of the term *ben torah* (in the singular) derive from Palestinian literature, either midrashic documents (mainly Amoraic, although there is a single, somewhat doubtful reference in *Sifrei Zuta* as preserved in *Midrash Ha-Gadol*) or the Yerushalmi. The Babylonian Talmud only attests the plural form *bnei torah*, and it appears there usually in descriptive statements. In the Palestinian sources, it is used more in the sense of a vocative.

53. See my article, "Agnon from a Medieval Perspective," in *History and Literature: New Readings of Jewish Texts in Honor of Arnold Band*, ed. William Cutter and David C. Jacobson (Providence: Brown Judaic Studies, 2002), 171–85. A revised version of the essay will appear in *Jewish Literature Cultures*, vol. 3: *The Modern and Contemporary Periods*.

54. On the following passages, see Zlotnick, *Ma'ase Yerushalmi*, 27–30; see also Gershom Scholem, "New Chapters in Regard to Ashmedai and Lilith" [in Hebrew], *Tarbiz* 19 (1948): 160–75.

55. Zlotnick, *Ma'ase Yerushalmi*, 28; Trachtenberg, *Jewish Magic*,
For the sources, see Zlotnick, *Ma'ase Yerushalmi*, 28; see also Scholem, "New Chapters," 160–65.

56. Dauber, *In the Demon's Bedroom*, 141.

57. It is worth noting as well that, in both episodes, one of the protagonists—the Rabbi in the first case, Ashmadai's daughter in the second—employ the same strategy of interrupting the prayers after the completion of *pesukei de-zimrah*; see my comments on the practice of "outcrying" in note 43 above.

CHAPTER 2

1. Israel Davidson, "Parody in Jewish Literature" (Ph.D. dissertation, Columbia University, 1907). Davison's treatment began only with the twelfth century, when, he claimed, "we first meet with parody in Jewish literature" (3).

2. In 2004, when this chapter first appeared as an article, RAMBI, the database for scholarly publications in Jewish Studies, listed a grand total of twenty-four publications for "parody." Of these, eight were in Bible (e.g., Jonah, Song of Songs); another eight in twentieth-century Jewish letters, mainly the usual suspects (e.g., Freud, Malamud, Agnon); and the remainder a hodgepodge of different topics. Only one publication was explicitly on a medieval Hebrew text, and none were in postbiblical or rabbinic Hebrew writing. As of this writing (November 15, 2015), Rambi lists fifty-three works (and, as this writer knows, does not list every article that has appeared). For some recent examples, specifically in regard to rabbinic literature, see Eliezer Diamond, "But Is It Funny? Identifying Humor, Satire, and Parody in Rabbinic Literature," in *Jews and Humor*, ed. Leonard J. Greenspoon (West Lafayette: Purdue University Press, 2007), 33–53; Daniel Stökl Ben-Ezra, "Parody and Polemics on Pentecost: Talmud Yerushalmi Pesaḥim on Acts 27," in *Jewish and Christian Liturgy and Worship*, ed. Albert Gerhards and Clemens Leonhard (Leiden: Brill, 2007), 297–311; Shlomo Naeh and Moshe Halbertal, "The Wells of Salvation: An Exegetical Satire and Polemic Against the Heretics" [in Hebrew], in *Higayon L'Yona: New Aspects in the Study of Midrash, Aggadah, and Piyut, In Honor of Professor Yona Fraenkel*, ed. Joshua Levinson, Jacob Elbaum, and Galit Hasan-Rokem (Jerusalem: Magnes, 2007), 192–97; and Aaron Amit, "A Rabbinic Satire on the Last Judgment,"

Journal of Biblical Literature 129 (2010): 679–97. Daniel Boyarin has used the term "Menippean Satire" in several articles and throughout his recent book, *Socrates and the Fat Rabbis* (Chicago: University of Chicago Press, 2009). For an example of the problems in distinguishing parody from satire or humor more generally, see *Vayikra Rabbah* 12, an entire chapter devoted almost exclusively to the prohibition addressed to priests in Lev 10:9, "Drink no wine or other intoxicants [. . . when you enter the Tent of Meeting]." As any reader of the chapter recognizes, the midrash tends to lurch, somewhat like the drunk father in 12:1, back and forth between praise and blame of wine (and drinking), without being able to make up its mind whether it is good or bad. In the final passage, the midrash cites the aggadot about Solomon who, it claims, never drank wine all seven years he was building the Temple until the night he completed the building, when he married the daughter of Pharoah, overdrank, and then overslept, with the keys of the Temple under his pillow, thereby making it impossible for the Temple service to begin until his mother, Bathsheba, came into his bedroom and harangued him for oversleeping! Is this parodic or merely satirical? As a further example of a possibly parodic passage, my colleague Yaakov Elbaum has called my attention to *Midrash Tehillim* 1:15, with Korah's complaint against Moses and Aaron. One should also mention here the examples cited by Saul Lieberman in *Midreshei Teiman*, 2nd ed. (Jerusalem: Wahrmann Books, 1970), 26–32, that I discuss at length later in this essay.

    3. See especially Holger M. Zellentin, *Rabbinic Parodies of Jewish and Christian Literature* (Tübingen: Mohr Siebeck, 2011), and Peter Schäfer, *Jesus in the Talmud* (Princeton: Princeton University Press, 2007). The literature on *Toledot Yeshu* is now enormous; most recently, see *Toledot Yeshu ("The Life Story of Jesus") Revisited: A Princeton Conference*, ed. Peter Schäfer, Michael Meerson, and Yaakov Deutsch (Tübingen: Mohr-Siebeck, 2011).

    4. M. H. Abrams, *A Glossary of Literary Terms*, 5th ed. (New York: Holt, Rhinehart, and Winston, 1988), 18. Clearly, the definition of literary terms is hardly absolute, and their use is essentially heuristic. It is, however, helpful to have a working definition, if only to differentiate the subject of this paper—what I call "literary parody"—from merely humorous or satirical works. Abrams's definition of literary parody is largely identical with "burlesque," which he defines "as 'an incongruous imitation'; that is, it imitates the matter or manner of a serious literary work or of a literary genre, but makes the imitation amusing by a ridiculous disparity between its form and style and its subject matter. The burlesque may be written for the sheer fun of it; usually, however, it is a form of *satire*. The butt of the satiric ridicule may be the particular work or general type that is being imitated, or (often) both of these together." (17). Other terms associated with both parody and burlesque are "lampoon," "travesty," "mock-epic," or "mock-heroic." As we shall see, most of these terms could be applied with justice to the *Alphabet of Ben Sira*.

    5. For parody in the Bible, see G. A. Yee, "The Anatomy of Biblical Parody: the Dirge Form in 2 Samuel 1 and Isaaiah 14," *Catholic Biblical Quarterly* 50 (1988): 565–86; Athalya Brenner, "'Come Back, Come Back, the Shulammite' (Song 7:1–10): A Parody of the 'Wasf' Genre," in *On Humour and the Comic in the Hebrew Bible*, ed. Yehuda T. Radday and Athalya Brenner (Sheffield: Sheffield Academic Press, 1990), 251–75. Judges 5:28–30, from Deborah's victory song, is sometimes cited as well as parody of the lament form.

    6. On parody in rabbinic literature, see Davidson's comments in "Parody in Jewish Literature," 1–2. For a good example of the problems in identifying whether or not a passage is parodic, see *Vayikra Rabbah* 12, an entire chapter devoted almost exclusively to the prohibition addressed to priests in Lev 10:9, "Drink no wine or other intoxicants [. . . when you enter the Tent of Meeting]"; as any reader of the chapter recognizes, the midrash tends to lurch, somewhat like the drunk father in 12:1, back and forth between praise and blame of wine (and drinking), without being able to make up its mind whether it is good or bad. In the final passage, the midrash cites the aggadot about Solomon, who, it claims, never drank wine all

seven years he was building the Temple until the night he completed the building when he married the daughter of Pharoah, overdrank, and then overslept, with the keys of the Temple under his pillow, thereby making it impossible for the Temple service to begin until his mother, Bathsheba, came into his bedroom and harangued him for oversleeping! As a further example of a possibly parodic passage, my colleague Yaakov Elbaum has called to my attention *Midrash Tehillim* 1:15, with Korah's complaint against Moses and Aaron. One should also mention here the examples cited by Lieberman in *Midreshei Teiman*, 26–32, which I discuss at length later in this essay.

7. M. M. Bakhtin, *The Dialogic Imagination*, ed. by Michael Holquist, trans. by Caryl Emerson and Michael Holquist (Austin: University of Texas Press, 1981), 374.

8. For the text of S. Buber, ed., *Midrash Abba Guryon*, see *Sifrei De-aggadeta ʿal Megillat Esther* (1886; repr., Jerusalem: Vagshall, 1989), 1–57, and Buber's brief introductory notes. For parodic sections, see the beginning of chapters 1 and 5. See also Z. M. Rabinovitz, *Ginze Midrash* (Tel Aviv: Tel Aviv University, 1976), 161–71, and Rabinovitz's comments ad locum. Interestingly, the manuscript he publishes there is written in a tenth-century Oriental (Babylonian or Iraqi) script, a fact that at least shows that such parodic texts circulated in those general environs.

9. Yosef Yahalom and Michael Sokoloff, *Shirat Bnei Maʿarava* (Jerusalem: Israel Academy of Sciences, 1999), poem 32, 196–201.

10. Giulio Bartolocci, *Bibliotheca Magna Rabbinica* (Rome: Sacrae Congregationis de Propaganda Fide, 1675–94), 1:683–89; cited in Eli Yassif, *Sipurei Ben Sira bi-Yemei Ha-Beinayim* (Jerusalem: Magnes, 1984), 130 n. 3.

11. J. Reifmann, *Ha-Karmel* (Vilna, 1873), 2:124–38.

12. Yassif, *Sipurei Ben Sira*.

13. Ibid., 19–29.

14. On Ben Sira, see M. Z. Segal, ed., *Sefer Ben Sira Ha-Shalem* (Jerusalem: Mossad Bialik, 53).

15. See Yassif, *Sipurei Ben Sira*, 7–12. So far as I understand Yassif, the question nonetheless remains whether the two versions are actually different texts or recensions. Yassif notes that Version A is preserved in Ashkenazic manuscripts of a northern French provenance; Version B is preserved in manuscripts written in Italian hands (and of a somewhat later date than the French Ashkenazic manuscripts). Nonetheless, Yassif believes that Version B (Italy) is probably closer to what the "original" text of the *Alphabet* looked like—if there ever was an "original" text.

16. I have also utilized the English translation by Norman Bronznick that Mark Jay Mirsky and I revised and published in *Rabbinic Fantasies* (1990; repr., New Haven, Yale University Press, 1998), 169–202, which was done (alas) before Yassif's edition was available.

17. Hebrew: *ʿarez myduhey*, which is *zeraʿ yehudim*, "Jewish seed," spelled backward. See Shraga Abramson, "Wisdom Says, People Say" (Hebrew), in *Minhah Le-Yehudah: Presented to Rabbi Y. L. Zlotnick* (Jerusalem: n.p., 1950), 28–29, cited in Yassif, *Sipurei Ben Sira*, 198 n. 6.

18. The text here seems to be corrupt. Version A reads, "Jeremiah began to reprove them until they stopped him and said, Why are you reproving us? You will not leave until you act like us."

19. It is unclear whether, in the *Alphabet*'s narrative, the "I" in the Jeremiah verse refers to Jeremiah or to Ben Sira; see the use of the verse in *Pesikta Rabbati*, to be discussed shortly in this chapter.

20. Yassif, *Sipurei Ben Sira*, 32.

21. Reifmann, *Ha-Karmel*, 2:133. See also A. Epstein, *Mi-Kadmoniyot Ha-Yehudim* (Vienna: n.p., 1887), 120.

22. Israel Levi, "La nativité de Ben Sira," *Revue des etudes Juives* 23 (1891): 197–205; Tal Ilan and Reuven Kiperwasser, "Virginity and Water: Between the Babylonian Talmud and Iranian Myth," in *A Thousand Judgements: Festschrift for Maria Macuch*, ed. Almut Hintze, Desmond Durkin-Meisterernst, and Claudius Naumann (Wiesbaden: Harrassowitz, 2019), 193–208; and James R. Russell, "The Nativity of Ben Sira Reconsidered," in *"Suddenly, Christ": Studies in Jewish and Christian Traditions in Honor of Alexander Golitzin*, ed. Andrei Orlov, Vigiliae Christianae Supplements (Leiden: Brill, forthcoming). I wish to thank my colleague James Russell for sharing his article with me.

23. Adolph Jellinek, *Beit Ha-Midrash* (1873; repr., Jerusalem:Wahrmann Books, 1967), 2.6:xi–xiii.

24. Yosef Dan, *Ha-Sippur Ha-ʿIvri bi-Yemei Ha-Beinayim* (Jerusalem: Keter, 1974), 74–76.

25. Yassif, *Sipurei Ben Sira*, 38–39.

26. Wayne Booth, *A Rhetoric of Irony* (Chicago: University of Chicago Press, 1974), 72.

27. For rabbinic parallels, see Yassif's notes in *Sipurei Ben Sira*, 197–98.

28. Rivka Ulmer, *Pesiqta Rabbati* (Atlanta: Scholars Press, 1997), 1:xiii. See also H. L. Strack and Guenter Stemberger, *Introduction to the Talmud and Midrash*, trans. Markus Bockmuehl, 2nd printing (Minneapolis: Fortress, 1996), 299–302. Chapter 26 is considered by some scholars to have originally been a separate work, but the specific questions of dating, etc. do not affect our argument here. Unfortunately, the second volume of Ulmer's critical edition containing chapter 26 has not yet appeared. My translation and references are all based on the edition of M. Friedmann [Meir Ish-Shalom], *Midrash Pesikta Rabbati* (1880; repr., Tel Aviv: n.p., 1963), 129b–30a. I have also consulted the translation of William G. Braude, *Pesikta Rabbati: Discourses for Feasts, Fasts, and Special Sabbaths* (New Haven: Yale University Press, 1968), 525–27. The passage is also cited in slightly different form in *Yalkut Shimeoni*, Jeremiah, para. 262—indicating, if nothing else, that the passage enjoyed wide circulation.

29. Yassif, *Sipurei Ben Sira*, 33–34.

30. Ibid., 37–38.

31. It is forbidden to mutilate any animal in such a way that the mutilation would made the animal unfit to be sacrificed in the Temple. A dog, however, cannot be sacrificed under any circumstance, nor can it be exchanged for a sacrifice. The question therefore arises whether or not the general prohibition against mutilation attaches to a dog; canine-lovers will be relieved to know that the Talmud decides that, regardless of a dog's sacrificial status, it is forbidden to castrate it.

32. To be sure, its improbability has not deterred halakhists from taking the story very seriously. See the *Taz* ad *Shulkhan Arukh, Yoreah Deʿah* 195:7, which cites our story in the *Alphabet of Ben Sira* as a putative authority for the halakhic permissibility of artificially inseminating a woman with her father's semen.

33. See Judah Goldin, "Several Sidelights of a Torah Education in Tannaite and Early Amoraic Times," in *Ex Orbe Religionum: Studia Geo Widengren Oblata* (Leiden: Brill, 1972), 176–91, esp. 184 on students learning aphorisms and on learning how to finish a verse that someone else has begun. For Greco-Roman parallels, see Stanley F. Bonner, *Education in Ancient Rome: From the Elder Cato to the Young Pliny* (Berkeley: University of California Press, 1977), 172–73, on the use of *sententiae* and *gnomai*—moral maxims, usually in short sentences—as the subject matter for learning to read and write. On 173–74, Bonner discusses the Bouriant papyrus of Menander, which has an entire series of such lines written out in alphabetical order according to the initial letter in the line. Yassif, *Sipurei Ben Sira*, 22–23, also cites the story about the king and his wife whom he orders to be executed from the Arabic collection *Kalilah and Dimnah*, chapter 11, as a source for the use of a similar structure in a tale; in the *Kalilah and Dimnah* tale, the king's counselor makes the king remember his love for his wife

by citing alphabetic maxims to him. The English translation of *Kalilah and Dimnah* that I consulted (T. B. Irving, trans., *Kalilah and Dimnah* [Newark, Del., Juan de la Cuesta, 1980) retells the story in chapter 7.B (133–47), but the translation does not follow an alphabetic series.

34. Steven M. Wasserstrom, *Between Muslim and Jew: The Problem of Symbiosis Under Early Islam* (Princeton: Princeton University Press, 1995), 167–69.

35. Lieberman, *Midreshei Teiman*, 26–31.

36. *Pirkei Derekh Eretz* 1 (= *Seder Eliyahu Zuta* 16), in Meir Ish-Shalom (M. Friedmann), ed., *Nispahim Le-Seder Eliyahu Zuta* (Vienna: Achiasaf, 1902), 5 and n. 21, reprinted in M. Ish-Shalom, ed., *Seder Eliyahu Rabbah VeSeder Eliyahu Zuta (Tanna DeBei Eliyahu)*, 3rd printing (Jerusalem: Wahrmann Books, 1969). Also cited and discussed in Lieberman, *Midreshei Teiman*, 28.

37. Ignaz Goldziher, "Education (Muslim)," in *Encyclopaedia of Religion and Ethics*, ed. James Hastings (New York: Charles Scribner's Sons, 1925), 5:201–2; the epigram quoted is on 201. See also Ulrich Marzolph, "The Qoran and Jocular Literature," *Arabica* 47 (2000): 478–87, and Franz Rosenthal, *Humor in Early Islam* (Philadelphia: University of Pennsylvania Press, 1956). I wish to thank my colleagues Everett Rowson, Roger Allen, and David Hollenberg for referring me to these sources and for enlightening me in general about the tradition of Majun (profligacy, libertinism) with its profane, quasi-blasphemous parodies of *hadith*.

38. Yassif, *Sipurei Ben Sira*, 39–44.

39. There are two exceptions to this rule: first, the maxim for the letter *daled* is not in the *Sanhedrin* passage (although the maxim's misogynistic idea certainly is), and second, the maxim for the letter *zayin*, which uses part of the verse cited by the Talmud's editor as a reason not to read Ben Sira ("A thin-bearded man is very wise; a thick-bearded one is a fool"), modifies the talmudic version so as to make it less offensive; according to Yassif (ibid., 43), these changes were made deliberately by the author of the *Alphabet* so as not to violate the apparent talmudic consensus that these verses are unworthy of being read.

40. Segal, *Sefer Ben Sira Ha-Shalem*, 44.

41. For discussion and other sources, see ibid., 36–46, and Sid. Z. Leiman, *The Canonization of Hebrew Scripture: The Talmudic and Midrashic Evidence* (Hamden, Conn: Archon, 1976), 92–101. While the question of the rabbis' attitude toward the book lies beyond the scope of this project, it should be noted that Akiba's phrase *ha-korei bi-sfarim ha-hitzoniyim* probably refers not to the mere "reading" of these books but to their "liturgical recitation" in the synagogue service in the same manner as the Pentateuch or other books of the Hebrew Bible were liturgically recited. On this, see Menachem Haran, *Ha-Asuppah Ha-Mikrait* (Jerusalem: Mosad Bialik and Magnes, 1996), 124–36.

42. Lieberman, *Midreshei Teiman*, 30–31.

43. See Ish-Shalom, *Seder Eliyahu Rabbah*, 5 n. 21, in which he collects numerous statements from rabbinic literature that both praise and condemn schoolteachers.

44. I want to thank Barry Scott Wimpfheimer for bringing this passage to my attention; see his analysis in *Narrating the Law: A Poetics of Talmudic Legal Stories* (Philadelphia: University of Pennsylvania Press, 2011), 97–105.

45. See ibid., 101 and n. 31. Wimpfheimer has informed me that this is the correct reading in all manuscripts (with the exception of Florence II 1 8) as well as the editio princeps; only the Vilna edition has *akpeid*.

46. Given the scope of the scholarship, it is impossible to give adequate bibliographical references here. The names most frequently associated with our new appreciation of the anonymous editors of the Talmud are David Weiss-Halivni and Shamma Friedman. For the Stammaim as storytellers, see Jeffrey L. Rubenstein's recent work, *Talmudic Stories: Narrative Art, Composition, and Culture* (Baltimore: Johns Hopkins University Press, 1999) and his bibliography there. For the best overview of Weiss-Halivni's approach, see Jeffrey Rubenstein's

"Translator's Introduction," in David Weiss-Halivni, *The Formation of the Babylonian Talmud*, introduced, translated, and annotated by Jeffrey L. Rubenstein (New York: Oxford University Press, 2013), xvii–xxxv.

47. For the best overview of the many developments in the field, see Robert Brody, *The Geonim of Babylonia and the Shaping of Medieval Jewish Culture* (New Haven: Yale University Press, 1998).

48. ibid., 334.

49. On piyyut in the Geonic period, see ibid., 323–32; Ezra Fleischer, *Shirat Ha-Kodesh Ha-ʿIvrit bi-Yemei Ha-Beinayim* (Jerusalem: Keter, 1975), 289–329.

50. Rabbi Moshe ben Maimon (Rambam), "Shemoneh Perakim- Hakdamah Lemasekhet Avot," chapter 5, in Rabbeinu Mosheh ben Maimon, *Ha-Kedamot le-Feirush Ha-Mishnah*, ed. M. D. Rabinovits (Jerusalem: Mosad Harav Kuk, 1961), 189. I want to thank Yaakov Elbaum for referring me to this passage; on its background and later literary echoes, see Elbaum, *Le-Havin Divrei Ḥakhamim* (Jerusalem: Mosad Bialik, 2000), 84 n. 28. The phrase *milei de-bedihuta* is found twice in the Babylonian Talmud, in a story about the sage Raba who would preface his lessons with such "words of amusement" (*b. Shabbat* 30b; *b. Pesahim* 117a), but Maimonides's statement about rabbinic entertainment is unattested elsewhere.

CHAPTER 3

Full-color versions of all the images in this chapter can be seen in the original version published in the *Jewish Studies Internet Journal* 11 (2012): 235–322 or at http://www.biu.ac.il/JS/JSIJ/11-2012/Stern.pdf.

1. Michele Dukan, *La Bible hébraïque: Les Codices copiés en Orient et dans le zone Sepharade avant 1280* (*Bibliologia* 22) (Turnhout: Brepols, 2006), 10.

2. The geographical regions cited are based upon Malachi Beit-Arié's well-known typology of Hebrew codicological traits; see Beit-Arié, *Hebrew Manuscripts of East and West: Towards a Comparative Codicology* (London: The British Library, 1992), 25–78. For a fuller exposition, see now Beit-Arié's new edition of *Hebrew Codicology*, found on the web at: http://web.nli.org.il/sites/NLI/Hebrew/collections/manuscripts/hebrewcodicology/Documents/HebrewCodicologycontinuouslyupdatedonlineversion.pdf, 61–66.

3. For Parma Palatina, see B. Richler, ed., with codicological description by Malachi Beit-Arié, *Hebrew Manuscripts in the Bibliotheca Palatina in Parma: Catalogue* (Jerusalem: Jewish National and University Library, 2001). For the British Library, see George Margoliouth, *Catalogue of the Hebrew and Samaritan Manuscripts in the British Museum*, 4 vols. (1899–1935; repr., London: British Museum, 1965); Ilana Tahan, *Hebrew Manuscripts: The Power of Script and Image* (London: The British Library, 2007); and John Reeve, ed., *Sacred: Books of the Three Faiths: Judaism, Christianity, Islam* (London: The British Library, 2007). For the Bodleian, see Adolph Neubauer, *Catalogue of the Hebrew Manuscripts in the Bodleian Library* (Oxford: Clarendon, 1886), 1:3–24, 808–13, and Malachi Beit-Arié, comp., and R. A. May, ed., *Catalogue of the Hebrew Manusripts in the Bodleian Library: Supplement of Addenda and Corrigenda to Vol. 1 (A. Neubauer's Catalogue)* (Oxford: Clarendon Press, 1994), 3–18, 452–56. For Spanish and Portuguese biblical manuscripts in Britain generally, see Bezalel Narkiss, *Hebrew Illuminated Manuscripts in the British Isles*, vol. 1: *The Spanish and Portuguese Manuscripts*, 2 parts (Jerusalem: The Israel Academy of Sciences and Humanities; London: The British Academy, 1982). For the Vatican, see B. Richler, ed., *Hebrew Manuscripts in the Vatican Library: Catalogue*, with palaeographical and codicological description by Malachi Beit-Arié in collaboration with Nurit Pasternak (Vatican City: Biblioteca Apostolica Vaticana, 2008); Philip Hiat, ed., *A Visual Testimony: Judaica from the Vatican Library* (Miami: Center for the Fine Arts and the Union of American Hebrew Congregations, 1987); and *Rome to Jerusalem: Four Jewish Masterpieces*

from the Vatican Library (Jerusalem: The Israel Museum, 2005). For the Jewish Theological Seminary of America, see the Lutzki Catalogue, Library of the Jewish Theological Seminary of America. For the Madrid and other Spanish books, see Francisco Javier del Barco del Barco, ed., *Catálogo de Manuscritos Hebreos de la Comunidad de Madrid*, 3 vols. (Madrid: Consejo Superior de Investigaciones Científicas Instituto de Filología, 2003–6). For the former Sassoon Collection, see David Solomon Sassoon, comp., *Ohel Dawid: Descriptive Catalogue of the Hebrew and Samaritan Manuscripts in the Sassoon Library, London* (London: Humphrey Milford and Oxford University Press, 1932), 1:1–37, 604–16, 1091–112. For the Ambrosiana, see Carlo Bernheimer, *Codices Hebraici Bibliothecae Ambrosianae* (Florence: S. Olschki, 1933); Aldo Luzzatto, *Hebraica Ambrosiana*, vol. 1: *Catalogue of Undescribed Hebrew Manuscripts in the Ambrosiana Library* (Milan: Edizioni il Polifilio, 1972); Luisa Mortara Ottolenghi, *Hebraica Ambrosiana*, vol. 2: *Description of Decorated and Illuminated Hebrew Manuscripts in the Ambrosiana Library* (Milan: Edizioni il Polifilio, 1972). For illustrated biblical manuscripts in France, see H. Zotenberg, *Catalogues des Manuscrits Hébreux et Samaritains de la Bibliothèque Impériale* (Paris: Imprimerie Impériale, 1866); Michel Garel, *D'une Main Forte: Manuscrits Hébreux des Collections Francaises* (Paris: Bibliotheque Nationale, 1991); and Gabrielle Sed-Rajna, *Les Manuscrits Hébreux Enluminés des Bibliothèques de France* (Leuven-Paris: Peeters, 1994).

4. This chapter is, in a very real sense, a victim of technological change. Since I first wrote it as an article, the number of manuscripts available digitally has grown exponentially; if I were to write the chapter today, I would do it entirely differently and be able to consult on the screen manuscripts I could only read about three years ago. Even so, I hope my major conclusions and arguments are still relevant.

5. To some extent, my typology was anticipated by that undertaken by Moshe Goshen-Gottstein, "The Rise of the Tiberian Bible Text," in *Biblical and Other Studies*, ed. A. Altmann (Cambridge: Harvard University Press, 1963), 35–44, who proposed three categories for Genizah fragments he studied in American collections—(1) "Massora [*sic*] Codices," by which he meant deluxe copies on parchment for "professional" usage, either copying or checking other Bible manuscripts; (2) "Study Codices," by which he referred to Bible manuscripts *without* Masorah that were "used for learning and study-purposes in general" and not prepared by professional scribes; (3) "Listener's Codices," by which he meant even less carefully produced manuscripts written "wholesale" by scribes for persons who wished to follow the Torah reading in the synagogue in their own copies. As this brief description suggests, Goshen-Gottstein's typology was based largely on the quality of the manuscript and less on their contents or structure.

6. For a large variety of such codices, see Margoliouth, *Catalogue of the Hebrew and Samaritan Manuscripts*, 1:82–118; Adolph Neubauer, "The Early Settlement of the Jews in Southern Italy," *Jewish Quarterly Review*, o.s., 4 (1892): 11–16.

7. For a helpful survey of the variations and for recent scholarship on the topic, see Michael Berenbaum and Fred Skolnik, ed., *Encyclopaedia Judaica*, 2nd ed. (Detroit: MacMillan Reference, 2007), 3:580–83.

8. See, however, the 1489 Ashkenazic "Tikkun Kor'im" Manuscript sold at the Sotheby's auction of Property from the Delmonico Collection of Important Judaica in New York City on December 17, 2008, lot 202; the lot is described in full in the auction catalogue. I wish to thank Dr. Emile Schrijver for calling my attention to this unusual codex that directly anticipates the modern *tikkun*.

9. For examples of model books, see Bodl. MS Opp. 186 (Neubauer, *Catalogue*, no. 37), a Pentateuch with Esther Scroll, Ashkenaz, ca. 1400; MS Parma 2025 (Beit-Arié, *Hebrew Manuscripts*, no. 38) Pentateuch with Masorah Toledo, 1256; MS Parma 2003–4, 2046 (Beit-Arié, *Hebrew Manuscripts*, nos. 74, 77), a liturgical Pentateuch with Onkelos, Scroll, *haftarot*,

Job, and Rashi, France?, 1311, and whose colophon states that the Targum was copied from a copy brought from Babylonia with supralinear vocalization (see my discussion under Ashkenazic liturgical Pentateuchs); and Bermuda Floersheim Trust Bible (formerly Sassoon, *Ohel Dawid*, no. 82), Soria (Spain), 1312, written by Shem Tov Ibn Gaon, and one of the few Bibles with numbered verses.

10. Most sources suggest that codices were used but scrolls were consulted (and decisions were made by following the majority of scrolls) in cases of doubt about particular readings or orthography. See the story recounted by Menahem Meiri summarized later in this chapter (annotated in note 27), who describes a scroll written by the Spaniard Meir Abulafia that was then used as a model for a specially commissioned *tikkun* from which to copy Torah scrolls in Germany. For other sources on using codices as model books for scrolls, see R. Isaac Alfasi (1013–1103) (cited by Menaḥem Recanati [Italy, late thirteenth to early fourteenth century] in *Piskei Halakhot* [Bologna, 1538], no. 43; Asher ben Yehiel (Germany 1250–59–d. Spain 1328) in *Shut Rosh* (Constantinople, 1517), 3:6; and Moshe ben David Chalawah (Spain, 1290–1370) in B. Herschler, ed., *Shut Maharam Chalawah* (Jerusalem: n.p., 1987), no. 144, all of whom allude in passing to copying scrolls from codices. Recanati's citation of Alfasi suggests that the practice of not using scrolls as models for copying arose out of the fear that the Torah would be left open disrespectfully if it were regularly used in this way. I wish to thank Rabbi Menaḥem Slae for assisting me in finding the latter sources.

11. According to Sfardata, the terms *ḥumash* or *ḥumshei torah* appear in some 140 colophons, 115 of them dated. In Ashkenaz the terms appear in two of the earliest manuscripts of the twelfth century, including Valmadonna MS 1 (1189, probably England; see my discussion below); in Italy, since 1260; and in Sefarad, since 1225 (Tiemçan). In the Near East and in Byzantium, the terms appear only in the fifteenth century.

12. See, for one example, *Vayikra Rabbah* 16:3; M. Margaliyot, ed., *Sefer Ha-Ḥilukim Shevein Anshei Mizrah u-Venei Eretz Yisrael* (Jerusalem: Hebrew University, 1937), 350.

13. Fragments of *haftarah lectionariés* are found already in the Cairo Geniza; see *Hebrew Bible Manuscripts in the Cambridge Genizah Collections* (Cambridge: Cambridge University Press, 1978–2003): vol. 2, ed. M. C. Davis, NS 32.4 (p. 62); NS 32.9 (pp. 62–63); vol. 3, ed. M. C. Davis and Ben Outhwaite, T-S AS2.236 [491] (p. 31); T-S AS28.167 (?) [6591] (p. 404); vol. 4, ed. M. C. Davis and Ben Outhwaite, T-S AS 60.96 [5821] (p. 383); AS60.160[5885] (p. 388). For an example of a medieval Scrolls codex, see Bodl. Laud 154 (Neubauer, *Catalogue*, no. 129), and for numerous examples of *haftarah* codices according to the Ashkenazic, Sefardic, and Italian rites, as well as codices with the *haftarot* and the Scrolls, see the numerous manuscripts cited in the Parma Palatina catalogue, pp. 55–60. For the methodological difficulties in identifying *haftarah* codices, see Judith Kogel, "The Reconstruction of a *Sefer Haftarot* From the Rhine Valley: Towards a Typology of Ashkenazi Pentateuch Manuscripts," in *Books Within Books: New Discoveries in Old Book Bindings*, ed. Andreas Lenhardt and Judith Olszowy-Schlanger (Boston: Brill, 2014), 43–68.

14. The best known of these books is the *Parashat Shelaḥ Lekha* (Numbers 13–15), Persia?, 1106/7 (Jerusalem, NLI 5702). See Bernheimer, *Codices Hebraici*, 3:60–61 (no. 50); a note on p. 60 describes three similar *parashah* books that Malachi Beit-Arié discovered in Meshad. I want to thank Professor Beit-Arié for calling my attention to these manuscripts.

15. For discussion and bibliography on these codices, see David Stern, *Jewish Literary Cultures*, vol. 1: *The Ancient Period* (University Park: Pennsylvania State University Press, 2015), 161–88.

16. A significant number of the early Near Eastern codices have two columns: St. Petersburg, National Library of Russia (NLR) MS EBP I B 3 (Bernheimer, *Codices Hebraicis*, 1:42–47, MS 3), dated 916, the earliest dated complete extant codex; St. Petersburg, NLR MS EBP I B 4 (1:98–107, MS 13); Cairo Karaite Synagogue Moussa Dar'I [Gottheil 13] (2:60–71, MS 23), dated

1028; St. Petersburg, NLR MS EBP I B 4, dated 1139/40; and St. Petersburg, NLR MS EBP II B 4, 1238–39. Almost one third of Oriental (Near Eastern) dated and datable colophoned Bibles have two columns. I wish to thank Professor Beit-Arié for supplying me with this information.

17. Stern, *Jewish Literary Cultures*, 1:184–85, and for bibliography, 230 n. 96.

18. Yosef Ofer, *The Babylonian Masora of the Pentateuch, Its Principles and Methods* (Jerusalem: The Academy of the Hebrew Language and Magnes, 2001), 26–27.

19. For a good sketch of the historical background, see Katrin Kogman-Appel, *Jewish Book Art Between Islam and Christianity: The Decoration of Hebrew Bibles in Medieval Spain* (Leiden: Brill, 2004), 10–56.

20. See Stern, *Jewish Literary Cultures*, 1:179–81, and bibliography cited on 227 n. 71, and, in particular, Rachel Milstein, "Hebrew Book Illustration in the Fatimid Period," in *L'Egypte fatimide: Son art et son histoire*, ed. Marianne Barrucand (Paris: Presses universitaires de Paris-Sorbonne, 1999), 429–40.

21. For a reproduction of a page from this codex, see Malachi Beit-Arié and Edna Engel, *Specimens of Mediaeval Hebrew Script*, 2 vols. (Jerusalem: The Israel Academy of Sciences and Humanities, 2002), pl. 14.

22. Most Spanish masoretic Bibles continue to use three columns, though there are a sufficient number of copies with two. For the influence of the Islamic book on these Bibles, see Kogman-Appel, *Jewish Book Art*, 38–50.

23. In an as-yet-unpublished article, Paul Saenger has made the attractive suggestion that the *seder* signs were preserved as a reference system, and Dukan, *Bible hébraique*, 107, similarly suggests that they may have been preserved to serve as Jewish equivalents to Christian chapters. Unfortunately, virtually no hard evidence for such use of *seder* signs exists.

24. On this manuscript, see Sed-Rajna, *Manuscrits Hébreux*, 5–7. This manuscript appears to be the first Sefardic Bible to have this particular decoration for Exod 15, which does not appear in early Near Eastern masoretic Bibles. It does appear, however, in an undated and unlocalized manuscript, BL MS Or. 2363. Margoulieth, *Catalogue*, 1:39 describes this Bible as either Persian or Babylonian and dates it to sometime between the eleventh and twelfth centuries, but Kogman-Appel, *Jewish Book Art*, 46–47, appears less certain. See also Jacob Leveen, *The Hebrew Bible in Art* (London: The British Academy; London: Oxford University Press, 1944), 70–71.

25. On their accuracy, see H. J. Zimmels, *Ashkenazim and Sepharadim* (London: Oxford University Press, 1958), 138; Nahum Sarna, "Hebrew and Bible Studies in Medieval Spain," in *The Sefardi Heritage*, ed. Richard D. Barnett (New York: Ktav, 1971), 329–31, 345–46; Sarna, "Introductory Remarks," in *The Pentateuch: Early Spanish Manuscript (Codex Hillely) from the Collection of the Jewish Theological Seminary* (Jerusalem: Makor, 1977), n.p.

26. The statement about the superior Spanish and Tiberian books is found in S. G. Stern, ed., *Teshuvot Talmidei Menaḥem le-Dunash* (Vienna: n.p., 1870), 67–68, cited in Sarna, "Introductory Remarks." For Meir of Rothenberg, see his Glosses to Maimonides's *Mishneh Torah, Hilkhot Sefer Torah* 8:2–4.

27. Menachem Meiri, *Kiryat Sefer*, ed. Moshe Hirschler (Jerusalem: Vagshel, 1996), 48.

28. Sarna, "Introductory Remarks." Sarna also discusses the various theories surrounding the origins of its name.

29. Sarna, "Introductory Remarks," [vii].

30. The following sections basically summarize Kogman-Appel, *Jewish Book Art*, which also contains extensive bibliography on additional scholarship. See also Bezalel Narkiss, *Hebrew Illuminated Manuscripts in the British Isles: A Catalogue Raisonné*, vol. 1: *The Spanish and Portuguese Manuscripts* (London: Oxford University Press, 1982), 20–41, 101–20, 153–76.

31. For an overview of these tendencies, see Kogman-Appel, *Jewish Book Art*, 54–56, 57–97, and for analysis, see Eva Frojmovic, "Jewish Mudejarismo and the Invention of Tradition," in *Late Medieval Jewish Identities: Iberia and Beyond*, ed. Carmen Caballero-Navas and Esperanza Alfonso (New York: Palgrave Macmillan, 2010), 233–58.

32. On this Bible, see Kogman-Appel, *Jewish Book Art*, 65–68.

33. For a reproduction of a carpet page from the same Bible that virtually repeats the same floral design, see Rafael Weiser and Rivka Plesser, eds., *Treasures Revealed* (Jerusalem: The Hebrew University and the Jewish National and University Library, 2000), 26, and Narkiss, *Hebrew Illuminated Manuscripts*, pl. 5.

34. On these carpet pages, see Kogman-Appel, *Jewish Book Art*, 65–68.

35. See Jerrilyn D. Dodds, "Mudejar Tradition and the Synagogues of Medieval Spain: Cultural Identity and Cultural Hegemony," in Vivian Mann, Thomas F. Glick, and Jerrilyn D. Dodds, *Convivencia: Jews, Muslims, and Christians in Medieval Spain* (New York: George Braziller with the Jewish Museum, 1991), 115, where she mentions the views of some scholars who seem to believe they were already found in thirteenth-century synagogues.

36. See, for example, Kogman-Appel, *Jewish Book Art*, pl. 2 (BnF MS Héb. 21, Tudela, 1301–2), pl. 8 (BL MS Add. 15250, Catalonia, second half of the fourteenth century), or Bodl. MS Add. Opp. 75 (Neubauer, *Catalogue*, no. 68; Soria or Tudela, late thirteenth century).

37. On this Bible and others composed in the same period (and probably in geographical proximity), see Kogman-Appel, *Jewish Book Art*, 131–40.

38. On this question, see Kogman-Appel, *Jewish Book Art*, 68–74, in which she supports Joseph Guttman's thesis that the pictures (if not the folios themselves) were added to the codex later; see Guttman, "The Messianic Temple in Spanish Medieval Hebrew Manuscripts," in *The Temple of Solomon: Archaeological Fact and Medieval Tradition in Christian, Islamic and Jewish art*, ed. Joseph Gutmann (Missoula: Scholars Press, 1976), reprrinted in Joseph Gutmann, *Sacred Images: Studies in Jewish Art from Antiquity to the Middle Ages* (Northhampton: Variorum, 1989), 125–45.

39. On these Bibles and their menorah illustrations, see note 115 below.

40. On this Bible, see Andreina Contessa, "An Uncommon Representation of the Temple Implements in a Fifteenth-Century Hebrew Sephardi Bible," *Ars Judaica* 5 (2009): 37–58, and a later companion article on that codex and other similar ones, Contessa, "Sephardic Illuminated Bibles: Jewish Patrons and Fifteen-Century Christian Ateliers," in *The Hebrew Bible in Fifteenth-Century Spain: Exegesis, Literature, Philosophy, and the Arts*, ed. Jonathan Decter and Arturo Prats (Leiden: Brill, 2012), 61–72.

41. The history of this scholarship and its bibliography are comprehensively summarized in Kogman-Appel, *Jewish Book Art*, 43–45, 68–88, 131–70, and esp. 156–70. See also the excellent analysis in Eva Frojmovic, "Messianic Politics in Re-Christianized Spain: Images of the Sanctuary in Hebrew Bible Manuscripts," in *Imagining the Self, Imagining the Other: Visual Representation and Jewish-Christian Dynamics in the Middle Ages and Early Modern Period*, ed. Eva Frojmovic (Leiden: Brill, 2002), 91–128.

42. Despite its colophon, the Bible bears no similarity to Bibles produced in the so-called Lisbon workshop and is fully in the tradition of the late fifteenth-century Castilian Bibles. The Bible may have been begun in Spain and completed in Lisbon, or it may have been commissioned by a Spanish Jew living in Lisbon who wished to own a "Castilian" Bible. For further discussion, see David Stern, *Chosen: Philadelphia's Great Hebraica* (Philadelphia: Rosenbach Museum and Library, 2007), 22–23. Note, too, the group of fifteenth-century Hebrew Bibles from Castile and Aragon that were probably brought to Italy by exiles from Spain (and are today preserved in Italian collections), discussed by Andreina Contessa in "Uncommon Representation" and "Sephardic Illuminated Bibles"; these Bibles contain Islamically derived

masoretic micrography produced by Jewish scribes, who evidently wished to revive the earlier Castilian Spanish Bibles, *and* lavish illustrations (probably including the Temple implement pages in the Imola Bible) that emulate contemporary Castilian Gothic-style illumination, almost certainly produced in Christian ateliers.

43. Gabriella Sed-Rajna, *Manuscrits hébreux de Lisbonne: Un atelier de copistes et d'enlumineurs au XVe siècle* (Paris: CNRS, 1970), and her introduction to *The Lisbon Bible, 1482* (Tel Aviv: Nahar Miskal and Yedi'ot Aharonot, 1988).

44. Sed-Rajna, *Lisbon Bible.*

45. Frojmovic, "Messianic Politics," 96.

46. The major proponent of this view has been Guttman; see "Messianic Temple"; and now, for a far more sophisticated formulation of the same idea, see ibid.

47. Kogman-Appel, *Jewish Book Art*, 176, 185–88. Note as well the fifteenth-century Bibles with Temple implement illustrations discussed by Andreina Contessa in "Uncommon Representation" and "Sephardic Illuminated Bibles"; the scribes and Jewish patrons of these Bibles also appeared to have wished to revive the thirteenth-century Islamicizing Bibles and their culture, and probably for the same reasons.

48. The literature on *convivencia* is immense, but for what is still a very good introduction, see Mann, Glick, and Dodds, *Convivencia.*

49. On El Transito and the symbolic cultural meanings of its Mudejar style, see Jane S. Gerber, "The World of Samuel Halevi: Testimony from the El Transito Synagogue of Toledo," in *The Jew in Medieval Iberia, 1100–1500*, ed. Jonathan Ray (Boston: Academic Studies Press, 2012), 33–59.

50. Dodds, "Mudejar Tradition."

51. Ibid., 125–26. Dodds explains the use of the Qur'anic inscriptions as proof of the comfort that the Jews of Toledo felt within the surrounding Islamic culture. See also Gerber, "World of Samuel Halevi."

52. John Williams, "A Castilian Tradition of Bible Illustration," in *Journal of the Warburg and the Courtauld Institutes* 28 (1965): 66–85, reprinted in Joseph Guttman, *No Graven Images* (New York: Ktav, 1971), 385–417.

53. Lawee, "Aharon Aboulrabi," 141, citing H. Bresc. My argument here is very close to the one made by Eva Frojmovic in several articles, such as "Messianic Politics," and "Jewish Mudejarismo."

54. Irven M. Resnick, "The Codex in Early Jewish and Christian Communities," *Journal of Religious History* 17 (1992): 1–17.

55. The Bible was not the only book in Spain to serve the Jews as a mode of responding to contemporary Christian culture. For an argument about the use of the haggadah along the same lines (albeit in a very different way), see Marc Michael Epstein, *The Medieval Haggadah: Art, Narrative, and Religious Imagination* (New Haven: Yale University Press, 2010), and Michael A. Batterman, "Bread of Affliction, Emblem of Power: The Passover Matzah in Haggadah Manuscripts from Christian Spain," in Frojmovic, *Imagining the Self*, 53–90; but for some criticism of the approach, see Katrin Kogman-Appel, *Illuminated Haggadot from Medieval Spain* (University Park: Pennsylvania State University Press, 2006), esp. 212–23.

56. Thus, for example, BnF MS Héb. 7, Perpignan, 1299.

57. Such a prayer is also found in the Paris Bible cited in the previous note, as well as in another closely related Bible codex, Copenhagen, Kongelige Bibliotek, Cod. Hebr. 2, written in 1301, possibly in Perpignan; see Kogman-Appel, *Jewish Book Art*, 133–38.

58. See, for example, Parma, Biblioteca Palatina MS Parma 2668 (Toledo, 1277); BL MS Kings 1 (Solsona 1385); Rome, Communita israelitica no. 19 (Barcelona 1325).

59. For the Jewish and Islamic sources in English translation as well as superb annotation and bibliographical information, see John C. Reeves, *Trajectories in Near Eastern Apocalyptic:*

A Postrabbinic Jewish Apocalypse Reader (Atlanta: Society of Biblical Literature, 2005), 106–32; Islamic sources do not mention the Temple implements specifically but do speak of the staff of Moses and the ark of the covenant. The key Jewish text is the *Otot Ha-Mashiach* (Portents of the Messiah); see, in particular, the sixth sign, p. 124, where the Temple vessels are said to have been deposited in the palace of Julianos Caesar. For Byzantine Christian traditions, see Ra'anan Boustan, "The Spoils of the Jerusalem Temple at Rome and Constantinople: Jewish Counter-Geography in a Christianizing Empire," in *Antiquity in Antiquity: Jewish and Christian Pasts in the Greco-Roman World*, ed. Gregg Gardner and Kevin L. Osterloh (Tubingen: Mohr Siebeck, 2008) and particularly his comments on their relation to the Jewish sources at the end of his article.

60. Williams, "Castilian Tradition"; Bianca Kuenel, "Jewish and Christian Art in the Middle Ages: The Dynamics of a Relationship," in *Juden und Christen zur Zeit der Kreuzzüge*, ed. Alfred Haverkamp (Sigmaringen: Jan Thorbecke Verlag, 1999), 1–15, esp. 13–14, and especially Carl-Otto Nordstrom, "The Temple Miniatures in the Peter Comestor Manuscript at Madrid," *Horae Soederblomianae* 6 (1964): 54–81, reprinted in Guttman, *No Graven Images*, 39–74, who argues that the Madrid manuscript illustrations were directly based on Jewish models.

61. For background on the 1263 disputation, see Robert Chazan, *Barcelona and Beyond: The Disputation of 1263 and Its Aftermath* (Berkeley: University of California Press, 1992), esp. 172–95, and Frojmovic, "Messianic Politics," to whose overall argument my own is strongly indebted. As Frojmovic notes, the key verse in predicting the messianic dates of 1358 and 1403 was Dan 12:12, a verse that is quoted in both the Paris 6 and Copenhagen Bible inscriptions.

62. C. Chavel, ed. *Peirush R. Bahya 'al Ha-Torah* (Jerusalem: Mosad Harav Kuk, 1966–68), 2:268.

63. Ibid., 2:288–89.

64. I take the word "icon" here from Frojmovic, "Messianic Politics," 125, who prefers to see the implements as "non-figurative icons of messianic belief."

65. Joseph Gutmann, "Masorah Figurata in the Mikdashyah," in *VIII International Congress of the International Organization for Masoretic Studies, Chicago, 1988* (Atlanta: Scholars Press, 1990), 71–77. The earliest extant biblical colophon to describe itself as a *mikdashyah* is Jerusalem, Jewish National and University Library MS 4° 780, but this Bible does *not* include Temple implement illustrations. The earliest *mikdashyah* Bible with Temple implements is the Farhi Bible, Hispano Provençal, 1366–82 (formerly Sassoon MS 368).

66. Very few of these Bibles, however, illustrate the Temple itself. Two exceptional codices that do contain diagram-like illustrations of the Temple are a Bible written by Joseph ben Judah Ibn Merwas (BL MS Or. 2201) in Toledo in 1300 and a map written by Joshua Ibn Gaon in Soria in 1306, now bound into the Second Kennicott Bible (Bodl. MS Kenn. 2, fol. 2r). The two maps are very similar and may have derived from a common source; see Kogman-Appel, *Jewish Book Art*, 107. Compare, however, the rarity of depictions of the Temple in Jewish Bibles to the many found in Christian Bibles going back to the Codex Amiatinus (eight century); see the discussion in Mary Carruthers, *The Craft of Thought: Meditation, Rhetoric, and the Making of Images, 400–1200* (Cambridge: Cambridge University Press 1998), 221–76. Gutmann, "Masorah Figurata," 73, also calls attention to eighth-century Qur'ans found in Yemen whose frontispieces had images of an ideal mosque.

67. Naphtali Wieder, "'Sanctuary' as a Metaphor for Scripture," *Journal of Jewish Studies* 8 (1957): 165–75, esp. 166–68. Wieder notes that the analogy is a metaphor for equivalent *sancta*, but, given the exceptional literacy of the Qumran sectarians and their devotion to the Bible, as evidenced by the huge number of biblical fragments found among the Dead Sea Scrolls, it is tempting to think that the Bible and attention to biblical study may actually have served them as a surrogate sanctuary and mode of worship.

68. Ibid., 171. For the King's Bible, see Kogman-Appel, *Jewish Book Art*, 154–55, and Margoulieth, *Catalogue of the Hebrew and Samaritan Manuscripts*, 1:26–28, no. 56.

69. See my article "On the Term *Keter* as a Title for Bibles: A Speculation About Its Origins," in *Festschrift for Menahem Schmelzer*, edited by Evelyn Cohen and Emile Schrijver (Leiden: Brill, 2017). In the article, I also discuss another term, *mishkan*; see the colophon to a northern Italian Bible written in 1499 (Parma, Biblioteca Palatina MS Heb. 2516, Margoliouth, *Catalogue*, no. 24) by the Spanish exile and scribe Moses ben Hayyim Akrish, who thus describes the book.

70. Profiat Duran, *Maase Efod: Einleitung in das Studium und Grammatik der Hebräischen Sprache von Profiat Duran*, ed. Jonathan Friedländer and Jakob Kohn (Vienna: J. Holzwarth, 1865). On Duran, see now Maud Kozodoy, *The Secret Faith of Maestre Honoratus: Profayt Duran and Jewish Identity in Late Medieval Iberia* (Philadelphia: University of Pennsylvania Press, 2015). For earlier studies, see Isadore Twersky, *Studies in Jewish Law and Philosophy* (New York: Ktav, 1982), 203–16; Eliezer Gutwirth, "Religion and Social Criticism in Late Medieval Rousillon: An Aspect of Profayt Duran's Activities," *Michael: On the History of the Jews in the Diaspora* 12 (1991): 135–56; Kalman Bland, *The Artless Jew: Medieval and Modern Affirmations and Denials of the Visual* (Princeton: Princeton University Press, 2000), 82–91; and Irene E. Zwiep "Jewish Scholarship and Christian Tradition in Late-Medieval Catalonia: Profiat Duran on the Art of Memory," in *Hebrew Scholarship and the Medieval World*, ed. Nicholas de Lange (Cambridge: Cambridge University Press, 2001), 224–39.

71. Duran, *Maase Efod*, 14.

72. Ibid., 10.

73. Ibid., 13. Cf. the similar statement on 11.

74. Ibid., 11.

75. Ibid., 14. On *shimush tehillim*, see Gutwirth, "Religion and Social Criticism," 151–52.

76. Duran, *Maase Efod*, 178. On this, Frank Talmage, "Keep Your Sons from Scripture: The Bible in Medieval Jewish Scholarship and Spirituality," in *Understanding Scripture: Explorations of Jewish and Christian Traditions of Interpretation*, ed. Clemens Thoma and Michael Wyschograd (New York: Paulist Press, 1987), 91 (but note that the page reference is incorrect).

77. Duran, *Maaseh Ephod*, 10.

78. Bland, *Artless Jew*, 83–84.

79. On this entire topic, see Zwiep, "Jewish Scholarship," the first important article to approach this dimension of Duran's work, which is a watershed moment in the history of Jewish reading practice. Zwiep overemphasizes the degree to which Duran sees reading as a solitary act. In point of fact, the very first of his rules of memorization emphasizes study with an important scholar and intellectual exchange with colleagues (18). Still, Zwiep is correct in stressing Duran's view that reading is the private act of an individual done from written texts.

80. Duran, *Maase Efod*, 18.

81. It should be noted that the type of memorized knowledge that Duran describes is very different from the type of memorized knowledge that it is likely students in the classical rabbinic period possessed from aural acquisition of the biblical text; in contrast, Duran's solitary reader memorizes Scripture from a written and read text.

82. Duran, *Maase Efod*, 19. Duran refers to the mnemonymic signs of the Masoretes, but see Zwiep's comments in "Jewish Scholarship," 233, connecting Duran to Hugh of Saint Victor's advice in the *Didascalion*. The use of *simanim* (and the term itself) goes back to the rabbinic period, but there, of course, it is used in regard to remembering the traditions of the Oral Torah.

83. Duran, *Maase Efod*, 19.

84. Ibid., 21.

85. Ibid., 19; translation adapted from Zwiep, "Jewish Scholarship," 236.

86. Duran, *Maase Efod*, 21.

87. Ibid., 21.

88. Ibid.

89. For the still classic account of this period and its social conflicts, see Yitzhak Baer, *A History of the Jews in Christian Spain*, trans. L. Schoffman, 2 vols. (Philadelphia: Jewish Publication Society, 1966), 2:35–158, and Eliezer Gutwirth, "Conversions to Christianity Amongst Fifteenth-Century Spanish Jews: An Alternative Explanation," in *Jubilee Volume for Shlomo Simonsohn* (Tel Aviv: Tel Aviv University Press, 1993), 97–121.

90. Frojmovic, "Jewish Mudejarismo," 241–46, quote from 244.

91. The information here is all based on Bezalel Narkiss and Aliza Cohen-Mushlin, introduction to *The Kennicott Bible* (London: Facsimile Editions, 1985); Cecil Roth, "A Masterpiece of Medieval Spanish-Jewish Art—The Kenicott Bible," *Sefarad: Revista de Estudios Hebraicos y Sefardíes* 12, no. 2 (1952): 351–68, reprinted in Roth, *Gleanings: Essays in Jewish History, Letters and Art* (New York: Hermon Press, 1967), 298–315; and Kogman-Appel, *Jewish Book Art*, 212–15.

92. Sheila Edmunds, "The Kennicott Bible and the Use of Prints in Hebrew Manuscripts," *Atti del XXIV Congresso Internazionale di Storia dell'Arte* 8 (1983): 23–29; Edmunds, "A Note on the Art of Joseph Ibn Hayyim," *Studies in Bibliography and Booklore* 11, nos. 1–2 (1975–76): 25–40. For a summary of her work, see Narkiss and Cohen-Mushlin, introduction, 55–56 and 70–71.

93. The entire Bible can now be viewed online at http://purl.pt/23405/3. For an extensive discussion of the book as well as for bibliography on earlier scholarship, see Kogman-Appel, *Jewish Book Art*, 98–110.

94. Kogman-Appel, *Jewish Book Art*, 98, 123–24.

95. Cecil Roth, "An Additional Note on the Kennicott Bible," *Bodleian Library Record* 6 (1961): 659–62, repr. in C. Roth, *Gleanings*, 318; Narkiss and Cohen-Mushlin, introduction, 18.

96. For reproductions of the two colophons, see Narkiss and Cohen-Mushlin, introduction, 13–14, and for the relationship between the two Bibles, see 16–18 and passim, esp. 25–27 and the table on 26 comparing the contents and sequence of sections in the two texts.

97. For these images, see Bodl. MS Kenn. 1 no. 2322, fols. 442v–43r. For brief comments, see Narkiss and Cohen-Mushlin, introduction, 41. On the animal battles, see Ursula Schubert, "Zwei Tierszenen am Ende der Ersten Kennicott-Bibel, La Coruña 1476, in Oxford," *Jewish Art* 12–13 (1986–87): 83–88.

98. See Beit-Arié, *Hebrew Codicology*, 64.

99. On the Ambrosian Bible, see Bezalel Narkiss, *Hebrew Illustrated Manuscripts* (Jerusalem: Keter, 1969), 1: pl. 25; and Ottolenghi, *Hebraica Ambrosiana*, 2:119–25. On the Wroclaw Bible, see Therese Metzger, *Di Bibel von Meschullam und Joseph Qalonymos* (Wuerzberg: Schoeningh, 1994). On their common scribe, Joseph Qalonymus, see Joseph Gutmann, "Joseph Ben Kalonymus: The Enigma of a Thirteenth-Century Hebrew Scribe," in *A Crown For a King: Studies in Jewish Art, History, and Archaeology in Memory of Stephen A. Kayser*, ed. Shalom Sabar, Steven Fine, and William M Kramer (Jerusalem: Gefen, 2000), 147–51.

100. See, for example, BnF MS Héb. 5–6 (southern Germany or southern Switzerland, 1294–95) and 8–10((southern Germany, 1304), both of which are multivolume masoretic Bibles like the Ambrosian and contain the interverse Targum in the Pentateuch volume. Both are also large if not giant codices (53.4 × 37.5 cm and 44.5 × 32.5 cm, respectively).

101. Jordan S. Penkower, "A Sheet of Parchment from a 10th or 11th Century Torah Scroll: Determining Its Type Among Four Traditions (Oriental, Sefardi, Ashkenazi, Yemenite)," *Textus* 21 (2002): 235–64. As the title of Penkower's article indicates, there are also Oriental (examples drawn mainly from tenth- to eleventh-century texts) and Yemenite (fifteenth to sixteenth century) traditions aside from Ashkenazic and Sefardic (thirteenth to fourteenth century).

102. For Spanish Bibles before 1280, see Dukan, *Bible hébraique*, 187–222, and particularly the helpful table on 222; most of the codices are either in what she calls "grand format" (between 369 × 295 mm and 299 × 277 mm) or "format intermédiare" (283 × 275 mm to 197 × 178 mm). My preliminary survey suggests that most fourteenth-century Spanish Bibles continue to adhere to these rough proportions.

103. The best single overview of the history of the Latin Bible in Europe as a material artifact is Christopher de Hamel, *The Book: The History of the Bible* (London: Phaedon, 2001), 64–139. For individual periods in separate essays, see *The Practice of the Bible in the Middle Ages: Production, Reception and Performance in Western Christianity*, ed. Susan Boynton and Diane J. Reilly (New York:Columbia University Press, 2011), esp. Richard Gyug, "Early Medieval Bibles, Biblical Books, and the Monastic Liturgy in the Benevantan Region," 34–60; Diane J. Reilly, "Lectern Bibles and Liturgical Reform in the Central Middle Ages," 105–25; Lila Yawn, "The Italian Giant Bibles," 126–56; and Laura Light, "The Bible and the Individual: The Paris Bible," 228–46.

104. Walter Cahn, *Romanesque Bible Illumination* (Ithaca: Cornell University Press, 1982), 64–91; Reilly, "Lectern Bibles"; Yawn, "Italian Giant Bibles." See also Sarit Shalev-Eyni, *Jews Among Christians: Hebrew Books Illumination from Lake Constance Region* (London: Harvey Miller; Turnhout: Brepols, 2010), 1–10, who was the first to connect the Hebrew Bibles to their Latin counterparts in Germany.

105. De Hamel, *Book*, 135–39; and now esp. Light, "Bible and the Individual," passim.

106. See Colette Sirat, "Le livre hébreu: Rencontre de la tradition juive et de l'esthétique française," in *Rashi et la culture juive en France du Nord au moyen Age*, ed. Gilbert Dahan, Gérard Nahon, and Elie Nicolas (Paris: Peeters, 1997), 242–59, where she shows how these changes affected Jewish books generally as well as Bibles. On the Bible in particular, see Shalev-Eyni, *Jews Among Christians*.

107. Oliver Hahn, with Timo Wolff, Harmut-Ortwin Feistel, Ira Rabin, and Malachi Beit-Arié, "The Erfurt Hebrew Giant Bible and the Experimental XRF Analysis of Ink and Plummet Composition," *Gazette du livre medieval* 51 (2007): 16–28. For illustrations and a short description, see Petra Werner, comp., *Kitwe-Jad: Jüdische Handschriften: Restaurien, Bewahren, Präsentieren* (Berlin: Staatsbibliothek zu Berlin- Preussischer Kulturbesitz, 2002), 18–25. The other giant Bibles include Erfurt 2 (SBB MS Or., fol. 1212).

108. Dianne J. Reilly, *The Art of Reform in Eleventh-Century Flanders: Gerard of Cambrai, Richard of Saint-Vanne and the Saint-Vaast Bible* (Leiden: Brill, 2006); Reilly, "Lectern Bibles"; and Yawn, "Italian Giant Bibles."

109. De Hamel, *Book*, 37–38, and Reilly, "Lectern Bibles," 108–9.

110. Malachi Beit-Arié, "The Individualistic Nature of the Hebrew Medieval Book: Production and Consumption" [in Hebrew], *Zion* 65 (2000): 441–51. Nearly all the best-known cases of individuals dedicating their books to synagogues relate to Karaites and the Karaite community. An exceptional case in Ashkenaz may be that of the Maḥzor Worms; see Malachi Beit-Arié, ed., "The Worms Mahzor-MS Jerusalem, Jewish National and University Library Heb 4° 781/1: Würzburg? (Germany), 1272," in *Worms Mahzor: MS Jewish National and University Library Heb. 4O 781/1*, ed. Malachi Beit-Arié (London: Cyelar; Jerusalem: Jewish National and University Library, 1985), intro. vol., 13–35, reproduced with corrigenda in Beit-Arié, *The Makings of the Medieval Hebrew Book: Studies in Palaeography and Codicology* (Jerusalem: Magnes, 1993), 16–17. As Beit-Arié suggests, the commissioner may already have intended, at the time he commissioned the book, to donate it to the community after his death.

111. Hahn et al., "Erfurt Hebrew Giant Bible," 18.

112. For the Schocken Bible and a reproduction of its famous opening initial word page for Genesis, see Narkiss, *Hebrew Illustrated Manuscripts*, pl. 31.

113. These include the Duke of Sussex German Pentateuch (BL MS Add. 15282), also from Lake Constance, ca. 1300.

114. BnF MS Héb. 33, described in Sirat, "Livre hébreu," 246–47 and illustration 9.

115. These include:

1. BnF MS Héb. 36, a liturgical Pentateuch written in Poligny in 1300 (reproduced and described in Garel, *D'une Main Forte*, 105), in which (fol. 283v) the Menorah, located at the end of Deuteronomy before the Five Scrolls section of the codex, is surrounded by scenes of Aaron, the binding of Isaac, and the judgment of Solomon. The page is reproduced in Narkiss, *Hebrew Illustrated Manuscripts*, pl. 24.

2. The Regensburg Pentateuch, Regensburg, Bavaria, ca. 1300 (Jerusalem, Israel Museum MS 180/52, fols. 155v–56r), which contains the array of Temple implements plus the figure of Aaron kindling the menorah (fols. 155v–56r). See Kogman-Appel, *Jewish Book Art*, 156–60, and now Kogman-Appel, "Sephardic Ideas in Ashkenaz—Visualizing the Temple in Medieval Regensburg," *Simon Dubnow Institute Yearbook* 8 (2009): 245–77, who has correctly characterized the very different shape of the utensil in the Ashkenazic MS from its Sefardic counterparts. Where the latter follow Maimonides's description, the Ashkenazic manuscripts seem to follow Rashi's.

3. BL MS Add. 11639, fol. 114r, the so-called French Miscellany, northern France, ca. 1288–98, about which, see my discussion below under the liturgical Pentateuch in Ashkenaz.

4. BnF MS Héb. 5–6 (southern Germany / southern Switzerland, 1294–95, fol. 118v), reproduced in Garel, *D'une Maine Forte*, with its very interesting full-page micrographic drawing of an olive tree from which (presumably) Aaron is picking olives while others are pressing them to make olive oil for the menorah; the olive tree itself is depicted as resembling a seven-branched menorah.

There are also several Italian Bibles with a picture of the Menorah:

1. BL MS Harley 5710, vol. 1, fol. 136r, Rome, Italy, around 1300, reproduced in Tahan, *Hebrew Manuscripts*, 30, and found also at the end of Deuteronomy. Note that in Margoliouth's British Library catalogue, this manuscript is incorrectly dated to 1240 on the basis of an owner's inscription; Bezalel Narkiss, in the unpublished "Catalogue of the Hebrew Illuminated Manuscripts in the British Isles," vol. 2: "Italian Manuscripts," corrected the date to 1340. I wish to thank Ms. Anna Nizza for supplying me with this information.

2. Parma, Biblioteca Palatina MS Heb. 1849, no. 64 in Richler's Parma Palatina catalogue (*Hebrew Manuscripts*), written in 1304, contains pictures of the Temple implements within an opening of two folio pages (fol. 91a), placed between Exodus and Leviticus. Reproduced in Luisa Mortara Ottolenghi, "Un gruppo di manoscritti ebraici romani del sec. XIII e XIV e la loro decorazione," in *Studii sull'Ebraismo Italiano in memoria di Cecil Roth*, ed. E. Toaff (Rome: Barulli Editore, 1974), 157, this illustration is more like a map of the Temple structure and bears little similarity to the design of the Spanish carpet page–like illustrations of the Temple implements.

To the best of my knowledge, neither of these Italian Bibles has figured in past scholarship about the history of the Temple implement imagery.

116. On the emergence of initial word panels in biblical manuscripts, as part of the development of modes of structural design and transparency to aid readers, see Malachi Beit-Arié,

Unveiled Faces of Medieval Hebrew Books: The Evolution of Manuscript Production—Progression or Regression? (Jerusalem: Magnes, 2003), 51–59, and on biblical manuscripts in particular, 55–57.

117. On the first illustrated initial word panels in Jewish books as found in Munich, Bayerische Staatsbibliothek (BSB) Cod. Heb. 5 (the Rashi *kuntras*, on which, see my discussion of study Bibles later in thic chapter), see Eva Frojmovic, "Jewish Scribes and Christian Illuminators: Interstitial Encounters and Cultural Negotiation," in *Between Judaism and Christianity: Art Historical Essays in Honor of Elisheva (Elizabeth) Revel-Neher*, ed. Katrin Kogman-Appel and Mati Meyer (Leiden: Brill, 2009), 281–305.

118. Garel, *D'une Main Forte*, 102–3, no. 70. For similar images in contemporary Christian books, see Lilian M. C. Randall, *Images in the Margins of Gothic Manuscripts* (Los Angeles: University of California Press, 1966), pl. LXV, no. 315 (Verdun, Bibliothèque municipale MS 107, fol. 19v, early fourteenth century, France) and no. 316 (BL Royal MS 10 E.IV, fols. 65v, early fourteenth century, England). For another example of a similar illustration in an early fourteenth-century book, see the Luttrell Psalter (BL MS Add. 42130), p. 10.

119. For an excellent illustration of the parallels between Christian and Jewish book art grotesques, see John Reeve, ed., *Sacred: Books of the Three Faiths: Judaism, Christianity, Islam* (London: The British Library, 2007), 150–51, which counterposes a folio from the Duke of Sussex's German Pentateuch (a liturgical Pentateuch), Germany ca. 1300 (BL MS Add. 15282, fol. 45v) with marginal grotesques, and an opening from the English Luttrell Psalter, fourteenth century (BL MS Add. 42130, fols. 179v–80r); the Pentateuch's monsters are, of course, micrographic pen drawings while the Luttrell Psalters are painted.

120. For other text illustrations in micrography in Ashkenazic Bibles, see SBB MS Or., quarto 9 (Rouen, 1233), fol. 19a, with a picture of Jacob's ladder to illustrate Gen 28:10–22, reproduced in Werner, *Kitwe-Jad*, 28–29; and BnF MS Héb. 85 (Lorraine, Franche Comte, ca. 1280–1300), fol. 112v, reproduced in Garel, *D'une Main Fort*, 104, which has a micrographic description of knights jousting, the two figures marked as "David" and "Naval" to illustrate their "contest" over Abigail in 1 Sam 25. The figures are very similar to the jousting knights in BnF MS Héb. 4, discussed above, and it is no surprise that both manuscripts are from the same area in France in the late thirteenth century.

121. For micrographic trees, see BnF MS Héb. 5–6 described above in n. 100.

122. Jehuda Wistinetzki, ed., *Sefer Hasidim* (1891; repr., Frankfurt: Wahrmann, 1924), para. 709 (= MS Parma, p. 137); R. Margoliot, ed., *Sefer Hasidim* (Jerusalem: Mossad Ha-Rav Kuk, 1956–57), para. 282 (= Bologna edition, 1538). On the prohibition and its background, see Beit-Arié, "Individualistic Nature," 565; and Shalev-Eyni, *Jews Among Christians*, 4–5. Note, however, that Judah—whether or not he was aware of it—does not complain that these images derive from Christian books.

123. Frojmovic, "Jewish Mudejarismo," 244–45.

124. Mary Carruthers, *The Book of Memory: A Study of Memory in Medieval Culture* (Cambridge: Cambridge University Press, 1990), 122–55 and esp. 245–48. The problem with this explanation is that most of the designs, particularly in Sefardic manuscripts, but also in Ashkenazic ones, are so conventional and recurring that it is hard to imagine how they would have helped readers remember particular items.

125. Suzy Sitbon, "L'espace, les forms dessinées par la letter, le texte dans les bibles Hébrauqyes espagnoles du XIIIe siècle," in *Jewish Studies at the Turn of the Twentieth Century*, ed. Judit Targarona Borrás and Angel Sáenz-Badillos (Leiden: Brill, 1999), 2:163–68, and Sitbon, "Intersections Between Artistic Visual Creation and Cosmogony in Some Spanish Bibles," *Iggud: Selected Essays in Jewish Studies* 3 (2007): *99–113.

126. Oleg Grabar, *The Mediation of Ornament* (Princeton: Princeton University Press, 1992), 155–93, in particular, 190.

127. On dragons in particular, Marc Michael Epstein, *Dreams of Subversion in Medieval Jewish Art and Literature* (University Park: Pennsylvania State University Press, 1997), 70–95. For observations on the problematic presence of such images, see Epstein's comments on 82–84; and now see also Ilia Rodov, "Dragons: A Symbol of Evil in European Synagogue Decoration?," *Ars Judaica* 1 (2005): 63–84, which, despite its title, deals extensively with dragons in manuscript art as well.

128. Cited in Michael Camille, *Image on the Edge: The Margins of Medieval Art* (Cambridge: Harvard University Press, 1992), 9.

129. Ibid.

130. Ivan G. Marcus, *Rituals of Childhood: Jewish Acculturation in Medieval Europe* (New Haven: Yale University Press, 1996), 11–12.

131. In addition to Ivan G. Marcus's book cited in the previous note, see Elisheva Baumgarten, *Mothers and Children: Jewish Family Life in Medieval Europe* (Princeton: Princeton University Press, 2004), and the various chapters on Ashkenazic culture in David Biale, ed., *Cultures of the Jews* (New York: Schocken, 2002).

132. In the case of Sefarad, I am speaking about the overall strategy of resistance to the hegemonic Christian culture of the Iberian kingdoms. The micrographic masoretic decorations that borrow elements of Mudejar design and reflect Islamic aniconism are, in fact, another instance of "inward acculturation," though now in relation to Islamic culture.

133. On this manuscript, Malachi Beit-Arié, *The Only Dated Medieval Hebrew Manuscript Written in England (1189 CE) and the Problem of Pre-expulsion Anglo-Hebrew Manuscripts* (London: Valmadonna Trust Library, 1985), 1–35 and pls. 1–10, reprinted in Beit-Arié, *Makings of the Medieval Hebrew Book*, 129–51, as "The Valmadonna Pentateuch," and now Judith Olszowy-Schlanger, *Les Manuscrits Hébreux dans L'Angleterre Médiévale: Étude Historique et Paléographique* (Paris: Peeters, 2003), 238–42.

134. Macho A. Diez "Introductory Remarks" [in Hebrew], in *The Pentateuch with Masorah Parva and the Masorah Magna and with Targum Onkelos, Ms. Vat. Heb. 448* (Jerusalem: Makor, 1977), n.p. As Diez remarks, the *Onkelos* text is a nonrepresentative version that is nonetheless represented in some Yemenite traditions and was reprinted in the Sabbioneta edition of 1557. So the version clearly remained in circulation.

135. Richler, *Hebrew Manuscripts in the Bibliotheca Palatina*, 18–19 (no. 74, MS Parma 2004, formerly de Rossi 12). See Neubauer, "Early Settlement," 615–16.

136. Jordan S. Penkower, "The Text of the Pentateuch in Manuscripts Written by Early Ashkenazic Sages in the Tenth Through Twelfth Centuries" [in Hebrew], in *Shnaton: Annual for the Study of Bible and the Ancient Near East* 17 (2007): 279–308.

137. For a brief overview of the influence of Eretz Yisrael traditions on Ashkenazic customs, see Israel M. Ta-Shma, *Creativity and Tradition: Studies in Medieval Rabbinic Scholarship, Literature, and Thought* (Cambridge: Harvard University Center for Jewish Studies, 2006), 1–37, and esp. 23–24.

138. Klein, *Genizah Manuscripts*, 1:xxii–xxiii; 2: pls. 4–9 (MS B), 10–19 (MS C), 20–49 (MS D). I wish to thank my colleague Steven Fraade for calling my attention to these Targum manuscripts and for pointing out to me the implications for reading practice that I describe at the end of the paragraph.

139. On the format of the Palestinian Targumim fragments, see Steven D. Fraade, "Rabbinic Views on the Practice of Targum, and Multilingualism in the Jewish Galilee of the Third-Sixth Centuries," in *The Galilee in Late Antiquity*, ed. Lee I Levine (New York: The Jewish Theological Seminary and Cambridge: Harvard University Press, 1992), 253–86; and Willem Smelik, *Rabbis, Language, and Translation in Late Antiquity* (Cambridge: Cambridge University Press, 2013); and Willem Smelik, "Orality, Manuscript Reproduction, and the Targums," in *Paratext and*

Megatext as Channels of Jewish and Christian Traditions: The Textual Markers of Contextualization, ed. August den Hollander, Ulrich Schmid, and Willem Smelik (Leiden: Brill, 2003), 49–81. I wish to thank Professor Fraade for calling these texts to my attention.

140. For French Pentateuchs that omit the Targum altogether, see BnF MS Héb. 53 (SedRajna, *Manuscrits Hébreux Enluminés*, no. 60); Héb. 19 (no. 64); Héb. 4 (no. 69); it may be significant that all three manuscripts also have Masorah. For French Pentateuchs that substitute Rashi for Targum, see BnF MS Héb. 1349 (no. 59) and BL MS Or. 2696. For Rashi's place as a commentator, see the section below on study Bibles. The first source to mention the substitution of Rashi for the Targum was the French Tosafist Moses of Coucy (first half of the thirteenth century) in *Sefer Mitzvot Gadol*, end of Positive Commandments no. 19, who already mentions that his teachers had advised reading Rashi over the Targum as being more profitable. See also Abraham Gross, "Rashi and the Tradition of Study of Written Torah in Sepharad," in *Rashi Studies*, ed. Zvi Arie Steinfeld (Ramat Gan: Bar Ilan University Press, 1993), 37.

141. I wish to thank Eva Frojmovic for correcting my description of this illustration as it appeared in the original version of this chapter. For a description of the page, see Sassoon, *Ohel Dawid*, 19–21. Note the red dot signifying the apple and that, in the picture inside the roundel, Eve has no breasts, while in the larger portrait next to the roundel, she does. This iconography is attested in a number of Byzantine Octateuchs, on which, see Mati Meyer, "Eve's Nudity: A Sign of Shame or Precursor of Christological Economy," in *Between Judaism and Christianity: Art Historical Essays in Honor of Elisheva (Elisabeth) Revel-Neher*, ed. Katrin Kogman-Appel and Mati Meyer (Leiden: Brill, 2009), 243–58. Whether or not this iconography is to be found in any Western manuscripts remains to be determined.

142. I have not been able to find any rhyme or reason as to when the Masorah is copied and when it is not; there is no obvious geographical or chronological pattern behind its presence or absence. Our earliest example of the genre, the Valmadonna Pentateuch, has the full Masorah parva and Masorah magna.

143. The remainder of this paragraph draws heavily on Gyug, "Early Medieval Bibles," esp. 35–38. I also wish to thank Mr. Andrew Irving for discussing the Latin Bibles with me.

144. See ibid., 37 and notes ad locum.

145. See Maimonides, *Teshuvot Ha-Rambam*, ed. Joshua Blau (Jerusalem: Mekitsei Nirdamim, 1957–61), no. 294. On the history of the problem as summarized below, see Israel Ta-Shma, *Early Franco-German Ritual and Custom* [in Hebrew] (Jerusalem: Magnes, 1994), 171–81. Note that in his responsum, Maimonides refers to "our ḥumashim," with certain reference to codices; this would appear to be one of our earliest sources for the use of the term in connection with liturgical Pentateuchs. In *b. Gittin* 60a, which Maimonides uses as a source for his view, the word ḥo[u]mashim refers to scrolls containing single books of the Bible; see Rashi ad locum.

146. An unusual example of such a study Bible is the Albenc Pentateuch (France, 1340) (Bodl. MS Opp. 14; Neubauer, *Catalogue*, no. 20; Beit-Arié, *Catalogue of the Hebrew Manusripts*, no. 20), with narrative micrographic illustrations in *carmina figurata* style and numerous ink-drawings for the biblical text *and* for Rashi's commentary in the same volume. Bezalel Narkiss, "The Seal of Solomon the Scribe: The Illustrations of the Albenc Pentateuch of 1340," in Kogman-Appel and Meyer, *Between Judaism and Christianity*, 319–51, suggests that the text illustrations "were probably added to induce young members of the family . . . to study the text of the Pentateuch and the commentary in order to understand their meaning" (325).

147. Isaac bar Moshe, *Sefer Or Zaruʿa*, part 1, "The Laws of Kriʾat Shema,'" para. 11 (Jerusalem: Yefe Nof / Y. Pozen, 2005), 22; cf. Shalev-Eyni, *Jews Among Christian*, 9–10. The same practice was already predicated as normative law in the Maḥzor Vitry of Simha ben Samuel (d. 1105), para. 117, which was especially influential in northern France. For the text, see S. Hurwitz, ed., *Machsor Vitry* (Nürnberg: Y. Bulka, 1923), 1:88.

148. Paul Saenger, "Reading in the Later Middle Ages," in *A History of Reading in the West*, ed. Guglielmo Cavallo and Roger Chartier (original French ed. 1995; English ed. trans by L. G. Cochrane; Amhert and Boston: University of Massachusetts Press, 1999), 133.

149. Saenger, "Reading in the Later Middle Ages," 133.

150. This extraordinary manuscript is now available in a facsimile edition, *The North French Hebrew Miscellany: British Library Add. MS 11639, with a Companion Volume*, ed. Jeremy Schonfield (London: Facsimile Editions, 2003).

151. For an elaboration of this argument, see chapter 6 in this volume.

152. For another example of a liturgical Pentateuch from the Lisbon workshop, see the Almanzi Pentateuch, Lisbon, 1480–90, BL MS Add. 27167, with pages reproduced in Tahan, *Hebrew Manuscripts*, 64–65.

153. Gross, "Rashi and the Tradition of Study," 37 and n. 44.

154. Israel Abrahams, ed., *Hebrew Ethical Wills* (Philadelphia: Jewish Publication Society, 1926), 65–66.

155. Gross, "Rashi," and Jordan S. Penkower, "The Process of Canonization of Rashi's Commentary to the Torah," in *Study and Knowledge in Jewish Thought*, ed. Howard Kreisel (Beer-Sheva: Ben Gurion University of the Negev Press, 2006), 2:123–46, and the citations in the following notes; and Eric Lawee, "Reception of Rashi's *Commentary on the Torah* in Spain: The Case of Adam's Mating with the Animals," *Jewish Quarterly Review* 97, no. 1 (2007): 33–66, esp. 36–45, where he traces Rashi's growing presence through citations of his commentary in the works of other Spanish exegetes and through the composition of supercommentaries; as Lawee notes (42), the first printed Hebrew book in Spain with a date was Rashi's *Commentary on the Torah* (Guadelajara, 1476). I should add, however, that the evidence of the codices themselves does not entirely reflect the textual sources. Most Spanish liturgical Pentateuchs do not have either Targum or Rashi, though for an exception, see New York, Jewish Theological Seminary of America Lutzki 191, a fragment of a large quarto-sized liturgical Pentateuch written in fourteenth-century Spain in which each verse is followed by the Targum, then Saadiah, then Rashi; the biblical verse is written in large square Sefardic script, the Targum and Saadiah in a significantly smaller semicursive, and then Rashi in an even smaller semicursive.

156. For the Rabbeinu Asher citation, see his novellae (*ḥidushim*) for b. Berakhot 1:8, and the work Orḥot Hayyim attributed to him and cited in Penkower, "Process of Canonization," 143 n. 86. For Jacob Ba'al Ha-Turim, see Tur Oraḥ Ḥayyim, no. 285. Note as well that Jacob's brother, Judah, also commended the regular reading of Rashi's commentary on the weekly parashah (Israel Abrahams, ed., *Hebrew Ethical Wills* (1926; Philadelphia: Jewish Publication Society of America, 1954), 1:174; cited in Lawee, "Reception," 38 n. 24.

157. Gross, "Rashi," 37–40; and Penkower, "Process of Canonization," esp. 138–46.

158. This manuscript and its importance particularly for Rashi studies has been hotly debated over the past twenty years. See, in particular Abraham Grossman, *Ḥakhmei Tzarfat Ha-Rishonim* (The Early Sages of France) (Jerusalem: Magnes, 1996), 184–93, which summarizes his earlier debate with Eliezer Touitou in Touitou, "Does MS Leipzig 1 Reflect the Original Version of Rashi's Commentary on the Torah?" [in Hebrew], *Tarbiz* 61 (1992): 115–85. Cf. Jordan S. Penkower, "Rashi's Corrections to His Commentary on the Pentateuch," *Jewish Studies, An Internet Journal* 6 (2007): 141–86, https://www.biu.ac.il/JS/JIJ, and Penkower's other articles on the masoretic notes in the codex listed in his bibliography there.

159. See the extensive discussion in Stern, *Jewish Literary Cultures*, 1:161–88.

160. The following discussion draws on Mordechai Breuer, "Keep Your Children From Higgayon" [in Hebrew], in *Mikhtam Le-David: Sefer Zikhron Ha-Rav David Ochs*, ed. Y. Gilat and E. Stern (Ramat Gan: Bar Ilan University Press, 1978), 242–64, Talmage, "Keep Your Sons from Scripture"; Kanarfogel, "On the Role of Bible Study"; and Gross, "Rashi." For the best

overall survey of the variety of types of medieval Jewish biblical exegesis, see the numerous chapters in Magne Saebo, ed., *Hebrew Bible / Old Testament: The History of Its Interpretation* (Goettingen: Vandenhoek & Ruprecht, 2000), vol. 1, part 2.

161. The Prophets and Hagiographa were often considered the proper subject of "advanced" biblical study, particularly in the Mediterranean area, and were therefore studied alone; see Talmage, "Keep Your Sons from Scripture, 85.

162. For further discussion of this page and its striking layout, see chapter 5.

163. See, for example, the manuscripts in the Bodleian Library listed in Neubauer, *Catalogue*, cols. 19–20, nos. 119–28,

164. Ephraim Kanarfogel, *Jewish Education and Society in the High Middle Ages* (Detroit, Wayne State U Press, 1992), 79–85; Kanarfogel, "On the Role of Bible Study"; and Grossman, *Hakhmei Tzarfat*, 457–506.

165. Kanarfogel, *Jewish Education*, 15–32.

166. On the development of the introduction in particular, see Eric Lawee's superb study, Lawee, Eric, "Introducing Scripture: The *Accessus ad auctores* in Hebrew Exegetical Literature from the Thirteenth through the Fifteenth Centuries," in *With Reverence for the Word: Medieval Scriptural Exegesis in Judaism, Christianity, and Islam*, ed. Jane Dammen McAuliffe, Barry D. Walfish, and Joseph W. Goering (New York: Oxford University Press, 2003), 157–79.

167. Elazar Touitou, "Concerning the Presumed Original Version of Rashi's Commentary on the Pentateuch" [in Hebrew], *Tarbiz* 56 (1987): 79–97.

168. On this, see ibid.; Grossman, *Hakhmei Tzarfat Ha-Rishonim*, and Penkower, "Rashi's Corrections to His Commentary."

169. On the term *kuntres*, see Malachi Beit-Arié, "Hebrew Codicology: Historical and Comparative Typology of Hebrew Medieval Codices Based on Documentation of the Extant Dated Manuscripts Using Quantitative Approach" [English version], updated preprint, internet version 0.2+ (November 2018), https://www.academia.edu/38097973, 315–44. As Beit-Arié notes, the word has both a codicological and bibliographical meaning; the former, as a gathering or quire; the latter, as a codex. The Tosafists nearly always refer to Rashi as *ha-kuntres*, and on occasion, Rashi appears to refer to his own commentary in that way (*b. Kerithot* 22b, s.v. "Akiba). See Beit-Arié, *Hebrew Codicology*, 236.

170. Leslie Smith, "Jews and Christians Imagining the Temple," in *Crossing Borders: Hebrew Manuscripts as a Meeting-Place of Cultures*, ed. Piet van Boxel and Sabine Arndt (Oxford: Bodleian Library, 2009), 104.

171. BSB Cod. Hebr. 5. For a description of the manuscript and its background, Malachi Beit-Arié, *Hebrew Manuscripts of East and West: Towards a Comparative Codicology* (London: The British Library, 1992), 21 and 111 n. 53, where he cites R. Suckale's study of the Latin instructions, and for analysis of the significance of the very complex and multiple dimensions of the Jewish-Christian collaboration in the manuscript, Frojmovic, "Jewish Scribes and Christian Illuminators."

172. Cited from BnF MS Héb. 184 in Uriel Simon, "Interpreting the Interpreter: Supercommentaries on Ibn Ezra's Commentaries," in *Abraham Ibn Ezra*, ed. I. Twersky and J. Harris (Cambridge: Center for Jewish Studies, Harvard, 1993), 92; see also the quote from Judah Ibn Mosconi cited on the same page of Simon's article.

173. For a full history of this page format from the Glossa Ordinaria through the Bomberg Talmud of 1520–21, see chapter 5, which complements the discussion of the format's impact here.

174. The earliest talmudic tractate with the glossed format is Arras, Bibliothèque municipal MS 889 (969); again, see chapter 5. The view that Leipzig 1 originated in France in the thirteenth century would appear to be that of Abraham Grossman, *Hakhmei Tzarfat*, 187–88. For the dissenting view, see Eliezer Touitou, "Ms. Leipzig."

175. See, for example, Bodl. MS Digby Or. 34, Italy, 1327 (Song of Songs with Targum, Rashi, and Ibn Ezra); Vienna, Österreichische Nationalbibliothek Cod. Hebr. 9, Ashkenaz fourteenth century; Bodl. MS Kenn. 5, Segovia, Spain 1487 (Former Prophets with Targum, Rashi, Radak, and Gersonides). Plates of these manuscripts can be seen in Beit-Arié, *Hebrew Manuscripts* (fig. 37, 38, and 39). For another remarkable example from Spain, see the so-called "Rabbinic Bible" (San Lorenzo de El Escorial, Real Biblioteca MS G-I-5), described and reproduced in *Biblias de Sefarad / Bibles of Sepharad*, ed. Esperanza Alfonso, Javier del Barco, et alia (Madrid: Biblioteca Nacional de España), 288–91. One should also note the case of glossed Psalters. While most medieval psalters were liturgical books and do not have commentariés, there are a sufficient number that do, the most famous being the Parma Psalter (MS Parma 1870 [de Rossi 510]), a lavishly illustrated late thirteenth-century (ca. 1280) codex from northern Italy, with the commentary of Abraham Ibn Ezra written in the three outer margins around the text. Interestingly, this particular page format parallels the Byzantine form used for some Christian psalters rather than the glossed form (with columns) used more widely.

176. On this manuscript, see the Bodleian catalogues of Neubauer and Beit-Arié, no. 129 (Neubauer, *Catalogue*, 20, and Beit-Arié, *Catalogue of the Hebrew Manusripts*, 16). On transparent layout, see Beit-Arié, *Unveiled Faces*, 49–59.

177. Sirat, "Livre Hébreu," 247.

178. Simon, "Supercommentaries," esp. 93–94. For examples of pages with a supercommentary using the *Glossa ordinaria* format, see Sirat, *Hebrew Manuscripts*, 128–31, esp. figs. 58 (Paris, Séminaire Israélite de France MS 1) and 59 (Nîmes, Bibliothèque municipale MS hébr. 22).

179. The glossed format appears already in the 1472 Bologne Pentateuch, but the page format reaches its full form first in the Second Rabbinic Bible (Venice, 1523–24).

180. The earliest European manuscript is Vatican Library MS Vat. ebr. 31, probably written in Apulia (very likely in Otranto) in 1072/3. In contrast, the earliest dated Ashkenazic manuscript is a Babylonian Talmud, Florence, Biblioteca Nazionale Centrale MS II 7, written in 1177.

181. Malachi Beit-Arié, "The Making of the Book: A Codicological Study," in *The Barcelona Haggadah (MS British Library Additional 14761)*, ed. Jeremy Schonfeld, 2 vols. (London: Facsimile Editions, 1992), 31–32.

182. On the Sefardic communities in Spain, primarily in southern Italy and the Kingdom of Naples in particular (until 1541), see Robert Bonfil, *Rabbis and Jewish Communities in Renaissance Italy* (London: Littman Library, 1993), 145–50, 155.

183. For an example of a complete Bible without the Masorah (even though it is written in two columns like a masoretic Bible), see Vatican Library MS Ross. 554, a complete Bible written in Rome in 1286. For a description, see Richler, *Hebrew Manuscripts in the Vatican Library*, 592–93, and pl. 13; according to the entry, there are brief masoretic notes on a very few pages in the entire codex. For additional illustrations, see *Rome to Jerusalem: Four Jewish Masterpieces from the Vatican Library* (Jerusalem: Israel Museum, 2005). As for the liturgical Pentateuch, none of the twenty-two examples in the Parma collection (just to cite one large corpus of the genre) have the Masorah.

184. The quantitative information in this passage was supplied to me by Professor Malachi Beit-Arié, based on the data in Sefardata, and I gratefully acknowledge his assistance.

185. On the development of the humanist text, see the excellent article by Martin Davies, "Humanism in Script and Print," in *The Cambridge Companion to Renaissance Humanism*, ed. Jill Kraye (Cambridge: Cambridge University Press, 1996), 47–62, esp. 49–51.

186. On the different modes of script and the increasing preference for the semicursive mode, see Beit-Arié, *Unveiled Faces*, 75–81.

187. See, for example, BnF MS Héb. 27, a Bible copied in 1294/95 in a semicursive script in two columns, again with headlines in a large square script,

188. Beit-Arié, *Unveiled Faces*, 80.

189. Thus MS Parma 1679 (de Rossi 509, Cat. 24), which has been attributed to Isaac b. Ovadiah b. David of Forli, who copied a good number of manuscripts in the mid-fifteenth century. On Isaac, see the end of this chapter and the publications of Nurit Pasternak cited in note 196 below.

190. Robert G. Calkins, *Illuminated Books of the Middle Ages* (Ithaca: Cornell University Press, 1983).

191. Ibid.

192. The three books are all annotated with a special system of *te'amim* or accents that distinguishes them from the rest of the Bible. Although it is not known what was its original purpose, this distinction helped foster the idea that these books were "poetic"—indeed, in medieval and renaissance treatments, these books were commonly believed to epitomize the essence of biblical poetry. Their status as poetry also probably lay behind the special ways in which their lines are laid out (with a division in the middle of each verse) in medieval manuscripts. On the history of these books as poetry and their page layout, see James Kugel, *The Idea of Biblical Poetry: Parallelism and Its History* (New Haven: Yale University Press, 1981), 114–15 and esp. 125–26, and for their later treatment, see the references in the index, s.v. *Sifrei EMeT*.

193. In terms of numbers, to give one example, the Parma collection alone contains nine Psalters written in Italy from 1391 through the end of the fifteenth century and twelve *Sifrei EMeT*.

194. Exactly how or why this view of the books developed is not clear, but perhaps it had something to do with their common title as *Sifrei EMeT* (originally an anagram of Iyov [Job], Mishlei [Proverbs], and Tehillim [Psalms]) being understood as "Books of Truth," that is, philosophical truth.

195. Fabrizio Lelli, "Christian and Jewish Iconographies of Job in Fifteenth Century Italy," in *Jewish Biblical Interrpetation and Cultural Exchange: Comparative Exegesis in Context*, ed. Natalie B. Dohrmann and David Stern (Philadelphia: University of Pennsylvania Press, 2008), 216.

196. Nurit Pasternak, "A Meeting Point of Hebrew and Latin Manuscript Production: A Fifteenth Century Florentine Hebrew Scribe, Isaac ben Ovadiah of Forli," *Scrittura e Civiltà* 25 (2001): 185 and passim; see also her Hebrew article, "Isaac ben Ovadiah ben David of Forli: An Extraordinary Jewish Scribe Who Converted to Christianity?," *Tarbiz* 68 (1999): 195–212; and her dissertation, "Together and Apart: Hebrew Manuscripts as Testimonies to the Encounters of Jews and Christians in Fifteenth-Century Florence, The Makings, the Clients, Censorship" (Ph.D. diss., Hebrew University, 2009). All of my remarks on Isaac ben Ovadiah are drawn from Pasternak's seminal work.

197. Pasternak, "Meeting Point," 199.

198. As Pasternak notes, sixteen of Isaac's extant works are biblical in genre. These include five full Bibles, several liturgical Pentateuchs, Psalters, and several *Sifrei EMeT*.

199. I wish to express my gratitude to Eva Frojmovic for identifying these images for me (and for correcting the incorrect explanations I provided for them in the original publication of this article).

200. For the beginning of an answer to this question, see the next chapter in this book, "The Making of the Rabbinic Bible."

CHAPTER 4

1. Elizabeth Eisenstein, *The Printing Press as an Agent of Change*, 2 vols. (Cambridge: Cambridge University Press, 1979); the full debate was ignited by Adrian Johns in *The Nature*

of the Book: Print and Knowledge in the Making (Chicago: University of Chicago Press, 1998), and continued with the exchange between Eisenstein and Johns in *The American Historical Review* 107 (2002): 87–121. For a vivid description of the differences in reading practice caused by print, see Anthony Grafton, "The Humanist as Reader," in *A History of Reading in the West*, ed. Guglielmo Cavallo and Roger Chartrier, trans. Lydia G. Cochrane (Amherst: University of Massachusetts Press, 2003), 179–212; and in the same volume, 22–33, the important methodological (and cautionary) remarks by the editors on the use of the term "revolution" as applied to the invention of print.

2. The most famous description of the social scene in the print house is found in Aldus Manutius's dedication of his edition of *Rhetorica ad Herennium*, cited and translated in Martin Lowry, *The World of Aldus Manutius* (Ithaca: Cornell University Press, 1979), 165–66, but more pertinent for our concerns is Henri Estienne's colorful picture of his father Robert's publishing house quoted and translated in Anthony Grafton, *Bring Out Your Dead: The Past as Revelation* (Cambridge: Harvard University Press, 2001), 142–43, and Grafton's analysis, 141–47. For a second-hand and somewhat overly vivid imagined but charming picture of the multicultural scene in Daniel Bomberg's printing house, see David Werner Amram, *The Makers of Hebrew Books in Italy: Being Chapters in the History of the Hebrew Printing Press* (1909; repr., London: Holland Press, 1963), 175–77. See also Eisenstein, *Printing Press*, 75–76, 250–54, and Amnon Roz-Krokotzkin. *The Censor, the Editor, and the Text: The Catholic Church and the Shaping of the Jewish Canon in the Sixteenth Century*, trans. Jackie Feldman (Philadelphia: University of Pennsylvania Press, 2007), 101–9.

3. Brian Richardson, *Print Culture in Renaissance Italy: The Editor and the Vernacular Text, 1470–1600* (Cambridge: Cambridge University Press, 1994), esp. 1–18. On correctors and their emergence during this period, see Grafton, "Humanist as Reader."

4. See Eisenstein, *Printing Press*, esp. "Part Three: The Book of Nature Transformed," 520–74.

5. The first polyglot, the Complutensian Bible, appeared between 1514 and 1517. To be sure, Origen's Hexapla (in six columns) and the Tetrapla (four columns), which survive only in small fragments, antedate and anticipate the layout and goal of the Complutensian—and perhaps partly inspired it—but even the Hexapla had at most two languages, Greek (primarily) and Hebrew. On the publication of the Complutensian Bible, see Julian Martin Abad, "The Printing Press at Alcala de Henares: The Complutensian Polyglot Bible," in *The Bible as Book: The First Printed Editions*, ed. Paul Saenger and Kimberly Van Kampen (London: The British Library, 1999), 101–15; Rosa Helena Chinchilla, "The *Complutensian Polyglot Bible* (1520) and the Political Ramifications of Biblical Translation," in *La Traduccióen España ss. XIV–XVI*, ed. Roxana Recio (Leon: Universidad de Leon, 1995), 169–90; and (though focusing more on the New Testament volume) Jerry H. Bentley, *Humanists and Holy Writ: New Testament Scholarship in the Renaissance* (Princeton: Princeton University Press, 1983), 70–111. The publication of the Complutensian coincided, it should be noted, with the nearly simultaneous publication of the Polyglot Psalter (Genoa, 1516), which included the Arabic translation as well.

6. This is not to suggest that it is—or was—in any way impossible to distinguish between Hebrew books produced *primarily* for Jews, and those produced *primarily* for Christians; on the latter, see Stephen G. Burnett, "Christian Hebrew Printing in the Sixteenth Century: Printers, Humanism, and the Impact of the Reformation," *Helmantica* 11 (2000): 13–42. My point is only that the once clear-cut category had become decidedly blurred.

7. The original title of the 1517 edition on its title page is *Arbaʿah ve-ʿEsrim*—namely, "the Twenty-Four" books of the Hebrew Bible. The title page of the 1524–25 edition has as its heading "Shaʿar Adonai He-Ḥadash" (The New Gate of the Lord) and then simply lists its contents as *Ḥumash (Pentateuch) . . . Neviʾim Rishonim . . . Neviʾim Aḥaronim . . . u-Ketuvim.* As Jordan S. Penkower has shown, the earliest sign of the later title "Mikraʾot Gedolot" is in

the 1548 Venice edition, where its title appears as *'Esrim ve-Arba' 'Gadol*—namely, the "large" (i.e., folio-sized) "Twenty Four" books, and beginning from that period, the edition was sometimes referred to as the *Mikra Gedolah*, "The Large (= folio-sized) Scripture." See Penkower, "Jacob Ben Ḥayyim and the Rise of the Biblia Hebraica" (Ph.D. dissertation, Hebrew University of Jerusalem, 1982), 1. In an article published shortly later, "The First Edition of the Hebrew Bible that Bomberg Published and the Beginning of His Publishing House" [in Hebrew], *Kirjat Sepher* 58 (1983): 586–604, specifically 601–2 n. 68, Penkower also cites two occurrences of the plural form *Mikra'ot gedolot* in the 1595 Mantua censorship list where the phrase means "copies of the *Mikra Gedolah.*" The earliest appearance of the phrase as the title of the Bible in its entirety is to be found in the Lemberg (?) 1808 edition. For an illustration of the page, see *Encyclopaedia Judaica* (New York: MacMillan, 1972), 2:783. The term "Rabbinic Bible," *Biblia rabbinica*, appears to be a Christian Hebraist name; it is not clear when it first came into usage.

8. The definitive work written to date on the first two RBs is Jordan S. Penkower's comprehensive doctoral dissertation, "Jacob Ben Ḥayyim"; unfortunately, Penkower's dissertation is not yet published, but pro tem, see Penkower's summary of his findings in the entry on "Rabbinic Bible," in *The Dictionary of Biblical Interpretation*, ed. John H. Hayes (Nashville, Tenn.: Abingdon Press, 1999), 2:361b–64a. In addition, see his valuable article "First Edition" cited in the previous note and his many other articles cited in later notes. Penkower's work is complemented by B. Barry Levy, "Rabbinic Bibles, MIKRA'OT GEDOLOT, and Other Great Books," *Tradition* 25 (1991): 65–81, which is the initial part of a work in progress on the history of the Rabbinic Bible in its entirety; I wish to express my gratitude to Professor Levy for allowing me to read his unpublished manuscript. See also his book *Fixing God's Torah: The Accuracy of the Hebrew Bible Text in Jewish Law* (New York: Oxford University Press, 2001), which contains important material on the Rabbinic Bible, to which I will return later in this chapter. Earlier works that remain valuable are Christian D. Ginsburg, *Jacob Ben Chajim Ibn Adonijah's Introduction to The Rabbinic Bible* (1867; repr., New York: Ktav, 1968), which includes both a Hebrew text of Jacob Ben Ḥayyim's introduction and an English translation and a long introductory essay; Ginsburg, *Introduction to the Massoretico-Critical Edition of the Hebrew Bible* (1897; repr., New York: Ktav, 1966), 922–76, with full descriptions of all the early printings; and Moshe Goshen-Gottstein, *Biblia rabbinica* (Jerusalem: Makor, 1972), 3–20. Additional comments on the Rabbinic Bible are also found in many of the works on sixteenth-century Hebrew printing in Venice cited in the next note.

9. In addition to the works cited in the previous note, see the recent works of Bertram Eugene Schwarzbach, "Les editions de la Bible hébraïque au xvie siècle et la création du texte massorétique," in *La Bible imprimée dans l'Europe moderne*, ed. Bertram Eugene Schwarzbach (Paris: Bibliothèque nationale de France, 1999), 16–67, and Giuliano Tamani, "Le Prime Edizioni Della Bibbia Ebraica," in *Bibel in jüdischer und christlicher Tradition* (Frankfurt: Anton Hain, 1993), 259–74. In earlier scholarship, see A. M. Haberman, *The Printer Daniel Bomberg and the List of Books Published by His Press* [in Hebrew] (Zefat: Museum of Printing Art, 1978); Yisrael Mehlmann, "The Printing House of Daniel Bomberg in Venice" [in Hebrew], in *Genuzot Sefarim* (Jerusalem: Jewish National and University Library, 1976), 13–42); Lazarus Goldschmidt, *The Earliest Editions of the Hebrew With a Treatise on the Oldest Manuscripts of the Bible by Paul Kahle* (New York: Aldus Book, 1950); and A. Berliner, "The Hebrew Publishing House of Daniel Bomberg" [in Hebrew], translated from the German (1904) in *Selected Writings* (Jerusalem: Mossad Harav Kuk, 1969), 163–75; Moses Marx, "Gershom (Hieronymus) Soncino's Wanderyears in Italy, 1492–1527: Exemplar Judaicae Vitae," *Hebrew Union College Annual* 11 (1936): 427–501, esp. 442–45; Joshua Bloch, *Venetian Printers of Hebrew Books* (New York: New York Publica Library, 1932); and Amram, *Makers of Hebrew Books*, 146–224.

10. The most important recent work on Bomberg is Bruce Nielsen, "Daniel van Bombergen, a Bookman of Two Worlds," in *The Hebrew Book in Early Modern Italy*, ed. Adam Shear and Joseph Hacker (Philadelphia: University of Pennsylvania Press, 2011), 56–75, 230–52. See also the works of Habermann, Mehlmann, Bloch, and Amram, all cited in the previous note.

11. The little-known Pratensis is best summed up in Paul Kahle, "Felix Pratensis—a Prato Felix: Der Bearbeiter der ersten Rabbinerbibel, Venedig, 1516–17," *Die Welt des Orients* 1 (1947): 32–36; and summarized in Kahle, *The Cairo Genizah* (Oxford: Blackwell, 1959), 69 n. 3; and Kahle, "The Hebrew Text of the Complutensian Polyglot," in *Homenaje a Millas-Vallicrosa* (Barcelona: Consejo Superior de Investigaciones Científicas, 1954), 742–44.

12. On Pratensis and Egidio da Viterbo, see Gi Signorelli, *Il Cardinale Egidio da Viterbo, Agostiniano, Umaniste e Reiformatore, 1469–1532* (Florence: Libreria Editrice Fiorentina, 1929), 203 n. 8, cited in Robert J. Wilkinson, *Orientalism, Aramaic and Kabbalah in the Catholic Reformation: The First Printing of the Syriac New Testament* (Leiden: Brill, 2007), 45.

13. The two kabbalistic works were Abraham Abulafia's *Imrei Shefer* and *Sefer Ha-Temunah*, a kabbalistic interpretation of the Hebrew alphabet. Both translations were apparently Pratensis. See Penkower, "First Edition," 597 n. 51.

14. Ibid.

15. On the difference between privileges and patents, see Christopher L. C. E. Witcombe, *Copyright in the Renaissance: Prints and the Privilegio in Sixteenth-Century Venice and Rome* (Leiden: Brill, 2004), 21–22, and for Pratensis and Bomberg, 43–44.

16. See Marx, "Gershom (Hieronymus) Soncino's Wanderyears," 441–42 and 445–56. On Aldus's Hebrew ambitions, see Martin Davies, *Aldus Manutius: Printer and Publisher of Renaissance Venice* (Tempe: Arizona Center for Medieval and Renaissance Studies, 1999), 50–55.

17. Marx, "Gershom (Hieronymus) Soncino's Wanderyears," 443. Bomberg's success is further confirmed by his successful application for permission for four Jews to live in Venice so as to assist him in the work, and for their release from the obligation of wearing the yellow hat; on the latter, see Horace Brown, *The Venetian Printing Press* (1891; repr., Amsterdam: Gérard Th. van Heusden, 1969), 105, and Penkower, "First Edition," 598–99 and n. 58 for the original Latin request and further bibliography.

18. See the statement of Marino Sanuto quoted in Witcombe, *Copyright in the Renaissance*, 44.

19. Ibid., 44–45.

20. On the frame, see Marvin Heller, *The Sixteenth Century Hebrew Book: An Abridged Thesaurus* (Leiden: Brill, 2004), 95. For other differences between the two editions, see my discussion below.

21. The English translation and original Latin are taken from Ginsburg, *Introduction to the Massoretico-Critical Edition*, 945–46.

22. On Egidio and his kabbalistic interests, see Wilkinson, *Orientalism, Aramaic and Kabbalah*, 29–54, and esp. 42–46.

23. Ibid., 45.

24. Ginsburg, *Introduction to the Massoretico-Critical Edition*, 945–46. This last claim has been the subject of much debate. Ginsburg vehemently criticizes it as misleadingly hyperbolic (945–47), but see Kahle's explanation, in *Cairo Genizah*, 123, and Penkower's explanation of Pratensis's statement in "Jacob Ben Hayyim" (187–88) as well as his post "A Note on the Latin Dedication in the Rabbinic Bible of Venice 1517," Seforim Blog, January 11, 2009, https://seforimblog.com/2009/01/noteonlatindedicationinrabbinic. See also the comments of Alberdina Houtman, "Targum Isaiah According to Felix Pratensis," *Journal for the Aramaic Bible* 1 (1999): 191–202, esp. 201–2, in regard to the text of the Targum.

25. Two books in the Hagiographa have the Targum and two commentaries—Proverbs (Radakand the commentary "Kav-venaki" by David Ibn Yahya ben Solomon [1455–1528]) and

Job (Nahmanides [1194–270] and Abraham Farisol [1451–1525?]). The Five Scrolls have the Targum and Rashi. Daniel has the commentary of Gersonides (1288–1344), and both Ezra-Nehemiah and Chronicles have the commentaries of Rashi and an abridgment of the late midrashic anthology *Yalkut Shimoni*, probably compiled in the late thirteenth century.

26. Schwarzbach, "Editions de la Bible hébraïque," 38–39, and 54; see also the brief history of the text in A. Darom's edition of R. David Kimchi (Radak), *Ha-Peirush Ha-Shalem ʿal Tehilim* (Jerusalem: Mossad Harav Kuk, 1979), 5–6. The specific verses in Psalms are 2:12; 19:10; 21:1; 22:32; 45:18; 72:20; 110:7.

27. The history of this single folio page is not entirely clear. Habermann, *Ha-Madpis*, 29, writes that the page was taken out of most copies. Schwarzbach, "Editions de la Bible hébraïque," 39–40, has proposed that the page Habermann saw was taken from a separate, unrelated edition of Radak's work and inserted into copies of RB 1517, but his proposal remains to be confirmed. For a complete text of the folio page in translation, see http://www.glaird.com /kim-comm.htm. It is worth noting that the folio also contains Radak's interpretations of Ps 87:7, which do not appear in Darom's edition of Radak's commentary.

28. See Jordan S. Penkower, "The Chapter Divisions in the 1525 Rabbinic Bible," *Vetus Testamentum* 48 (1998): 350–74, esp. 353–60, where he studies the variants in the divisions as based on the Vulgate, as established (if not introduced) by Stephen Langton in the thirteenth century. Verse divisions, also based on Christian enumerations, were not introduced into a Jewish Bible until the 1548 reprinting of the Rabbinic Bible in which *every fifth verse* is marked in the text. See also Penkower, "Verse Divisions in the Hebrew Bible," *Vetus Testamentum* 50 (2000): 279–393. As Jacob ben Hayyim Ibn Adoniyahu states at the end of his introduction (trans. Ginsburg, *Introduction to the Massoretico-Critical Edition*, 80–81), he adapted the chapter and verse numberings from R. Isaac Nathan's biblical concordance, *Netiv Meir* (written in 1437–1445, first published by Bomberg, with Adoniyahu's editing, in 1523), which, in turn, adapted the chapter and verse numberings from Arlotti's Latin Concordance (ca. 1290); Isaac Nathan compiled his work in order to assist Jews in rebutting Christian polemical attacks. See, however, Penkower, "Chapter Divisions," 362–65, where he shows that Ibn Adoniyahu actually took the numerations from the chapter list at the beginning of the Concordance.

29. This estimated number is primarily based upon the figures and reasoning in Zipora Baruchson, "Money and Culture: Financing Sources and Methods in the Hebrew Printing Shops in Cinquecento Italy," *La Bibliofilia* 92 (1990): 23–39, in particular, 28 and n. 9, there with additional bibliography on print runs in contemporary Christian printing houses; see also her complementary article, published under Shifra Z. Baruchson-Arbib, "The Prices of Hebrew Printed Books in Cinquecento Italy," *La Bibliofilia* 97 (1995): 149–61. In an older study, A. M. Haberman, *Toledot Ha-Sefer Ha-ʿIvri* (Jerusalem: Rubin Mass, 1945), 79, gives a range of 800–1500 for the output of sixteenth-century Hebrew presses; in his later work, "Printer Daniel Bomberg," 21, he proposes a range of 500–1000 copies. See also Marvin J. Heller, *Printing the Talmud: A History of the Earliest Printed Editions* (Brooklyn: Im Hasefer, 1992), 159, and 191 for some important economic considerations determining size of print runs. See also Bruce Nielsen, "A Note About Book Prices in the Sixteenth Century," in *The Valmadonna Trust Library*, part 1: *Magnificent Manuscripts and the Bomberg Talmud* (New York: Sotheby's, 2015), 65–66. For print runs of non-Jewish/Hebrew books in early sixteenth-century Italy, the most extensive discussion remains Rudolph Hirsch, *Printing, Selling, and Reading: 1450–1550* (Wiesbaden: Otto Harrassowitz, 1967), 61–68, who concludes with a quote from F. Kapp (*Geschichte des deutschen Buchhandels* [Leipzig: Börsenvereins der deutschen buchhändler, 1886]): "Up to the middle of the XVIth century no rule can be established for the size of editions. Available data are too incomplete." See also Brian Richardson, *Printing, Writers and Readers in Renaissance Italy* (Cambridge: Cambridge University Press, 1999), 21, where he estimates the norm

to have been about one thousand copies. A serious study of print output in sixteenth-century Hebrew publishing is an important desideratum.

30. On the 1521 edition, see Marvin Heller, *The Sixteenth-Century Hebrew Book: An Abridged Thesaurus*, 2 vols. (Leiden: Brill, 2004), 1:143.

31. See the material collected and analyzed by Penkower, "Jacob Ben Ḥayyim," 8–12, and in his appendixes on 396–99.

32. The two kabbalistic commentaries are the *Tzror Ha-Mor* by Abraham Saba (Venice, 1522–23) and the *Commentary on the Torah* by Menaḥem Recanati (Venice, 1523). For the most complete list of the books Ibn Adoniyahu worked on, see Penkower, "Jacob Ben Ḥayyim," 7, which supercedes the listings in Haberman, *Printer Daniel Bomberg*. On *Meir Netiv*, see Penkower, "Jacob Ben Ḥayyim," 389–91.

33. For a detailed investigation, see Penkower, "Jacob Ben Ḥayyim," chapter 4 in its entirety, 148–90, and for a summary, 177–78.

34. See the table with references in Penkower, "Jacob Ben Ḥayyim," 284 n. 25.

35. Ibid., 52–53; as Penkower notes, Ibn Adoniyahu did not, strictly speaking, invent the Masorah finalis (*mesorah sofit*)—the term had been used throughout the Middle Ages to describe the masoretic material—lists of differences, treatises, etc. that were copied at the back of massoretic codices. What he did "invent" was a new use for the term and a new form for it.

36. For a single indication of the importance attributed to Ibn Adoniyahu's text, see the statement in 1897 by Christian D. Ginsburg in *Introduction to the Massoretico-Critical Edition*, 963–64, that Ibn Adoniyahu's text "is the only Massoretic recension. No textual redactor of modern days who professes to edit the Hebrew text according to the Masorah can deviate from it without giving conclusive justification for so doing." Ginsburg himself, in his own edition of the Hebrew Bible, exactly reproduced the 1524–25 text, and in this light, it is hardly surprising that the first two editions of Rudolph Kittel's *Biblia Hebraica* (1906, 1913) also essentially reproduced Jacob Ben Ḥayyim's text from RB 1524–25. It was only the third edition (1929–37) that for the first time deviated from the four-hundred-year-old convention and, at the urging of Paul Kahle, replaced RB 1524–25 with the text of the famous Leningrad Codex (NLR MS Evr. B 19a). For a somewhat partisan account of the history behind this third edition, see Paul E. Kahle, *The Cairo Geniza (The Schweich Lectures of the British Academy, 1941)* (London: For the British Academy by Oxford University Press, 1947), 72–78.

37. As noted earlier, Bomberg received his *privilegia* in 1515. In August 1517, the Venetian Senate declared that privileges would only be granted for new works and to works that had not been printed before. After the revocation, Bomberg had his *privilegia* reconfirmed in 1518, but he may have anticipated the problems he faced in 1525, detailed earlier in this chapter. He possibly hoped to convince the Senate that RB 1525 was indeed a new book and therefore did not fall under the strictures of the 1517 revocation. On this background, see Witcombe, *Copyright in the Renaissance*, 41–45.

38. For a discussion of the question as to whether Jewish complaints against the 1517 edition on account of Pratensis's editorship motivated Bomberg to publish the second Rabbinic Bible, see Penkower, "Jacob Ben Ḥayyim," 410–12.

39. On the page format, see both chapter 3 above and, for a complete history of the format, chapter 5 below.

40. Translation and Latin text cited in Ginsburg, *Introduction to the Massoretico-Critical Edition*, 945–46. For the deficiencies that Ibn Adoniyahu may have seen in Pratensis's edition, see Penkower, "Jacob Ben Ḥayyim," 15–24. For a summary and the entirety of chapter 4, see 148–90 and Penkower, "Rabbinic Bible," 362.

41. Penkower, "Jacob Ben Ḥayyim," 8–14, and Penkower, "Rabbinic Bible," 362. Penkower's primary explicit evidence for Ibn Adoniyahu's belief in the kabbalistic significance of the

Masorah is his note on Exod 10:5 in which he used kabbalistic (Zoharic) criteria to determine whether the word *lir'ot* is written plene or defectively (with or without a *vav*).

42. On Bomberg's introduction, see Penkower, "Jacob Ben Ḥayyim," 13–14. The classic study of Christian Kabbalah remains F. Secret, *Les Kabbalistes Chrétiens de la Renaissance* (Paris: Dunod, 1964).

43. Hebrew: *ha-to'elet ha-gadol*. He is explicitly referring here not to kabbalistic secrets but to halakhic laws and homiletical lessons, as described on pp. 76–77, where he cites the Mordechai and Maharam of Rothenberg as previous authorities who used the Masorah as the basis for legal decisions.

44. As translated by Ginsburg, *Jacob Ben Chajim Ibn Adonijah's Introduction*, 77–78, with slight stylistic revisions.

45. Ibid., 37. The last phrases are taken from Num 11:25–26, with reference to the charismatic prophets Eldad and Meidad. Ginsburg translates: "And as if by prophecy they wrote down their labours in books, to which nothing is to be added."

46. For the phrase, see *m. Avot* 3:13 and David Stern, "The First Jewish Books and the Early History of Jewish Reading," in *Jewish Literary Cultures*, vol. 1: *The Ancient Period* (University Park: Pennsylvania State University Press, 2015),161–88, specifically 179–80.

47. Alton was a wealthy Venetian Jew who is mentioned in several of Bomberg's colophons and title pages as having been instrumental in helping to gather and acquire manuscripts. See Penkower, "Jacob Ben Ḥayyim," 285–86 n. 28.

48. At this point and for the remainder of the paragraph, Ibn Adoniyahu's language switches from the Hebrew rhymed narrative prose to a talmudic idiom of Aramaic mixed with Hebrew phrases.

49. Hebrew *keli mapatzo* (Ezek 9:2).

50. The meaning of this last sentence is unclear. The phrase about "the builders" alludes to Ps 118:22; the word *bonim*, "builders," may allude to those who "understand" (*bun*)—namely, the wise. See the midrash recorded in *b. Berakhot* 64a ad Isa 54:17 and Ḥanoch Yalon, *Pirkei Lashon* (Jerusalem: Mossad Bialik, 1971), 123–55.

51. See also Ezra 1:5 and Isa 41:2, *mi hei'ir mi-mizraḥ tzedek*, which is probably the source for the use of the phrase in Ezra.

52. Compare, for example, the introduction of Abraham ben Meir de Balmes to his *Mikneh Avram* (Venice: Daniel Bomberg, 1523), in which he, too, describes his personal troubles as well as how he was rescued by Bomberg (whom he praises in terms similar to those Ibn Adoniyahu uses), but far more vaguely.

53. The density of allusion here is in fact close to the kind of *shibutz* so typical of medieval Hebrew poetry; my notes cite only some of the most obvious cases, but virtually every one of Ibn Adoniyahu's sentences contains an allusion.

54. A second edition, printed by Gershom's son Eliezer, appeared in Constantinople in 1535.

55. On this narratological ambiguity and the use of the phrase, see Matti Huss, "The 'Maggid' in the Classical *Maqama*" [in Hebrew], *Tarbiz* 65 (1996): 129–72.

56. For the edition and text, see Dov Jarden, ed., *Maḥberoth Immanuel Ha-Romi*, 2nd ed. (Jerusalem: Kiryat Moshe, 1984), 1:9–10. I want to thank Raymond Scheindlin for drawing my attention to Immanuel's poems and their similarity to Ibn Adoniyahu's narrative.

57. On this chapter, see David Malkiel, "Eros as Medium: Rereading Immanuel of Rome's Scroll of Desire," in *Donne nella storia degli ebrei d'Italia: Atti del IX Convegno internazionale, Lucca, 6–9 giugno 2005* (Florence: Giuntina, 2007), 35–59; Malkiel touches upon the question of the identity of the *sar*, though mainly in terms of ascertaining his historicity.

58. Malkiel, "Eros as Medium," 46–50.

59. Literally, "shook out the bosom of my garment"; cf. Neh 5:13.

60. Ginsburg, *Jacob Ben Chajim Ibn Adonijah's Introduction*, 41.

61. On Ibn Adoniyahu's conversion, see Ginsburg, *Jacob Ben Chajim Ibn Adonijah's Intro-duction*, 11–14. The main evidence for his conversion is Elijah Levita's famous slur in his poetic introduction to *Massoreth Ha-Massoreth*, ed. Christian D. Ginsburg (1867; repr., New York: Ktav, 1968), 94, where he refers to Ibn Adoniyahu as one "whose name was formerly Jacob, let his soul be bound up in a bag with holes." See also Penkower, "Jacob Ben Ḥayyim," 412–14 n. 12.

62. Joseph Hakohen, *Divre Ha-Yamim le-Malkhei Tzarfat u-Vet Otoman Ha-Tugar* (Sabionetta, 1554), 137b, quoted in Habermann, *Ha-Madpis*,12. For a collection of other encomia paid to Bomberg by his Jewish correctors, editors, and printers, see Habermann, *Ha-Madpis*, 16–17.

63. The main scholar to raise this speculation is Mehlmann, "Printing House," 18–19; but for an overview of the positions, see also Meir Benayahu, *Copyright, Authorization, and Imprimatur for Hebrew Books Printed in Venice* [in Hebrew] (Jerusalem: Machon Ben-Zvi and Mosad Rav Kuk, 1971), 17 and n. 4 ad locum, and Heller, *Printing the Talmud*, 138–39.

64. I need to emphasize that I am not making a historical claim here but solely addressing Ibn Adoniyahu's self-perception and representation of himself vis-à-vis a specific Christian, Daniel Bomberg. For the historical "reality," and the complications in speaking about it, see Robert Bonfil, *Jewish Life in Renaissance Italy*, trans. by Anthony Oldcorn (Berkeley: University of California Press, 1991), esp. 101–24.

65. The description that follows is based upon the typology set forth in the previous chapter on the Hebrew Bible in the Middle Ages, previously published as "The Hebrew Bible in Europe in the Middle Ages: A Preliminary Typology," *Jewish Studies Internet Journal* 11 (2012): 235–322, or at http://www.biu.ac.il/JS/JSIJ/112012/Stern.pdf. As its subtitle indicates, the typology does not claim to be comprehensive; it is restricted to Europe and does not include Bibles written in either the Orient or Yemen, and it is based on an inspection of Bibles described in the catalogues of many of the major collections of Jewish books, not on direct inspection of the manuscripts themselves. As a preliminary typology, it aims to set out the general parameters of the history of the medieval European Hebrew Bible as a book, not its specifics; I have therefore refrained from offering specific numbers or percentages of each subtype or feature and have limited my comments to deliberately vague adjectives like "most" or "many" or "a few." It is my hope that future research will both fill in these details and correct the inaccuracies that my preliminary typology almost certainly contains.

66. On the halakhic permissibility of liturgical reading from a codex rather than from a Torah scroll, see Israel Ta-Shma, *Early Franco-German Ritual and Custom* [in Hebrew] (Jerusalem: Magnes, 1994), 171–81.

67. Two Spanish liturgical Pentateuchs have Ibn Ezra's commentary: Parma, Biblioteca Palatina MS [176] Pal. 2 (Spain, fifteenth century), in addition to Rashi, *Onkelos*, Masorah magna and Masorah parva, and *Patshegen*, a commentary on the Targum; and Bodleian 2327 (Oxford, Bodleian Library [Bodl.] Opp. Add. 37, Spain or Provence, fourteenth century), in addition to *Onkelos*. New York, Jewish Theological Seminary of America Lutzki 191, assigned to fourteenth-century Spain, has *Onkelos* and Saadiah's Judeo-Arabic *tafsir*, and then Rashi, all written interverse in graded-size scripts.

68. See, for a splendid example, New York, Jewish Theological Seminary of America Lutzki 206, a luxurious mid-fifteenth-century Italian Pentateuch with Nahmanides's commentary.

69. This manuscript and its importance, particularly for Rashi studies, has been hotly debated over the past twenty years. See in particular Abraham Grossman, *Ḥakhmei Tzarfat Ha-Rishonim* (The early sages of France) (Jerusalem: Magnes, 1996), 184–93, and Elazar Touitou, "Does MS Leipzig 1 Reflect the Original Text of Rashi's Commentary to the Torah" [in Hebrew], *Tarbiz* 61 (1992): 315. See also Jordan S. Penkower, "Rashi's Corrections to His Commentary on the Pentateuch," *Jewish Studies, An Internet Journal* 6 (2007): 141–86, www.biu.ac.il/JS/JIJ.

70. On the development of the format, see Christopher de Hamel, *Glossed Books of the Bible and the Origins of the Paris Booktrade* (Woodbridge: D. S. Brewer, 1984); Collete Sirat, "Le livre hebreu: Recontre de las tradition juive et de l'esthetique francaise," in *Rashi et la culture juive en France du Nord au moyen Age*, ed. Gilbert Dahan, Gérard Nahon, and Elie Nicolas (Paris: Peeters, 1997), 242–59.

71. The question of their transmission and preservation is separate from the question as to how they were initially composed. Both Geonic and Sefardic commentaries appear to have been composed as *ḥibburim*, compositions in their own right. The genesis of Ashkenazic commentaries, like those of Rashi and his tosafistic successors, is less clear; scholars disagree as to whether these commentaries were even initially composed as full commentaries or whether they originated as marginal glosses in response to comments of earlier commentators.

72. On the development of the humanist text, see the excellent article by Martin Davies, "Humanism in Script and Print," in *The Cambridge Companion to Renaissance Humanism*, ed. Jill Kraye (Cambridge: Cambridge University Press, 1996), 47–62, esp. 49–51.

73. On the early printed Hebrew Bibles, Christian D. Ginsburg's survey in his *Introduction to the Massoretico-Critical Edition* remains in many ways the most extensive discussion of early printed Bibles between 1477 and 1528, but it must be supplemented by Herbert C. Zafren, "Bible Editions, Bible Study and the Early History of Hebrew Printing," *Eretz Yisrael* 16 (1982): *241–51; the various entries in David Sandler Berkowitz, *In Remembrance of Creation: Evolution of Art and Scholarship in the Medieval and Renaissance Bible* (Waltham: Brandeis University Press, 1968), esp. items 121–49 and 165–71; and the excellent survey by Adrian Schenker, "From the First Printed Hebrew, Greek, and Latin Bibles to the First Polyglot Bible, the Complutensian Polyglot, 1477–1517," in *Hebrew Bible / Old Testament: The History of Its Interpretation*, vol. 2: *From the Renaissance to the Enlightenment*, ed. Magne Saebo (Goettingen: Vandenhoeck & Ruprecht, 2008), 276–91. See also the still useful and shorter survey by Richard Gottheil in "Bible Editions," in *The Jewish Encyclopaedia* (New York: Funk & Wagnalls, 1903) 3:154–62 (with a useful chart diagramming a stemma of influences).

74. Zafren, "Biblical Editions," *240–41. Among the earliest dated Hebrew books printed in both Italy and Spain were commentaries on the Bible by Rashi.

75. See both ibid. and Alexander Marx, "The Choice of Books by the Printers of Hebrew Incunabula," in *To Doctor R. Essays Here Collected and Published in Honor of the Seventieth Birthday of Dr. A. S. W. Rosenbach, July 22, 1946*. (Philadelphia n.p., 1946), 155–57.

76. Goldschmidt, *Earliest Editions of the Hebrew Bible*, 12–13.

77. I have excluded from my survey books of Psalms alone or other individual books.

78. Zafren, "Biblical Editions," also lists two other editions of the Pentateuch with *haftarot* and Scrolls: no. 63, Spain or Portugal, no date; and no. 64, Hijar, no date.

79. See, however, Zafren, "Biblical Editions," *243, no. 34, a Pentateuch with Targum, *haftarot*, and the Five Scrolls from Italy 1480–90 (see *Ha-Otzar li-Melekhet Ha-Defus Ha-ʿIvri Ha-Rishona ʿad Shenat Reish-Samekh* [*Thesaurus Typographiae Hebraicae Saeculi XV*], ed. Aron Freimann and Moses Marx [1924; repr., Jerusalem: Universitas-Booksellers, 1967–69], B40); and no. 37, a Pentateuch with Rashi, *haftarot*, and the Five Scrolls, Naples, 1491 (*Ha-Otzar* B20).

80. These are Proverbs with Gersonides and Menaham Meiri (1492) and Former Prophets with Gersonides and Radak (1494).

81. This point would seem to be borne out as well by Penkower's reconstruction of the early publication history of Bomberg's various editions of the Bible between 1515 and 1517, in Penkower, "First Edition," esp. 595–96.

82. Like the 1517 edition, the only thing it lacked was the convenience of the haftarot in the Pentateuch volume, but see Penkower, "First Edition," esp. 591–92, where he argues convincingly that RB 1517 began as a folio-sized liturgical Pentateuch, with the *haftarot*, the Five

Scrolls, Targum, and Rashi, which was then expanded into the full Rabbinic Bible on the Bible; the only complete copy of this edition that Penkower was able to locate is preserved today in two separate volumes: Bodl. MS Opp. Fol. 23 and Bodl. MS Opp. Fol. 41.

83. On Rashi in Sefarad, see Abraham Gross, "Rashi and the Tradition of Study of Written Torah in Sepharad," in *Rashi Studies*, ed. Z. A. Steinfeld (Ramat Gan: Bar Ilan University Press, 1993), 27–55, and Jordan S. Penkower, "The Process of Canonization of Rashi's Commentary to the Torah," in *Study and Knowledge in Jewish Thought*, ed. Howard Kreisel (Beer-Sheva: Ben Gurion University of the Negev Press, 2006), 2:123–46.

84. On Sephardim in Spain, see Bonfil, *Jewish Life*, 59–62.

85. See B. Barry Levy on the Rabbinic Bible, unpublished manuscript. Again, I want to thank Professor Levy for his willingness to share his important work-in-progress with me.

86. Elhanan Reiner, "'A Jew Does Not Need to Study Anything Except Talmud': On Study and Subjects of Study in Ashkenaz in the Early Print Period," in *Ta Shema͑: Scholarly Articles in Jewish Studies in Memory of Israel M. Ta-Shema͑*, ed. Avraham Reiner et al. (Alon Shevut: Tevunot—Herzog Seminary, 2012), 705–46, esp. 735–40. I wish to thank Professor Reiner for allowing me to read an early draft of this important article.

87. Jerome Friedman, *The Most Ancient Testimony: Sixteenth-Century Christian-Hebraica in the Age of Renaissance Nostalgia* (Athens: Ohio University Press, 1983), 13–14. For a balanced survey of Christian knowledge of Hebrew and of Christian Hebraist biblical study from Nicholas de Lyra on, see Saebo, *Hebrew Bible / Old Testament*, specifically the chapters by Lesley Smith on "Nicholas de Lyra," 49–63; Arjo Vanderjagt on "Early Humanism," 154–89; Sophie Kessler Mesguich on "Early Christian Hebraism," 254–75; and Stephen G. Burnett, on "Later Christian Hebraism," 785–826; see also Alastair Hamilton, "Humanists and the Bible," in Kraye, *Cambridge Companion to Renaissance Humanism*, 100–117.

88. For a cautionary statement about overestimating Hebraic literacy among Christian Hebraists, see Burnett, "Later Christian Hebraism," and Burnett, "Christian Hebrew Printing."

89. On Muenster, see E. I. J. Rosenthal, "Sebastian Muenster's Knowledge and Use of Jewish Exegesis," in *Essays in Honor of the Very Reverend J. H. Hertz*, ed. I. Epstein et al. (London: Goldston, 1943), 351–69. Note, too, that Muenster was not alone. According to Mesguich in her article "Early Christian Hebraism," 267 n. 59, Pellican translated into Latin both Ibn Ezra's commentary on the Pentateuch and Rashi on Genesis and Exodus, although the translations were never published, and the Hebraist Wolfgang Fabricius Caputo (1478–1541) was familiar with Ibn Ezra's biblical commentary and used him in his work (268).

90. For the correspondence and generous translations into English of the Latin texts, see Amram, *Makers of Hebrew Books*, 164–67. For additional correspondence, see Penkower, "Jacob Ben Ḥayyim," 298 n. 90. I wish to thank Jordan S. Penkower for reminding me of this correspondence.

91. The history of the various editions and their multiple commentaries is treated in B. Barry Levy's work-in-progress on the Rabbinic Bible / Mikraʾot Gedolot as well as the question of the definition of the genre.

92. Precisely how exactly scribes in the Middle Ages copied Torah scrolls—whether from another scroll or from special codices like a *tikkun*, and/or whether there was preference for using scrolls or codices—is a topic still to be explored. Most sources suggest, somewhat paradoxically, that codices were used but, in cases of doubt about particular readings or orthography, scrolls were consulted (and decisions were made by following the majority of scrolls). Menahem Meiri in *Kiryat Sefer*, ed. M. Hirschler (Jerusalem: n.p., 1996), 48, describes a scroll written by the Spaniard Meir Abulafia that was then used as a model for a specially commissioned *tikkun* in order to copy Torah scrolls in Germany. R. Isaac Alfasi (1013–1103) (cited by Menaḥem Recanati [Italy, late thirteenth to early fourteenth century] in *Piskei Halakhot*

[Bologna, 1538], no. 43), Asher ben Yehiel (Germany 1250/59–Spain 1328) (*Shut Rosh* [Constantinople, 1517], 3:6), and Moshe ben David Chalawah (Spain, 1290–1370) (*Shut Maharam Chalawah*, ed. B. Herschler [Jerusalem, 1987], no. 144) all allude in passing to copying scrolls from codices. Recanati's citation of Alfasi suggests that the reason may have been that it was feared that the Torah would be left open disrespectfully if it were used as a regular model. I wish to thank Rabbi Menaḥem Slae for assisting me in finding the latter sources.

93. See *m. Menahot* 3:7; *b. Menahot* 29a on *kotzo shel yod* (regarding a *mezuzah*) and 34a (regarding *tefillin*), from both of which the halakhah about a Torah scroll is extrapolated; *Mishneh Torah, Hilkhot Sefer Torah* 10:1; cf. *Hilkhot Tefillah u-Mezuzah ve-Sefer Torah* 1:19, 2:2, 3; *Tur Yorah Deʿah* 275:6 (end); *Shulḥan ʿArukh Yorah Deʿah* 275:6; *Oraḥ Ḥayyim* 32:4. For the most extensive discussion of the halakhic conflicts between rabbinic statements and the masoretic text, see Sid. Z. Leiman, "Masorah and Halakhah: A Study in Conflict," in *Tehillah le-Moshe: Biblical and Judaic Studies in Honor of Moshe Greenberg*, ed. M. Cogan et al. (Winona Lake, Ind.: Eisenbrauns, 1997), 291–306, esp. 292–94.

94. As is well known, there are many differences in the various codices; on differences in Torah scrolls, see Jordan S. Penkower, "A Sheet of Parchment from a 10th or 11th Century Torah Scroll: Determining Its Type Among Four Traditions (Oriental, Sefardi, Ashkenazi, and Yemenite)," *Textus* 21 (2002): 235–64.

95. See also *b. Soferim* 6:4 for the account of the three Torah scrolls kept in the Temple court where they corrected anomalous readings in each one according to the text found in the other two.

96. The most extensive discussion of these competing authorities for deciding the correct form and reading is Levy, *Fixing God's Torah*, in his detailed analysis of the various responsa of Rabbi David Ben Solomon Ibn Abi Zimra (Radbaz, 1479–1573). For the position of the Masorah in particular as an authority, see 67–88, as well as Leiman, "Masorah and Halakhah," in regard to conflicts between the Masorah and the Babylonian Talmud. Jordan S. Penkower has revisited the responsa literature in regard to the problem of biblical variants and the types of solutions offered for it, noting that the few examples always cited appear to be derived from Rashi's citations in his biblical commentaries; see Penkower, "The Bible Text Used by Rashi as Reflected in His Commentaries on the Bible" [in Hebrew], in *Rashi—The Man and His Work*, ed. by Avraham Grossman and Sara Japhet, 2 vols. (Jerusalem: Merkaz Shazar 2009), 1:99–122, in particular, 99–104.

97. Levy, *Fixing God's Torah*, esp. 102–55.

98. Abraham Ibn Ezra, introduction to his commentary on the Torah, "Ha-Derekh Ha-Ḥamishit," in *Torah Ḥayim* (Jerusalem: Mossad Harva Kook, 1986), 10; cited and translated in Levy, *Fixing God's Torah*, 21.

99. Meir ben Todros Ha-Levi Abulafia, introduction to *Masoret Seyag la-Torah* (1754; repr., Israel, n.p., 1969). On Abulafia, see Bernard Septimus, *Hispano-Jewish Culture in Transition: The Career and Controversies of Ramah* (Cambridge: Harvard University Press, 1982), 35–38, and on the complicated reception history of the book, see Israel Ta-Shma, "The Literary Oeuvre of R. Meir Halevi Abulafia," *Kiryat Sefer* 45 (1969–70), 119–26. Note as well Abulafia's Torah scroll described in note 92 above.

100. The responsum is published in *She'eilot u-Teshuvot Ha-Rashba Ha-Meyuḥasot le-Ha-Rambam* (1883; repr., Bnei-Braq: n.p., 1958), no. 232. The text as printed, however, is corrupt. For the corrected text, see Leiman, "Masorah and Halakhah," 299; Jordan S. Penkower, "Maimonides and the Aleppo Codex," *Textus* 19 (1982): 403. For a lengthy, comprehensive discussion of the entire responsum, its different versions, and its subsequent influence, see Levy, *Fixing God's Torah*, 103–30. As Levy notes (109–10), Rashba did not rule out the Masorah's value in determining other paratextual matters, like majuscular and miniscular letters, open and closed spacings, etc. His main reason for dismissing the Masorah's authority in deciding questions of

consonantal spelling was due to its own corruption and many disagreements. Jordan S. Penkower has also called to my attention the fact that Rashba's opinion had little effect on Sefardic scribes who, even in their codices, continued to copy the text as it was handed down in their tradition. On this phenomenon in general, see Leiman, "Masorah and Halakhah," esp. 302–5.

101. Meiri's formulations are to be found in both his commentary on the Talmud, *Beit Ha-Behirah ʿal Massekhet Kidushin*, ed. A. Schreiber (Jerusalem: Kedem, 1971), ad 30a, and in his scribal manual *Kiryat Sefer*, introduction, esp. 14–15. For a discussion of the two texts, see Levy, *Fixing God's Torah*, 122–30, who notes that, in *Kiryat Sefer*, Meiri granted greater authority to the Masorah than he did in his talmudic commentary, where it has virtually none. As with the Rashba, Meiri seemed to discount the Masorah's authority largely because of its corruptions and inconsistencies (*Beit Ha-Behirah ʿal Kiddushin*, p. 15), not because he doubted the Masorah's ultimate worth. As Jordan S. Penkower has noted to me, Meiri did not invalidate Torah scrolls except where he could decide that the source (upon which the disputed case was based) was clearly in error; *Kiryat Sefer* is devoted to determining correct spellings and which sections are open and closed.

102. Note Levy's concluding statement in *Fixing God's Torah*, 132: It remains to be demonstrated that, other than in fairly limited circles, until the sixteenth century the Masorah ever really totally controlled undisputed spellings of all works in Torah scrolls the way it did control most peripheral, non-orthographic details." The last statement must refer primarily to vocalization and accentuation.

103. It is worth noting in passing that, whatever his view of the origins of the *keri/ketiv* system, Radak's attitude toward the Masorah and its importance was extremely positive; on his attitude, see Frank Talmage, *David Kimchi: The Man and the Commentaries* (Cambridge: Harvard University Press, 1975), 83–94.

104. Ginsburg, *Jacob Ben Chajim Ibn Adonijah's Introduction*, 42.

105. On the "humanistic" dimensions of Abravanel's exegesis, see the excellent treatment of the Spanish commentator by Eric Lawee, in Saebo, *Hebrew Bible / Old Testament*, esp. 208–14, and esp. 208–10 on this particular example.

106. Ginsburg, *Jacob Ben Chajim Ibn Adonijah's Introduction*, 48–49. Note that in the *b. Nedarim* passage, R. Isaac's statement follows an alternative interpretation of the last part of the Nehemiah verse that understands it as referring not to "verse ending" but to "masorot." Whether or not R. Isaac's statement was associated by the Talmud's editor with that last opinion, perhaps Ibn Adoniyahu understood it that way.

107. For the phrase, see the discussion of Shmuel Safrai in *Literature of the Sages* (Assen: Van Gorcum, 1987), 182–83; Martin S. Jaffee, *Torah in the Mouth: Writing and Oral Tradition in Palestinian Jordan, 200 BCE–400 CE* (New York: Oxford University Press, 2001), 80–83 and 188–89 n. 55 for additional bibliography; and, most recently, N. Danzig, "The Ruling of Sacred Books: The Origins of the Halakhah and Its Repercussions" [in Hebrew], in *Atara L'Haim: Studies in the Talmud and Medieval Rabbinic Literature in Honor of Professor Haim Zalman Dimitrovsky*, ed. Daniel Boyarin et al. (Jerusalem: Magnes, 2000), 283–359, esp. 283 n. 1. It is worth noting that one can trace virtually the entire history of the material text of the Torah from the early rabbinic through the Amoraic and later periods by following the successive assignment of the status of *halakhah le-moshe mi-sinai* to each of its material features, from its script and parchment to its glue, etc. The assignment of this status to the Masorah by Ibn Adoniyahu in the early sixteenth century appears to be the very last stage in this history.

108. For further analysis of Ibn Adoniyahu's logic in extending the Sinaitic status to all of the Masorah, see Levy, *Fixing God's Torah*, 144–47.

109. This is a point that Penkower makes throughout chapter 3 of his dissertation, "Jacob Ben Ḥayyim," 51–147; see, for example, 60–61.

110. Again, this is a point that Penkower emphasizes throughout chapter 3 of "Jacob Ben Ḥayyim," and it is one that Ibn Adoniyahu himself made in the introduction to the Rabbinic Bible (Ginsburg, *Jacob Ben Chajim Ibn Adonijah's Introduction*, 39). The editorial policy Ibn Adoniyahu followed in not relying on speculation but on written sources was his normative one, not limited to biblical texts, as is shown by the colophon he wrote for the edition of Maimonides's *Mishneh Torah* (1524), in which Ibn Adoniyahu stated the same position, "I do not rely upon my judgment because it is weak (*kalisha*)." For the text of the colophon and discussion, see Yaakov Shmuel Spiegel, *Chapters in the History of the Jewish Book: Scholars and Their Annotations* [in Hebrew] (Ramat-Gan: Bar-Ilan University Press, 1996), 213–14 (end) and 219. On this, see also Penkower, "Jacob Ben Ḥayyim," 290–91 n. 38b, who had earlier made the same connection between Ibn Adloniyahu's statement in the introduction to the Rabbinic Bible and the *Mishneh Torah* colophon, in both of which he also cited as precedents for himself both Nahmanides (Spain, ca. 1195–ca. 1270) and Rashba; the identity of the latter is not entirely clear, but as Penkower notes there, Ginsburg misnamed Rashba in his English translation as Rashbam, Rashi's famous grandson. For the difference in attitude toward classical Greek and Latin texts and the excessive use of conjecture by editors in contemporary Italy, see Richardson, *Print Culture*, 21–23.

111. Ginsburg, *Jacob Ben Chajim Ibn Adonijah's Introduction*, 76–77.

112. Ibid., 77.

113. Penkower, "Jacob Ben Ḥayyim," 45–50.

114. As an indication of the impact of Ibn Adoniyahu's view of the homiletical and kabbalistic significance of the Masorah, it is worth noting that, in the 1548 edition, the so-called shorter commentary of the Baʿal Ha-Turim (Jacob ben Asher [1269–1343]), a homiletical and mystical commentary based on the Masorah, was first printed and has subsequently been reprinted in virtually every edition of the Rabbinic Bible .

115. Part of this was due to the expert testimony to its excellence by other scholars of the Masorah like Elia Levita (1469–1549), particularly in his laudatory poem appended to the last volume of RB 1524–25; and still later by Menaḥem di Lonzano (1550–before 1624), author of *Or Ha-Torah* and Yedidyah Norzi (1560–1626), author of the Minḥat Shai. Even if the latter figures sought to "improve" Ibn Adoniyahu's text, they nonetheless accepted it as the standard. See also Penkower's discussion of the responsum of R. Jacob b. Israel Levi (Venice, 1614) in "Jacob Ben Ḥayyim," 44–45.

116. This fact—important especially from a modern scholarly perspective—is one of the major implicit themes of Penkower's definitive study of the text types in his dissertation, but I want to thank him for explicitly calling my attention to it in a personal communication. The triumph of the Sefardic text type over the Ashkenazic in the case of Bomberg's Rabbinic Bible is also worth comparing to the near-opposite case that occurred with Bomberg's edition of the Babylonian Talmud (1521–23). That edition was based on the previous, "Ashkenazic" editions the Talmud printed by Joshua and Gershom Soncino, with their particular choice of the Tosafot in addition to the commentary of Rashi; once Bomberg's edition became the definitive, virtually universal one, it effectively spelled the demise of the Talmud as printed in Spain that sometimes contained Sefardic commentators like Nahmanides as well as, on occasion, different page layouts.

117. Moshe Goshen-Gottstein, "Foundations of Biblical Philology in the Seventeenth Century: Christian and Jewish Dimensions," in *Jewish Thought in the Seventeenth Century*, ed. Isadore Twersky and Bernard Septimus (Cambridge: Harvard University Center for Jewish Studies, 1987), 77–94; Goshen-Gottstein, introduction to *Biblia rabbinica*, esp. 9–13. More recent studies include Edward Breuer, *The Limits of Enlightenment: Jews, Germans, and the Eighteenth-Century Study of Scripture* (Cambridge: Harvard University Center for Jewish

Studies, 1996), esp. 77–107; the essays by Mesguich and Burnett in Saebo, *Hebrew Bible / Old Testament*; and Schwarzbach, "Editions de la Bible hébraïque," esp. 54–67.

118. For a summary, see Penkower, "Jacob Ben Ḥayyim," appendixes 14 and 15 (415–18). As Goshen-Gottstein perceptively argued ("Foundations," 83), the concept of a "masoretic Bible" or "masoretic text" was Christian, not Jewish. For Ibn Adoniyahu, the text he edited was the traditional biblical text "exact according to the Masorah," not one created by the Masoretes, as the term "masoretic Bible" suggests.

119. On the Haskalah project, see the definitive study of Breuer, *Limits of Enlightenment*, 109–75, and his summary in Saebo, *Hebrew Bible / Old Testament*, 1006–21. For a minor but fascinating English footnote to Breuer's underacknowledged work, see David Ruderman's account of the Anglo-Jewish reaction to Kennicott in *Jewish Enlightenment in an English Key* (Princeton: Princeton University Press, 2000), 23–56.

120. Moses Mendelssohn, *Gesammelte Schriften* (Stuttgart: Friedrich Frommann, 1971–2000), 15,1 (1990), 39–40; cited and translated in Breuer, *Limits of Enlightenment*, 161; Saebo, Hebrew *Bible / Old Testament*, 1016.

121. Esth 1:11. Given the verse's original reference in context, there is something decidedly playful about Ibn Adoniyahu's citation of it here.

CHAPTER 5

1. The history of this phrase is not clear. The earliest source I have been able to locate is in the Hebrew introduction to the *editio princeps* of Maimonides's *Commentary to the Mishnah* (Naples: Joshua Solomon Soncino, 1492), 2a (*u-mi-yam ha-talmud meshitihu*). According to the bibliographer Tuvia Preschel, the same reading is found in the Copenhagen manuscript of the *Commentary*, but in later printed editions the phrase was changed (for unknown reasons) to *mi-yam kadmoneinu* ("from the sea of our predecessors"). Preschel also notes a passage in *Shir Ha-Shirim Rabbah* (5:14:2, Vilna ed. 31b) (fifth to sixth century) that compares the Talmud to the great sea (*zeh ha-talmud she-hu ke-yam ha-gadol*). See http://www.toviapreschel .com/he/מידומלתה. I wish to thank Ephraim Kanarfogel for alerting me to Preschel's site.

2. See, for example, the Vilna editions of Maimonides's *Mishneh Torah* and the *Shulḥan ʿArukh*; the Mossad Ha-Rav Kuk edition of the mystical classic *Sefer Ha-Bahir* (Jerusalem: Mosad Harav Kook, 1950); numerous editions of the Passover Haggadah with commentaries since the late seventeenth century. For more recent attempts by Jewish authors to use the format for different purposes, see David Blumenthal, *Facing the Abusing God: A Theology of Protest* (Louisville: Westminster / John Knox, 1993), who uses the traditional format to advance an untraditional argument; Avraham Holtz, *Marʾot u-Mekorot: Mahadurah Muʾeret u-Meyuʾeret shel Ha-Khnasat Kalah shel Shai Agnon* (Jerusalem: Schocken, 1995), which effectively uses the format to elevate Agnon to a semicanonical status; and in fictional novels, Benjamin Zucker, *Blue* (Woodstock: Overlook, 2000), and Ruby Namdar, *Ha-Bayit Asher Neḥerav* (Or-Yehuda: Zemorah Bitan, 2013), and its English translation, *The Ruined House* (New York: Harper Collins, 2017). Most famously, Adin Steinsaltz used the traditional talmudic page format in the original editions of the Talmud with his own commentaries in both Hebrew and English versions (as well as other vernaculars): Jerusalem: Ha-Makhon Ha-Yisraeli le-Firsumim Talmudiyim, 1981, repr. in 1997; English edition, New York: Random House, 1989. Interestingly, the most recent editions published by Koren Publishers in Jerusalem (since 2012) have abandoned the traditional page format.

3. The first person explicitly to call attention to this connection was Collette Sirat in *Hebrew Manuscript of the Middle Ages*, ed. and trans. Nicholas de Lange (Cambridge: Cambridge University Press, 2002), 60: see also Sirat, "Le livre hebreu: Recontre de las tradition

juive et de l'esthetique francaise," in *Rashi et la culture juive en France du Nord au moyen Age*, ed. Gilbert Dahan, Gérard Nahon, and Elie Nicolas (Paris: Peeters, 1997), 242–59; and Colette Sirat, "Looking at Latin Books, Understanding Latin Texts. Different Attitudes in Different Jewish Communities," in *Hebrew to Latin, Latin to Hebrew: The Mirroring of Two Cultures in the Age of Humanism* (Berlin: Institut für Judaistik, Freie Universität; Turin: Nino Aragno Editore, 2004), 12–15. Malachi Beit-Arié, in *Hebrew Manuscripts of East and West: Towards a Comparative Codicology* (London: The British Library, 1992), 86–98, calls attention to the phenomenon of multilayered texts but does not deal specifically with the talmudic page. So far as I know, Sirat and Beit-Arié are virtually the only ones even to note the connection, though see now the remarks of Justine Isserles, "Les parallèles esthétiques des manuscrits hébreux ashkenazes de type liturgico-légal et des manuscrits latins et vernaculaires médiévaux," in *Manuscrits hébreux et arabes: Mélanges en l'honneur de Colette Sirat*, ed. Nicholas de Lange and Judith Olszowy-Schlanger, Bibliologia 38 (Turnhout: Brepols, 2014), 85–86. Most other treatments of the talmudic page deal solely with the history of its contents, not its form; see Marvin J. Heller, *Printing the Talmud: A History of the Earliest Printed Editions of the Talmud* (Brooklyn: Im Hasefer, 1992); Marvin J. Heller, "Designing the Talmud: The Origins of the Printed Talmudic Page," in *Studies in the Making of the Early Printed Book* (Leiden: Brill, 2008), 92–105; Haym Soloveitchik, "The Printed Page of the Talmud: The Commentaries and Their Authors," in *Printing the Talmud: From Bomberg to Schottenstein*, ed. Sharon Liberman Mintz and Gabriel M. Goldstein (New York: Yeshiva University Museum, 2005), 37–42; Marvin Heller, "Earliest Printings of the Talmud," in Mintz and Goldstein, *Printing the Talmud*, 61–78, repr. in Heller, *Further Studies in the Making of the Early Printed Book* (Leiden: Brill, 2013), 421–49; and Javier del Barco, "Hebrew Manuscripts: The Ashkenazi Glossed Bible," https://www.bl.uk/hebrewmanuscripts/articles/theashkenaziglossedbible. One exception is Edward Fram, "In the Margins of the Text: Changes in the Page of the Talmud," in Mintz and Goldstein, *Printing the Talmud*, 91–96. All these articles deal with the printed Talmud, none with its manuscripts.

4. Modern scholarship on the Glossa Ordinaria essentially began with Beryl Smalley in *The Study of the Bible in the Middle* Ages (Notre Dame: University of Notre Dame Press, 1964), 46–66. In the last two decades, the field has grown enormously with numerous articles on individual books and various aspects of the work. The first full-scale treatment of the Glossa as a material text was Christopher de Hamel, *Glossed Books of the Bible and the Origins of the Paris Book Trade* (Woodbridge: D. S. Brewer, 1984), which remains an essential source. The most recent book-length study, which complements de Hamel, is Lesley Smith, *The Glossa Ordinaria: The Making of a Medieval Bible Commentary* (Leiden: Brill, 2009). For a briefer treatment, see Lesley Smith, "The Glossed Bible," in *The New Cambridge History of the Bible*, vol. 2: *From 600 to 1450*, ed. Richard Marsden and E. Ann Matter (Cambridge: Cambridge University Press, 2012), 363–79, and Smith, "Biblical Gloss and Commentary: The Scaffolding of Scripture," in *The Visualization of Knowledge in Medieval and Early Modern Europe*, ed. Marcia Kupfer et al. (Turnholt: Brepols, forthcoming). Other excellent and more focused studies that deal specifically with the material dimension include Margaret T. Gibson, "The Place of the *Glossa Ordinaria* in Medieval Exegesis," in *Ad litteram: Authoritative Texts and Their Medieval Readers*, ed. Mark D. Jordan and Kent Emery Jr. (Notre Dame: University of Notre Dame Press, 1992), 5–27; Gibson, "The Twelfth-Century Glossed Bible," in *Studia Patristica Vol. XXIII: Papers Presented to the Tenth International Conference on Patristic Studies Held in Oxford 1987*, ed. Elizabeth A. Livingstone (Leuven: Peeters Press, 1989), 232–44; Gibson, "The Glossed Bible," in *Biblia Latina cum Glossa Ordinaria: Facsimile Reprint of the Editio Princeps, Adolph Rusch of Strassburg 1480/81*, ed. Karlfried Froehlich and Margaret T. Gibson (Turnhout: Brepols, 1992), vii–xi; Karlfried Froehlich, "The Printed Gloss," in Froehlich and Gibson, *Biblia Latina cum Glossa Ordinaria*, xii–xxvi.

5. Earlier scholarship misattributed the invention of the Glossa to Walafrid Strabo (d. 849), but this has now been conclusively disproven. For an alternative to Anselm and the School of Laon, see Gibson, "Twelfth-Century Glossed Bible," who proposes Hugh of Saint Victor as the key figure in its development. The work in its entirety was, in any case, the product of multiple figures, not a single individual.

6. De Hamel, *Glossed Books*, 14–27; Smith, *Glossa Ordinaria*, 91–140.

7. Smith, *Glossa Ordinaria*, 101–2.

8. Ibid., 106–7.

9. Ibid., 114–16. As she notes, because every scribe's hand is different, it would have been virtually impossible to produce exact or identical copies.

10. There are also cases where a fourth column of gloss appears on the page as a kind of insert within one of the gloss columns, or where there are two columns of Vulgate and two columns of gloss, one accompanying each Vulgate columns. The variations are innumerable.

11. For an example of such a page, see Margaret T. Gibson, *The Bible in the Latin West* (Notre Dame: University of Notre Dame Press, 1993), 60–61 (pl. 17, Peter Lombard's Magna Glosatura).

12. Gibson, "Twelfth Century Glossed Bible," 233–37; Gibson, "Place of the *Glossa Ordinaria* in Medieval Exegesis," 8–12, and especially the plates of manuscripts: pl. 1 (Frankfurt, Stadt und Universitätsbibliothek MS Barth. 32) is a glossed eighth-century Carolingian Psalter, pl. 10 (London, British Library MS Harley 3095) is a glossed Boethius ca. 1000. Cf. Richard H. Rouse and Mary A. Rouse, "*Ordinatio* and *Comilatio* Revisited," in Jordan and Emery, *Ad litteram*, 126. Some of these texts have an interlinear commentary as well, but it was not a regular feature until after 1050 C.E.; see Gibson, "Place of the *Glossa Ordinaria*," 5–6. Legal texts also use the glossed format and eventually develop a standard commentary, but that development is later. On the legal glosses, see Hermann Kantorowicz, "Note on the Development of the Gloss to the Justinian and the Canon Law," in Smalley, *Study of the Bible in the Middle Ages*, 52–55.

13. Gibson, "Place of the Glossa Ordinaria," 12–14.

14. Cited in Smith, *Glossa Ordinaria*, 5–6.

15. Ibid., 109.

16. Ibid., 114.

17. See, again, Gibson, *Bible in the Latin West*, 60–61 (pl. 17, Peter Lombard's Magna Glosatura) and 54–55 (pl. 15, Nicholas of Lyra's *Postillae*), and see especially Gibson's comments on the problem behind the page and the various solutions found for it on 62–63 (pl. 18, Stephen Langton, Commentary on Ruth). As she notes, on the Nicolas of Lyra and Langton pages, Scripture reverts to being mere lemmata on the page.

18. Colette Sirat, "Le livre hébreu: Recontre de la tradition juive et de l'esthétique française," in *Rashi et la culture juive en France du Nord au Moyen Âge*, ed. Gilbert Dahan, Gerard Nahan, and Elie Nicolas (Paris: Peeters, 1997), 248; Colette Sirat, "Notes sur la circulation de livres entre Juifs et Chrétiens au Moyen Âge," in *Du Copiste au collectionneur: Mélanges d'histoire des textes et des bibliothèques en l'honneur d'André Vernet*, ed. Donatello Nebbiae-Dalla Guarda and Jean-François Genest, Bibliologia 18 (Turnhout: Brepols, 1999), 383–403; Colette Sirat, "En vision globale: Les Juifs médiévaux et les livres latins," in *La tradition vive: Mélanges d'histoire des textes en l'honneur Louis Holtz*, ed. Pierre Lardet, Bibliologia 20 (Turnhout: Brepols, 2003), 19–23; Joseph Shatzmiller, *Cultural Exchange: Jews, Christians, and Art in the Medieval Marketplace* (Princeton: Princeton University Press, 2013), 22–26.

19. Sirat, "Livre hébreu," 248.

20. The earliest example of the form may be Leipzig 1. The dating of this manuscript has been debated, with views ranging from the early thirteenth to the mid-fourteenth century; see Abraham Grossman, *Ḥakhmei Tzarfat Ha-Rishonim* (The early sages of France) (Jerusalem:

Magnes, 1996), 184–93, and Elazar Touitou, "Does MS Leipzig 1 Reflect the Original Text of Rashi's Commentary to the Torah" [in Hebrew], *Tarbiz* 61 (1992): 315. See also Jordan S. Penkower, "Rashi's Corrections to His Commentary on the Pentateuch," *Jewish Studies, An Internet Journal* 6 (2007): 141–86, www.biu.ac.il/JS/JIJ. The *humash* is a specific genre of the medieval Hebrew Bible that contains, in addition to the Pentateuch, either all of the following texts or a combination of them—the Aramaic Targum, the *haftarot* (readings from the Prophets recited weekly after the public Torah reading in the synagogue), the Megillot (the Five Scrolls), and a few other texts that were read in the synagogue. For further discussion of the genre, see Stern, *Jewish Bible*, 89–90.

21. On the masoretic notes and their presence in different types of Jewish Bibles, see Stern, *Jewish Bible*, 68–116.

22. See Abraham Gross, "Rashi and the Tradition of Study of Written Torah in Sepharad," in *Rashi Studies*, ed. Z. A. Steinfeld (Ramat Gan: Bar Ilan University Press, 1993), 27–55, and Jordan S. Penkower, "The Process of Canonization of Rashi's Commentary to the Torah," in *Study and Knowledge in Jewish Thought*, ed. Howard Kreisel, 2 vols. (Beer-Sheva: Ben Gurion University of the Negev Press, 2006), 2:123–46.

23. Beit-Arié, *Hebrew Manuscripts*, 89. Beit-Arié also discusses an offshoot of the Glossa-influenced page layout, the "non-functional multi-layered manuscripts," where the scribe combines on the page different completely unrelated texts and whose main motive must have been "the compelling scribal quest for form and design" (88). These texts are beyond the scope of this work, but they are an extreme expression of at least some of the motivations that must have led scribes to produce some of the most creatively designed Bible and Talmud pages.

24. The most recent comprehensive census of the manuscripts, Yaacov Sussmann, *Thesaurus of Talmudic Manuscripts*, 3 vols. (Jerusalem: Yad Ben Zvi and the Friedberg Genizah Project, 2012), 3:6, lists sixty-eight, but I have subtracted six Yemenite manuscripts that clearly belong to a different scribal tradition altogether. See also "The Complete Manuscripts of the Babylonian Talmud," ed. Menachem Katz et al., https://fjms.genizah.org, 4, and Michael Krupp, "Manuscripts of the Babylonian Talmud," in *The Literature of the Sages, First Part*, ed. Shmuel Safrai (Aasen: Van Gorcum; Philadelphia: Fortress, 1987), 346–61, where he lists sixty-three manuscripts. To be sure, there are also more than 2,700 fragments of lost Talmud codices, the vast majority from the Cairo Genizah. The small number of surviving Talmud codices is partly due to the destruction of volumes in the various burnings of the Talmud, the most infamous of which occured in Paris in 1241 and in Rome in 1553. Most manuscripts of the Talmud, however, were destroyed not through acts of violence or in the course of the forced expulsions of their owners and subsequent travails, but through *overuse*; the codices were read and studied until the letters (almost) literally fell off the pages.

25. On Munich 95, see the description in Raphael Nathan Nata Rabbinowicz, *Sefer Dikdukei Soferim* (Variae Lectiones in Mischnam et in Talmud Babylonicum), 15 vols. (Munich: H. Roesl and E. Huber, 1867–1886), 1:27–35. On the uniqueness of this codex, and the likelihood that it was the only codex in the Middle Ages to contain the entire Talmud, see Shamma Friedman, "Variant Readings in the Babylonian Talmud—A Methodological Study Marking the Appearance of 13 Volumes of the Institute for the Complete Israeli Talmud's Edition," *Tarbiz* 68 (1999): 131 n. 12, and Norman Golb, *The Jews in Medieval Normandy: A Social and Intellectual History* (Cambridge: Cambridge University Press, 1998), 529–31. Golb suggests that Munich 95 is actually a copy of an earlier codex compiled by the late Tosafist Simson of Chinon as an attempt to preserve the best talmudic readings; that original codex was, Golb argues, the last major project of the Tosafist movement, an attempt to produce a kind of definitive copy of the Talmud. As we will see, one of the main thrusts of the Tosafist endeavour was to resolve every contradiction and inconsistency throughout the entire talmudic corpus and thereby to unify the entire work as a whole. If Golb is correct, Munich 95 may be seen as an attempt literally to

realize this project of unification by placing the entire Talmud within the covers of a single codex.

26. On the Florence Talmud, see David Rosenthal, introduction to *Babylonian Talmud: Codex Florence* [in Hebrew] (Jerusalem: Makor, 1972), 1–6. On the Hamburg Talmud, see the catalogue description by Gottfried Reeg in *Manuscript Cultures*, ed. Irina Wandrey (Hamburg: Centre for the Study of Manuscript Cultures, 2014), 81–84. Both page formats are found in both Ashkenazic and Sefardic manuscripts, but there appears to be a decided preference in Ashkenaz for the two-column format and in Sefarad for the single page-wide layout. In Yemen, all Talmud manuscripts have the single page-wide format.

27. *Ba'alei Ha-Tosafot*, 29 n. 72*, also lists Gratz MS III 142, which has a single leaf from a glossed MS of Shabbat, and Augsburg, Staats- und Stadtbibliothek Augsburg Fragm. rel 1, a single page from *Bava Metzi'a*. Vatican Library MS Vat. ebr. 111, which he also lists, only has the Tosafot written in some margins. Urbach apparently was unaware of Moscow, Lenin Library Cod. 594 at the time he was writing because the Russian collections had not yet been opened to Western scholars.

28. Vatican Library MS Vat. ebr. 127 (Ashkenaz, second half of the fourteenth century); Vatican Library MS Vat. ebr. 140 (Ashkenaz, fourteenth century); Oxford, Bodleian Library (Bodl.) Opp. 38 (Ashkenaz, fourteenth century); and Bodl. MS Opp. 726 (Ashkenaz, fourteenth century). The surviving leaves of some *printed* Sefardic Talmuds published in Guadalajara, Spain, and Porto, Portugal, before the expulsion in 1492 also have only Rashi and use the same "late" Glossa format.

29. The reader familiar with the printed Talmud may be surprised to find the tractate *Berakhot* in the middle of the Talmud, not at its very beginning. In fact, in the Middle Ages, the order of the tractates varied between manuscripts; in Munich 95, *Berakhot* is placed at the end of *Seder Mo'ed* (the Order of Holidays) and before *Seder Nashim* (the Order of Women).

30. This manuscript, as yet virtually unstudied, is in visual terms one of the most remarkable manuscripts written in the Middle Ages. While many of the pages utilize the straightforward three-column format illustrated in the page reproduced here, many other pages vary the format and write the Tosafot (or Rashi, or even the Gemara) in complicated geometric forms.

31. This page, Bodl. MS Opp. 248, fol. 204v, demonstrates the difficulties scribes had in coordinating all the various elements on the glossed page. The majuscule letters in the Mishnah and the Tosafot column both contain the same formulaic expression used to signify the end of one chapter and the beginning of the next: *hadran 'aleikha* (may you go back [and study again] the chapter). In this case, the chapter that concludes on this page is *Yebamot* 11, *Nos'in 'al Ha-Anusah* (which in the Bomberg and Vilna editions ends on fol. 101a). In both printed editions, this chapter is followed by the chapter beginning *Mitzvat Halitzah*. During the manuscript age, however, the sequence of chapters could vary from one codex to another, and in this manuscript, Bodl. MS Opp. 248, *Nos'in* was followed by *Heresh She-Nasa* (which in the printed editions appears as chapter 14, beginning on fol. 112b). On the page, the Mishnah, Tosafot, and Rashi columns all record texts at the end of *Nos'in* and the beginning of *Heresh*. The scribe, however, could not fit the beginning of the Gemara for *Heresh* on the page because of the length of the previous section's text. (Here, again, one also sees the fluidity of the textual tradition; the two final paragraphs of the Gemara appears in this codex in an order opposite to how they appear in the printed edition; the paragraph in a smaller script on the top is actually the final paragraph of the chapter, while the one in the slightly larger hand beneath it is the penultimate.) Note as well that elsewhere in this codex, the halakhic compendium *Sefer Mordechai* regularly appears on the page as a separate element; it is not present on this page.

32. For a description of this codex, see Rabbinowicz, *Dikdukei Soferim* 4:7–8, and the entry in the catalogue of the Institute for Microfilmed Hebrew Manuscripts at http://aleph.nli.org.il /F/XETA34LQQCR82C7USN7KUIP9GYE6YI6XY12TAAH3PEGN7L6SPP18969?func=find

acc&acc_sequence=021791545. This is an unusual manuscript for several reasons. As I will note, the Tosafot were generally not studied in Sefarad, and it is therefore more than slightly ironic that the one handwritten Talmud with a page format that most closely resembles the printed format is inscribed in a Sefardic hand and was probably written in Spain itself. The Tosafot on the page in the codex, however, are not the conventional Ashkenazic Tosafot but the Tosafot of R. Asher ben Yehiel (1250–1327), known as Tosafot Ro"sh. Asher ben Yehiel was a German Tosafist, probably born in Cologne, and a student of R. Meir of Rothenburg. After the latter was imprisoned, R. Asher emigrated to Spain and eventually settled in Toledo, where he became the community's rabbi and an immensely important religious leader throughout Sefarad. Among other things, he is credited with introducing tosafistic dialectical analysis to Sefarad, and his own Tosafot were the ones studied in Sefarad, hence their presence in this codex. At the same time, the page layout in this codex is powerful testimony to how the glossed format had spread throughout the Jewish world by the mid-fifteenth century. Also worth noting is the unusual fact that the Talmud text and the secondary texts on the page are both written in a Sefardic semicursive hand.

33. While we should pause before taking these percentages too seriously because of the small number of surviving Talmud manuscripts, fragments of lost Talmud manuscripts that survive as recycled binding material confirm the small percentage of glossed manuscripts. Among the 199 leaves described and reproduced in Mauro Perani and Saverio Campanini, *I Frammenti Ebraici di Bologna: Archivio di Stato e Collezioni Minori* (Florence: Leo S. Olschki Editore 1997), there are some thirty leaves from Talmud manuscripts. Of those thirty, twenty-one use the single page-wide format (and, except for three, all use Sefardic script); nine use the double-column format (and are all written in Ashkenazic script); and only two, both in Ashkenazic script from the thirteenth century, use the glossed format. In addition, there are three leaves from paratalmudic works that also use the Glossa format—two from copies of Alfasi's code and one from a *Sefer Mordechai*, all inscribed in Ashkenazic script. Taken together, the five examples of the Glossa format represent 18 percent of the Talmud fragments.

34. In this observation, I am deliberately excluding printers in the Iberian Peninsula—about whom, see my comments later in this chapter—because their editions did not figure in the subsequent printing history of the Talmud. Joshua Soncino was the first to print a tractate of the Talmud, *Berakhot*, in 1482–83.

35. The primary source for the use of the *sefer ha-ʿatakah* is the colophon of R. Gabriel of Strassbourg, Joshua Solomon Soncino's editor and proofreader, at the end of his edition of the tractate *Betzah*, Soncino, 1484; reproduced in *Ha-Otzar li-Melekhet Ha-Defus Ha-ʿIvri Ha-Rishona ʿad Shenat Reish-Samekh (Thesaurus Typographiae Hebraicae Saeculi XV)*, ed. Aron Freimann and Moses Marx (1924; repr., Jerusalem: Universitas-Booksellers, 1967–69), 62. On the use of the *sefer ha-ʿatakah*, see Haim Z. Dimitrovsky, introduction to *S'ridei Bavli: An Historical and Bibliographical Introduction* [in Hebrew] (New York: Jewish Theological Seminary, 1979), 1:61–69, and Heller, *Printing the Talmud*, 63–64.

36. The source for this geneology is a statement by Gershom Soncino in the colophon to his edition of David Kimchi's (Radak's) *Sefer Mikhlol* (Constantinople, 1532–34), where he writes that Moses Mentzlan, the great-grandfather of Gershom's grandfather, Israel Nathan Soncino (the true founder of the printing dynasty), was a fifth-generation descendant of Moses of Speyer, "who is mentioned in Tosafot Tukh" (on which, see my discussion later in this essay). See A. M. Habermann, *The History of the Hebrew Book* [in Hebrew] (Jerusalem: Rubin Mass, 1968), 86–87. For more on the family history, see Heller, *Printing the Talmud*, 53–54.

37. For the definitive account of the Soncino's publishing history of Rafael Natan Neta Rabinowitz, *Maʾamar ʿal Hadpasat Ha-Talmud*, ed. By A. M. Habermann (Jerusalem: Mosad Ha-Rav Kuk, 1952), 7–31. See also Heller, *Printing the Talmud*, 51–133. For a briefer version, see

Marvin J. Heller, "The Earliest Printings of the Talmud," in Mintz and Goldstein, *Printing the Talmud*, 61–78.

38. The complaint is on the title page of Soncino's 1533 Constantinople edition of Radak's *Sefer Mikhlol*. For a translation, see Moses Marx, "Gershom (Hieronymus) Soncino's Wanderyears in Italy, 1498–1527: Exemplar Judaicae Vitae," in *Hebrew Union College Annual*, 11 (1936): 485.

For more on Soncino's relationship with Bomberg, 479–84. For a new perspective on the complexity of the rivalry between Gershom Soncino and Bomberg, see Angelo M. Piattelli, "New Documents Concerning Bomberg's Printing of the Talmud," in *A Tribute to Menahem Hayyim Schmelzer*, ed. Evelyn M. Cohen, Angelo M. Piattelli, Michael Reuveni, Emile G. L. Schrijver, and Tamas Turan (Leiden: Brill, forthcoming).

39. For a comprehensive description of the Tosafot in the printed editions, see E. E. Urbach, *Baʿalei Ha-Tosafot* (The Tosafists), 4th exp. ed. (Jerusalem: Mosad Bialik, 1980), 600–75. See also Heller, *Printing the Talmud*, 102–3. The Tosafot in the printed editions, known colloquially as "our Tosafot," are mainly those edited by Eliezer of Touques, which were based on the collection of R. Samson of Sens. The many other collections of Tosafot were essentially doomed to oblivion by not making it into print until they were rediscovered in manuscript in the twentieth century.

40. On foliation for a Christian audience, see Bruce Nielsen, "Daniel van Bombergen, a Bookman of Two Worlds," in *The Hebrew Book in Early Modern Italy*, ed. Joseph R. Hacker and Adam Shear (Philadelphia: University of Pennsylvania Press, 2011), 72.

41. See Yaakov S. Spiegel, "On Methods of Citation and Reference by Names of Tractates Among Rishonim (Early Medieval Rabbinic Sages)" [in Hebrew], *Alei Sefer* 14 (1987): 29–53.

42. Only single leaves or gatherings of these manuscripts survive, but, as we will note later, Sefardic Jews studied Nahmanides's novellae on the Talmud in place of the Tosafot. So far as we know, however, no Iberian editions ever published Nahmanides on the page with the Talmud. For a description of the Iberian editions, see Dimitrovsky, *S'ridei Bavli*, vols. 1 and 2, including photographic facsimiles of all the surviving leaves, and Heller, *Printing the Talmud*, 31–49.

43. On Bomberg's finances, see Nielsen, "Daniel van Bombergen," 56–67.

44. To be sure, later editions of the Talmud added additional paratexts to the margins of the page. These include citations of parallel passages in other tractates and rabbinic texts, cross-references to halakhic codes, emendations and glosses, and various other commentaries. In still later editions, various other texts like Isaac Alfasi's *Sefer Halakhot* were added to the back of the book. For a helpful overview, see Fram, "In the Margins of the Text."

45. The first homily related in the preceding paragraph is cited in Heller, *Printing the Talmud*, 61 n., from a lesson that Heller's son's Talmud teacher gives him. For more homiletical interpretations along the same lines, see S. Y. Agnon, *Sefer, Sofer, ve-Sippur* (Tel Aviv: Schocken, 1978), 206–7. I wish to thank Shalem Yahalom for pointing me to Agnon. The same reification of the talmudic page is reflected in the fantastic accounts (or are they shtetl legends?) of the "pin test," wherein students in the celebrated yeshivot of Eastern Europe would test their talmudic erudition (and entertain themselves in their spare time) by sticking a pin through one letter of a word on the page, and then identifying the letters that the pin went through on the other pages in the volume. In other words, these students memorized not only the text of the Talmud but its precise layout on the page.

46. For the most extensive recent treatment of "visual epistemology" or "the materiality of reading," see Johanna Drucker, *Graphesis: Visual Forms of Knowledge Production* (Cambridge: Harvard University Press, 2014); on the Talmud and other ancient and medieval texts, see 161–79. The classic article on the subject is D. S. McKenzie, "The Book as an Expressive

Form," from his *The Pannizi Lectures, 1985: Bibliography and the Sociology of Texts* (London: The British Library, 1986), 1–20. For two other seminal articles especially relevant to our subject, see Malcom B. Parkes, "The Influence of *Ordinatio* and *Compilatio* on the Development of the Book," in *Scribes, Scripts, and Readers* (London: Hambledon Press, 1991), 121–42, and Roger Chartier and Peter Stallybrass, "What Is a Book?," in *The Cambridge Companion to Textual Scholarship*, ed. Neil Fraistat and Julia Flanders (Cambridge: Cambridge University Press, 2013), 188–204.

47. Quoted in Avraham Grossman, *The Early Sages of France: Their Lives, Leadership and Works* (Jerusalem: Magnes, 1996), 178. For the process of the canonization of Rashi's Talmud commentary, see 175–81.

48. Drucker, *Graphesis*, 3 and passim. See also Peter Storkenson, "Explicit and Implicit Graphs: Changing the Frame," *Visual Language* 26, nos. 3–4 (1992): 389–436, and on the Talmud specifically, 425–27. I wish to thank Jeffrey Hamburger for bringing Storkenson's article to my attention.

49. While there is a large body of classical works on talmudic methodology (*darkhei ha-talmud*), there is as yet no single definitive modern study of how the *sugya* works. Pro tem, see Shamma Friedman, "General Introduction to Research on the Sugya" [in Hebrew], in *Talmudic Studies: Investigating the Sugya, Variant Readings and Aggada* (New York: Jewish Theological Seminary of New York, 2010), 3–36.

50. On these textual assumptions and their application, see David Stern, "On Canonization in Rabbinic Literature," in *Jewish Literary Cultures*, vol. 1: *The Ancient Period* (University Park: Pennsylvania State University Press, 2015), 140–60, esp. 150–60.

51. The most comprehensive treatment of Tosafist methodology is Urbach, *Ba'alei Ha-Tosafot*, 676–752; see also Israel M. Ta-Shema, *Ha-Sifrut Ha-Parshanit le-Talmud be-Eiropa u-ve-Tzefon Afrika: Ḥelek Sheini, 1200–1400 (Talmudic Commentary in Europe and North Africa: Literary History Part Two, 1200–1400)* (Jerusalem: Magnes, 2000), 94–115. For the most succinct and lucid exposition in English, see Soloveitchik, "Printed Page of the Talmud," 38–42.

52. On Tosafist adjudication, see Ephraim Kanarfogel, "Progress and Tradition in Medieval Ashkenaz," *Jewish History* 14 (2000): 287–315. For an insightful contextualization, see Talya Fishman, *Becoming the People of the Talmud: Oral Torah as Written Tradition in Medieval Jewish Culture* (Philadelphia: University of Pennsylvania Press, 2011), 121–54.

53. On the emergence of pilpul as a distinctive mode of dialectical analysis, see Israel M. Ta-Shema, "Tosfot Gornish—Their Character and Relations to the Methods of Pilpul and Ḥilluk" and "New Information about Tosfot Gornish and Their Importance," in *Knesset Meḥkarim (Studies in Medieval Rabbinic Literature)*, vol. 1: *Ashkenaz* (Jerusalem: Mossad Bialik, 2004), 345–55 and 356–71. For a recent attempt to date the beginning of pilpul even earlier, to late Tosafists living in the second half of the thirteenth century, see Shalem Yahalom, "The *Pilpul* Method of Talmudic Stude: Earliest Evidence" [in Hebrew], *Tarbiz* 84 (2017): 543–74. Note that an analogous mode of casuistic Talmud study developed in Sefarad known as *Iyyun Sefaradi*, most famously in the school of R. Isaac Canpanton (1360–1463), the author of *Darkhei Ha-Talmudi*, but because this school had no impact on the history of the talmudic page, it is beyond the scope of this chapter. On Canpanton, see Daniel Boyarin, *Ha-Iyyun Ha-Sefaradi le-Farshanut Ha-Talmud shel Megureshei Sefarad* (Jerusalem: Ben Zvi Institute and Hebrew University, 1989), and Sergey Dolgopolski, *What Is Talmud? The Art of Disagreement* (New York: Fordham University Press, 2009), 69–110, 179–229.

54. For talmudic sources, see *m. Avot* 6:6 and *b. Bava Batra* 145b. On the meaning of the root, *p-l-p-l*, as referring to "the act of turning to one side, then to the other," see Hanoch Yallon, *Studies in the Hebrew Language* [in Hebrew] (Jerusalem: Mossad Bialik, 1971), 89–93, esp. 89–90. See also Dov Raffel, *Ha-Vikkuaḥ 'al Ha-Pilpul (The Debate Over the Pilpul)* (Jerusalem: Dvir, 1979), 11 n. 1. As Raffel notes, the mistaken claim that *pilpul* derives from *pilpel*, "pepper,"

is based on a Talmud passage (*b. Yoma* 85b) that compares a certain sage's scholastic acuity to "pepper." In fact, the two words, *pilpul* and *pilpel*, are not related.

55. On the rise of pilpul in the late Middle Ages and early modern period, see Mordechai Breuer, "The Rise of Pilpul and the Ḥilukim in the Yeshivot of Ashkenaz" [in Hebrew], in *Sefer Zikaron le-Yeḥiel Yaʿakov Weinberg* (Jerusalem: Feldheim, 1970), 241–55; Mordechai Breuer, "Pilpul," in *Encyclopaedia Judaica*, ed. Michael Berenbaum and Fred Skolnick (Detroit: Macmillan Reference, 2007), 16:161–63; H. Z. Dimitrovsky, "On the Method of Pilpul" [in Hebrew], in *Salo Wittmeyer Baron Jubilee Volume*, ed. Saul Lieberman and Arthur Hyman (Jerusalem: American Academy for Jewish Research, 1975), 111–81; Elhanan Reiner, "Changes in the Yeshivot of Poland and Ashkenaz in the 16th and 17th Centuries and the Controversy over Pilpul" [in Hebrew], in *Studies in Jewish Culture in Honour of Chone Shmeruk*, ed. Israel Bartal, Ezra Mendelsohn, and Chava Turniansky (Jerusalem: Shazar Center, 1993), 9–80. For an overview of the entire phenomenon of analytic study over a thousand years, see Raffel, *Ha-Vikkuah*. The "invention" of pilpul and its introduction into the Polish yeshiva is conventionally attributed to Jacob Pollack (1460–1541), about whom, see Elhanan Reiner, "'The One Whose Students Are the Giants On This Earth,' Rabbi Jacob Pollack: The First and Foremost of the Sages of Cracow," in *Kroke-Kazimierz-Cracow: Studies in the History of Cracow Jewry* (Tel Aviv: The Center for the History of Polish Jewry, The Diaspora Research Institute, Tel Aviv University, 2001), 43–68.

56. For descriptions of these techniques and assumptions, see Breuer, "Rise of Pilpul," 247–49; and Dimitrovsky, "On the Method of Pilpul," 116–22.

57. Dimitrovsky, "On the Method of Pilpul," 116–18.

58. Reiner, "Changes in the Yeshivot." Reiner's argument is much more expansive and subtle than my brief summary suggests. He ties the controversy over pilpul both to the changing status of rabbinic leadership and to the impact of print upon study and practice of adjudication.

59. Eliyahu ben R. Elkanah Capsali, *Seder Eliyahu Zuta*, ed. A. Shmuelavitz, S. Simonsohn, and M. Benayahu (Jerusalem: Ben Zvi Institute, 1977), 2:246–47. On the passage, see Reiner, "Changes in the Yeshivot," 16–24; Breuer, "Rise of Pilpul," 245–46; and Dimitrovsky, "On the Method of Pilpul," 119–22.

60. Capsali, *Seder Eliyahu Zuta*, 2:246–47.

61. Quoted from *Begidat Ha-Zeman* by Breuer, "Rise of Pilpul," 246, from a manuscript in the Bibliotheque nationale de France.

62. Natan Neta Hannover, *Sefer Yeven Metzulah, Megilat ʾEifah, Gezeirot T"Ḥ ve-T"T* (Tel Aviv: Ha-Kibbutz Ha-Meuchad, 1966), corr. ed. by I. Heilprin (Toronto: n.p., 1991). For an English translation (with some inaccuracies), see Abraham J. Mesch, *Abyss of Despair (Yeven Metzulah)*, with a new forward by William B. Helmreich (1950; repr., New Brunswick: Transaction Books, 1983), 113.

63. Reiner, "Changes in the Yeshivot," 37–43.

64. On the *ḥiluk*, see Dimitrovsky, "On the Method of Pilpul," 117–19.

65. Reiner, "Changes in the Yeshivot," 43–47.

66. Dimitrovsky, "On the Method of Pilpul," 117, notes that the pilpul itself has two stages. In the first, the student is supposed to attempt to explain the meaning of the talmudic passage on his own, without looking at Rashi and the Tosafot, in order to discover the logic of the discourse by himself, and so that the student can then "test" Rashi's understanding more objectively, as it were.

67. Hebrew: *kitzurim u-setirot*. For my translation, see Dimitrovsky's explanation of the meanings of these terms, in "On the Method of Pilpul," 155–60.

68. Hannover, *Sefer Yeven Metzulah*, 85.

69. Reiner, "Changes in the Yeshivot," 41–43.

CHAPTER 6

1. Among the more prominent works are Marc Michael Epstein, *Dreams of Subversion in Medieval Jewish Art and Literature* (University Park: Pennsylvania State University Press, 1997); Richard I. Cohen, *Jewish Icons: Art and Society in Modern Europe* (Berkeley: University of California Press, 1998); Vivian B. Mann, *Jewish Texts on the Visual Arts* (Cambridge: Cambridge University Press, 2000); Kalman P. Bland, *The Artless Jew: Medieval and Modern Affirmations and Denials of the Visual* (Princeton: Princeton University Press, 2001); Anthony Julius, *Idolizing Pictures: Idolatry, Iconoclasm, and Jewish Art* (London: Thames and Hudson, 2001); Samantha Baskind and Larry Silver, *Jewish Art: A Modern History* (London: Reaktion Books, 2011); Margaret Olin, *The Nation Without Art: Examining Modern Discourses on Jewish Art* (Lincoln: University of Nebraska Press, 2011); Rachel Neis, *The Sense of Sight in Rabbinic Culture: Jewish Ways of Seeing in Late Antiquity* (Cambridge: Cambridge University Press, 2013); Marc Michael Epstein, ed., *Skies of Parchment / Seas of Ink: Jewish Illuminated Manuscripts* (Princeton: Princeton University Press, 2015).

2. For primary texts, including rabbinic responsa, see Mann, *Jewish Texts*, 19–34; Kalman Bland, "Defending, Enjoying, and Regulating the Visual," in *Judaism in Practice: From the Middle Ages Through the Early Modern Period*, ed. Lawrence Fine (Princeton: Princeton University Press, 2001), 281–97.

3. The locus classicus for rabbinic opposition to the making of images in books in particular is the famous responsum of Meir of Rothenburg (1215–93) (*Responsa Maharam of Rothenburg* [Jerusalem: Bet Mishmar Sefarim Yahadut, 1986], no. 56, translated in Mann, *Jewish Texts*, 111–12), in which he objects to illustrations because they are distracting and detract from concentrating upon prayers; he explicitly states, however, that illustrations are not prohibited on account of idolatry. The same criticism is often made of micrography; see the remarks of R. Judah He-Ḥasid in *Sefer Ḥasidim*, ed. Judah Wistinetzki (1891; repr., Frankfurt: M. A. Wahrmann, 1924), 184; on which, see Malachi Beit-Arié, "Ideals Versus Reality: Scribal Prescriptions in *Sefer Ḥasidim* and Contemporary Scribal Practices in Franco-German Manuscripts," in *RASHI, 1040–1990: Hommage à Ephraïm E. Urbach*, ed. Gabrielle Sed-Rajna (Paris: Editions du Cerf, 1993), 559–66. The ubiquitous presence of illustrations in prayerbooks, especially in those that are Ashkenaz, and of micrographic illustrations particularly in Ashkenazic masoretic Bibles is vivid testimony to how little artists or patrons paid attention to the rabbinic objections. For discussion of this topic, see Bland, *Artless Jew*, 59–91; see also Bezalel Narkiss, "The Illuminations of the Worms Maḥzor," in *Worms Maḥzor: MS Jewish National and University Library Heb. 4° 781/1*, ed. Malachi Beit-Arié (London: Cyelar; Jerusalem: Jewish National and University Library, 1985), intro. vol., 88–89. On micrography, see Leila Avrin, "Micrography as Art," in Colette Sirat and Leila Avrin, *La lettre hébraïque et sa signification: Micrography as Art* (Paris: Centre National De La Recherche Scientifique, 1981), 51–53.

4. This is not to say that Jewish art is found only in liturgical contexts. The earliest dated illustrated Hebrew manuscript is the famous Rashi commentary, Munich, Bayerische Staatsbibliothek (BSB) Cod. Heb. 5, composed in 1232/33, on which (specifically about its aniconism), see Eva Frojmovic, "Jewish Scribes and Christian Illuminators—Interstitial Encounters and Cultural Negotiation," in *Between Judaism and Christianity: Art Historical Essay in Honor of Elisheva (Elisabeth) Revel-Neher*, ed. Katrin Kogman-Appel and Mati Meyer (Leiden: Brill, 2009), 281–305. A number of Bibles with illustrations were composed in both Ashkenaz and Sefarad, though the illustrations in these books are typically small in number and appear mainly as organizational and structural markers at heads of books. The most commonly illustrated nonliturgical text is Maimonides's *Mishneh Torah*, particularly in Ashkenaz (somewhat ironically, given Maimonides's lack of enthusiasm for illustrated books); see, for examples, the Kaufmann Mishneh Torah (Cologne, 1295–96), the Jerusalem Mishneh Torah (copied in

Spain, fourteenth century, illustrated in Italy, ca. 1400), and the Frankfort Mishneh Torah (northern Italy, fifteenth century). For further discussion of these manuscripts, see the notes ad locum in Bezalel Narkiss, *Hebrew Illuminated Manuscripts* (Jerusalem: Leon Amiel, 1992).

5. Lebanon is a common epithet in rabbinic literature for the Temple, which was built out of the cedars of Lebanon.

6. Nearly the entire line is quoted from Song 4:8, which in context is spoken by the lover to his beloved; in the poem, the line is spoken, it seems, by the prayer leader reciting the poem.

7. Hebrew: *amanah*, a place-name, but used here as a synonym for the covenant.

8. See Isa 57:9. The "king" here may be both a reference to God and to the Messiah. In the Song of Songs, Solomon was often identified as "the king."

9. On the identity of these figures, see Narkiss, "Illuminations," 83. For a recent discussion of the Jew's hat, see Sara Lipton, *Images of Intolerance: The Representation of Jews and Judaism in the Bible moralisée* (Berkeley: University of California, 1999), 15–20 and the bibliography cited on 158 nn. 4 and 5.

10. For the most recent and satisfying discussion, see Marc Michael Epstein, *The Medieval Haggadah: Art, Narrative, and Religious Imagination* (New Haven: Yale University Press, 2011), 45–63. For an earlier summary of the differing views, see Narkiss, "Illuminations," 87–89, with bibliography. For an earlier exchange on the vexed question, see Ruth Melinkoff, *Antisemitic Hate Signs in Hebrew Illuminated Manuscripts from Medieval Germany* (Jerusalem: Center for Jewish Art, 1999), and the sharp critique of Marc Michael Epstein, "Representations of the Jewish Image: Three New Contributions," *AJS Review* 26 (2002): 327–40.

11. On the place of the maḥzor's composition and original home, see Beit-Arié, "The Worms Maḥzor: Its History and Its Palaeographic and Codicological Characteristics," in Beit-Arié, *Worms Maḥzor*, intro. vol., 13–35, esp. 19–20, repr. in Beit-Arié, *The Makings of the Medieval Hebrew Book: Studies in Palaeography and Codicology* (Jerusalem: Magnes, 1993), 152–75.

12. For an excellent overview of views on the history of Jewish prayer, see Stefan C. Reif, *Judaism and Hebrew Prayer: New Perspectives on Jewish Liturgical History* (Cambridge: Cambridge University Press, 1993), 88–121.

13. Classic texts on the early development of rabbinic prayer include Joseph Heinemann, *Prayer in the Talmud: Forms and Patterns*, trans. Richard Sarason (Berlin: de Gruyter, 1977), and Ezra Fleischer, "On the Beginnings of Obligatory Jewish Prayer" [in Hebrew], *Tarbiz* 69 (1990): 397–441; see also Reif, *Judaism*, 88–21; Ruth Langer, "Revisiting Early Rabbinic Liturgy: The Recent Contributions of Ezra Fleischer," *Prooftexts* 19 (1999): 179–94.

14. On the orality of early prayer, see Stefan C. Reif, "Written Prayer from the Genizah: Its Physical Aspect and Relationship to Its Content," in *From Qumran to Cairo: Studies in the History of Prayer* [in Hebrew], ed. Joseph Tabory (Jerusalem: Orhot Press, 1999), 121–30. See the statement of Ḥaninah ben Dosa in *m. Berakhot* 5:5 and its continuation: "If an individual errs in his prayers, it is a bad sign for him, and if the prayer leader errs, it is a bad sign for him and for his congregation." Note also the following story, in which Ḥaninah says that he can tell if his prayer has been accepted or not by how fluently it flows from his lips. On the phrase, "shegurah/shagrah tefillati be-fi" and its relevance for understanding the phenomenology of prayer, see Shlomo Naeh, "'Creates the Fruit of Lips': A Phenomenological Study of Prayer According to Mishnah Berakhot 4:3, 5:5" [in Hebrew], *Tarbiz* 63 (1994): 185–218. For Greco-Roman attitudes toward the advantages of reciting a speech from memory rather than from a written text, see Quintillian, *Institutio Oratoria* 11.3.132–33: "The same remark also applies to the practice of being prompted aloud or reading from a manuscript as though uncertain of our memory. For all these mannerisms impair the force of our speaking, chill the effect of emotional appeals and make the judge think that he is not being treated with sufficient respect." Translation from Quintillian, *The Institutio Oratoria of Quintillian*, trans. H. E. Butler (Cambridge: Harvard University Press, 1922), 4:315. See also Pliny the Younger, *Epistulae* 2.19:

"I know very well that speeches when read lose all their warmth and spirit, almost their entire character." Translation from Pliny the Younger, *Letters and Panegyricus*, trans. Betty Radice (Cambridge: Harvard University Press, 1969), 1:147.

15. For discussion of this topic, see Jakob J. Petuchowski, "Some Laws of Jewish Liturgical Development," *Judaism* 34, no. 3 (Summer 1985): 312–26.

16. See Fleischer, "On the Beginnings," 426–27. The main source for a quorum is *m. Megillah* 4:3.

17. On the beginnings of piyyut, see the classic article of Ezra Fleischer, "Studies in the Problems of the Liturgical Function of the Types of Early Piyyut" [in Hebrew], *Tarbiz* 40 (1970–71): 41–63.

18. For the Hebrew text, see Jacob Mann, "Genizah Fragments of the Palestinian Order of Service," *HUCA* 2 (1925): 323. For the English translation, see Joseph Heinemann, *Literature of the Synagogue*, ed. Jakob J. Petuchowski (New York: Gorgias Press, 1975), 217.

19. For sources of the imagery, see Ps 80:9 (for Israel as a vine); Ps 78:16 and Prov 5:15 (for water); *Shir Ha-Shirim Rabbah* 1 (for Torah as water). For Horeb, see also *Shemot Rabbah* 2:4 and 51:8.

20. On opposition to piyyut, see Ruth Langer, *To Worship God Properly: Tensions Between Liturgical Custom and Halakhah Judaism* (Cincinnati: Hebrew Union College Press, 1998), 110–87. For earlier treatments, see Louis Ginzberg, ed., *Ginzei Schechter* [Hebrew], 2 vols. (New York: Jewish Theological Seminary of America, 1929), 2:504–73 (vol. 2 includes the text of *Pirkei ben Baboi*'s famous attack on piyyut).

21. See Ezra Fleischer, *Hebrew Liturgical Poetry in the Middle Ages* [in Hebrew] (Jerusalem: Magnes, 1975), 279–83, 311–16.

22. For a few examples, see the famous piyyut composed by the ninth-century southern Italian *paytan* Amittai b. Shefatyah in honor of the marriage of his sister Cassiah (in *Megillat Ahima'atz* [in Hebrew], ed. Benjamin Klar [Jerusalem: Sifrei Tarshish, 1974], 606); the piyyutim composed in the wake of the earthquake in Tiberias (tenth to twelfth century); and the heartbreaking *kerovah* of R. Yehoshua He-Haver R be-R. Natan on the death of his son (published in Menachem Zulay, *Eretz Israel and Its Poetry: Studies in Piyyutim from the Cairo Geniza* [in Hebrew] [Jerusalem: Magnes, 1995], 153–77, supplemented by Ezra Fleischer, "Matters of Piyyut and Poetry," in *Studies in Literature Presented to Simon Halkin* [in Hebrew], ed. Ezra Fleischer [Jerusalem: Magnes, 1973], 183–89). I wish to thank Professor Yosef Yahalom for pointing me to these last references.

23. For a caveat to this general rule, however, see Ezra Fleischer's remarks relating to the Ashkenazic mahzor (and Worms Mahzor in particular) in his "Prayer and Piyyut," in Beit-Arié, *Worms Mahzor*, intro. vol., 53.

24. Yosef Yahalom, *Mahzor Eretz Yisrael: A Geniza Codex* [in Hebrew] (Jerusalem: Magnes, 1987); Fleischer, "Piyyut and Prayer"; and Joseph Yahalom, "Eretz-Israel *MAHZORIM* in the Genizah: From Palaeography to Liturgy," in *"From a Sacred Source" Genizah Studies in Honour of Professor Stefan C. Reif*, ed. Ben Outhwaite and Siam Bhayro (Leiden: Brill, 2010), 357–75.

25. On *Seder Rav Amram*, see Robert Brody, *The Geonim of Babylonia and the Shaping of Medieval Jewish Culture* (New Haven: Yale University Press, 1998), 191–93 and the references there to the earlier works of Daniel Goldschmidt, Louis Ginzberg, and Jacob N. Epstein.

26. Joseph Tabory, "The Prayer Book (Siddur) as an Anthology of Judaism," in *The Anthology in Jewish Literature*, ed. David Stern (New York: Oxford University Press, 2004), 143–58.

27. Again, a recent study is Robert Brody, "The Enigma of *Seder Rav 'Amram*," in *Knesset Ezra: Literature and Life in the Synagogue: Studies Presented to Ezra Fleischer* [in Hebrew], ed. Shulamit Elitzur, Moshe D. Herr, Gershon Shaked, and Avigdor Shinan (Jerusalem: Ben-Zvi Institute, 1994), 21–34.

28. On Siddur Saadiah, see Brody, *Geonim*, 260 and esp. 153–54; the quoted words are from Brody's translation of the introduction to the siddur on its latter pages. See also Reif, *Judaism*, 187–89.

29. On the development of the medieval rites, as alluded to here and discussed briefly in the next paragraph, see Reif, *Judaism*, 153–206; Ismar Elbogen, *Jewish Liturgy*, trans. Raymond Scheindlin (Philadelphia: Jewish Publication Society, 1993), 271–85. In *Hebrew Manuscripts of the Middle Ages* (Cambridge: Cambridge University Press, 2002), Colette Sirat displays two illustrations of Maḥzor Vitry—the prayerbook of the School of Rashi—that vividly illustrate the history of the prayerbook; see illustrations 140 (p. 197, late twelfth century) and 53 (p. 124, thirteenth century, with a commentary in micrographic zoomorphic decoration).

30. The discussion here and in the following paragraphs draws extensively upon the published works of Malachi Beit-Arié and Colette Sirat, especially Beit-Arié, *Hebrew Codicology: Tentative Typology of Technical Practices Employed in Hebrew Dated Manuscripts* (1977; repr., Jerusalem: Israel Academy of Sciences and Humanities, 1981); Beit-Arié, *Hebrew Manuscripts of East and West: Towards a Comparative Codicology* (London: The British Library, 1993); Beit-Arié, *Unveiled Faces of Medieval Hebrew Books: The Evolution of Manuscript Production—Progression or Regression?* (Jerusalem: Magnes, 2003); and Sirat, *Hebrew Manuscripts*. See also Stefan C. Reif, "Codicological Aspects of Jewish Liturgical History," *Bulletin of the John Rylands University Library* 75 (1993): 117–31.

31. Beit-Arié, *Hebrew Manuscripts*, 84.

32. On this manuscript, see George Margoliouth, *Catalogue of the Hebrew and Samaritan Manuscripts in the British Museum*, 4 vols. (1899–1935; repr., London: British Museum, 1965), 2:218–33.

33. On the layout of glossed pages as well as multilayered ones, see my discussion in chapter 5 of this volume on the topography of the talmudic page.

34. The earliest surviving codex with representational illustrations is the famous Rashi codex, BSB Cod. Heb. 5, on which, see Frojmovic, *Jewish Scribes and Christian Illuminators*. The appearance of Jewish book art at that time is typically attributed to the movement of artistic workshops out of monasteries and their establishment in urban centers where most everyone could have access to them. An earlier view whose most vocal spokesperson was the eminent art historian Kurt Weitzmann sought to trace a continuous history of Jewish book illustration back to antiquity; see Weitzmann, *Illustrations in Roll and Codex: A Study of the Origin and Method of Text Illustration* (Princeton: Princeton University Press, 1947), and Weitzmann, "The Illustration of the Septuagint," in *Studies in Classical and Byzantine Manuscript Illumination*, edited by Herbert L. Kessler (Chicago: University of Chicago Press, 1971), 45–75. For Jewish art historians who followed Weitzman, see Narkiss, *Hebrew Illuminated Manuscripts*, 14, and Joseph Gutmann, *Images of the Jewish Past: An Introduction to Medieval Hebrew Miniatures* (New York: Society of Jewish Bibliophiles, 1965). For a reappraisal, see Katrin Kogman-Appel, "Bible Illustration and the Jewish Tradition," in *Imaging the Early Medieval Bible*, ed. John W. Williams (University Park: Pennsylvania State University Press, 1999), 61–96; Katrin Kogman-Appel, *Illuminated Haggadot from Medieval Spain: Biblical Imagery and the Passover Holiday* (University Park: Pennsylvania State University Press, 2006), 135–45. The Weitzmann theory has largely been discarded in most recent scholarship.

35. My discussion of the Worms Maḥzor is based on the magnificent facsimile edition, Beit-Arié, *Worms Mahzor*. The entire facsimile, including its introductory volume with scholarly essays, is now accessible digitally at http://www.jnul.huji.ac.il/dl/mss/worms.

36. Beit-Arié, "Worms Maḥzor," 15–17 (= *Makings*, 154–56).

37. Mainly on fol. 224v, but in various other places as well; see Beit-Arié, "Worms Maḥzor," 28–29 (= *Makings*, 167–68).

38. For the full account, see Beit-Arié, "Worms Maḥzor," 29–30 (= *Makings*, 168–69).

39. On the Worms rite, see E. Daniel Goldschmidt, "The Worms Maḥzor" [in Hebrew], *Kirjath Sepher* 34 (1959): 388–96, repr. in Goldschmidt, *Studies in Prayer and Liturgical Poetry* (Jerusalem: Magnes, 1979), 9–30, and Fleischer, "Prayer and Piyyut," esp. 66–78. Our major source for knowledge of the Worms rite is the famous *Customs of the Holy Community of Worms* [in Hebrew], comp. Rabbi Yuzpa Shamash, ed. Benjamin S. Hamburger and Eric Zimmer (Jerusalem: Mifʿal torat ḥakhme Ashkenaz, Mekhon Yerushalayim, 1988).

40. For other appearances of *ein omrim* in the maḥzor, see fols. 131r, 131v, and 156r. Goldschmidt, *Studies*, 10–11, notes that in some instances the punctuator left unpunctuated sections of prayers that were no longer recited in Worms.

41. See Fleischer, "Prayer and Piyyut," 44–45. For another example, see fols. 219–20, which were inserted in order to replace fols. 89–90.

42. For such a book, see the Esslingen Maḥzor (Ashkenaz, 1290), Library of the Jewish Theological Seminaryof America MS 9344.

43. For wax stains, see fols. 154–76 and esp. 158r–v, 160r, and 163v. For references to the custom, see Beit-Arié, "Worms Maḥzor," 30 (= *Markings*, 169) and nn. 103–4.

44. The literal translation, according to Chone Shmeruk, "The Versified Old Yiddish Blessing in the Worms Maḥzor," in Beit-Arié, *Worms Maḥzor*, intro. vol., 100), is "May a good day be available (or lit up) for him who carries this *mahzor* to the synagogue."

45. The manuscript is National Library of Israel (Jewish National and University Library) MS 38°4281 (Record No. 000042830). In the margins of the pages containing the chronicle of the earthquake in Norcia, later writers added chronicles of earthquakes in Larippa in 1291 and in Tocco in 1457. The maḥzor also contains a *seliḥah* "On the Earthquakes," by Matityah of Larippa, published in Hayim Schirmann, ed., *Selection of Hebrew Poetry in Italy* [in Hebrew] (Berlin: Schocken, 1934), 179–81. For the library list, see Ephraim E. Urbach, "A List of Hebrew Books from Early Printing Times" [in Hebrew], *Kirjath Sepher* 15 (1938): 237–39.

46. Most of the information here and in the subsequent paragraphs is culled from Narkiss, "Illuminations," 83–86. See also Gabrielle Sed-Rajna, *Le Mahzor enluminé: Les voies de formation d'un programme iconographique* (Leiden: Brill, 1983), 32–37; Sed-Rajna, "The Image in the Text: Methodological Aspects of the Analysis of Illustrations and Their Relation to the Text," *Bulletin of the John Rylands University Library* 75 (1993): 25–32.

47. On these floors, see Steven Fine, *Art and Judaism in the Greco-Roman World: Toward a New Jewish Archaeology* (Cambridge: Cambridge University Press, 2005), 196–205; Lee I. Levine, *The Ancient Synagogue: The First Thousand Years* (New Haven: Yale University Press, 1999), 572–78; and Rachel Hachlili, "The Zodiac in Ancient Jewish Synagogal Art: A Review," *JSQ* 9 (2002): 219–58.

48. For the most recent and comprehensive treatment of the zodiac in synagogue floor mosaics, see Lee I. Levine, *Visual Judaism in Late Antiquity: Historical Contexts of Jewish Art* (New Haven: Yale University Press, 2012), 318–36.

49. See Joseph Yahalom, "The Zodiac in the Early Piyyut in Eretz-Israel" [in Hebrew], *Meḥkerei Yerushalayim be-Sifrut ʿIvrit* 9 (1986): 313–22, and Yahalom, *Poetry and Society in Jewish Galilee of Late Antiquity* [in Hebrew] (Tel Aviv: Ha-Kibbutz Ha-Meuchad, 1999), 22–23; see also Seth Schwartz, *Imperialism and Jewish Society, 200 B.C.E. to 640 C.E.* (Princeton: Princeton University Press, 2001), 270–72, and Fine, *Art and Judaism*, esp. 201–5. Throughout his book, though (e.g., 184–95 in addition to the pages cited earlier), Fine offers a nuanced and thoughtful portrait of the role of art in the ancient synagogue and its relation to the classical Jewish liturgy and especially to piyyut.

50. See Narkiss, "Illuminations," 84. For example, Aquarius—in Hebrew, *deli*—is illustrated in Jewish texts as a bucket (the literal meaning of *deli*) rather than as a water carrier, the typical Christian illustration. Aries, "ram" in Latin—the sign for Nisan—is called *taleh*, "lamb" in Hebrew, and illustrated accordingly.

51. It is worth noting that the zodiac, despite the apparent incongruity of its presence in a Jewish prayerbook, is essentially the only illustration from medieval Jewish prayerbook art to remain in the prayerbook after the advent of the printing press. In my personal library, I own copies of maḥzorim printed in Sulzbach (1762, 1795) and in Offenbach (1797), both of which continue to print woodcuts of the zodiac and the monthly labors (though combined into a single image) that follow the Worms Maḥzor's style; the woodblocks in the two printings differ from each other, however. I have also seen an American prayerbook from the beginning of the twentieth century that likewise contains the zodiac signs for the piyyut (but not the labors) in a far more schematic style that would seem to befit twentieth-century representations, just as the eighteenth-century illustrations seem to reflect contemporary models. A full study of Jewish zodiac illustration from antiquity to the modern period is a scholarly desideratum.

52. A striking example of the phenomenon behind this problem is found in the "Iti mi-Levanon" illustration, as it is found in other thirteenth-century manuscripts that contain Benjamin b. Zeraḥ's piyyut; in these other illustrations, the bride and the groom are pictured as human lovers seated next to one another on a pedestal—a representation that, as Sarit Shalev-Eyni has shown ("Iti mi-Levanon Kalah" [in Hebrew] [Come with me from Lebanon my bride], *Rimonim* 6/7 [1999]: 6–20), derives either from illustrations in such works as the Codex Menasse, a collection of secular lovesongs known as the Minnelieder, or from a long Christian iconographical tradition depicting Christ crowning the virgin or the church.

53. See Sed-Rajna, "Image in the Text."

54. Narkiss, "Illuminations," 80–81.

55. The phrase itself comes from the twelfth-century meditational treatise *Gemma Anima*, which may or may not have been composed by Honorius of Autun. As Mary Carruthers shows, the phrase is picked up by Gregory the Great (seventh century) and then acquires a wide currency. For a full discussion, see Carruthers, *The Book of Memory: A Study of Memory in Medieval Culture* (Cambridge: Cambridge University Press, 1990), 340 n. 3, and for a more general discussion of the entire topic, see 221–23.

56. Ibid., 222.

57. To be fair, the midrashic model has more often been implicitly invoked than explicitly discussed. It appears most frequently in the context of scholarly discussions over the history of various iconographical motifs that seem to be borrowings from ancient exegetical traditions, and usually in connection with debates over the question of whether the motif was originally Jewish (i.e., midrashic) or Christian. These questions have also been deeply implicated in speculations about the origins of Jewish and Christian art; see the literature cited in note 34 above. Nonetheless, the basic model in these discussions for understanding the function of the art has been through its midrashic content, with the understanding that the content served as a kind of exegetical or pedagogical tool. See, for example, Gabrielle Sed-Rajna, "The Image as Exegetical Tool: Paintings in Medieval Hebrew Manuscripts of the Bible," in *The Bible as Book: The Manuscript Tradition*, ed. John L Sharpe III and Kimberly van Kampen (London: Oak Knoll Press, 1998), 215–22. For a comprehensive review of the scholarship, see Kogman-Appel, "Bible Illustration and the Jewish Tradition."

58. Rachel Wischnitzer-Bernstein, "The Money-Changer with the Balance: A Topic of Jewish Iconography," *Eretz-Israel* 6 (1960): 23–25.

59. The biblical phrase *kofer nafsho* (Exod 30:12) is repeated several verses later in *le-khapeir ʿal nafsheteikhem* (Exod 30:16), "to ransom their persons." In the piyyut, this is explicated as "they give ransom (*kofer*) without shame or contumely, in order to atone for their sins (*beʿad ʿavonam le-khapeir*)."

60. On the Jewish or Christian identity of illustrators of Jewish books, see Bezalel Narkiss, *The Golden Haggadah* (London: Pomegranate, 1997), 67, but see also Epstein's comments in

his review essay, "Representations of the Jewish Image," 336–37. As we now know, the illustrations in the earliest dated illustrated Jewish manuscript, the famous Rashi commentary BSB Cod. Heb. 5 (written near Würzburg, 1232/33), were drawn by a Christian artist, a fact made evident by the discovery of instructions to the artist in Latin next to the pictures; see Beit-Arié, *Hebrew Manuscripts*, 21.

61. Since this chapter first appeared as an article in 2010, a number of important studies of Jewish art in liturgical books have appeared that, without using my terminology of visual piyyut, nonetheless adapt an analogous approach that seeks to treat text, image, and liturgical function in tandem as part of the "whole book." See Sarit Shalev-Eyni, *Jews Among Christians: Hebrew Book Illumination from Lake Constance* (London: Harvey Miller, 2010); Eva Frojmovic, "Early Ashkenazic Prayer Books and Their Christian Commentators," in *Crossing Borders: Hebrew Manuscripts as a Meeting-Place of Cultures*, ed. Piet van Boxel and Sabine Arndt (Oxford: Bodleian Library, 2010), 45–56; Epstein, *Medieval Haggadah*, esp. 19–128; Katrin Kogman-Appel, *A Mahzor from Worms: Art and Religion in a Medieval Jewish Community* (Cambridge: Harvard University Press, 2012); Sara Offenberg, *Illuminated Piety: Pietistic Texts and Images in the North French Hebrew Miscellany* (Los Angeles: Cherub Press, 2013); and Dalia-Ruth Halperin, *Illuminating in Micrography: The Catalan Micrography Maḥzor MS Heb 8°6527 in the National Library of Israel* (Leiden: Brill, 2013).

CHAPTER 7

1. The slavish republishing and recycling of the 1695 Amsterdam Haggadah and its illustrations in the two subsequent centuries have been noted and dicussed by nearly all scholars who have dealt with the printed haggadah; see Cecil Roth, "The Illustrated Haggadah," in *Studies in Books and Booklore* (New York: Gregg International, 1972), 177–79; Yosef Hayim Yerushalmi, *Haggadah and History* (Philadelphia: Jewish Publication Society, 1975), 47–48; and Richard Cohen, *Jewish Icons: Art and Society in Modern Europe* (Berkeley: University of California Press, 1998), 94–97. Worth noting, too, is that its wide diffusion continued even into the twentieth century in America, thanks to the fact that the several early editions of the Maxwell House Haggadah also reprinted its illustrations.

2. The biographical information on Abraham bar Jacob is very scanty. The key source appears to be the entry in J. C. Wolfius, *Bibliotheca Hebraea* (Hamburg/Leipzig, 1727), 3:39 (who received his information from a certain Theodorus Hasaeus), who writes that bar Jacob was originally a "Verbi Divini Minister in litoribus Rheni" and now lives in Amsterdam where he converted to Judaism. See Rachel Wischnitzer, "Von der Holbeinbibel zur Amsterdamer Haggadah," *Monatsschrift für Geschichte und Wissenschaft des Judentums* 75 (1931): 269–86, repr. in Wischnitzer, *From Dura to Rembrandt: Studies in the History of Art* (Milwaukee: Aldrich; Vienna: IRSA; Jerusalem: Center for Jewish Art, 1990), 29–48, esp. 31–32; and Wischnitzer, "Zur Amsterdamer Haggadah," *Monatsschrift für Geschichte und Wissenschaft des Judentums* 76 (1932): 239–41, repr. in *From Dura to Rembrandt*, 53–54; and Abraham Ya'ari, *Mehkerei Sefer* (Jerusalem: Mosad Harav Kuk, 1958), 250–51, who lists other works done by bar Jacob. According to Bezalel Narkiss, "The Illustrations of the Amsterdam Haggadah and Its Place in the History of Hebrew Printing," in *Facsimile Edition of the Amsterdam 1712 Haggadah* (Jerusalem: Makor, 1972), 1, a more complete list of the works is found in the papers of Narkiss's father, Mordechai Narkiss, but to the best of my knowledge it has never been published. Professor Harold Brodsky of the University of Maryland has kindly shared with me an email correspondence he received from Dr. Adrian K. Offenberg of the Bibliotheca Rosenthaliana (October 2002) in which he relayed additional information he had received that bar Jacob was from Bochum (Baukem) in Westphalia, that he was twenty-six when he came to Amsterdam in 1695, and that his second wife was Deborah Proops, a sister of the famous Jewish

printer Solomon ben Joseph Proops. Proops's printing house published the 1712 edition of the Amsterdam Haggadah in which bar Jacob's name was left out of the title page(!). An unresolved question remains as to the name Abraham bar Jacob and why it is not Jacob bar Abraham (the latter being the more typical patronym for a convert). According to Offenberg, some of his children are mentioned in the burial register of the Jewish cemetery at Muiderberg, but he is never called a *ger* (convert) as would be expected. There is little question, however, that he was a convert, since on the haggadah's title page he names himself as "*Avram* [*sic*] *bar Yaʿacov mi-mishpaḥat Avraham Avinu*" (Abram bar Jacob from the family of Abraham our forefather).

3. There is as yet no definitive study of the Ashkenazic haggadah, but see Mendel Metzger, *La Haggada Enluminée* (Leiden: Brill, 1973); Bezalel Narkiss, *Hebrew Illuminated Manuscripts* (Jerusalem: Leon Amiel, 1992), 33–35; Narkiss, "The Art of the Washington Haggadah," in *The Washington Haggadah*, ed. Myron M. Weinstein (Washington: Library of Congress, 1991), text vol., 51–54; and my introductory essay, "The Washington Haggadah: The Life of a Book," in the facsimile edition of *The Washington Haggadah* (Cambridge: Harvard University Press, 2011).

4. There exists no comprehensive study of the illustrations in the early printed haggadah. Pro tem, see Roth, "Illustrated Haggadah."

5. For discussion of this image and its transformations, see Joseph Gutmann, "The Messiah at the Seder," in *Studies in Jewish History Presented to Professor Raphael Mahler on His Seventy-Fifth Birthday*, ed. Shmuel Yeivin (Merhavia: Sifriat Poalim, 1974), 29–38; Cohen, *Jewish Icons*, 91–93; and Stern, "Washington Haggadah." For the 1609 image of the Temple, see Shalom Sabar, "Messianic Aspirations and Renaissance Urban Ideals: The Image of Jerusalem in the Venice Haggadah, 1609," in *The Real and Ideal Jerusalem in Jewish, Christian and Islamic Art*, ed. Bianca Kuehhnel (Jerusalem: Journal of the Center for Jewish Art, 1998), 295–312.

6. Ibid., 40–41; Roth, "Illustrated Haggadah," 49.

7. Roth, "Illustrated Haggadah," 178.

8. Wischnitzer, *From Dura to Rembrandt*, 36; note, however, that figures 4 and 5 in her article are mistitled; Yerushalmi, *Haggadah and History*, pl. 60, has the correct sequence.

9. For discussion of the image and reproductions, see James Clifton and Walter S. Melion, eds., *Scripture for the Eyes: Bible Illustration in Netherlandish Prints of the Sixteenth Century* (New York: Museum of Biblical Art, 2009), 19–20 and fig. 6. The woodcuts were all the work of Martin de Keyser. Note as well figure 7, "Suppliant Before a King," and the discussion of image that includes a dove signifying the Holy Spirit in a radiant cloud above the king; this image is effectively the reverse of David praying before the Holy Spirit.

10. Wischnitzer, "Von der Holbeinbibel," 36, drew attention to the Merian connection, but the fullest exposition of this illustration and the previously unnoted connection to the Lutheran Bible is in Falk Wiesemann, *"Kommt heraus und schaut"—Jüdische und christliche Illustrationen zur Bibel in alter Zeit (Katalog zur Ausstellung, Universitäts- und Landsbibliothek Düsseldorf)* (Essen: Klartext Verlag, 2002), 30, and the Dutch/English version of the catalogue, *Ondanks het Tweede Gebod / Despite the Second Commandment* (Amsterdam: Bijbels Museum, 2003), 28–29.

11. Wiesemann, *"Kommit heraus"*; Wiesemann, *Ondanks het Tweede Gebod / Despite the Second Commandment* (Amsterdam: Bijbels Museum, 2003), 28–29; Milly Heyd, "Illustrations in Early Editions of the Tsene-U'rene: Jewish Adaptations of Christian Sources," *Journal of Jewish Art* 10 (1984): 64–86; R. Wischnitzer, "Gleanings: The Zeena U-Reena and Its Illustrations," in *From Dura to Rembrandt*, 130–33; and N. Feuchtwanger-Sarig, "How Italian are the Venice Minhagim of 1593? A Chapter in the History of Yiddish Printing in Italy," in *Schöpferische Momente des Europäischen Judentums in der frühen Neuzeit*, ed. Michael Graetz (Heidelberg: C. Winter, 2000), 177–205.

12. Clifton and Melion, *Scripture for the Eyes*, 15–17.

13. Wiesemann, *Despite*, 22–26, but see also Wiesemann's notes regarding instances in which the publishers either did not remove the offending signs or missed them.

14. I owe the discovery of this detail to my colleague and good friend Marc Epstein. At the Dr. Steven Ungerleider Haggadot Symposium at the Brown University Library on October 19, 2018, I presented a version of this chapter with the requisite Powerpoint presentation of the images. On the blown-up image on the screen, Marc noticed the tiny figures sketched in the background. To the best of my knowledge, this is the first time anyone has noticed this detail, and it is all thanks to Powerpoint!

15. The peculiarity of the detail should not be dismissed. For one thing, it is much more poorly drawn than the rest of the engraving; indeed, it looks almost like someone added it as an afterthought. Moreover, the messiah appears to be holding in his hands something that looks suspiciously like a cross, but it is impossible to make out exactly what the object is.

16. As Wiesemann notes (*Despite*, 27), bar Jacob "slipped" in copying this engraving from Merian and inadvertently left a tiny cross on the roof of the inner Temple that Merian had placed there as a sign that the place would be the site of the church of the Final Judgment. Later eighteenth-century scribes who hand-copied and hand-illustrated haggadot that mimicked the Amsterdam haggadah, like Joseph Leipnik, corrected bar Jacob's mistake, removed the cross, and sometimes substituted a Star of David in its place.

17. The most complete treatment of the 1695 Amsterdam map and its predecessors is the article by Harold Brodsky, "The Seventeenth-Century Haggadah Map of Avraham Bar Yaacov," *Journal of Jewish Art* 20 (1993): 149–57. The best facsimile of all the maps treated in Brodsky's article is Kenneth Nebenzahl, *Maps of the Holy Land* (New York: Abbeville, 1986), which also contains valuable commentary. For listings of the maps in Nebenzahl and additional bibliography, see Brodsky, Seventeenth-Century Haggadah Map, 149 n. 1, and Michel Garel, "La Première Carte de Terre Sainte en Hébreu (Amsterdam, 1620/21)," *Studia Rosenthaliana* 21 (1987): 131–39. See also Yerushalmi, *Haggadah and History*, pl. 69 (where he erroneously describes the map as "the first Hebrew map ever published").

18. The description of Adrichem's and bar Jacob's maps in this paragraph are based on the careful descriptions in Nebenzahl, *Maps of the Holy Land*, 94, pl. 35 (Adrichem), and 138–39, pl. 52 (bar Jacob); Brodsky, "Seventeenth Century Haggadah Map"; Ariel Tishby, ed., *Holy Land in Maps* (Jerusalem: The Israel Museum, 2001), 96–97, 122–23; and Yerushalmi, *Haggadah and History*, pl. 69 (on the 1712 Amsterdam edition). The standard reference work on cartography, David Woodward, ed., *The History of Cartography*, vol. 3: *Cartography in the European Renaissance* (Part 2) (Chicago: University of Chicago Press, 2007), has only a few pages on German maps of the Holy Land (pp. 1216–17); there is otherwise little mention of the subject, only a few lines devoted to Christian van Adrichem [*sic*], and no mention of Abraham bar Jacob.

19. Nebenzahl, *Maps of the Holy Land*, 113, pl. 40.

20. Ibid.

21. As Brodsky, "Seventeenth-Century Haggadah Map," 153, notes, the Bible actually lists forty-two stations, not forty-one; why bar Jacob omitted *Iye-Abarim* is not clear, but see Brodsky for one explanation.

22. Wischnitzer, *From Dura to Rembrandt*, 36 and 39, figs. 7–8.

23. Brodsky, "Seventeenth-Century Haggadah Map," 156–57.

24. See the copperplate engraving map of Nicholas Visscher the Elder (Amsterdam, 1659), in Nebenzahl, *Maps of the Holy Land*, 132–33, pl. 49; and Brodsky, "Seventeenth-Century Haggadah Map," 150–51. Brodsky offers a "midrashic" explanation for the number of rafts in bar Jacob's map.

25. Hebrew: *eretz ha-kedoshah*, "the holy land," an unintended Christianism (from *terra sancta*), which appears nowhere else in Hebrew literature; see Brodsky, "Seventeenth-Century Haggadah Map," 155.

26. Translation from Yerushalmi, *Haggadah and History*, pl. 69.

27. See, for example, the comment of Roth, "Illustrated Haggadah," 49, who notes that the map's connection "with the subject matter is difficult to see" and demands explanation.

28. Note that bar Jacob has *yevinam* and had added the suffix "them" to the verb.

29. Don Isaac Abravanel, *Commentary on the Pentateuch*, standard version (repr., Jerusalem: Bnei Arbal 1964), 4:160 ad Num 33.

30. Abraham Saba, *Tzeror Ha-Mor* (1879; repr., Brooklyn, 1961), Numbers, fol. 46b. See also Abraham Gross, *Iberian Jewry from Twilight to Dawn: The World of Rabbi Abraham Saba* (Leiden: Brill, 1995), 161–63.

31. See Gross, *Iberian Jewry* 161.

32. For the early period on the Jewish side, see Gershom Scholem, *Sabbatai Sevi: The Mystical Messiah*, trans. by R. J. Z. Werblowsky (Princeton: Princeton University Press, 1973), 893–95; Matt Goldish, *The Sabbatean Prophets* (Cambridge: Harvard University Press, 2004), esp. 162–70; and Yosef Kaplan, *An Alternative Path to Modernity* (Leiden: Brill, 2000), esp. 211–33. On the Christian side, see R. H. Popkin, "Some Aspects of Jewish-Christian Theological Interchanges in Holland and England, 1640–1700," in *Jewish-Christian Relations in the Seventeenth Century: Studies and Documents*, ed. J. van der Berg and Ernestine G. E. van der Wall (Dordrecht: Kluwer, 1988), 3–32; and Popkin, "The Sabbatean Movement in Turkey (1703–1708) and Reverberations in Northern Europe," *Jewish Quarterly Review*, n.s., 94 (2004): 300–317.

33. For this remarkable text, see Zalman Shazar, ed., *Sippur Maʿasei Shabbetai Tzevi (Beshreibung fun Shabbesai Tzvi)* (Jerusalem: Merkaz Zalman Shazar, 1978). On R. Leib and the date of the work, see 19–26. I wish to thank Professor Shlomo Berger for calling my attention to the importance of R. Leib's work for my subject.

34. Meir Benayahu, "'The Holy Society of Rabbi Judah Ḥasid and Its Emigration to the Land of Israel" [in Hebrew], *Sefunot* 3/4 (1959–60): 131–82.

35. For some indication of the Christian views, see Popkin, "Some Aspects," and LeRoy Edwin Froom, *The Prophetic Faith of our Fathers: The Historical Development of Prophetic Interpretation* (Washington, D.C.: Review and Herald, 1948), 783–96, and esp. the tables on 784–87. I wish to thank Professor Matt Goldish for referring me to this source and discussing the Christian reactions.

36. On the curious figure of Leon, see A. K. Offenberg, "Jacob Jehuda Leon (1602–1675) and His Model of the Temple," in van der Berg and van der Wall, *Jewish-Christian Relations*, 95–115; and Offenberg, "Dirk van Santen and the Keur Bible; New Insights into Jacob Judah (Arye) Leon Templo's Model Temple," *Studia Rosenthaliana* 37 (2004): 401–22.

37. Offenberg, "Dirk van Santen," 497; see also Offenberg, "Jacob Jehuda Leon," 101. For a detailed consideration of the architectural history of Templo's Temple and the question of its relation to the architecture of contemporary Portuguese synagogues in the Netherlands, see Gary Schwartz, "The Temple Mount in the Lowlands," in *The Dutch Intersection: The Jews and the Netherlands in Modern History*, ed. Yosef Kaplan (Leiden: Brill, 2008), 111–479. Schwartz deals at length with Christian representations of the Temple's architecture, in particular that of the Nieuwe Kerk in Haarlem, which is ultimately based on the design and iconography of the Escorial, the great palace of Philip II outside Madrid, built in the later sixteenth century. A bird's eye view of the Escorial was printed in Willem and Joan Blaeu's *Atlas Maior*, vol. 9 (1662), repr. in Schwartz, Temple Mount, 467, fig. 10. The resemblance between the overall layout of the Escorial in that illustration and bar Jacob's Temple is striking.

38. Nebenzahl, *Maps of the Holy Land*, 42–45, pl. 15; Tishby, *Holy Land in Maps*, 74–75.

39. Menasseh ben Israel, *The Hope of Israel: The English Translation by Moses Wall, 1652*, ed. Henry Méchoulan and Gérard Nahon, trans. Richenda George (Oxford: Littman Library, 1987), esp. 156–59 (paras. 34–37). Christians, of course, were no less fascinated by the subject of the ten lost tribes, since the restoration and conversion of all Jewry was seen almost

universally as an unconditional prerequisite for the Second Coming of Christ. For a recent summary of the subject and relevant bibliography, see Goldish, *Sabbatean Prophets*, 27–34.

40. Simon Schama, *The Embarrassment of Riches: An Interpretation of Dutch Culture in the Golden Age* (New York: Knopf, 1987), 93–125, quotes from 104 and 96, respectively. For his discussion of Vondel's epic *Passcha* (Passover), which concludes with a specific "comparison Between the Redemption of the Children of Israel and the Liberation of the United Provinces of the Netherlands," see, in particular, 105. For important qualifications of Schama's view, see Paul Regan, "Calvinism and the Dutch Israel Thesis," in *Protestant History and Identity in Sixteenth-Century Europe: The Medieval Inheritance* (Aldershot: Scolar Press, 1996), 91–106, though even Regan appears to acknowledge that by the mid-1600s "the changing character of the Reformed church and the increasing strength and self-confidence of the Dutch Republic would have made it easier for some Dutch Calvinists to formulate a notion of a Dutch Israel" (105).

41. Larry Silver, "Mapped and Marginalized: Early Printed Images of Jerusalem," in Kuehhnel, *Real and Ideal Jerusalem*, 313–24, esp. 323–24.

INDEX OF BIBLICAL AND RABBINIC SOURCES

INDEX OF MANUSCRIPTS

GENERAL INDEX

Abulafia, Meir Ha-Levi. *See* Ramah
Abravanel, Isaac, 141–42, 205, 216–17
von Adrichem, Christian, 218
  Theatrum terrae sanctae (Amsterdam, 1590), 211, *213*
Agnon, S. Y., 23
Akiba, Rabbi, 41
Aleppo Codex (*Keter Aram Tzova*), 50, 52, 70
Almanzi Pentateuch, 64–65
Alphabet of Ben Sira, 3, 28ff.
Amat Di Itztalvu, 28
Ambrose, 151
Ambrosian Bible, 78–79
Anselm of Laon, 151, 155
Arba'ah Turim, 96
Arba'ah ve-'Esrim (First Rabbinic Bible) (Venice, 1517). *See also* Rabbinic Bible
Augustine, 151

Bakhtin, Mikhail, 28
de Balmes, Abraham, 124
bar Jacob, Abraham, 205, 207, 209–18
bar Makhir, R. Nathan, 88–89
bar Moses, Isaac, 92
Bartolocci, Giulio, 29
Bavli. *See* Talmud and *Talmud Bavli*.
Bede , 151
Beit-Arié, Malachi, 5, 79–80, 107, 160, 188–90
Beit Ha-Midrash, 33
Bekhor Shor, Joseph, 99, 137
Ben-Amos, Dan, 15
ben Asher, Aaron, 56, 70, 78, 120, 133
ben Asher, Bahya, 69
ben Baruch, Meir. *See* Maharam
ben Gershon, Levi, 99, 159
ben Ḥayyim, Jacob, 121, 129
ben Hillel, Mordechai, 143
ben Ḥofni, Samuel, 98
ben Israel, Manasseh, 218
ben Judah, Simḥah, 193, 195, 198–99, 202–03
ben Kalonymus, Isaac Nathan, 121
ben Meir, Samuel, 99

ben Moses Halevi, Isaac. *See* Duran
ben Qilir (Killir), Eleazar, 198
ben Rabbi Oizer, Leib, 217
Ben Sira
  author, 29, 37, 40
  book of, 29–40, 42
ben Yakar, Jacob, 99
ben Yehiel, Asher, 96
ben Yekutiel, Immanuel ben Solomon, 129
ben Zeraḥ, Benjamin, 180–81
ben Zoma, 38
Beshreibung fun Shabbesai Tzvi, 217
Biblia Rabbinica. *See* Rabbinic Bible
Boethius, 155
Bomberg, Daniel, 114–46, 150, 168–69, 170–71, 178
  Arba'ah ve-'Esrim (First Rabbinic Bible) (Venice, 1517), ii, 114–121, *117*, 123, 125, 137–38; verso of title page (papal approbation), *118*; 1 (Genesis 1), *119*; insert with commentary of Kimḥi, *120*; *Talmud Bavli with Rashi and Tosafot*, Massekhet (Tractate) Berakhot (Venice, Bomberg, 1520), 168–170, *169*
  Torah, Nevi'im, Ketuvim (Second Rabbinic Bible) (Venice, 1524–25), 114, 122–24, 132, 136–39, 144
Book of Antiochus, 133
Book of the Righteous. See *Sefer Ḥasidim*
Booth, Wayne, 34, 41
Brody, Robert, 45

Calkins, Robert, 109
Camille, Michael, 86
Capsali, Eliyahu, 175–77
Carruthers, Mary, 85, 200
Cassiodorus, 151
Cervera Bible, 60, 74–76
Circle-Maker, The. *See* Ha-Me'ageil, Ḥoni
Codex Amiantinus, 68
Codex Grandior of Cassiodorus, 68
Cohen, Arthur, 4

Talmud
  as Ashkenazic document, 171
  Arras MS, 164, 263n30, *164*
  Babylonian, 19, 147, 150, 161
  Florence MS, 161–62, *163*
  Hamburg Codex, 161-62, *163*
  page layout, 147–78
  Palestinian, 147
  Printed editions of: Bomberg (Daniel), 168–
      78. See also *Talmud Bavli* (Venice,
      1520); Soncino (Joshua Solomon and
      Gershon), 167–168; Spanish and Por-
      tuguese editions, 170
  Widow of Romm and His Brothers, *148, 149*.
      See also *Talmud Bavli* (Vilna,
      1880-86).
  "Sea of Talmud," 147, 259n1
Talmud Bavli with Rashi and Tosafot, Massekhet
    (Tractate) Berakhot (Venice, 1520), 168–
    170, *169*
Talmud Bavli with Rashi and Tosafot, Massekhet
    (Tractate) Berakhot (Vilna, 1880-86) 147–
    150, 170, *148*
Tanakh. *See* Hebrew Bible
Tarfon, Rabbi, 39
Targum(im), 50, 78, 88–90, 92, 96, 99, 103, 116,
    158
  Aramaic, 95, 115–16, 119, 133–134
  lack of, 105
  Jerusalem Targum, 116, 120
  omission of, 133–34
  Palestinian, 89
  placement and formatting of, 107–08, 118, 125
  Pseudo-Jonathan, 123
  Rashi and/or, 133–36, 158–159
  Second Targum to Esther, 120
  Targum Neofiti, 116
  Targum Onkelos, 50, 78, 89, 116, 123
  Tiberian vocalization, 88
  with commentary, 115–116, 123, 135
Ten Commandments, The. *See* Decalogue, The
Theatrum orbis terrarium (Antwerp, 1570), 215
Theatrum terrae sanctae (Amsterdam, 1590),
    211–214
  map of Holy Land, *213*

Toledo Bible, 53–54
Toledot Yeshu, 27
Torah, Nevi'im, Ketuvim (Second Rabbinic
    Bible), (Venice, 1524-25) 122, *124*
Torah scrolls (*Sifrei Torah*)
  controversies over correct inscription,
      139–41
  text-types, 78
  weekly reading in synagogue, 92, 133.
Tzene u-Rene, 209
Tzeror Ha-Mor, 217

Van Gennep, Ernold, 86
Vesconte, Petrus, 211, 218
Veyne, Paul, 10
Vulgate, 144–45, 151–55, 171

Wieder, Naphtali, 70
Wiesel, Moses, 205
Wiesemann, Falk, 209
Wilde, Oscar, 34
Williams, John, 67
Wimpfheimer, Barry, 44
Wischnitzer-Bernstein, Rachel, 202, 207, 209,
    214
Worms Mahzor, 179–80, 193–97, 200–01, 203–4
Writings. *See* Ketuvim
Wroclaw Bible, 78–79

Yahalom, Yosef, 28, 186
Yassif, Eli, 29–31, 33–35, 38, 40
Yerushalmi. *See* Talmud
Yeven Metzulah, 176
Yitzhaki, Shlomo. *See* Rashi
Yonatan Sheida, 23

Zafren, Herbert, 135
Zarathustra, 33
Zedekiah, 31
Zevid, Rabbi, 13–14
Zeira, Rabbi, 31, 35
Zeresh, 28
Zlotnick, J. L., 20
Zohar, 24
Zwiep, Irene E., 72